Christmas in Pennsylvania

Compliments of
SHAUB & BURNS,

Christmas in Pennsylvania

A Folk-Cultural Study

Alfred L. Shoemaker

Introduction and
New Foreword and Afterword by
Don Yoder

STACKPOLE
BOOKS

Originally published in 1959 by the Pennsylvania Folklife Society
Foreword and Afterword © 1999 by Don Yoder

Published by
STACKPOLE BOOKS
5067 Ritter Road
Mechanicsburg, PA 17055
www.stackpolebooks.com

Printed in the United States of America

10 9 8 7 6 5 4 3 2 1

FIRST STACKPOLE EDITION

*Frontispiece: St. Nicholas and donkey with plenty of gifts for good
children and a switch, like the Belsnickel, for the naughty ones.
Trade card, Shaub and Burns, circa 1880.* ROUGHWOOD COLLECTION

Library of Congress Cataloging-in-Publication Data

Shoemaker, Alfred Lewis, 1913–
    Christmas in Pennsylvania : a folk-cultural study / Alfred
L. Shoemaker ; introduction and new foreward and afterword
by Don Yoder. — 1st Stackpole ed.
      p.   cm.
    Includes bibliographical references and index.
    ISBN 0–8117–0328–2
    1. Christmas—Pennsylvania.   2. Pennsylvania—Social
life and customs. I. Title.
GT4986.P4S56   1999
394.2663'09748—dc21
                                  99–29757
                                      CIP

Contents

Publisher's Note vi

Foreword vii

Foreword to the First Edition xi

Introduction to the First Edition:
The Folk-Cultural Background xiii

Open-Hearth Christmases 1
    Christmas Mummers 3
    Barring Out the Schoolmaster 7
    Metzel Soup and Christmas Money 15
    Matzabaum, Moshey, and Bellyguts 21
    Christmas Dew 25

Woodstove Christmases 29
    Christ-Kindel to Kriss Kringle 33
    The Christmas Tree in Pennsylvania 45
    Trimming the Christmas Tree 57
    Among the Christmas Trees 67
    Belsnickling 75
    Carnival of Horns 91
    Of Cookies and Cookie Cutters 99
    Christmas Day 107
    Second Christmas 115
    Of Pyramids and Putzes 119
    Firecracker Christmases 129

Conclusion to the First Edition 131

Afterword 133

Notes 149

Further Reading 155

Index 159

Publisher's Note

Stackpole Books is proud to bring back into print Alfred L. Shoemaker's *Christmas in Pennsylvania*. Forty years after its original publication by the Pennsylvania Folklife Society, the work remains vital as both a document of Pennsylvania's rich Christmas traditions and a prototype of folk-cultural studies in America.

In this edition, the Shoemaker text has been reset with a new design; however, with the exception of minor corrections of spelling and punctuation, it remains unchanged.

The project was made possible primarily by Dr. Shoemaker's longtime colleague, Don Yoder, who wrote the 1959 introduction to the book, which is included here. In addition to contributing an insightful new foreword and afterword, Dr. Yoder has also translated several Pennsylvania Dutch passages that had not been furnished in the original, added numerous illustrations from his extensive Roughwood Collection, and assembled the comprehensive bibliography.

The republication of *Christmas in Pennsylvania* reflects a strong tradition of publishing in Pennsylvania, as it commemorates the Pennsylvania Folklife Society, which preserved Pennsylvania's folk heritage in monographs, such as the original *Christmas in Pennsylvania*, and the remarkable journal, *Pennsylvania Folklife*, which sadly is now defunct. This edition also marks the commitment of Stackpole Books—a publisher in Pennsylvania for nearly seventy years—to producing quality books on Pennsylvania history and life.

KYLE R. WEAVER, EDITOR
1999

Foreword

For a decade and a half I had the pleasure of working closely with the late Alfred L. Shoemaker on several joint projects: the Pennsylvania Dutch Folklore Center at Franklin and Marshall College, and its successor, the Pennsylvania Folklife Society; our journal, first called *The Pennsylvania Dutchman* and later *Pennsylvania Folklife*; and the Pennsylvania Dutch Folk Festival at Kutztown. With the republication of his groundbreaking *Christmas in Pennsylvania* after forty years, it is fitting to review his career and its effects on Pennsylvania studies and American scholarship.

Born in 1913 in Lehigh County, Pennsylvania, into a family whose first language of the home was Pennsylvania Dutch, Alfred Lewis Shoemaker was descended from colonial emigrant families from Germany and Switzerland. Among his ancestors was the colorful Lutheran preacher and fraktur artist Daniel Schumacher. Raised in a Pennsylvania Dutch–speaking community, Alfred Shoemaker spoke fluent *Pennsylfaanisch* all his life, although he once confessed to me that in his early school days he had made some conscious efforts to rid himself of what he considered a handicap—a Pennsylvania Dutch accent in speaking English. His mature English thus bore no trace of a "Dutchified" flavor, and he was an eloquent and moving platform speaker, with more than a touch of the preacher about his style.

As a student at Muhlenberg College in Allentown, he was inspired by both Preston A. Barba and the inimitable Harry Hess Reichard of the German department, two leaders in the "renaissance" of Pennsylvania Dutch studies in the 1930s. There he developed a compelling interest in studying his own culture. His horizons were broadened by an unforgettable junior year abroad spent at the University of Munich and a graduate year at the University of Heidelberg. His German in fact became so proficient

that, despite much theological training along the way, at Crozer and Mount Airy theological seminaries, he decided to become a Germanist. He chose the University of Illinois at Urbana because the German department there favored research in German dialectology. In 1940 he turned out a pioneering dissertation on the Pennsylvania Dutch dialect of Arthur, Illinois, an Amish settlement. It was also at Illinois that he had the good fortune of meeting J. William Frey, a younger York County Dutchman who also got his Ph.D. there with a dissertation on the Pennsylvania Dutch dialect of York County, Pennsylvania.

Dr. Shoemaker, the new Ph.D., returned to Pennsylvania, where he first taught German at Lafayette College at Easton, and then served a brief but productive term as director of the Historical Society of Berks County in Reading. There he started a Pennsylvania Dutch column in the local newspaper under the title *"Der Rote Gaisbort Schumacher"* (The Red Goat-Beard Shoemaker), which referred to the goatee he had grown, probably reflecting European influence. He was then called to Franklin and Marshall College, at Lancaster, where he joined J. William Frey on the faculty. While there Shoemaker founded the first academic program in American folklore in the United States, achieving a reputation locally by sending students out into the field to interview old-timers on their memories of Pennsylvania Dutch culture.

I had met both Dr. Shoemaker and Dr. Frey in Bethlehem some years before, at an annual meeting of the Pennsylvania Dutch Folklore Society, an organization on whose board of directors all three of us eventually were elected to serve. When I joined the faculty of Franklin and Marshall, my alma mater, in 1949, the triumvirate of Shoemaker, Frey, and Yoder was formed. This force produced the Pennsylvania Dutch Folklore Center in 1949, a research institute modeled on the European university institutes of folk-cultural studies; the journals *The Pennsylvania Dutchman*, in 1949, and *Pennsylvania Folklife*, in 1958, which became clearinghouses for both Pennsylvania Dutch studies and research on all of the state's ethnic groups; and the Pennsylvania Dutch Folk Festival at Kutztown, in 1950, the first folklife festival in the United States.

Dr. Frey eventually dropped out of the team, but Dr. Shoemaker and I continued the work on all fronts, researching and archiving ethnographic and genealogical data, publishing books, editing the journal (everything down to proofreading and pasteup), and each year planning the special events of the festival. We honored scholars and public figures with citations, including, one stellar year, the governor of the commonwealth.

In the 1950s both Dr. Shoemaker and I were "converted," one might say, from the narrowly defined Anglo-American concept of "folklore" to the much broader continental European concept of "folklife" and "folklife studies," as practiced in Scandinavian and Central European universities, and eventually also in the British Isles, beginning in Ireland. This approach involves studying an entire culture, not just its verbal lore. It differed from anthropology at the time in that folklife scholars analyzed their own cultures in both present and past, relating their development to the key concepts of tradition and community. Dr. Shoemaker had been influenced by the ethnographic methods of Åke Campbell and other Swedish scholars, as well as the British folklife movement, from which we imported the term *folklife*. I was influenced in turn by my visits to the Rhineland and an all-day interview at the University of Zürich with Richard Weiss, Switzerland's foremost folklife scholar, whose seminal book, *Volkskunde der Schweiz* (The Folk-Culture of Switzerland), published in 1946, has been a major influence on my own teaching career. With this broadened perspective, Dr. Shoemaker and I decided in 1958 to change the Folklore Center to the Pennsylvania Folklife Society. At the same time we adopted a new title for the journal, *Pennsylvania Folklife*, in order to promote research on all the ethnic and religious cultures of Pennsylvania.

Christmas in Pennsylvania grew out of Dr. Shoemaker's fascination with Pennsylvania Dutch folk customs, their history in the past, and their place in present-day culture. At his request I contributed the introduction, "The Folk-Cultural Background," dealing with the history of Christmas celebration (or noncelebration) among Pennsylvania's religious groups. This essay brought to light the fact that in the past, a great many Pennsylvania groups, led by the Quakers and other Puritan-derived sects, refused to join in the folk celebration of the holiday, accepting it only in the minimal sense of a religious rather than a traditional holiday with all the folk-cultural trimmings that had come down to Pennsylvania from medieval and even pagan times.

Dr. Shoemaker's chapters—the bulk of the book—present what can be called an historical ethnography of the Pennsylvania Dutch Christmas festival in all its manifestations, from the Belsnickel to the Christmas tree. The information was derived first from Dr. Shoemaker's ethnographic interviewing of Dutchmen he met here and there over the Dutch Country, who shared with him their memories of Christmas from their childhood days. He also delved deeply into Pennsylvania Dutch source materials, particularly the German and English weekly newspapers of nineteenth-century upstate Pennsylvania. These proved a treasure trove of Christmas data, with dated and localized descriptions of Belsnickling, of Christmas tree decoration, of Christmas candies and cookies and other foods—the entire range of Pennsylvania Dutch Christmas customs as well as the lore associated with them. *Christmas in Pennsylvania* was in fact the pioneer book in America analyzing Christmas in one particular American regional culture. And as a pioneer work presenting fresh data on every aspect of Christmas celebration, it has been widely quoted in the books that followed it.

Alfred Shoemaker had a vision for his Pennsylvania Dutch people: to promote research in every aspect of their culture; to encourage their self-expression; and to foster a sense of their own identity as an American ethnic group. He saw his people and their culture with the double understanding that resulted from his growing up within the culture, and then analyzing it from without using all the scientific tools of his broad education in Europe and America.

Through his work with all classes of Pennsylvanians, college and university colleagues, museum personnel, ministers and schoolteachers, yes, and the

Berks and Lehigh County farm folk who supported the Pennsylvania Dutch Folk Festival at Kutztown from its very beginning, he united diverse elements of Pennsylvania's population. But above all, with his charisma, his enthusiasm, and his genuine interest in all things Pennsylvania Dutch, he inspired others to carry on his work. Among these were Russell and Florence Baver, founders of the Pennsylvania Dutch Folk Culture Society; the Goshenhoppen Historians group in Montgomery County; Historic Schaefferstown in Lebanon County; and the Council of the Alleghenies in Western Pennsylvania and Maryland. All of these groups promote research, publish periodicals, and conduct festivals on the Shoemaker models. Our festival that he so capably directed in its first decade had by 1960 become the largest folk festival in the United States. As the first folklife festival in America, it influenced, among others, the Texas Folklife Festival, the Low German Festival in Kansas, and the National Festival of American Folklife in Washington, D.C.

In addition, academic research centers, such as the Center for Pennsylvania German Studies at Millersville University in Lancaster County, directed by C. Richard Beam, and the Pennsylvania German Cultural Heritage Center at Kutztown University in Lancaster County, founded and directed by David Valuska, have been influenced by the work of Shoemaker. And the Department of Folklore and Folklife at the University of Pennsylvania, of which I was the first chairman, has carried on folk-cultural research in the Shoemaker tradition for more than three decades.

Christmas in Pennsylvania, finally, reflects directly the mind and spirit of Alfred L. Shoemaker, whose work thus continues in many areas in Pennsylvania and other states. It is both a pleasure and an honor for me, as his longtime colleague, to write the new Foreword and the Afterword to the Fortieth Anniversary Edition of this significant book.

DON YODER
THREE KINGS DAY
JANUARY 6, 1999

Foreword to the First Edition

The purpose of a subtitle in a book is not so much an attempt on the part of an author to say what his book is about as it is to say what it is *not* about.

Christmas in Pennsylvania: A Folk-Cultural Study is, needless to say, not an account of the way Christmas is celebrated in the commonwealth today. For nowadays Christmas in Pennsylvania differs not an iota from Christmas in, say, Maine, or Minnesota.

Nor is it the object of the author of this volume to explore institutional Christmas practices in Pennsylvania, whether religious in nature (as in church or Sunday school) or secular (as in all its commercial aspects). Nor, we add, is this book concerned with how the creative arts—music, literature, and painting—have utilized the Pennsylvania Christmas theme.

As the subtitle would indicate, our approach to Christmas in Pennsylvania is a folk-cultural one. However, since academic folklore—the realm in which our subject rightfully belongs—has not as yet evolved scientific techniques peculiar to itself, we have taken recourse to a sister discipline, cultural anthropology. And we have applied its most recently developed technique in studying regional cultures—acculturation—to this study. Now so new a word, perhaps, needs to be defined. By acculturation we mean simply the process of cultural assimilation—the give and take that is constantly taking place where two or more differing cultures are brought face to face.

That the acculturational approach is so well adapted to any folk-cultural study in Pennsylvania is owing to an historic factor: Pennsylvania was settled by peoples representing different folk cultures, one British Isles in background, the other Continental—bearing names: Quaker, Scotch-Irish, and Pennsylvania Dutch.

The purposes of this volume are (1) to describe the folk-cultural background of Pennsylvania as it relates to Christmas, (2) to describe the many colorful folk practices at Christmas time in the Commonwealth, and (3) to show how these Christmas folk practices fared in the acculturation process.

ALFRED L. SHOEMAKER
1959

Introduction to the First Edition
THE FOLK-CULTURAL BACKGROUND

It is always somewhat of a shock to learn that the Puritans did not celebrate Christmas.[1] It will be somewhat of a shock to learn that in the eighteenth and early nineteenth centuries, most Pennsylvanians did not celebrate Christmas either. Puritanism is a thing of the spirit, and Pennsylvania's Puritans—who included the Quakers, Scotch-Irish Presbyterians, Baptists, and Methodists, as well as the Mennonites and other plain groups, who were Puritans in spirit—shared New England's aversion to paying special honor to the 25th of December.[2]

Shall we have holidays? asks the *Democratic Press* of Philadelphia, December 18, 1810. "[F]or the greater part of the citizens of Pennsylvania pay no regard to such days as Christmas, Easter, Whitsuntide, Hallow-eve, etc. . . ."

Let us take a look then at Pennsylvania's complex folk-cultural pattern in the eighteenth and nineteenth centuries, and attempt to sort out the Christmas people from the non-Christmas people, the pro-Christmas party, so to speak, from the anti-Christmas party.

Eighteenth-century Pennsylvania presented to the observer a very mixed pattern, folk-culturally speaking.[3] There were British Isles groups and Continental groups. The three dominant groups were the English and Welsh (Quakers and others), the Scotch-Irish (principally Presbyterians), and the German and Swiss groups (the so-called Pennsylvania Dutch). Among the English and Welsh there were of course a few Anglicans, in Philadelphia, Lancaster, York, and at scattered points in the country throughout the eastern counties. There were small settlements of German, Irish, and English Catholics, at Goshenhoppen (Bally) and Conewago, and in Philadelphia and the towns, but their influence then was small, on the common culture, that is.

Religiously speaking, those groups who organized their year around a liturgy—who in other words pre-

served some semblance of the Catholic church year—celebrated Christmas. These were the Lutherans, Reformed, Moravians, Episcopalians, and of course the small Catholic group. Those groups who exalted the Sabbath—or the revival season of the conversionists—or who shared the Puritan aversion to revelry and "waste"—made up the anti-Christmas party. These were the Quakers, the Scotch-Irish Presbyterians, the Methodists,[4] the Baptists, and the Plain Dutch groups (Mennonites, Brethren, and Amish).

The groups who celebrated Christmas had two elements in their celebration. The first element was the basic religious Christmas, rooted in the liturgy and sanctified by Catholic tradition, involving Christmas services, Christmas communions, decorated churches, Advent hymns, and Christmas carols. And a folk Christmas or popular Christmas, a Christmas of the home and of the streets rather than the church, was the second element. In the case of the Episcopalians this folk or popular Christmas brought something of the "Merry England" Christmas spirit to early Pennsylvania. In the case of the Gay Dutch (Lutherans and Reformed) it brought such Rhineland customs as Belsnickling and Second Christmas revelry and other customs, which will be discussed in detail in other parts of this volume.

In this chapter we shall be concerned with the first of these elements rather than the second, except where the folk Christmas interfered or tended to merge with the religious Christmas, and thus came under the censure of the clergy. In the nineteenth century the Sunday school, an Anglo-American church development, entered the world of the churches, and with it came the Sunday school Christmas festival and "celebration." It is not our purpose to tell that story, since it is a case of a general American Christmas custom which was adopted by Pennsylvania's churches.[5] We shall have to mention, however, the clerical reaction against this invasion of Santa Claus and Kriss Kringle into the church sanctuary.

Nor will we deal with the Roman Catholic celebration of Christmas as such in Pennsylvania, except to say generally that Catholics always celebrated it with the great joy that it is accorded in all Catholic cultures. Catholics were small in number during the formative period of Pennsylvania's folk culture (to 1850), and by the time they began to influence the common culture morally and educationally the Pennsylvania Christmas, which had grown out of the pro-Christmas Protestant groups, had reached its full proportions.[6] But although Catholics had little to do directly with shaping Pennsylvania's Christmas observance, except adding a little statistical weight to the pro-Christmas factions of the Episcopalians and Gay Dutch, it is perhaps a tribute to the old mother of Western Christendom that one of her favorite holidays, which she herself had named Christ-mass, the mass of Christ, was never discarded by some of her Protestant children and finally came, through them, to general acceptance in Pennsylvania as well as America as a whole.

With this introduction we can look briefly at Pennsylvania's Colonial Christmas.

ECHOES OF THE COLONIAL CHRISTMAS

Because of the great religious and folk-cultural variation in Colonial Pennsylvania, there was no uniform eighteenth-century "Pennsylvania Christmas." If one belonged to the Episcopalians or Lutherans or some other pro-Christmas denomination, one celebrated Christmas; if one was a Quaker or a Mennonite or a Presbyterian, one did one's best, like the Puritans, to ignore it.

That there were memories of happy Christmases in the eighteenth century shines through an article published in the weekly newspaper of the Quaker community of West Chester in 1833. Writing from Harrisburg, a correspondent said:

Christmas was here yesterday, but there was not much made of it—the church bells rang, and a few youngsters tippled egg-nog; but it was nothing like the "merry christmas" of olden times, when our grandfathers, in their three cornered hats and eel-skinned ques, marched solemnly to church with our grandmothers in the morning, and feasted and frolicked most devoutly all the rest of the

day. But the times are changed—old folks say, degenerated. (*American Republican,* West Chester, December 31, 1833)

The reference to the ringing of the bells brings us to an Episcopalian contribution to Christmas joy in Quaker Philadelphia. From the minutes of the vestry of Christ Church, Philadelphia, April 3, 1758, we learn of special provision for holiday bell-ringing:

Resolved, that the ringers of the bells be paid the sum of 10 pounds yearly, as usual, for ringing the bells for the service of the church on Sunday, etc. And for their ringing on the following holy days, viz: Christmas, Circumcision, on New Year's Day, Easter, Whitsuntide . . . they are to receive from the church wardens fifteen shillings for each of said days.[7]

On the Western Pennsylvania frontier, where Virginian customs had an influence, Christmas was also a time of joy and revelry. The Presbyterian minister David McClure (1748–1820), describing his visits among the Virginia settlements in Western Pennsylvania "early in 1773," writes: "Rode 7 miles to Mr. Stevenson's & preached. The hearers mostly Virginians. . . . Several present, appeared almost intoxicated. Christmas & New Year holly days, are seasons of wild mirth & disorder here."[8]

That some Philadelphians were in the custom of feasting on Christmas Day is evident from the journal of Christopher Marshall. Marshall was of Quaker background and while his journal (1774–1785) is mostly negative in regard to Christmas, he does furnish us one good reference. December 25, 1777: "No company dined with us today save Dr. Phyle one of our standing family[;] we had a good roast turkey, plain pudding and minced pies."[9] And again, note the Christmas invitation from Hannah Thomson, wife of Charles Thomson, Secretary of Congress, writing from New York, where Congress was then in session, to John Mifflin and young Isaac Norris in Philadelphia, September 17, 1786:

I wish cousin Isaac and you would come & eat yr Christmas dinner here. I will give you as good mince pies & as fat a turkey as you can procure either from Molly Newport or Market Street. You w[oul]d be delighted with the Visiting parties a wishing a happy New Year.[10]

The conflict between pro- and anti-Christmas groups is nowhere better seen than in the memoirs and journals of the Pennsylvania Quakers. The Joseph

An early Pennsylvania Madonna with Child—a broadside entitled "The Birth of Christ," printed by Gustav S. Peters in Harrisburg about 1845.

Price Journal at the Historical Society of Pennsylvania contains four references to Christmas, all negative. December 25, 1790: "This Christmas day so called." December 25, 1796: "This is . . . what they call Christmas day." December 25, 1797: "Turkey Christmasday." And finally, December 25, 1818: "This Christmas spent not as ought to do." The Diary of George Nelson of Philadelphia, also at the Historical Society of Pennsylvania, tells us, under date of Monday, December 26, 1791: "After breakfast open'd my store door but not the window being an Holiday and most of my neighbours shut up. . . ." A nice evidence of Quaker respect for dissident opinion.

As Philadelphia's secular Christmas began to get out of hand with "frolicking" and night revelries, the Quakers began recording their distaste for it. A glimpse into the Elizabeth Drinker home at various "Christmasses," through the pages of the Elizabeth Drinker Diary, gives us plenty of this sort of evidence.

December 25, 1793: Christmass, so call'd, keep't by some pious well minded people religiously, by some others as a time of Frolicking.

December 25, 1794: Such a Christmas day is but seldom known, 'Tho I wont attempt to say, I n'er saw such a one—a green Christmas it is, but I trust it does not follow that we shall have *fatt Church Yards*. James was busy in the Washhouse cutting up 6 Hoggs.

December 25, 1795: Called Christmass day: many attend religiously to this, others spend it in riot and dissipation; We as, a people, make no more account of it than another day.

December 25, 1805: About one o'clock this morn'g I heard a dull heavy thumping, I could not account for after listening some time I heard musick, then concluded that ye first Noise was a Kittle-drum—a strange way of keeping Christmass.

December 25, 1806: Last night or rather this morn'g I heard the kettle-drum for a long time it is a disagreeable noise in my ears, it was after one o'Clock, and at two, I sat up, and took a pinch of snuff, which I do not do, but when I feel unwell and uncomfortable—I had sleep't none, nor for some length of time after. . . .[11]

With this brief glimpse of frontier revelries, Episcopalian bells ringing out over the rooftops of Colonial Philadelphia, and Quaker ladies being roused from honest sleep by the "kittle-drums" of worldly mummers, let us take a look at a subject which agitated Pennsylvania's anti-Christmas forces in 1808–1814.

CHRISTMAS AND THE LEGISLATURE, 1808–1814

Like everything else in Pennsylvania's mixed colonial culture, the Christmas controversy, for that is what it amounted to, reached the legislature in Harrisburg, where members of the different colonial cultures met to make laws for the new commonwealth.

In the period 1808–1814 the Christmas question came up in regard to Christmas adjournment. Such a common matter today was not universally acceptable in Pennsylvania in 1808. "Herr Spangler remarked," a Lancaster newspaper tells us in 1808, reporting a debate at Harrisburg on the 15th of December, "that among the Germans Second Christmas is regarded as a holiday, just like Sunday." It was his opinion therefore that "no business could be transacted in the House on that day, since the Germans would not be present" (*Der Volksfreund*, Lancaster, December 27, 1808).

When it became customary at this time to dismiss the legislature for an extended "Christmas holiday," a Quaker-dominated West Chester paper expressed nothing but scorn for legislators who wasted tax money by adjourning on Christmas. The question was particularly acute in that America was then engaged in the War of 1812.

But perhaps the volunteers have only returned to keep Christmas, in imitation of their brother soldiers in the legislature, who this season, it seems, have adjourned for two weeks, all but a day, (from Dec. 23 to January 4). There is one trifling difference, in the two cases: The poor soldier gets only 30 cents a day, in the field, for having (in the language of the seat-of-government paper) "bayonets poked through his ribs and his sides bored with bullets," while his brother legislators draw *three dollars* a day for eating Christmas pies. (*American Republican*, West Chester, December 29, 1812)

West Chester again attacks the legislature for Christmas indolence in the year 1814:

They adjourned on the Christmas holydays, as they are foolishly called, and shamefully received pay when they unjustly absented themselves from our employment. This fraud cost the state more than two thousand dollars for doing nothing. . . . Had the Devil been born at the beginning of these holydays, the manner they are kept would better suit his character than Christ's. A festival to honor Christ by drinking, cursing, swearing and fighting. Fie for shame,—that legislators should countenance such wickedness. Who hath required this at your hand? You may justly answer Anti-Christ, and none else. There is not a man on earth, knows when Christ was born. In the Eastern world, they pretend it was on the 9th of January—in the Western world they imagine it was on the 25th of December. But the subject was never mentioned, before our holy religion was ruined by blending heathenism with christianity. I have read *Eusebius, Socrates, Scholasticus, Eviginus,* and *Dorotheus,* and not one word is said about Christmas. The above authors bring us to the sixth century. The word mass was not in use among Christians. This heathenish phrase is of a latter date. Plutarch, a heathen, says the word mass meant the ceremonies used by the heathen priests. A good origin for Christmas indeed! Should any superstitious person keep a Christmas, let him do it. But in the name of common sense, let not our legislators tax our state between two and three [six and seven] thousand dollars, to honor Anti-Christ. (*American Republican,* December 27, 1814)

All of which illustrates the power of the anti-Christmas forces in Pennsylvania in the first half of the nineteenth century.

THE QUAKERS AND
THE DAY CALLED CHRISTMAS[12]

Pennsylvania's Quakers called Christmas "the Day called Christmas," to show that they did not countenance any papal or superstitious undertones in the word itself. In general Quakers treated Christmas like any other day. If it fell on a business day, their shops and factories were open as usual. As late as 1862 the Philadelphia Quakers were noted for this disregard of Christmas. "There were no places of business open save the fancy goods stores," writes a reporter in a Philadelphia newspaper, "and a few establishments belonging to Friends, who, eschewing Christmas, look upon all days alike, except the Lord's." (*North American,* December 27, 1862)

A Doylestown paper in 1874 enlarges on this attitude:

Forty years ago, in Quaker Pennsylvania there were hundreds of people who would not have known what was meant had you told them that you were going away to spend the *Holidays.* Most of them knew that the 25th of December was Christmas, but that the day should be considered as different from any other day hardly entered their heads. In a few families, here and there, the children hung up their stockings, but closing schools and places of business, making presents to friends, and observing the day as a holiday, were things undreamed of. (*Bucks County Intelligencer,* December 22, 1874)

By 1889 Friends who employed others on Christmas began to see that a Christmas holiday might be justifiable after all:

We well know how the customs of the present age have cast their toils around us. We know when those in our employ are not willing to carry on the regular work on that day, it may be better to yield to them for the sake of peace and good feeling. We know also, that when the general arrangement for business is thrown out of its course to suit that day, we must arrange our business to meet the emergency. (*Friend,* Third Month 30, 1889)

It was a losing battle, but the editor still thought Friends could salve their conscience with the distinction between passive compliance and active participation.[13]

The Quaker periodicals reveal for us the trend of nineteenth-century Quaker attitudes to Christmas. Beginning with the *Friend* (organ of Orthodox Quakerism) in 1828, and with the *Friends' Intelligencer* (organ of the Hicksite type of Friends) beginning in 1845, we can trace Quaker attitudes to Christmas throughout the nineteenth century.[14]

The results are negative, of course. Christmas, like all "holy" days, did not exist in Quakerism. To the Quaker there was nothing holy but the Spirit. Even "Firstday," when Friends were accustomed to meet for worship like the others who called it the "Lord's Day" and the "Sabbath," was not any holier than any other day in the calendar.[15]

Hence year after year ministers and editors urged Friends not to "observe days and times," like the "foolish Galatians." The editors of the Quaker periodicals could be counted on for an annual editorial on why Friends should not celebrate Christmas.

In the earlier period these annual editorials are general, using the older Puritan reasons for condemning "holy days," occasionally connecting Christmas—Christ-mass—with Roman Catholic superstition, rationalistic in that they deny that the exact date of the birthday of Jesus is known at all. Toward the end of the century, the editors had to caution Friends not to adopt the worldly Christmas customs of their Episcopalian and Pennsylvania Dutch neighbors. Here the analogy was no longer the "foolish Galatians" but rather the "apostate Israelite."

Let us look at the evidence.

"That portion of the year that has just opened upon us," remarks a writer in the *Friend* for First Month (January) 3, 1835,

is welcomed by the generality of persons in easy circumstances, as a season of peculiar social enjoyment. While the more sober have looked forward to it as a time that shall again assemble their long scattered family around the cheerful fireside. . . ."

Friends are urged to witness against the "luxurious entertainments during the present winter." The constant note of the necessity of helping the poor is sounded as the Quaker substitute for the feasting and celebration that the more worldly groups yielded to in the holiday season.

The editor of the *Friends' Intelligencer*, in an article entitled "The Season," appearing First Month 3, 1846, gives us the full and typical Quaker rationale of opposition to Christmas. Let us listen to his words in full:

That particular period of time, especially, called Christmas, viewed as a Religious festival, has, we fully believe, tended more to open licentiousness of manners, than to the increase and encouragement of sound morality and religion. The mummery which takes place in some of the churches, so called, at this season, under the ministration of a class of hireling teachers, and the childish and superficial ideas which are propagated through this corrupt and interested medium, concerning the nature and mode of Christian redemption, are wonderfully calculated to enlarge the sphere of stupidity, and to increase the shades of moral darkness over the minds of mankind. The testimony of the Society of Friends against the observance of days and times, had its origin in sound views of Truth, and has reference to the best interests of the community. We are therefore very desirous that none of our members, while they indulge in innocent acts of conviviality, may give their countenance, in any way, to these anniversary institutions as having any real connection with true piety and religion.

Christmas entertaining was in particular a temptation to Philadelphia Friends. While entertaining of visiting Friends was an accepted and welcome part of "Yearly Meeting Week" in the Spring, when Jersey and upstate Pennsylvania Friends filled the Quaker residences to overflowing and Quaker tables vied with one another to produce evidence of Quaker culinary superiority, the same sort of thing at Christmastime served no practical purpose, and

A Pennsylvania Dutch Madonna from the first half of the nineteenth century. The Madonna and angels were obviously copied from a Renaissance print, but the stars could double as Pennsylvania hex signs.

might encourage the neighbors in their own too lavish entertainment practices.

In particular Friends were cautioned in the 1850s against the "Evening Parties" which had become fashionable in Philadelphia for the holiday season. J. M. E., commenting on an editorial in the *Public Ledger* on these "Fashionable Parties"—with their terrapins and oysters, champagne and brandy, ice-cream and calves'-foot jelly, claret punch and hock—expresses his opinion that

while it behooves *Friends* individually to examine how far this evil is making inroads into the real welfare of their families, I would by no means be looked upon as setting my face against a well-regulated social intercourse. (*Friends' Intelligencer,* Twelfth Month 3, 1853)

The editor, reviewing "Evening Parties" shortly afterwards, expressed his fear that "the contagion is gradually spreading . . ." and felt that women were chiefly to blame, and gave as his firm opinion that where such gatherings did take place, and Friends were involved, guests should leave for home at 10 P.M. (*Friends' Intelligencer*, First Month 7, 1854).

Country Friends were being tempted by Christmas too. The voice of an old-fashioned country Friend is heard in 1889. Writing from Pennsville, he voices his testimony against "falling into the ways of an evil world, either in eating or drinking, or in the vain amusements and pastimes so prevalent in the world." "And," he adds, putting the moral weight of his nearly 79 years behind it,

I fear that many under our name [meaning Quakers] are too much falling into the practice of making the time called Christmas a day of feasting and mirth, instead of being engaged as we all ought to be, to be prepared for the solemn change that awaits us all. We have need, all of us, to be found watching so that that day may not come upon us unawares and find us unprepared. (*Friend*, letter dated Twelfth Month 15, 1889)

Which is a genuine Quaker sermon, and could also have passed as a Puritan sermon on the subject in the seventeenth century.

The editor of the *Friend* took time in 1900 to outline the familiar Puritan-Quaker argument against holy days:

Certain conventional days are defended as objects of devout observance, because of the graces and benevolent qualities of heart which they are supposed to inspire. No matter if Christmas-time was observed under other names as days began to lengthen in the year, and by nations however heathen, long before the advent of Christ personally on earth; no matter whether the day is of Scriptural appointment or not, we will cherish it, say its advocates, for the good-cheer, the unselfishness, the thankfulness, and other graces that it is charged with, and that come out of it. (*Friend*, Twelfth Month 29, 1900)

This, which amounted to depending upon a day for grace, was, concluded the editor, a superstition.

Santa Claus makes a brief and unwelcome appearance on the pages of the *Friend* in 1906, in a quotation from the *Evangelical Friend:*

We, as a people, are prone to wink at tradition and mythology and smile approvingly at the children's momentary enjoyment of Santa Claus and his gifts. We talk about mythology, and about tradition, but the Bible warns against these things, against falsehood and

hypocrisy. The time has surely come in the history of the church and of Christianity when we should banish this myth from our midst. A little girl in my home town, like the vast majority of children, has been taught that Santa Claus was her Christmas friend; but finally some one told her there was no Santa Claus. She was disappointed. A few days later she refused to go to Sabbath School. When pressed for a reason why, she replied, "Likely as not this Jesus Christ business will turn out just like Santa Claus." (*Friend*, Twelfth Month 1906)

And, adds the editor of the *Friend*, "Parents, teachers, let her words dwell with you."[16]

The *Friend* also reported in 1906 (quoting the *Christian Instructor*) that news had reached it from Des Moines, Iowa, that one of the Protestant churches "is reported to have had a baby in a manger as part of the Christmas doings," and the correspondent thought that "we as a nation are going Romeward very fast."

In all the churches there is need for watchfulness against such foolish nonsense as is often practiced in the name of Christ during holiday times specially. Christians, like the Israelites of old, often have a desire to be like their neighbors in religious as well as in other things. (*Friend*, First Month 13, 1906)

The best of the Quaker accounts of attitudes to Christmas, and Friends' reactions to practices of neighboring groups, comes from the *Friend* in 1904, in which a Quaker, following all the stiff Quaker aversion to Christmas celebration, writes of an experience he had with two neighbors' families in Fernwood, in the Philadelphia area:

Having occasion to call on some of our neighbors a few days after the day called Christmas, the writer was brought into some exercise of mind to know how to acquit himself of what seemed an unpleasant duty to parents and children, seeing that the lesson which duty would point out, in love of right and in love of both, would much conflict with that in which they had been occupied with great delight. In one of these houses tattered clothing and general appearances denoted a shortness of the necessaries of life. The father was unwell and partly out of employment, yet in one corner of the occupied room was a green bush or tree called "a Christmas tree," the lading of which had cost both money and time. A little boy approached me saying, "Chris Kinkle did not bring me anything, although I hung my stocking up."

In another house where everything bespoke plenty, the father having a good trade, a much larger and more costly laden pine bush filled a corner of the room, and a number of children around it. A lit-

This fraktur by a Quaker schoolmaster from Bucks County, circa 1800–1810, presents pointed evidence of the Quaker opposition to the Christmas celebration. The piece is entitled "Verses on the Vanity and Superstitious Manner of Some People's Keeping of Christmas Day. Done by Henry Hill schoolmaster from London. For Mrs. Jane Fell Living in the County of Bucks in Pennsylvania."

tle son of the occupant of the house came to me greatly delighted with the false stories he had been made to believe, what "Chris Kinkle" (which is taken from the German meaning the Christ-child) had done, and made demonstrations showing how he got in at the top of the chimney, and tumbled out at the bottom of it.

It is not supposed that any of the readers of THE FRIEND are guilty of so deceiving their children; and we hope that the fewer number are guilty of setting the example of needless waste of means on any of the so-called "holy days." But we could but feel sorry for both parents and children of the said families. And on reflecting how, no doubt, many thousands are doing after the same manner, the query arose whether we, the people called Friends, are as clear as the Truth requires that we should be in order that we may, by example and words, by patterns and rightful helpers in these and other things, by heeding the teaching of Divine Grace, which teaches to deny "ungodliness and the world's lusts," all that will not work for the glory of our Heavenly Father, and to the furtherance of his cause of truth and righteousness in the earth. We have for years believed that the increase of waste of money in unnecessary and even useless things, as well as the other evils which are getting more and more to abound, calls for a plain and open testimony against the keeping of all so-called "holy days," and especially against the manner in which they are kept.[17]

That the Quakers were originally anti-Christmas but eventually succumbed to a modified attention to Christmas at least as a family festival, is plain from the records. That some of them succumbed earlier than our Friend from Fernwood who watched his neighbor's child demonstrate how "Kriss Krinkle" came down the chimney, is the implication of an editorial in the *Public Ledger* in 1847:

Some say that the custom was introduced into Philadelphia from New England, and is neither more nor less than an imitation of a Yankee Thanksgiving. But this is entirely improbable. The Puritans were a hard-faced set of fellows, and never laughed at anything, and devoured their spare-ribs and pumpkin-pies, their thanksgiving dinners, as solemnly as if they were awaiting the execution of the law. The only difference between their thanksgiving and their fast-days was that, on the first they looked solemn and crammed, and on the second they looked sour and went to bed hungry. Whoever will scan the sunny, joyous, full-fed visage of a Philadelphian on a Christmas day, would peremptorily declare that he never could have borrowed himself from the solemn looking phizzes of Connecticut or the Bay State, and hence that Christmas could not have sprouted from thanksgiving. Besides, Philadelphia is a Quaker city; and whoever knows how the Broadbrims were treated by the long-sided Jonathans, almost as badly as if they had been witches, will never believe that they would have imitated anything in Yankeedom. But we shall be told that the Quakers do not keep Christmas, and therefore that this argument fails. But they keep it quite as much as other Philadelphians. They do not rig out in spruce or hemlock; but they cram themselves with stuffed turkeys, devour mince-pies, and look quite as full and as fat and as rosy and as happy, and as satisfied with the inner man, as the devotees of the green boughs. Therefore we say that, whatever be the origin of Christmas elsewhere, in Philadelphia it began in High Street market, and as the Quakers founded the city and established that market, they must have had something to do with its contents. We believe, beyond all doubt, that, in our city, Christmas is of Quaker origin. (*Public Ledger,* December 25, 1847)

Which goes against all that we have said but is quoted not only for its caricature of the New Englander at Thanksgiving[18] and the well-fed Philadelphian at Christmas, but for its valuable suggestion about the place of the Farmers' Market in linking Christmas customs of upstate Pennsylvania with those of the city.

THE CHRISTMAS OF THE SCOTCH-IRISH

The Scotch-Irish Presbyterians from Ulster, who settled possibly a third of colonial Pennsylvania, transplanted Puritan attitudes to Christmas wherever they settled.

A descendant of one of them wrote in 1888:

You know I was brought up Presbyterian and as I now look back through misty recollection I half smile at the semi-grimness of the old time Christmas day. What Macaulay said of the Puritan was true of the ancient Presbyterian as I knew him in childhood—"He objected to bear baiting, not because it hurt the bear, but gave pleasure to the

spectators." In a large measure this has changed and now the day has more of human enjoyment than any special religious significance.[19]

Like their Quaker neighbors, the Presbyterians made very little of the Christmas festival in earlier years. A West Chester paper informs us as late as 1867 that

neither the Methodist, Baptist or Presbyterian congregations held religious services in their churches. Some of these, if not all, we believe, hold that the observance of any day than the Sabbath, is not enjoined by the Scriptures. (*American Republican,* December 31, 1867)

A Reading newspaper tells us that

for the first time in many years every church in the city was open for public worship. Even our Presbyterian friends who have hitherto steadfastly ignored Christmas—threw open their church doors and assembled in force to celebrate the anniversary of the Saviour's birth. (*Berks and Schuylkill Journal,* December 28, 1861)

The official view of Christmas as a rival to the Sabbath is outlined in the *Presbyterian Banner* in 1852, which greatly regretted "that the day is ordinarily spent so irreverently by those who would observe it, and who would dignify it with the Saviour's name." The editor continues, and here we hear the Puritan voice of Pennsylvania Presbyterianism:

We would that Christians, since Christ hath left no information and no injunction, could drop the name and cease to regard the season. Alas! how fond men are to do things not enjoined, and to disregard their Lord's very plain commandments! The *Sabbath* is the LORD'S DAY, by positive enactment; and the *Sacramental supper* is the LORD'S FEAST by express command. The *day* is fixed. The feast is *enjoined.* The observances of these seasons are all of divine prescription. Let then these be kept—sacredly kept—kept by all. But, if any will also regard *Christmas,* let them regard it as *Christians.* Let them thereon and therein, adorn their profession and honour their lord. (*Presbyterian Banner,* Philadelphia, December 25, 1852)

That the Presbyterians had made some accommodation to Christmas by mid-nineteenth century is evident from the reminiscences of Robert Blair Risk. Writing in a Lancaster paper in 1912, he draws a nostalgic picture of Christmas among the Lancaster County Scotch-Irish Presbyterians in the nineteenth century, who while they restrained themselves from too exuberant a Christmas celebration, had already adopted some of the customs of the Pennsylvania

Dutch neighbors.[20] Let us listen as the old gentleman describes his boyhood Christmas:

I was brought up in a Scotch-Irish Presbyterian family and neighborhood. If Christmas is overworked now, it was somewhat underdone in the days I speak of, as the community regarded the celebration as a somewhat Pagan custom involving too much hilarity. It was more inclined to make Thanksgiving a festive occasion, as it had a Puritan flavor, and at all times regarded the Sabbath as the Hindoo does his idol—great, although sometimes ugly and harsh. I never saw a Christmas tree till I had almost reached my majority. Such a symbol of Christmastide was too Germanic for Scotch-Irish appreciation. Still, the legend of Santa Claus was told in every household and believed in by every child. But I now think the genial saint was invoked by my elders more for disciplinary purposes than for any poetic appreciation of the myth. About the first of December I was duly told that if I was not a good boy my stockings in the big fireplace would get little or no recognition. To keep out of boyish pranks and mischief for three weeks took some of the charm out of Christmas enjoyment for us young lads. The restraint oft made us feel lonesome and that the great day was coming very slowly and seemed very far off. We also felt we were paying pretty dear for what might turn out inadequate reward. Still, we lads were as good as we could be, even if it did make us lonesome when we saw a fine chance for a prank or some boyish fun. In due time Christmas eve came and hopeful little heads went to bed early in order to be up at the first peep of dawn. Our stockings had been hung on the crane of the big fireplace in the firm belief that Santa Claus would visit them, as he had plenty of chimney room to get down to them, however big his pack might be. Our faith was never deceived, as in the morning we found our hosiery packed full of home-made candies, candles and nuts bought at the village store, a simple toy or two, but no games; a pair of gloves, and, perhaps, some useful wearing apparel. In short, the day, so far as parents were concerned, was one devoted to the children. There was little or no exchanging of gifts between members of the family, or with neighbors or distant relatives. Post cards were unknown, and so friendly greetings were not sent or received. One thing the children missed[:] In those stern old days, the Puritan Presbyterian underdone Christmas by not furnishing the youngsters fairy tales or reading that appealed to the imagination. It was not the day for children's books as now, but if it had been, stern theology would not have given them through the Christmas stocking. Such books as were made presents had some kind of sermon or moral attached to them which did not appeal to the youthful mind. The imaginative in story or novel was looked at with as much disfavor as was a deck of cards or a glass of wine. This was not right, as I believe I would have earlier acquired a taste for reading and for books had I

been furnished with Grimm's Fairy Tales instead of the Life of Benjamin Franklin—something unsuited for a child. But with it all the simple Christmas the child of sixty years ago received was wholesome. He did not expect too much or get too much. He was not surfeited by too many toys, and so what he received gave him long enjoyment. If he had little to love, he loved it much. He was not taught to save his pennies for one day's splurge, and so Christmas was more an episode than the greatest day in the year.

But how did the elders observe the day? Well, in a hearty, simple way. They did not wear themselves out in spirit and purse shopping, or become distracted about exchanging gifts. Very leisurely home preparations went on in the shape of extra baking of cakes and dainties, from a doughnut to a mince pie. The house was set in order with some decorations from the nearby swamp in the line of evergreens. The big turkey had been penned up for double feed, one of Charles Lamb's "sucklings," a fine little pig, was a-ripening for the slaughter, and, perhaps, a brace of ducks were in preparation for the feast of fat things. On Christmas morn all work on the farm ceased and man servant and maid servant donned their best attire, for they shared in the coming banquet the same as did the invited relative or near neighbor. The farm house then was a democratic centre and did not draw social distinctions as now. Every one was in good humor, for expecting no gifts they had no regret over none sent in exchange. In due time the feast graced the table and all but the colored folks sat down to it. Hearty appetites and souls free from care, with all the simplicity of honest good will and friendship, took their places and joyous merriment prevailed from the first carving till the dessert completed repletion.

Next came the peaceful pipe for the men and gentle talk among the women till nightfall approached. Then the poor of the neighborhood, few in numbers, would call and each would go home with cakes and the remains of the Christmas feast. It was all very simple and heartsome and without a heartburn or disappointment.[21]

THE EPISCOPALIAN CHRISTMAS

In the nineteenth century the Episcopalians grew into a more influential group in Pennsylvania than they had been in the eighteenth century. With the exception of some of the more low-church rectors—who thought there was too much levity among Episcopalians at Christmas—churchmen were wholeheartedly in favor of Christmas, both church and secular. With their decorated churches, bells ringing out through the December air, and Christmas feasting, it is a pleasant picture.

The short story, "Christmas in S———," which appeared in the *Church Register* (Philadelphia), February 17 and 24, 1827, will illustrate Episcopalian attitudes in the early nineteenth century.

First we are given a description of the church decorations.[22]

The Episcopal church of S——, at all times well attended, exhibited to the eye of the hasty observer, a spectacle truly gratifying. The taste of the ladies had been busy in devising and executing plans for the most graceful distribution of those symbols of gladness, which are admitted into our places of worship at this season. Wreaths of the richest evergreen were disposed in festoons along the railing of the chancel, entwined around the pillars which supported the pulpit, and hung amidst the rich carving, and the purple drapery which covered it.

The decorations were so elaborate, in fact, that the "pastor" feared his people's exertions

had been animated by no better motive than that "esprit de corps," which made them anxious *their* church should support the character of being always tastefully decorated, and of having better music than any other in S——.

The village of S—— was awaiting the Christmas holiday with mixed feelings.

Scarcely a dwelling could be found in S—— where preparations had not been made to distinguish a season custom has rendered almost synonymous with festivity. Even those whose creed prevented them from hallowing it by a religious service, seemed not unwilling to receive it as a domestic holiday, on which they loved to collect together the different branches of their families at the same festive board, mingling in the same assemblage the experience of age, the vivacity of youth, and the playfulness of childhood.

At the Christmas service the preacher, after laying before his people the religious significance of Advent,

commented with marked disapprobation on the habitual inconsideration, with which too many of those who were now within the sanctuary, would hasten to engage, as soon as they left its precincts, in every sort of levity, feasting and frivolity, thus hastily effacing every serious impression, the duties in which they had been previously occupied, might be made.

After the sermon one member said to another, "I think your aunt will not coincide exactly with the sentiments of the sermon. It is sadly against our having any more merry Christmas parties." And apropos of the minister's remarks, he said (speaking of poor

Mrs. Owen, who used to sit in the next pew to his mother) that

one Christmas I overheard her whisper to a friend, that she had been so hurried preparing for company, she feared she should have been detained from church; she had even been obliged to make a pie before she came, and she believed that she could not stay to commune.

In the Christmas party, which makes up the remainder of the story, one guest supports the minister, and adds her disapproval of card playing and theatergoing and novel reading (she *is* low church!). But the rest give themselves up to the enjoyment of the day's festivities—perfectly content to be at one moment "occupied in the most solemn services of religion, and the next, apparently as deeply engaged in the frivolous chit-chat of ordinary dinner party conversation." Which is perhaps a good summary of the Catholic approach to life in general.

CHRISTMAS AMONG THE GAY DUTCH

Among the Pennsylvania Dutch the only groups who celebrated Christmas with joy and abandon were (1) the so-called Gay Dutch—the Lutherans and Reformed, who brought the Catholic approach to life and worship to Pennsylvania from the Rhineland; and (2) the Moravians, those emotional sectarians, with their emphasis on their beloved *Jesulein*, the Baby Jesus, whose glories they sang in some of the most beautiful carols ever sung in America.

The approach to life that the Gay Dutch had was one of acceptance of the world. They said yes to life and work. They did not attempt to set up a holy community apart from the world, as did the early Quakers and the Plain Dutch groups, the Mennonites, Amish, and others. The world was God's world as it was, to the Lutheran and the Reformed.

While there was among them some influence of the Pietist movement, especially among the ministry, the people reacted to the American situation by reproducing the attitudes that had been customary among their forefathers in the tolerant and *gemütlich* Rhineland. In fact the world *gemütlich*—the very opposite of "Puritan"—can be used to describe these groups and their culture far into the nineteenth century.[23]

While in general the Gay Dutch (secular or folk) Christmas and the Moravian Christmas are described elsewhere in this volume, a few details need general treatment here.

The Lutherans and Reformed in Pennsylvania had a double basis for their Christmas. Because they came from Protestant traditions with a liturgical base, traditions that paid more than usual Protestant attention to the church year, Christmas was defended by the ministry. This pro-Christmas attitude on the part of Lutheran and Reformed religious leaders, allowed the people, in the first century and a half after the first settlement (1700–1850) to establish and develop a folk Christmas of their own, most elements of which had been brought from the Rhineland.

In the second half of the nineteenth century, when a significant proportion of the Lutheran and Reformed clergy had become either Puritan or High Church in outlook, when also the folk Christmas showed some signs of taking over in the Sunday school—when, as the church papers put it, Kriss Krinkle and Santa Claus began to crowd out the Christ Child—the clergy and the clergy-dominated church press changed their tolerance of the folk Christmas into opposition.

To illustrate what happened, let us look at the case of Second Christmas.

SECOND CHRISTMAS

If the English celebrated Twelve Days of Christmas, as the carol has it, the Gay Dutch celebrated at least two, Christmas Day and Second Christmas, which was the day after Christmas itself.[24]

In general Second Christmas was a day of relaxation, not quite so much of a religious holiday as Christmas. Ezra Keller, Lutheran minister in Hagerstown, Maryland, in 1842 attempted to make it a religious holiday. "My German communion I appointed on the second Christmas day," he tells us; "this displeased some, who although they deem it proper to observe the 26th as a holy day, yet do not think it as holy as the 25th."[25] A Lancaster news item from 1849 gives us the popular attitude to Second Christmas: "On the second day of Christmas we had a fox chase and other amusements. . . ." (*Pennsylvanian*, Philadelphia, January 2, 1849)

In the attempt to sanctify Second Christmas, other ministers held church consecrations and Sunday school exercises on the day. William A. Helf-

Zur Chriſtnacht

1 7 8 8

In Litiz.

Chorus.

Freuet euch und ſeyd frölich, die ihr Seinen Tag ſehet, den Tag unſers Heils. Der uns beſucht hat iſt GOtt mit uns, der Schönſte unter den Menſchenkindern. Licht iſt ſein Kleid, das Er an hat. GOttes Klarheit leuchtet aus Seinem Angeſichte. Alle Lande müſſen Seiner Ehre voll werden.

Gemeine.

Moravian Christmas Eve service for 1788 at Lititz in Lancaster County. The Moravians were among Pennsylvania's most avid celebrators of the Christmas holidays.

frich, the widely known Reformed leader of Lehigh and Berks Counties, tells us in his autobiography of the consecration of the new Longswamp Church on Saturday and Sunday, the 25th and 26th of December, 1852:

Preached on the first day. . . . The church was at that time the finest in the country. I thought on Christmas, when frost and snow covered the earth, that the sutlers would stay away—but no! even though in not such large numbers, yet the Devil brought them hither. There they stood, behind their "ginger cakes and sugar sticks" [*Lebkuchen und Zuckerstängeln*], stamping their feet and pulling their coat-collars closer on account of the frost, and used all their arts to entice buyers.[26]

What is significant about this is that the people were reacting in the old traditional ways. Second

Christmas was to them a day of relaxation. Even though they answered the call of their minister to gather at the church, they wanted to make it a social affair. The sutlers (*Marketender*) with their cakes and wares reacted also in the traditional manner. It was much like the traditional *Kerwe* (*Kermess, Kirchmess*) of the Rhineland villages from whence the Gay Dutch forefathers had emigrated a century before.[27]

The people, then, reacted in their usual way. The clergy too, perhaps, were acting in what was a traditional role for them. With their fear of the secular, with their growing dislike for the folk aspects of the culture, they forbade the popular practices.[28]

THE CHURCH VERSUS SANTA CLAUS

While the Sunday school Christmas festival was not of course part of the Gay Dutch folk Christmas, it did become increasingly popular in both Lutheran and Reformed parishes in the second half of the nineteenth century. This again produced tension between the layman's interpretation of Christmas (the Sunday school was a typically American layman's church organization) and clerical attitudes. Increasingly in the 1880s, the Lutheran and Reformed leadership became critical of some of the practices of the Sunday school celebration. While the *Lutheran Observer* for January 26, 1883, comments approvingly on the "Santa Claus pails," full of candies and dates, which were featured at a recent Christmas celebration in Blairsville, the *Lutheran and Missionary* of Philadelphia—representing the High Church wing of Pennsylvania Lutheranism, in a stern article on "Christmas Presents for Sunday Schools"—urges the giving of *religious* gifts rather than clay pipes, jumping jacks, and other secular delights (*Lutheran and Missionary*, December 9, 1880).

The folk Christmas practices were bitterly opposed by the Lutherans of the growing High Church school. "Let it be *Christmas* indeed," writes the editor of the *Lutheran and Missionary* in 1881,

and make Christ more prominent everywhere. It is His Day, and old and young should remember it. The sooner you present the *Christ child* to your children, the better. Do not suffer this lovely picture to be hidden by the hideous caricature of a Kriss-Kringle, that odious corruption of the German expression *Christkindchen,* or *Christkindle;* and do not substitute for the Babe of Bethlehem, the figment of a Santa Claus. . . . (*Lutheran and Missionary,* 1881)

Even the *Lutheran Observer* was ready to attack the Sunday school celebrations by 1883. It did so in an article entitled "The Heathenism of Christmas. A Protest Against Santa Claus," signed by "Germanicus" and written expressly for its columns. After giving a biography of St. Nicholas, whose birthday, more than incidentally, was pointed out to fall on "Luther's birthday too," "Germanicus" continues as follows:

The curious customs of St. Nicholas eve, as they obtain in the old country, are interesting and pleasant, and they do not at least partake of the nature of sacrilege. But when the Dutch brought their Sante Klaas to this country, and the Germans during this same month celebrated the feast of the *Christ-Kindlein,* the Christ-Child, they came in contact with people who gazed in astonishment on these superstitious customs. The New England Puritans had for years been forbidden by law to celebrate Christmas, and even the adherents of the English established church were accustomed to look upon Christmas as a day of feasting and jollity, rather than as a sacred religious festival.

Thus it was natural for them to combine the customs of the foreigners, the Dutch and the Germans; and Santa Claus and Kriss Kringle, as in their barbarous ignorance of the language they called the Christ-Child, became hopelessly intermingled in the American mind. The festival for both gradually came to be fixed on Christmas.

And now our correspondent gives us his view of the state to which the American Protestant Sunday school Christmas festival had attained by 1883:

And now, in a week or two, we shall read notices like the following:

"Santa Claus in the flesh.—The merry time made by his appearance in the Fourth P. Q. Church.—How Christmas was kept.—Santa Claus held a reception and made a special distribution of gifts in the Fourth P. Q. Church last evening. An army of children was present, whose faces shone with anticipation. The exercises began with a Christmas carol entitled 'Who comes this way so blithe and gay?' after which Master William Robinson marched boldly to the front and delivered a speech of welcome. Little Miss Florence Montague then told a story of her last doll, which caused much amusement. Miss Genevieve Parkington then recited the beautiful verses

'Twas the night before Christmas
When all through the house.

The Hon. Willard Brown then read a letter from the good saint, expressing that gentleman's perfect satisfaction with the Fourth P. Q. Sunday-school, its minister, its superintendent, and all its children.

At this moment a great commotion was heard outside. The rattle of sleigh bells was heard, and suddenly Santa Claus himself came dashing into church, and with a hop skip and jump stood on the platform, amid the wildest cheers and shouts of the children. After giving a history of himself he began to distribute presents to the children.

After the distribution the children sang the following beautiful hymn:

'Oh, this is Santa Claus' man,
Kriss Kringle with his Christmas tree.
Oh ho, Oh ho, ho, ho, ho, ho, ho, ho, ho, ho,
Then jingle, jingle, jing, jing, jing,
Right merry shall we be,
Then jingle, jingle,
Come Kriss Kringle,
Come with your Christmas tree;
And welcome, welcome, welcome Kriss,
Right welcome shall you be,
O there he is, yes, yes, 'tis Kriss,
'Tis Kriss with the Christmas tree,
The Christmas tree, the Christmas tree,
The Christmas tree, the Christmas tree.'"

Now this is no overwrought, fancy picture. It is a scene that will be witnessed in hundreds of churches in city and country, and judging from some reports that reached us last year through the OBSERVER, will not be wanting even in some Lutheran churches.

Not that we have learned it from our ancestors, or from our German brethren. In Germany and in the German churches of this country, Christmas is a sacred day. It commemorates the birth of Christ, God's unspeakable *gift*. Through him all good gifts came to men. The mummery of Santa Claus has no place in the ritual of the Lutheran church, excepting where some of our congregations have borrowed the folly from their neighbors.

Neither is it common among Protestant Episcopal churches, as far as I have observed. Churches that have a *Christian* year and whose liturgy provides for sacred hymns and services on such occasions, are less tempted to pervert the day to improper uses. But it is among the denominations that have had no other holy-day but Sunday, and that have only recently adopted the Christmas, and then only its outward and oftentimes most objectionable features, that these customs prevail. And as they constitute the great majority, the Santa Claus folly has infected family life, literature, church services, everything almost, at this season.

On aesthetical grounds alone this commingling of St. Nicholas eve and Christmas is objectionable. But it is on religious grounds that we ought to raise a solemn protest against this widespread cultus of Santa Claus.

Instead of the sacred hymns which our fathers sang, such as: "All my heart this night rejoice," "Good news from heaven the angles bring," "A Babe is born in Bethlehem," "Come hither ye faithful, triumphantly sing," and all the other angelic melodies, the children of the present time are fast getting their heads full of Santa Claus and of Kriss Kringle, Santa Claus' man.

"With cakes and plums, trumpets and drums,
And lots of pretty things he comes;
So now be quick, your places take,
And all a merry circle make:
For now he's near, he'll soon appear,
And we his jolly face shall see;
Oh, welcome Santa Claus' man,
Kriss Kringle," etc.

The Holy Christ-Child has in very truth been made to take the place of Santa Claus' man.

But not only from the churches should this pernicious heathenism be expelled: it should also find no place in the family. Christian mothers, you can do better than to deceive your little ones with ridiculous stories of the chimney saint. Present your gifts in whatever way you please, in the stockings or in the shoes; but be sure to tell your children that every good gift and every perfect gift is from above, and that Christ is God's gift to men. But do not let Santa Claus take the place of the blessed Saviour in the hearts and imaginations of your children.[29]

In 1894 both Lutheran and Reformed groups in Eastern Pennsylvania finally put their foot down on the invasion of the popular Christmas into the Church and Sunday school. In that year the Allentown Conference of the Lutheran Ministerium of Pennsylvania

resolved, that it is the unanimous opinion of the Conference, that many of the so-called Christmas festivals and entertainments are unbiblical, unchristian, a coarse distortion of the name and character of Christ, and are injurious in their influence on future generations. Resolved, that the Conference censure and condemn all these half-heathen exhibitions and customs and demand that they be banned forever from Christian churches and Sunday Schools. (*Allentown Friedens-Bote,* January 2, 1894)

An article entitled *"Der arme Weihnachtsmann"* in the *Friedens-Bote* for January 16, 1894, reports that the Reformed followed suit and "Poor Santa Claus" was banned from both Church and Sunday school.

HENRY FRANCIS DUPONT WINTERTHUR MUSEUM, INC.

This watercolor drawing depicts a Pennsylvania Dutch family gathered around their tabletop Christmas tree, complete with fenced manger scene, festive baked goods, and toys, circa 1812. The artist, John Lewis Kimmel (1786–1821), was a German emigrant who worked in Philadelphia between 1809 and 1821, except from 1817 to 1818, when he was revisiting his Swabian homeland. He has been called America's first genre painter.

NEW LUTHERAN ATTITUDES

There were two kinds of Lutherans in nineteenth-century Pennsylvania. The majority of Lutherans represented the Old Lutheran, *gemütlich*, or Gay Dutch approach to life: the Catholic outlook that life was good and religion sanctified all of life, from birth to death. These would later contribute to the High Church Lutheranism of the Philadelphia Seminary. A minority, with its citadel at Gettysburg Seminary, were known as New Lutherans and were at one time so revivalistic and so conversion-conscious that they resembled Methodists with Dutch accents more than the older Pennsylvania Lutheranism. So there were Old and New Lutheran attitudes to Christmas.

Typical of the New Lutheran attitude toward Christmas—which was the Puritan attitude applied on the Lutheran scene—are two editorials in the *Lutheran Observer* in 1854 and 1855, both from the pen of the somewhat irascible editor, Benjamin Kurtz (1795–1865).

In 1854, in an "editorial" on Christmas, Brother Kurtz sets forth the sour doctrine:

Before this number of our paper reaches our subscribers, Christmas will have gone by, and New-Year's Day shall be near at hand. We have nothing special to say in regard to the "holidays." To repeat for the hundredth time, the stereotyped remarks to which the occasion has so often given rise, is repugnant to our taste and would be naught but a weariness to our readers; they will thank us for our silence. (*Lutheran Observer,* December 29, 1854)

And again the following year he took pen in hand to write an editorial on "The Holidays":

It is customary to tender "the compliments of the season," but we have no inclination at present to conform to this practice. *First,* because *compliments* are for the most part empty things, and of no value; *second,* because we have nothing new to add to what we have again and again given expression to, on former similar occasions; *third,* because we are on the eve of leaving home to be absent a week or longer, and therefore have no time to string together a list of congratulations, or to prepare an argument on the hackneyed question, whether the 25th of December is the real day of Christ's birth, and ought to be celebrated as a holliday or not; and last though not least, because we have no disposition whatever, just at this time, either to write or talk. . . . (*Lutheran Observer,* December 28, 1855)

In other words, Benjamin Kurtz was not interested in Christmas.

Ezra Keller (1812–1848), one of the New Lutheran leaders, expressed not only the New Lutheran attitude but perhaps with it the general clerical attitude toward the relaxations of the people on Christmas, in his journal for 1840, when he was pastor at Hagerstown, Maryland:

Dec. 27. My prayer has been answered by the Lord, and to-day I was enabled to preach with much freedom and solemnity. I resolved boldly to reprove the Germans in this community for dancing and other accompanying sins, perpetrated on Christmas Day; in which duty the Lord blessed me with inward strength and power, giving evidence that it is always best to do what judgment and conscience pronounce to be right.[30]

In his attempt to sanctify the Christmas season, he reports in 1841 of preaching on Christmas morning at four o'clock, and again at eleven o'clock holding a "missionary meeting," at which "the children of the Sabbath school presented their gifts to the Lord." In all, in connection with the "Christmas festival," he writes, "I have preached four times." In 1842 and 1847 he reports holding a revival, in the latter year "between Christmas and New-Year," and in 1842 in appointing his German communion on Second Christmas Day, he displeased some of his parishioners, who "although they deem it proper to observe the 26th as a holy day, yet do not think it as holy as the 25th."[31]

In other words, his ideas of what was holy and proper on the "Christmas festival" were in conflict with the folk Christmas of some of his parishioners. This would prove to be a growing source of tension throughout the rest of the nineteenth century, in the Lutheran and Reformed Churches.

REFORMED CHURCH ATTITUDES

Possibly through the influence of Henry Harbaugh (1817–1867) the Reformed Church—which for some reason seems to have been in general more congenial to the folk elements in Gay Dutch life than the Lutherans—paid more attention to Christmas. At least it seems so as one reads through the Reformed periodicals.

Throughout the 1870s, '80s, and '90s of the last century, the December and January pages of the

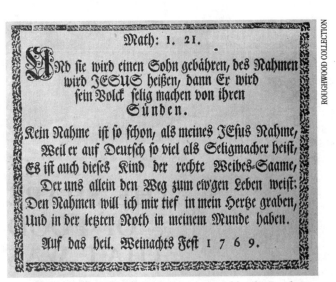

An early American Christmas greeting, printed by the Brotherhood at the Ephrata Cloister in 1769.

Reformed Church Messenger are full of Christmas items, which, like so "many little Christmas chimes" reverberated through the columns week after week (*Reformed Church Messenger*, February 2, 1870). The Christmas decorations are described in detail—as they were at Harvest Home earlier in the fall—the two occasions when the farm and the forest came to church. References to "Holy Christmas," "the joyous Christmas festival," and the "bright holiday season" appear in profusion. Glowing accounts by grateful pastors detail the many "donation visits"[32] that brought them and their families practical Christmas gifts, in one instance "schnitz" and "metzel soups" from the congregation (*Reformed Church Messenger*, January 26, 1870).

That there was a negative strain in the Reformed acceptance of Christmas, and that it occasionally, as among the Lutherans, came to the surface among the clergy, is seen in the writings of George Russell. In speaking of Christmas giving he writes,

Only when Christmas gifts refer with thankful devotion, to the Gift of Christ to sinners, can they have any true and proper significance. Let the Christian, as the child of God, have his joy. But evil subverts the good. The wicked caricature, mocking the goodness of God, turns the religious devotion intended in the true Christmas-gift, to a worldly mimicry and devil service. There is something shocking in the representation of the gift bestowing *Krist-Kindlein,* or Christ-Child, as the "belsnickel" or the evil spirit counterfeiting the gifts of God.[33]

CHRISTMAS AMONG THE PLAIN DUTCH

Contrasted with the Gay Dutch, who made up the majority of the Pennsylvania Dutch, were the Plain groups—Mennonites, Brethren, Amish, and related sectarian groups. These were intensely biblical, agreeing only to those church practices commanded by the Bible, particularly the New Testament. Like Puritans in general, they were antisacramental and therefore anticatholic in their approach to worship, and agreed to keep as holy only those days which are sanctioned in the Bible, not by the medieval church. Also their sense of personal discipline, their restraint of manners, would not let them "enjoy" anything quite so secular as Christmas. Christmas was for the "world's people," not for those whose goal was to be "little and unknown, loved by God alone."

While these groups had a minimal church observance of Christmas, and while their hymnals contained some of the standard German (Lutheran and Reformed) hymns for Advent,[34] Christmas among them was a negative affair, as it was among their Quaker brethren, whom they resembled in so many outward and inward ways.

An ex-Lancaster County Mennonite, writing of his boyhood Christmases near Lititz, has this to say and this is typical:

Christmas was just another day in this Mennonite family. No gaily decorated tree, no presents, unless Moravian uncles and aunts came through, which they often did. Santa Claus was a man in a picture, or perhaps a figure in a red coat and a beard that looked like a horse's mane, bobbing about in Brobst's drugstore window in Lititz. Playmates, whose parents did not belong to Meeting, explained that there also was a Belsnickle, Santa's opposite, who filled bad boys' and girls' stockings with ashes.

Lizzie, the genial hired girl, occasionally received a Mennonite frown "from her employers because she brought home some candy for 'der glae' [the little boy] at Christmas or Easter. 'No use spoiling him,' she was told."[35]

In their attempt to sanctify all their customs and preferences by references to the Bible, Mennonites turn to Jeremiah 10:1–6, which seems to the fundamentalist mind a clear reference to the "heathen" Christmas tree:

Hear ye the word which the Lord speaketh unto you, O house of Israel: Thus saith the Lord, Learn not the way of the heathen, and be not dismayed at the signs of heaven; for the heathen are dismayed at them. For the customs of the people are vain: for one cutteth a tree out of the forest, the work of the hands of the workmen, with the axe. They deck it with silver and with gold; they fasten it with nails and with hammers, that it move not. They are upright as the palm tree, but speak not: they must needs be borne, because they cannot go. Be not afraid of them; for they cannot do evil, neither also is it in them to do good. Forasmuch as there is none like unto thee, O Lord; thou art great, and thy name is great in might.[36]

DON YODER
1959

A drawing of a Pennsylvania Open-Hearth Christmas, which was prepared by Ralph D. Dunkelberger, of Berks County, for the original 1959 edition of this book.

OPEN-HEARTH CHRISTMASES

Of all the holidays in the year, Christmas, more than any other, evokes memories of home ties, kitchen memories, many of them: memories of one's mother (or grandmother, perhaps) busily engaged readying the Christmas dinner, and, oh, what aromas of roasting turkeys, sizzling chestnut filling, and rum-drenched mince pies—all emanating from memory's old-time woodstoves.

No name—in view of memories such as these—could be more appropriate, we feel, than the name "Woodstove Christmases" to designate nineteenth- and turn-of-the-century Christmases.

In like manner, we have chosen the name "Open-Hearth Christmases" to designate eighteenth- and early nineteenth-century Christmas practices in Pennsylvania.

Henry Harbaugh, a native of Franklin County, in 1858 described the Open-Hearth Christmases of his childhood as follows:

There comes to us, over the waste of years, pleasant memories of Christmas cheerfulness and unrestrained joy. Though a cold sheet of snow covered the fields and the mountains, and the sharp tingle of sleigh bells was heard ringing through the icy air, yet how warm and homelike was the scene within doors! A fire, such as was only known in what we now call the olden time, before the dull reign of coal began, blazed upon the wide, deep hearth. The broad, old-fashioned stone pavement, between the fire and the floor, afforded abundant room for the most extensive nut-cracking operations. The "ancient people" in the house, preferred their chestnuts boiled, and for their accommodation a kettle swung over the blaze. The "young folks" favored roasting, and not a little did we joy to watch them while one and another hissed, and bursted, and ran like a crazy bombshell over the floor, amid leaping, and shouting, and clapping of hands.

To introduce our two divisions—Open-Hearth Christmases and Woodstove Christmases—we shall lead off each of the two sections with what we like to call a literary theme song, in each instance a reminiscence. The literary theme song we have selected for Open-Hearth Christmases in Pennsylvania is a wandering umbrella mender's recollection of early Christmas observations in Pennsylvania. It is from an old manuscript in the Berks County Historical Society:

OPEN-HEARTH CHRISTMASES

The old "umbrella man" was occupying the wood chest back of the big, gray stove of one of the old village store stands of Berks County.

He had just enjoyed a big supper that the genial merchant had given him in consideration of repairing an old yellow umbrella.

It was cold and snowing. The evening was so unpleasant outside that none of the older habitués of the place were present. The younger element, however, were not to be kept back by the weather. This evening, instead of going as usual to the saddler shop, the young men came to the store, mainly to hear the itinerant mender of umbrellas.

He was an old man with a wise look and a kind heart. In Berks and several of the adjoining counties he was a familiar figure in every town, village and hamlet. Hundreds of farmers and others, whom he visited regularly, were always glad to have him sleep in some warm shop or outhouse of theirs or in the "beggar men's" bed in the garret. Everybody loved to hear the aged wanderer give his impressions of the many localities he had gone through, the people encountered and the changes that constantly took place.

The night the old man in the faded clothes sat by the glowing fire, surrounded by the young men in the village store, he was exceptionally happy and talkative, doubtless because he had secured such excellent quarters on a night so cold and snowy. The big sugar lions and elephants, the pail of mixture candy, the sugar pretzels and canes suspended from a string stretched before the windows, and the cheese box filled with peanuts, together with the piles of hog bristles, which had been brought by the small boys in exchange for holiday sweetmeats, all of these caused the conversation to turn toward Christmas topics. In response to a request from the boys the old traveler gave them the following talk in his own peculiar style:

It is about forty years now that I began going around over here in Pennsylvania patching and fixing umbrellas. From that time to this day I always made for some place in Berks County when it was near Christmas and New Year's. But, my, how things have changed about Christmas since I first came here to you people. I know when sugar was high up in price, about thirty years back, that there were very few children that got more for Christmas presents than a little candy toy and two or three cookies.

They sometimes got a few *snitz,* which the young children liked to eat between meals, for they were then not thrown around as much as now. *Snitz* was from two to three dollars a bushel. The children of poor people got nothing from their parents. Those old Belsnickel parties used to go to the rich people and get things and then carry them to the poor children. I went Belsnickling several times when I was young. We went to every house in half a township where poor children were. When we had given what we could get from people who could afford it better, we went to some of the big farm houses for fun. Cider and wine and apples we had all we could get down. We got a little cake but not much. About the only Christmas cake there was around in those days was *Leb-kucha.*

When we were done visiting the poor children and scared many of them before we did give them the things, we made our headquarters on one farm. We had fiddles and other music. Nearly always there was music and dancing till daytime, and sometimes till almost dinner time. Young ladies did come to the farmhouse the evening before. Then when we was come back from Belsnickling they joined in the frolic.

One Christmas fun twenty-five years ago that you don't hear much of nowadays was watching the Christ rose. They did say that time a certain variety of rose bush would blossom every year the night before Christmas. Well, those parties that did watch these roses was doing it to have luck. It was said that anybody who did see the Christ rose would be very much lucky all his life. Young girls and fellows went together to see the rose on the coldest night. They stood sometimes deep in the snow with their feet. If a boy and a girl saw the Christ rose while out together it was said they would sure get married. But when the Christ rose would not come out

when a young couple so did watch it, it was believed that they indeed would never come together. I know yet the time that most every garden had a Christ rose stalk. Almost all people believed much in it. Some planted the rose stalk so in the garden that it could be easily watched from a window. But year after year they did less believe in the old Christ rose belief. The rose stalks did grow less, and now there are very few of them any more. When you speak of Christ roses to the young people now they do not know at all what you mean.

Instead of Sunday School Christmas festivals in churches the Christmas amusements of the olden times were more outdoors. Fox chases, shooting matches, and such things were kept at most every hotel; there were most mighty big crowds at them. At many hotels, drinks were given for nothing the whole day, and on New Year, when there was sleighing. I tell you the big sleigh bells of those times rattled one almost deaf on Christmas. So many parties went over the holidays.

Christmas evening was a great time for spelling bees. There was always big crowds on this day and the person who did stand up longest, did get the Kriss Kingle. Then there was singing school contests on Christmas day and evening. You know there was singing schools in every township in that time. They would sing against each other for a present on Christmas. These things were done in school houses where there was some and also in churches and farm houses.

I know yet well the time when I first heard of the woman who baked two kinds of Christmas cookies. My, but all the people did talk about such big notioned people. They said such a thing must make almost any man break up. Then, when red, yellow and blue-colored sugar first come out and the women did begin to put that on their cookies the children did think it was wonderful.

The parents didn't give their children some money to buy Christmas things, but some of the best natured fathers and mothers allowed their boys and girls to keep what they did earn during the December month. How these boys and girls did scratch to clean hog bristles and catch muskrats and skin them. But they did not often spend all the money they earned. Those chaps and lassies did have an eye in business.

But in those olden times the Christmas dinners were mighty good, but not so much trashy as now, with fancy things. A good fat turkey and potato filling, and gravy, and bread and apple butter. That was about all; none of this sweet stuff that is now so the go. But there was always provision made for all the hungry in the neighborhood in those days. The big farmers all invited a great many persons. Of course, they do that this times, too, but not so much as one time.

CHRISTMAS MUMMERS

Though we frequently speak of Philadelphia as the Quaker City in the eighteenth century, there were other elements in its population, of course—Episcopalians, for one thing.

It is to the Episcopalians that we owe the custom of mumming on Christmas Eve in early Philadelphia, a custom which they brought with them from England.

Christmas mummers were the counterpart of the Belsnickel, brought to Pennsylvania by the settlers from German-speaking Europe: Germany, Switzerland, and from what is French Alsace today. Though both were masked, they differed radically in purpose. The mummers were groups of folk performers, each one impersonating a specific character. They presented their bit of theatre as they went from house to house. Their motive in presenting the Christmas Eve performances was the expected handout: good things to eat, or lacking this, a remuneration in small coin.

The rural Belsnickel, as often as not, made his rounds of the neighborhood alone. Supplied with cookies and nuts, chestnuts usually, and with whip in hand, he went from house to house, rewarding children who were well behaved and frightening and punishing with slashes from his whip those little boys and girls who did not obey the orders of their parents.

When the British Isles Christmas Eve tradition of mumming and the Continental tradition of Belsnickeling met in Pennsylvania, a new tradition evolved, one that continued in practice in Pennsylvania inland cities to the opening decades of the present century. Christmas Eve masqueraders—whether they were of English background or not—from the latter eighteenth century on took the name of Belsnickels or Belsh-nickels. The word "mummers" itself became restricted in Pennsylvania usage eventually solely to Philadelphia, where it no longer referred to Christmas masqueraders but New Year's masqueraders. (Else-where in Pennsylvania, be it noted, New Year masquerading went *not* by the name of mumming but by that of fantasticals or fantastics.)[1]

In the acculturation process *urban* Belsnickels, under the influence of the British Isles Christmas Eve mumming tradition, became members of a performing group—not theatrical, but musical—who went about the community, visiting private homes and public places to entertain, expecting in return to be rewarded with Christmas delicacies or small coin. (It is important to observe that the *rural* Belsnickels generally continued true to their original European purpose as punishers of naughty children, though they, under city influence, too finally expected to be treated by the families they visited.)

There is evidence that *urban* Belsnickels continued to keep alive traditional eighteenth-century English mummers' pieces in our Pennsylvania inland cities into the first decades of the present century. In a conversation the author had in July 1958 with David W. Thompson of Carlisle, Mr. Thompson reported that when he went Belsnickling along with other boys in the county seat of predominantly Scotch-Irish Cumberland Country around 1910 to 1915 they used to repeat the following traditional greeting at every home they entered:

> Christmas is coming; geese are getting fat,
> Please put a penny in the old man's hat.
> If you haven't got a penny, half a penny will do;
> If you haven't got a half a penny, God bless you!

Below, we shall now present the evidences of eighteenth-century mumming on Christmas Eve in Pennsylvania.

Francis B. Brandt in his account of early mumming in Philadelphia (Philadelphia *Evening Ledger*, November 17, 1930) quotes the following Quaker item, without, however, disclosing its source:

It was considered the proper thing in those days to give the leading mummers a few pence as a dole, which in the language of the present time they would pool, and buy cakes and beer. It was also regarded as the right thing to do to invite them into the house and regale them with mulled cider, or small beer, and homemade cakes. It was considered a great breach of etiquette to address or otherwise recognize the mummer by any other than the name of the character he was assuming. I remember a little girl, who, with all the curiosity of her sex, had discovered a neighbor's boy in the party; and with childish impetuosity she broke out with, "Oh, I know thee, Isaac Simmons. This is not George Washington!"

The Philadelphia *Public Ledger* of December 25, 1844, recorded one of the speeches used by the early Christmas mummers in the Quaker City:

Room, room, brave gallants, give us room to sport,
For in this room we wish for to resort.
And to repeat to you our merry rhyme,
For remember, good sirs, this is Christmas time.
The time to cut up goose pies now doth appear,
So we are come to act our merry Christmas here;
At the sound of the trumpet and beat of the drum,
Make room, brave gentlemen, and let our actors come.
We are the merry actors that traverse the street;
We are the merry actors that fight for our meal;
We are the merry actors that show pleasant play,
Step in then, King of Egypt, and clear the way.

From the Philadelphia *Sunday Dispatch* of December 27, 1857.
The mummery referred to by Scott was practiced in Philadelphia within recollection. We have frequently seen gangs of young fellows parading the streets of a Christmas eve, with their shirts outside of their lower garments and their faces blackened over. They would visit homes, and, after going through a series of "mumming," as it was called, they would put the master of the place under contribution for money or drink, and then go somewhere else to go through the same foolery. We have a glimmering recollection, too, of some of the uncouth rhymes recited by these Mummers, and we incline to the opinion that they must have originated about the time of the Restoration in England, when it was fashionable to poke fun at "Oliver Cromwell and his long copper nose." In our own city the Mummers were finally voted a nuisance, and all doors being shut against them, the Mummers became metamorphosed into Calithumpians, and these noisy Christmas-keepers now go about at night creating all sorts of discord, and "making night hideous with their yells."

From the *Moravian* of January 1, 1863.
Philadelphia Correspondent: Another old custom, now discontinued, I may mention to preserve its history from oblivion. When I was a boy (no matter how many years ago) much amusement among the young was found in parading as "mummers." Squads of from five to ten dressed themselves fantastically, and visited the houses of those who they imagined would receive them kindly. Amid these, they in turn recited some verses, or sang an amusing song, or perhaps enacted some drama got up for the occasion. Their reward generally followed in the shape of a few pennies, or cakes, according to circumstances. It is generally admitted that the now famous, and world renowned, Edwin Forrest here found the first field for the display of his even then wonderful powers; at all events the amusement was a very favorite one with him.

From the Philadelphia *Sunday Dispatch* of December 23, 1866.
The customs of Christmas Eve, derived by our ancestors from England and Germany, have pretty much passed away in the progress of time, which has changed all things save the hearts of the people. The last of these, known as mummers' sports, was in vogue within the recollection of many persons now living. The mummers were dressed in a grotesque manner, and went from house to house, where they enacted a mock play, entitled "Alexander and the King of Egypt," or recited humorous poems. No doubt the discontinuance of this custom arose out of the annoyance it subjected those to who had no fancy for such sport; for though the players first obtained the consent of the occupants before entering, it was of course often given reluctantly, and when once in the mummers remained as long as they pleased—much longer than was agreeable.

From the Philadelphia *Sunday Dispatch* of December 24, 1876.
The Mummers exist among us in degenerated forms as "Fantasticals" or "Calithumpians"—men who render the night hideous by their yelling, drum-beatings, and horn-tootings, and the day disgusting by their outrageous masking and foul disguises. Yet the Mummer formerly occupied a prominent place in the old-time Christmas revels, enacting those rude and irreverent mysteries, and miracle-plays which have been superseded by charades, parlor-games, dancing, and other refined amusements.

From *Recollections of Samuel Breck with Passages from his Note-Books (1771–1862)*, edited by H. E. Scudder (Philadelphia, 1877), pages 35–36. (Breck died in Philadelphia, August 31, 1862, aged 91 years.)

This scene of Philadelphia mummers is the illustration accompanying Egan's "A Day in the Ma'sh" in Scribner's
Monthly, *July 1881. It bears the caption: "Bell Snicklin."*

I forget on what holiday it was that the Anticks, another exploded remnant of colonial manners, used to perambulate the town. They have ceased to do it now, but I remember them as late as 1782. They were a set of the lowest blackguards, who, disguised in filthy clothes and ofttimes with masked faces, went from house to house in large companies, and, *bon gré, mal gré,* obtruding themselves everywhere, particularly into the rooms that were occupied by parties of ladies and gentlemen, would demean themselves with great insolence. I have seen them at my father's, when his assembled friends were at cards, take possession of a table, seat themselves on rich furniture and proceed to handle the cards, to the great annoyance of the company. The only way to get rid of them was to give them money, and listen patiently to a foolish dialogue between two or more of them. One of them would cry out, "Ladies and gentlemen sitting by the fire, put your hands in your pockets and give us our desire." When this was done and

they had received some money, a kind of acting took place. One fellow was knocked down, and lay sprawling on the carpet, while another bellowed out,

> See, there he lies,
> But ere he dies
> A doctor must be had.

He calls for a doctor, who soon appears, and enacts the part so well that the wounded man revives. In this way they would continue for half an hour; and it happened not infrequently that the house would be filled by another gang when these had departed. There was no refusing admittance. Custom has licensed these vagabonds to enter even by force any place they chose. What should we say to such intruders now? Our manners would not brook such usage a moment. Undoubtedly, these plays were a remnant of the old Mysteries of the fourteenth and fifteenth centuries.[2]

From an article "A Day in the Ma'sh" by Maurice F. Egan in *Scribner's Monthly*, July 1881, page 350.
On New-Year's Eve, crowds of men and boys dress themselves in fantastic costumes, and roam through the Neck and lower part of the city all night. This custom, doubtless a remnant of the old English Christmas "mumming," grows year by year in Philadelphia, and the mummers, becoming bolder, penetrate as far north as Chestnut street. This custom, attributed in New York to the Dutch, is not unknown in Brooklyn, where troops of fantasticals parade on Thanksgiving Day, Christmas, and New Year's.

From the Doylestown *Democrat* of January 6, 1885.
One of the English customs which obtained a foothold in Philadelphia was the masque of the mummers—a custom kept up from the middle part of the last century to within fifty or sixty years of the present day. The mummers were usually young fellows, who dressed in fantastic costume, took upon themselves characters and went from house to house reciting certain rhymes and expecting a "dole," which they generally received in the shape of pennies or something to eat and drink. The English Christmas masque of "St. George and the dragon" was the foundation of their little play. With patriotic feeling, however, they Americanized the piece. St. George was not recognized, but George Washington took his place; the dragon became Beelzebub and sometimes "Old Noll with his copper nose" (Cromwell) was superseded by Cooney Cracker, who "chawed tobacker." The rhymes were rude and simple:

> Here comes I, old Beelzebub,
> On my shoulder I carry a club,
> In my hand a dripping pan.
> Don't you think I'm a jolly old man?

The Father of his Country was inferior in importance in the piece to the father of evil. His speech commenced:

> Here am I, great Washington,
> On my shoulder I carry a gun.

The mummers were an attractive feature; there were mysteries about their coming and going, and it was a point of etiquette that however transparent their disguises might be none who saw them should be allowed to address them by their proper names. Southwark, Kensington and Northern Liberties were the favorite circuits of these companies when they were "on the road." It is surprising how completely they have ceased, so that even the memory of them has been but partially preserved.

From the Philadelphia *North American* of December 21, 1913.
The mummers, direct from anciently merrie England, have been shouldered off by Philadelphia's Christmas on to its New Year. In the early part of the nineteenth century the mummers appeared on Christmas eve, instead of New Year's eve, and they went from house to house, after the homely English fashion, singing their waits' songs and seeking dole of pence and cakes—and got it. That practice lasted right on up to twenty years ago, although transferred to December 25. During the last two decades the magnificent New Year pageant has developed on a scale that leaves humble petitioners at doorsteps too much beneath the mummers' dignity.

Probably the man who did most to keep alive the old spirit of sheer comic humor was Eph Horn, in after years famed as the most popular nigger minstrel. Eph organized a band of mummers that belonged around Sixth and South streets, and it was he who supplemented the character of George Washington—the patriotic substitute for the British Saint George—with our own peculiar Cooney Cracker, with Beelzebub and with the Prince of Egypt—all mummers' roles which held sway for years in the streets of Philadelphia.

BARRING OUT
THE SCHOOLMASTER

In the early period of the one-room rural schools, children throughout Pennsylvania used to lock out their teacher a day or two before Christmas.[1] They would permit him to enter the schoolroom only provided he promised, usually in writing, to give each pupil a Christmas gift—ordinarily candy or cookies. Frequently, in addition to extorting goodies to eat, the children also demanded of the teacher that he declare the rest of the day a holiday. This custom goes by the name of barring out[2] the schoolmaster.

The custom of barring out the schoolmaster has its roots in the eighteenth-century pay schools, parochial schools for the most part. Under this system, prior to the introduction of the public schools in the 1830s, each pupil paid the teacher by the day. A penny or a penny and a half was the going amount.

Under this subscription school system, the pupil-teacher-parent relationship was quite different from what it is today. The children of the time well realized that the schoolmaster could not make a living without their daily tuition, small though it may have been. They were, you see, in an ideal position to extort a gift. And, logically, the Christmas season—the traditional gift-giving time of the year—became the customary time to put the annual squeeze on the local teacher. One of our early Pennsylvania folklorists even suggests that the gifts the schoolmasters "gave" were a species of blackmail, or graft, paid by the pedagogue to retain the patronage of the parent.

Barring out the schoolmaster is a custom which is documented in all parts of the Commonwealth. Whether we are dealing with a custom brought from the British Isles or from the Continent, how widely it was observed in other parts of the nation—these are all questions to which there are as yet no answers.[3] That the custom is an early one in Pennsylvania becomes apparent from an article in the Philadelphia *Democratic Press* of December 18, 1810, which, inci-

dentally, is the earliest known description of this custom to date. The author—clearly a Quaker—wrote that this "very absurd and wicked practice has *long* prevailed in this country." (The italics are added.)

With the passing of the pay schools and the advent of free schools and compulsory attendance, the props, so to speak, were knocked out from under this custom. Under the public school system the teacher became the recipient instead of the giver of Christmas gifts. Generally, this custom disappeared in the latter part of the nineteenth century.

Barring out the schoolmaster is no longer practiced anywhere in Pennsylvania. But there are old-timers aplenty who recall participating in the custom. J. Steffy of near Red Run, Lancaster County, tells of helping to lock out the teacher of the White Hollow school about the year 1888. One old grandfather from Reamstown, also Lancaster County, tells of the teacher's Christmas gift of a mintstick, a whole one to the well behaved and half a one to all others.

The very last evidence we have located to barring out the schoolmaster in Pennsylvania is from the year 1928. Playwright Paul R. Wieand, then a rural school teacher in Lowhill Township, Lehigh County, found himself locked out, though on Shrove Tuesday, the traditional barring-out day in the Lehigh Valley.

From the Philadelphia *Democratic Press* of December 18, 1810.

A very absurd and wicked practice has long prevailed in this country, namely, that of Scholars barring out the Schoolmasters a little before the 25th of December, commonly called Christmas day, in order to extort permission from him to spend a number of days called the Christmas holidays in idleness or play. A scene of this kind took place last year in our school in this place: a few of the scholars took possession of the school-house, and so completely fortified it, that it was impossible to reduce it except by a regular siege, and the caitifs had provided against this also by laying in a large quantity of provisions. Thus was not only the Teacher shut out, but also all those Scholars not concerned in the plot, and who wished to occupy their time in learning, and not in idleness and riot.

Hearing of the insurrection, and having some children at school, who were thus shut out, I went with some of my neighbors to the place, to try if we could not by reason persuade the keepers of the garrison to surrender. They were prevailed to raise one of the windows a little. I asked them why they shut up the school house. One of them, who seemed to be the commander in chief, replied they wished to have ten days of Christmas-play.

From the York *Pennsylvania Republican* of January 8, 1840. This issue carries a lecture on Christmas delivered by Thomas E. Cochran (born in 1813) before the Columbia Lyceum on December 25, 1839.
[Cochran said:] An occasional pedagogue may meet with a barring-out from his sturdy vassals, who claim a prescriptive right to a week's holiday.

From *Autobiography of Rev. Abel C. Thomas* (Boston, 1852), pages 37–40. (Thomas taught school at Pine Barrens in York County about 1820.)
The scamps once played me the customary trick of "barring out." They had all antiquity as authority, and I was not in a position to prevent its exercise. It was on St. Valentine's Day. I had spent the evening previous in a company of young folks at a farmer's house, and was late in my arrival at the "wigwam" the next morning. I saw the smoke cheerfully issuing from the chimney, and half a score of happy faces at the window. Springing up the steps, I smartly applied my thumb to the door-latch—but all was fast, and the rebels shouted within. They had taken advantage of my late nap, and had barred me out! The girls had come as usual, but seeing how matters stood, had returned home.

"You won't get in there to-day, unless you agree to their terms," said one of my patrons who was passing by; and he laughed heartily as he added, "They understand the business. Every master we have had these five years has been barred out, and kept out; and they were all older and stronger than you are."

"I'll throw brimstone down the chimney, put a board over the top, and so smoke them out," said I.

"Look first that they have not water to put out the fire," was his reply.

I looked in at the window, and saw several buckets by the fire place; and the rogues mocked me as they witnessed my disappointment.

"I'll besiege the fortress till I starve out the garrison," said I.

Immediately the rebels pointed to sundry baskets of provisions standing on my table. And they grinned at me most provokingly as they took off the white napkins, and showed me pies and cakes and cheese in abundance. It therefore behooved me to try "a stratagem of war."

About a hundred and twenty yards distant was the smithshop of a young friend. Thither I repaired, and being joined by several companions, we commenced pitching quoits as though nothing extraordinary had happened. Presently came a messenger with a flag of truce, offering terms of capitulation. The paper was duly drawn up, and stipulated as follows: They would agree to surrender on condition, 1st. That I should pardon all hands; 2d. That I should grant a holiday; 3d. That I should furnish the garrison with all convenient dispatch, with two buckets of cider, a bushel of apples, fifty ginger-cakes, and one hundred cigars! Large supplies were demanded with a view to entertain sundry invited guests.

I returned a verbal answer that I would not treat with my subjects in rebellion, and that I would accept of nothing short of an unconditional surrender.

In the course of half an hour the lads were out in the field at play. They had posted a sentry to watch the movements of the hostile party. There were about fourteen in all, some of them fully my own age. After calculating the chances of cutting them off from the open window of egress, I started and ran with all speed. The alarm was instantly sounded, and they tumbled in, some of them "heels over head." Nevertheless I should have been in time to tumble in among them, had it not been for an intervening fence. I caught the last of them—a lad of about eight years—by the leg, the sash was pressed down by the party within, until he shrieked with both pain and fright, and I retired a few paces, so that he might be released. The straggler was drawn in, the window secured as before by nails over the under-sash.

Meanwhile I scanned "the port," and discovered that were the outer casings removed, the sashes might be withdrawn, with little danger to be apprehended from the besieged. They had however provided themselves with stout sticks, sharpened in the fire, and these they brandished in high glee. With an axe, I removed the casing, then the sashes and "the port" was open.

"Boys," said I, "I am coming in at that window, in a run-and-jump heels foremost; look out, stand from under."

I leaped in boldly, the rebels standing aside lest they should harm me with their sticks, or be harmed by my heels—reserving the resolution to pick me up and thrust me out. But I was too quick for them. Reaching my desk, and rapping on it, my authority was acknowledged, according to the established usage of "barring out." Every one went to his seat in silence,—and then, in obedience to orders, two of the largest pulled out all nails, removed all barriers, and put in the sashes. Shortly a hearty laugh from the "master" was rapturously joined by the late rebels, and the affair

Artist Ralph D. Dunkelberger did this drawing of a barring-out based on the Lancaster County account below.

ended in my compliance with the first two stipulations, namely, pardon and a holiday. They lost the cider, cakes, apples and segars, and I assisted them in eating the nice pies and provisions prepared for the extremity of a siege.

From the Lancaster *Inland Daily* of December 23, 1854.

"The Yankee Schoolmaster" by J . . . . of Lancaster.

In the year 183 . ., when I was a boy of fourteen years of age, I attended the district school in A . . . . township, L . . . . county, Pa. Our teacher was a man far advanced in years, and had taught school for the last twenty-five years in that one old and dilapidated school house. Many were the freaks played by us upon the old master, and often were we severely chastised. Old age and the constant murmuring of parents of the slow progress of their children in learning, induced the old gentleman to relinquish the

arduous duties of school teaching. The directors were prompt in securing the services of a young gentleman of considerable intelligence, of moral habits, and withal a gentleman in every respect.

The vacation ended and the school was convened under the charge of the new teacher. In a stern and commanding voice he called us to order, and silence—sepulchral silence reigned through the old building for once in many years. We were fairly awed at the strange proceedings, being always, under the old school teacher, accustomed to the pretty free use of our tongue during school hours. But times had changed. The rules were laid down in a plain style and strictly were they enforced, and we progressed with marked rapidity under the new discipline. Now the first quarter ended and the teacher being pleased with the situation remained, and the winter session opened. The cold and dreary month of December came, and with it the recollections of our yearly sport of *locking out* the teacher at Christmas.

"Boys," said one of my school companions as a number of us were together, "I think it is soon time to make arrangements for locking out our master."

"I'll give you my opinion, boys," responded another, who was always very cautious and would seldom assist us in any such undertaking, "I think it a very dangerous procedure with our present teacher, and besides he is a *Yankee*. They are up to these tricks, depend on it."

"P'shaw," bawled out Joe Slimp, after relieving his mouth of a large quid of tobacco, "what do these 'down east' folks know about it; he may kick up a fuss, but we will give him to understand that a lot of *good things* will set all to rights."

"I think that's as good a plan as we can arrive at, but we must stick to it and not let him in unless he has the necessary *passports*," said Jake Doty, who, in our inexperienced judgment, was considered an extraordinary bright boy.

Thus, in high expectation of pleasure, we separated.

From this time forward, until after Christmas, our lessons were very imperfectly recited, our minds being constantly occupied with the "locking out." At last the long wished for day came, and early in the morning, all of us repaired to the school house; soon everything was topsy-turvy; benches were propped against the door, the poker was run under the latch, and the windows were well secured, until everything was perfectly barricaded and apparently in a state of siege! The hour of school arrived and the teacher's measured steps resounded over the pavement—within not the slightest noise was heard—all was quiet. He put the key into the lock, but it was no go; he tried to force the door with the same success. Some boys becoming afraid and fearing severe punishment, made a noise and leapt out one of the back windows. The teacher not knowing the customary rule, presently Joe Slimp from within informed him what was required before he could be permitted to enter. The teacher smiled and immediately left; we, aware of it, opened the door. Now a general consultation was held on this all important subject—the question was will he return or not? At last it was agreed upon that one must serve as a look-out and report as soon as he (the teacher) came into sight, and the rest go within. So our previous spokesman, Joe Slimp, was selected. Joe mounted a post in front of the school house, looking down the long and narrow street in anxious expectations, constantly dodging right and left to get a clear sight. "By Jove," says he to himself, "there he comes," and down came Joe pell-mell into the school room, exclaiming—"he is coming with a great *big* basket covered with a cloth!"

The greatest noise and confusion was now created in replacing the benches, &c, and arranging everything properly. We all took our seats, quietly as if nothing in the least had happened, the door opened and in stepped the master with a large basket on his arm, tugging at it, apparently, for dear life. He placed it under the desk and opened school as usual. One lesson after another was now imperfectly recited, and the tittering and talking by us concerning the contents of the basket became so loud that he could not proceed.

"Silence!" came like a thunder-clap from the lips of the teacher, and all was quiet. "Jacob Doty and Joseph Slimp," he continued, "come forward and distribute the contents of this basket equally among the scholars."

Both were up in the twinkling of an eye, and eagerly grasped the basket, and then very proudly walked to the first bench and uncovered it for distribution, but without proceeding any further they stood still and looked each other steadily in the face, their countenances becoming pale as statues, and all of a sudden they flung the basket with all force into the corner of the room, when out rolled a small *nail keg and a few biscuits!*

Roar after roar of laughter came from the teacher and scholars, and Jake and Joe, you may judge, returned to their seats rather chop-fallen. School was dismissed for the remainder of the day, and ever afterwards Joe and Jake would turn a deaf ear to anything mentioned concerning the "locking out" of the Yankee Schoolmaster.

From an article "Our Schoolmasters" by the Reverend Benjamin Bausman in the June 1873 *Guardian*, pages 169–170.

On the day before Christmas some country schoolmasters were locked out of their castles by the scholars, and kept out until they would consent to furnish the whole school with Christmas presents. We had often heard how gloriously the scholars of other schools had fared by this plan. Unfortunately, our Master was a Squire. And a Squire, some thought, might take us right off to prison, if we provoked him in this way. One Christmas season, a few brave boys led the way, and the rest followed. In the morning the scholars took possession of the school-house. The door locked, and if I remember rightly, the shutters, too. How some trembled like an aspen leaf, with fright! Others peeped through the key-hole, and listened for the master's coming tread. We had reason to tremble. Our master was distant to his scholars; besides, he did not seem to relish a joke as much as some people do. He might just that morning be in one of his ill humors. You may smile at the scene, but I question whether the people of besieged Troy, or those of Vicksburg, felt the seriousness of their situation more keenly than did that group of children in a besieged country school-house.

At length we heard his tread. "Hush," was whispered round. Silent as the grave, was the school, for once. Such order the master had perhaps never produced before. In vain he tried to open the barred door. He commanded us to open. To disobey his command usually brought a storm about our ears. Such an act of disobedience, refusing to let him enter his own school-house, was a daring feat. A paper was slipped out under the door, solemnly setting forth our demands—candies, cakes, nuts and the little nick-nacks that make up the ordinary Christmas presents of country children. It was a fearful suspense, this deliberation of the school-master on this stately requisition. What could we do if he should fly into a passion, force the door open, and lay about him with the rod! There was no way to retreat left open, no open window through which to leap out. Ah, dear reader, to children such a performance has all the momentous importance, which historic events have to older people. At length the Master proposed to surrender, upon our terms, as specified in the paper. The door was opened. He entered with a smile, and we hardly knew whether to smile or scream from fear, lest after all he might visit us with dire punishment. He ordered us to our seats, wrote a note containing a list of the articles promised, and sent a few of the larger boys to the village to buy and bring them. Studying was impossible during their absence. The joy was too tumultuous to be bottled up, even for an hour. And the kind-hearted Master was as mirthful as we. At length the boys came, with great baskets, full of the spoils of our victory. Each one got a nice Christmas present. Never before had our Master seemed to us such a good man. For months this great siege in our school-house, and the grand victory of the besieged, was the daily topic of talk among the scholars. And in all the country round about, it was soon noised abroad, that Squire S . . . . . . had been locked out by his school. And the scholars, even the most timid and worst frightened, shared the glory and renown of the victory.

From *Lykens Twenty Years Ago,* Charles H. Miller (Lykens, 1876), page 13.

Barring-out was a custom not well established in this region. When it occurred at all it was generally upon Shrove Tuesday—the *Fastnacht* of the native Germans,—and not upon the Christmas of other localities. Once upon a time it befell the master of this school. The windows were nailed fast, one and all; the benches were dragged from all parts of the room and piled against the door,—a long row extending to the stove, as a prop; the terms of treaty were already thrust without, and all awaited the anxious moment with throbbing expectancy. For one brief hour the scholars were master,—the tables turned, as it were, and riot ran high and wild. For one brief hour only. Then came a rap upon the door which quaked the stoutest hearts and struck conviction to the very core. A voice soon followed after still more effective; the hiding-places emptied themselves as if by magic; the windows swarmed with hands and faces eager to escape; somehow, the doors flew open; the terms of treaty disappeared; the benches grew dangerous

with life and animation, never so suddenly evinced before or since; all things moved to their accustomed places with marvelous speed.

From the Lancaster *New Era* of December 28, 1878.

Bareville had no special services on Christmas; but was disgraced by the revival of an old custom—the barring out of the teacher of the primary and grammar schools. It is a disgrace for that community that would-be young men are yet to be found who have no common sense and are ignorant of the simplest forms of politeness. It may, however, be said to the credit of the seventy pupils of these schools that only one was found who was willing to do such work and he had to accomplish it by entering the school building at midnight.

From the Carlisle *American Volunteer* of January 6, 1881.

The old time custom of barring teachers out has lost its grip in Penn. But one was barred out this season, and he only for a half day. Teachers have been known to get their pupils to bar them out, but they instead of the teachers, are the losers, and consequently the custom is dying out.

From *Danville, Montour County, Pennsylvania,* D. H. B. Brower (Harrisburg, 1881), page 132.

There was one day in the year when the "master's" anger was braved, and that was in the time-honored custom of "barring out the master" on Christmas. On that great occasion, the plot being previously laid, the scholars assembled long before school time, and piled up the seats to barricade the door. All preparations made, they waited the coming of the "master." At last he came, and with threats alarmed the more timid, but the "big boys," no less determined, withstood the onset. An agreement to give free pardon and a general treat to the school was slipped out under the door, with the offer of opening the door if the "master" would sign and return the paper. Sometimes he returned it with his signature at once, and other times he kept them imprisoned for the day and punished them besides. "Barring out the master" was a common custom all over the county, but it has long since been abandoned, though many who read these lines will remember the exciting scenes connected with the old custom.

From *Pennsylvania Dutch,* P. E. Gibbons (Philadelphia, 1882), page 420.

The custom of barring out the teacher at Christmas appears not yet to be extinct in Lancaster County. The scholars demand a Christmas gift, but are not always successful. One teacher near here walked calmly home, and allowed the scholars to open the door at their leisure. An acquaintance, born in Northampton County, tells me that at his native place the teacher was locked out not at Christmas, but on Shrove-Tuesday, and merely for sport.[4]

From George R. Barr's "History of Ephrata" in the Ephrata *Review* of June 27, 1883.

It used to be the practice in those days to bar out the teacher several days before Christmas, and only permit him to enter the schoolroom upon the condition of his promising each pupil a Christmas gift.

Some tried the game on Mr. Ranck, by fastening the windows and shutters securely from the inside, and then locking the door and secreting the key. At first on his arrival at school, he seemed to be dumbfounded; then he assumed a slightly menacing attitude; then he became obstinate, unwilling to yield to our demands; gradually he seemed to relent, abandoning his imperative position by assuming a somewhat argumentative and pleading attitude, resorting to persuasion and all that sort of thing; and, finally, when he became convinced that we were unyielding in our demands, he compromised the difficulty by agreeing to buy us each "two cents worth" of Christmas cakes. And we got them, too, rejoicing in the glorious victory which our powers achieved.

From *Olden Times*, Henry L. Fisher (York, 1888), page 469.

It was the common practice for the larger "scholars" to assemble and get possession of the school-house in advance of the "master's" arrival, very early on the morning of the day preceding Christmas, and "bar" him out and keep him out until he subscribed his name to a paper something like the following, (which I give from memory founded on my own observation, having, like many others of my age, more than once participated in the popular and exciting game of barring out the master):

"Three dozen Ginger-Cakes; Six Dozen Sugar-Cakes; Six dozen Molasses-Crackers; Four dozen Ginger-Horses; do. Ginger-Rabbits; Six dozen Mintsticks; Three dozen Belly-guts; one hundred Loveletters; 2 Galls of Beer; one half bushel of some kind of Nuts, and one weeks Holidays."

But this he did only in the last resort—after having fruitlessly exhausted all ordinary means for effecting an entrance. So popular was the custom at one time that many, even of the parents, guardians, and others in *loco parentis*, aided and abetted the pupils in the contest by furnishing them provisions, and thus enabling them to "hold the fort" for several days; and seldom, indeed, if ever, did the Master even so much as attempt to inflict punishment upon those, who, it was deemed had neither done nor demanded aught but what was their legal right; that is, by immemorial custom; for whence the custom, no man knoweth any more than he does of the sepulchre of Moses.

From the Philadelphia *Public Ledger* of December 24, 1891.

A correspondent from Stony Run, Berks County: Those were the days when many of the school teachers boarded round. The female teacher was unknown, and these male instructors ruled with a rod of iron. On the day before Christmas the scholars indulged in their annual barring out. The boys and girls, big and little, gathered early at the school house on that day. All wanted to see the fun. The large boys were the leaders, and, after all the scholars had gathered in the school house, the doors and window shutters would be locked and barricaded. All were on the tip-toe of expectancy. Soon the teacher would be observed coming down the road, probably forgetful that it was so near Christmas, but he was soon reminded of something unusual going on by the fact that the door would not yield to his efforts to force it open. Then came the shouts and merry voices from within, telling him that Christmas was at hand and that he would be compelled to pay his annual tribute. Sometimes he became angry, but if he was a sensible man he would enter into the spirit of the frolic and demand to know the terms of capitulation. The answer came from within in the shape of a note, stipulating how many ginger cakes and pieces of candy were needed to go round, and soon the terms were arranged and the master would be admitted. He would probably bring with him the booty which he had promised on the following day, and no candy or cakes ever tasted as those earned in this manner.

From an article "Christmas When I Was a Boy" by the Reverend A. R. Kremer in the *Reformed Church Messenger* of December 24, 1896.

But still there are many things now connected with the observance of Christmas that were not dreamed of then. There were no Christmas vacations of a whole week or more, and not even on Christmas day were the schools closed. Doesn't it seem too bad that children had to go to school on Christmas day? Don't be too sure about that. The fact is, the scholars from the oldest to the youngest were almost sure not to be sick on that day, so they could go to school. Because part of the day in the school-room was given up to the distribution of the teacher's gifts of cakes and candies—the Christmas gift that every teacher was expected to give to the scholars. Sometimes it happened that a master refused to treat; and no wonder, as he received only fifteen dollars a month for his services, and had to support himself and family on so small a salary. But the boys and girls could not see it in that light; so, what do you think? They would go early on Christmas morning into the schoolhouse, bolt the door, and would not let the teacher in until he promised to give them a treat. Dr. Harbaugh, in a poem on the old schoolhouse where he had been a pupil, tells the story of the locking out of the teacher, in this wise:

Old Christmas brought a glorious time—
 Its memory still is sweet!
We barred the Master firmly out,
 With bolts, and nails, and timbers stout—
The blockade was complete.

And so the master was brought to terms, and as that was the custom in those days, he took it all in good part, though it cut off quite a slice from his income.

From the York *Gazette* of November 13, 1897.
Lewisberry news item: One thing was considered great sport among the boys, and that was to occasionally bar out the teacher, but one pedagogue proved himself equal to the occasion. After all persuasive methods had met with failure he climbed to the roof and let a piece of burning sulphur drop down the chimney to prevent the fumes from escaping. Very soon he was let in and ever after that they gave him no trouble in that line.

From a little volume of poetry, *Lancaster—Old and New,* James D. Law (Lancaster, 1902), page 8.

I had forgotten—so he sadly said—
To "make a mention" of the old-time school,
When boys and girls would bar their teacher out
Until he treated them to sweets and fruit.

From an article "The Schools of our Fathers" by M. R. Alexander in *Proceedings of the Kittochtinny Historical Society*, volume 2, Chambersburg, 1903, pages 179–180.
Holidays were few and far between and, more than that, most masters kept school six days a week. When, later, a concession was made granting alternate Saturday afternoons as a holiday joy reigned supreme in the hearts of Young America.

Sometimes the pupils "culled out" a holiday for themselves by "barring the teacher out." It was a well established custom in many places for the master about Christmas time, to treat his pupils not only to a holiday, but to a "lay out" consisting of candy, apples, and gingerbread. In case the master refused to conform to this custom the older boys took it upon themselves to bring him to terms by locking him out. This was revolution, of course, but considered justifiable under the circumstances; and while no violence was used upon the master yet he was not expected to yield without at least a show of effort to regain control. If by strategy or by forcing a lock or shutter he gained entrance the revolution failed, work was resumed, and no questions asked; otherwise the master yielded, furnished a treat and gave a holiday.

From an article "Folklore and Superstitious Beliefs of Lebanon County" by Dr. Ezra Grumbine in *Lebanon*

County Historical Society Proceedings, volume 3, 1905, pages 257–258.
A day or two before Christmas it was the custom for the pupils to bar out the schoolmaster and to demand gifts from him. To have the doors re-opened he was obliged to bring a basketful of fancy-shaped cookies and distribute them among his scholars, share and share alike. This was in the days of the subscription school, and the gifts were a species of blackmail, or graft, paid by the pedagog to retain the patronage of the parent.

Since the advent of free schools, compulsory attendance and minimum salary laws, the custom has passed away and the teacher now is the recipient instead of the giver of presents.

From *A Pioneer Outline History of Northwestern Pennsylvania,* W. J. McKnight (Philadelphia, 1905), page 413.
"Barring the master out" of the school-room on Christmas and New Year's was a custom in vogue in 1840. The barring was always done by four or five determined boys. The contest between the master and these scholars was sometimes severe and protracted, the master being determined to get into the school-room and these boys determined to keep him out. The object on the part of the scholars in this barring out was to compel the master to treat the school. If the master obtained possession of the school-room, by force or strategy, he generally gave the boys a sound flogging; but if the boys "held the fort," it resulted in negotiations for peace, and in the master eventually signing an agreement in writing to treat the school to apples, nuts, or candy. It took great nerve on the part of the boys to take this stand against a master. I know this, as I have been active in some of these contests.

From an article "The Myerstown Academy" by J. H. Bassler in *Lebanon County Historical Society Proceedings,* volume 3, 1906, page 391.
On another occasion the students indulged in the time-honored privilege of locking out the teacher on the last day of school, preceding Christmas. Mr. Witmer, instead of taking it good humoredly, armed himself with a formidable looking bunch of shoots from an apple tree in the yard, and, after vainly trying to force a window, scared one of the more timid scholars into unlocking the entrance door. As he stalked up the aisle to his desk, his threatening look betokened a fearful trouncing for the guilty party, if found. In an icy tone he demanded to know who had locked him out. The high tension of feeling in the schoolroom was instantly relaxed and followed by a ripple of amusement, when the calm, clear voice of Miss Annie Bockius, a quiet, studious young lady, and deservedly a favorite of the teacher's announced: "It was I, Mr. Witmer." The irate teacher felt the awkwardness of the situation and backed down as gracefully as circumstances permitted.

From an article "Palmyra, Its History and Its Surroundings" by the Reverend J. W. Early in *Lebanon County Historical Society Proceedings*, volume 4, 1908, page 257.

One incident of those early school days will never fade from memory. It was during the first or second winter. There had been much talk and even some considerable boasting about locking the teacher out before Christmas. This was an old time custom. But it had not occurred for some years. The scholars were frequently warned that it would prove a most unfortunate movement for which they would certainly be sorry, if they locked Mr. Dasher out. Finally a number of the larger scholars decided to try the experiment. So one afternoon, a few days before Christmas, the smaller scholars being sent home, they bolted the doors and fastened the shutters tightly. When the teacher came he could not get in. The scholars refused to open for him, unless under promise of liberal presents for Christmas. Not being able to get into the schoolhouse, he went home to await results. Of course they could not keep him out forever. Finding that they could not accomplish anything the scholars also went home.

From an article "Descriptive and Historical Memorials of Heilman Dale" by the Reverend U. Henry Heilman in *Lebanon County Historical Society Proceedings*, volume 4, 1909, page 456.

On or near Christmas it was the custom of the children to lock the door and bolt the shutters of the school house, in the morning, or at noon, while the master was absent, in order to extort candy and cakes from him. This was done on the day before Christmas at the Humberger school house, William Stewart, master. When he arrived in the morning and found it closed against him he was not slow to take in the situation, and to turn the tables on his naughty scholars. From a nearby worm fence he got a sufficient number of rails which he set up against the door and shutters, and imprisoned boys and girls until late in the afternoon, and this was the last time this little trick was played on their schoolmaster.

From *Old Home Week Letters*, C. H. Leeds (Carlisle, 1909), page 43.

Extract from a poem of Dr. George Duffield to J. Brown Parker, Esq.:

> Don't you mind the crowded school room for girls and boys, above?
> . . . .
> There Gad Day with his whiskers, and his ruler in his hand
> Sat like Olympian Jupiter, as one born to command.
> How often we barred him out, and then, what noise and din,
> How much more often, safer, too, that he would bar us in.

Letter from Dr. Colsin R. Shelly to Dr. Alfred L. Shoemaker, dated Lancaster, February 3, 1949.

I am a native of the western part of York County. After reading your article on local folklore I thought of several customs in western York County which took place every Shrove Tuesday and Ash Wednesday.

The last one out of bed on Shrove Tuesday was the old cluck, the first one the little peepie. The last one at school was the old cluck and was frequently reminded of the fact during the day by calling him the old cluck. Every pupil tried to get to school early before the teacher. Then if at all possible they would get on the inside of the building and barricade the door with benches and chairs so the teacher could not get in. Sometimes he was kept out the greater part of the forenoon. I recall of one teacher who smashed in a window-pane, which frightened the pupils so badly they opened the door.

If the teacher got there before the pupils everything was alright until nature compelled him to go outside, then the door was locked. The effect was the same as above. I had heard that one teacher went home for the day.

I have asked several people around Lancaster about it, but no one seems to know about the custom. When I was a youngster this was a general practice in my home section.

METZEL SOUP
AND CHRISTMAS MONEY

Round about the Christmas holiday season most people killed the porkers which they had raised and fattened during the year, and this period or season became known locally, and in Berks, Dauphin, York, and Lebanon counties, as the *metzel soup* season. The metzel soup was a portion of sausage, pudding or small cut of spare ribs, and was as much a courtesy among the rural people as an elegant present of jewelry or wine and cake among the residents of the city.

In quite early days it was customary to invite numerous friends to assist in the killing and dressing of the porkers, and the broth in which the pudding meat was boiled was used as a soup. Rye bread was broken into the savory liquor and the guests were then invited to partake of the metzel soup.

In time this custom became offensive, because with the intoxicating drinks added to this soup the people became beastly drunk. To escape such orgies and scenes the metzel soup became converted into a present of sausage and meat, which the neighbor enjoyed as much as anything else.

The metzel soup, as originally known, was customary in Germany, and had been brought to this country by our forefathers. It is related that on one occasion the father of Frederick the Great was riding near Strasburg, and seeing the drunken revelry attending the supping of a metzel soup, became so incensed that he sprang from his horse and, grasping a cudgel, began belaboring the men and women indiscriminately breaking a number of arms before he was induced to desist.

The description of a metzel soup, above,[1] stems from the pen of Samuel M. Sener, one of the earliest folklorists of Pennsylvania. It appeared in an article "Matzabaum and Metzel Soup" in the *Christian Culture* of January 1, 1892, pages 171–172. Sener presented the very same material in an address before the American Historical Society. (A report of his remarks before this society appears in the Lancaster *Intelligencer* of December 29, 1894.)

Excellent on the meaning of the metzel soup is this description from the Norristown *National Defender* of December 22, 1857:

Right well do we remember Christmas in the old farm house where we were born. It is true the glare and polish of wealth were not there, but the huge fire place with its famous back-log, its brightly polished andirons, and its huge crane, roared and cracked with the bright fire which threw its ruddy glow on the time stained rafters of our "best room." There were stacks of apples in the basket, and hickory nuts and butter-nuts in profusion, which we boys were cracking on the great hearth regardless of the fierce heat of the fire, while a gray haired grandfather sat in the "old arm chair" with its high wooden arms and straight back, looking kindly over his spectacles at the boys enjoying their "Happy Christmas!" What were silks and satins, jewelry and broadcloths, to us? Had we not a delicious home-made pudding for dinner, and a rare young gobbler fresh from our own poultry yard, and were we not surrounded by warm hearts and loving friends on those Christmas days in "Auld Lang Syne!" Then, there were great baskets of provisions sent to the poor family at the foot of the hill; we carried them to the door on our home-made sleds, and it was not the least of the pleasure of those holidays to see the smile of joy and thankfulness which shone in the faces of our "poor neighbors," at the welcome gift, and hear their eager expressions of grateful surprise, and when "Dobbin" and "Grey" were hitched to the old yellow sleigh, and we curled up in our stout woolen clothes and comforters and mittens, while we dashed away over the light fleecy snow to the village church, interchanging the "Happy Christmas" with friends and neighbors, we never thought of the toil in the summer heat, or the loss of our crops or the absence of glittering wealth, but our hearts went up in gratitude and love for the blessing we did enjoy, and bright hopes of those which were to come.

When a mist arises from the ground or from a wooded area, frequently following upon a thunderstorm, our Pennsylvania old-timers can be heard to say: "Die fix sin am kaffi kocha" (the foxes are brewing their coffee) or "De hawsa sin am damp-gnepp kocha" (the rabbits are cooking dumplings). Schuylkill County's folklorist, the late William H. Newell, tells us that when the mists arose from the Blue Mountains in his area, the people used to say the wolves were cooking their metzel soup.

Mrs. R. W. Fackenthal, of Springtown, Pennsylvania, wrote the author in 1950 that some sixty years earlier at the Lehigh County Teachers' Institute someone gave out the following Pennsylvania Dutch jingle for the teachers to translate into English:

Metzel-supp, un schnitz un gnepp
Macht die parra schnippsa, schnickera un schniffela.

[Metzel soup and Schnitz un Gnepp
Make the preachers weep for joy, dress up for the party,
   and sniff all the way.]*

She added: "Not one of them could do it."

In her article "Pennsylvania Dutch" in the Atlantic Monthly for October 1869, page 483, Phebe Earle Gibbons describes a butchering: "The friends who have assisted receive a portion of the sausage, etc., which portion is called the 'Metzel-sup.' The metzel-sup is also sent to poor widows and others."

In Samuel S. Haldeman's volume, Pennsylvania Dutch (London, 1872), the first linguistic study of the Pennsylvania dialect, page 57, appears this definition: "Metsel-soup, originally pudding broth, the butcher's perquisite, but subsequently applied to the gratuity for the animals he has slaughtered."

They tried something new in Lebanon in 1880— a metzel-soup banquet. It is to be regretted that the idea did not catch on. What a marvelous opportunity this would have been for the sort of thing that goes on in the Pennsylvania Dutch Country today under the name of Groundhog Lodges. The Lebanon Daily Times of December 22, 1880, writing of the affair, had this to say: "The bill of fare at a 'metzel-soup' banquet consists of fried sausage and pudding, sour krout and pork, with 'sy-reesel' and pig-tail as side dishes."

The Lancaster Daily Examiner of December 25, 1884, carries an article on the metzel soup, copied from the Harrisburg Independent:

There was a time when in the towns and cities of Berks, Dauphin, Lancaster, Lebanon and York counties, every man of family raised a pair or more of hogs. Forty years ago a pig sty at the end of the lot of every residence of the then borough of Harrisburg was more common than grape vines are now on such premises. Two or three weeks before Christmas, or earlier, the owners of these hogs had them slaughtered, sausage and pudding made, the hams, shoulders and sides pickled and then smoked, which furnished the meat of many families for the next summer. Then the old custom of exchanging pudding and sausage was in vogue. When a man slaughtered his hogs, he always sent a portion of his spare ribs, pudding and sausage to his neighbors. It was an act of courtesy which no neighbor could omit without losing his status as a gentleman. If a man omitted what was called the metzel soup, when he slaughtered his hogs, his neighbors would have tabooed him, and his good fellowship would have ceased. The metzel soup is an old German custom—metzel meaning, to make fine by chopping, hence the gift of pudding and sausage is called the metzel soup. This old custom has passed out of practice, as have many others of the quaint and generous practices of the Pennsylvania Dutch of the Christmas days' indulgences.

Henry L. Fisher, of York, described a metzel soup in his Olden Times (York, 1888), page 465:

The term metzel-soup is the Anglicised form of the German, Metzel-suppe. Metzeln, means to kill and cut to pieces, animals for meat— preeminently, for sausage. In the olden time, a time-honored custom (doubtless brought by our German ancestors from the fatherland,) prevailed, of sending to each near neighbor, at butchering time, a taste of the delicious sausage and puddings which were made in such great abundance on butchering occasions, which occurred, as they still do among our country-folk, at least twice during each winter; this "taste" usually consisted of a good sized dish—holding eight or ten pounds—heaping full, and was regarded as the pledge of continuing friendship between the families immediately concerned; for, if the metzelsoup was either omitted or not reciprocated, there was surely something wrong; and the preacher in charge, who always took a deep interest in keeping up the good custom, was sure to hear of the matter; and he generally succeeded in effecting a reconciliation over a love feast of fat things. This metzelsoup-custom became general among our rural folk of all nationalities, but is now gradually falling into desuetude together with many others.

Alice Morse Earle in her Home Life in Colonial Days (New York, 1898), page 419, describes the metzel soup:

---

* This little rhyme, which has to be paraphrased to give its full meaning, relates to the many "preachers' jokes" that the Pennsylvania Dutch delight in telling. Hardworking Pennsylvania farmers did not consider preaching "work," and sometimes criticized their pastors for freeloading. However, they were always welcome guests at their parishioners' tables, and from the preachers' standpoint, it was obvious that they believed in the Central Pennsylvania saying, "A strange bite always tastes good."

D.Y.

In rural Pennsylvania a charming and friendly custom prevailed among country folk of all nationalities—the "metzel-soup," the "taste" of sausage-making. This is the anglicized form of *Metzel-suppe; metzel* means to kill and cut in pieces—especially for sausage meat.

When each farmer butchered and made sausage, a great dish heaped with eight or ten pounds of the new sausages was sent to each intimate friend. The recipient would in turn send metzel-soup when his family killed and made sausage.

If the metzel-soup were not returned, the minister promptly learned of it and set to work to effect a reconciliation between the two offended parties. The custom is dying out, and in many towns is wholly vanished.

In the interval 1901–1911 the reminiscences of W. W. Davis and Abram Setley appeared in the New Holland *Clarion:*

Butchering Time. When it came to hog killing time in New Holland the boys looked forward for the fun. All the hog raisers tried to raise the largest hogs. What a time in the old town on New Year's Day, when the largest hogs were killed. They were brought to the hotel. People came from Lancaster, Reading and surrounding villages to see and have fun. Then the betting went on in regards to the weight of the porkers. We also had guessing boxes. The one coming nearest the weight of the porker was to receive a prize. The boxes would be full of guesses at ten cents a guess and when you went away from and answered, "New Holland," "Yes, you mean Sei Swamp, don't you?"

But one thing had to be done before the holidays. Every family kept hogs, and the poor animals had to be sacrificed. How keep Christmas without sausage and spareribs?

One unwritten law was observed. The first family that butchered was expected to send a "metsal-soup" to the neighbors, and when the neighbors butchered they, of course, returned the compliments. In that way for about two weeks we had a taste of all kinds of fresh meat.

Then we made "ponhaus," another delicacy that Taft, I suppose, knows nothing about. A solid breakfast food, beats corn flakes all hollow!

"DON'T FORGET THE POOR"

"Don't forget the poor"—this was one of the newspaper themes each recurring Christmas season in the time of the Open-Hearth Christmases in Pennsylvania. And we have seen the rural folk didn't forget. They sent metzel soups. The theme of giving to the poor found expression, also, in one of the earliest bits of Christmas verse in Pennsylvania, in Hannah More's "A New Christmas Hymn" appended to *The Two Wealthy Farmers* (Philadelphia, 1800), page 35:

> Come ye rich, survey the stable
> > Where your infant saviour lies;
> From your full o'erflowing table
> > Send the hungry good supplies.

But by the mid-nineteenth century this call "Don't forget the poor" became less and less frequent. A new way of life had come over the land, over all parts of it. And with its coming, the metzel soup season began to be forgotten, too, more and more. By the end of the century the custom was a mere memory.

We have one more significant item to relate on the theme of poverty and the metzel soup. It comes out of the days of the Great Depression of the 1930s. G. W. Stauffer of Charlottesville, Virginia, told it in the *Pennsylvania Dutchman* of March 1, 1953:

I was born in York County, in 1890, and moved South with a textile mill in 1928. I soon learned it was true what they say about Dixie. Yet I may meet a stranger any day. We may talk a few minutes and he may cut in with, "Are you from Pennsylvania or Ohio?" The wife still dishes out supper. After supper, she will redd up the kitchen. But the grandchildren say, "You all must come up to our house and set a while."

During the winter of 1932 I was living in Rockwood, a small town in Tennessee. A feed warehouse and farm owner decided that the quickest way to dispose of an oversupply of hogs was to slaughter them and retail the parts for what he could get for them. He spread the parts on tables in his feed warehouse. The call went out, "Pick out what you like and give me what is right."

I quickly bargained for several heads, livers, etc. A friend met me as I was on my way home. Said he, "Yankee, where you all going with them pig jowls? I thought that was a Southern dish." I agreed that he was right, but I told him these heads were to be cooked into a dish for a man who wanted to eat long and fast; they would be served on the table as Ponhaws or Scrapple.

"Come over to the house tomorrow evening," I said to my friend, "maybe it gives a metzelsoup."

He came and we gave him a liberal portion. The next evening he returned with several friends. Their proposition was this: There were several hundred families in that town in which the head of the family had been out of work for some time. So many were short of food. The warehouse man would contribute those heads, livers, feet, etc. The business men of the town would supply the bal-

A butchering scene from Henry L. Fisher's Olden Times: Or, Pennsylvania Rural Life Some Fifty Years Ago *(York, 1888).*

ance of the supplies. Would I supervise the preparing and cooking of Ponhaws?

Some delivered a load of wood, others contributed cornmeal, flour, salt, pepper, three cast iron kettles. The blacksmith made stirring irons. We put five to work with knives, cutting up the heads. I started the pots boiling.

Then we send word around the town, "Come and get it!" They came, with dishpans, cook pots, and pans, or what they had. Each was told to let it cool overnight, then slice it and fry it on a griddle.

Some came back within an hour. "It war no use to let it cool and then make hit hot again, it's good to eat now," they said.

That was Ponhaws cooking as you never saw before. Five days. The heads, livers, hearts, and feet from eighty hogs! And we scraped the last kettle to the bottom.

In fine, there are two literary items out of the turn-of-the-century period which we wish to offer at this point. One is from "The Butchering" in Henry L. Fisher's *Olden Times* (York, 1888), page 178:

But one thing more, and, though the last, yet, not the least—
There was the gen'rous, old-time metzel-soup,
Which, 'twas the custom, at such times to send
To every neighbor, relative, and friend;
Not lent, nor given with grudge, or, less *recoup,*
But by the goodly dame, as Heav'n had taught her,
In faith and hope, as bread cast on the water.

The other literary piece is a dialect poem "Die Metzel Soup," by J. J. Behney. The poet's introduction (it appeared in the Lebanon *Evening Report* of February 5, 1900) reads:

My object in writing on "Die Metzel Soup" is to call to mind several old customs which have gone out of date. When I was a boy on the farm, we used to have the evening meal for friends on butchering day; and in the days of my grandparents, the preacher received his share.

Die Metzel Soup

Am ovet gebt's die metzel-soup,
Es sommelt sich an grosy droop;
An yaders sitst sich in die roy;
S gebt frishy warsht, kucha un boy.

Der porra, nemohls foldt ehr kots,
Die metzel-soup kumdt on der blots;
Fimf yard brodewarsht un leverfilsel
Un knucha flashe, ware wase we feel.

An ormer mon, sie lue is glay,
Ferlusdt sich net gons uf die gmay;
Die metzel-soup is nee'n surprise,
An nadlich ding we'n yader wise.

[The Metzel Soup

For supper there's the metzel soup,
There gathers for it quite a crowd.
Everyone sits in a row at the table,
There's fresh sausage, cakes, and pie.

The preacher, too, does not fall short.
Some of the metzel soup goes to his place:
Five yards of sausage and liverwurst,
And soup bones, who knows how many?

The preacher's a poor man, his salary is small,
He can't quite rely on what the church pays,
So the metzel soup is never a surprise,
It's a friendly thing, as everyone knows.]

CHRISTMAS MONEY

Besides metzel soup, butchering time had yet another Christmas implication in years gone by: Country boys and girls would gather the hog bristles after butchering; they would clean them and then sell them to a local brush maker or saddler or they would take them to the village store where they bartered them for as much Christmas candy—clear toy candy, usually—as their value would buy. This clear toy candy, more often than not, was the only candy rural children got at Christmas time.

Hog bristles found a ready market throughout the first two hundred years of Pennsylvania history. In the eighteenth and early nineteenth centuries brush makers frequently ran advertisements in the newspapers requesting to buy them. The principal brush maker about 1800 in the commonwealth was one John Fisher of Lancaster. He advertised for hog bristles in newspapers all over the state. Here is part of an advertisement he inserted in the Carlisle *Gazette* of December 19, 1787:

Although the article [hog bristles] may not appear of consequence to some, yet he can assure the public, that many hundred pounds are exported in specie annually, to Great Britain, in payment for said article.

Another brush maker, Samuel Wright, advertised in the Reading *Berks and Schuylkill Journal* of January 5, 1822: "The subscriber, in North Callowhill Street, will give 40 cents a pound for clean combed bristles and 50 cents if taken in brushes. N.B. His brushes are all stamped S. Wright."

The Doylestown *Democrat* of December 27, 1881, has the earliest reference we have been able to find on bartering hog bristles for Christmas candy:

Years ago, a few toy candies, with several fancy shaped, frosted, home-made molasses cakes, decorated with the juice of red beets, besides, perhaps, some other trifling article, constituted a child's presents. In many instances, the children were obliged to gather up the hog-bristles left from butchering, comb them out, so as to appear marketable, and convert them into money, wherewith to purchase; thus they really bought part of their presents themselves.

Another account is from the Reading *Weekly Eagle* of December 21, 1895:

The first three weeks of December bring the country boys and girls pleasures cherished as the merry holidays. Gathering hog bristles is the best source of income the boys and girls of the country have. When there's a butchering on the place, the eight and ten-year-olds get up as early as the grown people, and when, at dawn, the hogs are scraped, the youngsters stand close by and pick up the bristles as fast as the men can take them off. They take the bristles on boards, and butt ends all one way, and when, after a few days, they are dry, the bristles are combed and cleaned, tied up into small bundles, and then taken to the village store, where a ready market always awaits them. Nice bristles, such as are long and stiff, most usually are worth seventy-five cents or more per pound. But when the ends are mixed and the bristles are thin and short, they are worth only half that amount. The children who use care in preparing them for market are always well paid for their pains.

In a recent letter to the author, Jaret L. Snyder of Wernersville, Berks County, wrote:

In the locality where I was raised, after the fall butchering, we children would gather the pig-bristles, clean and bunch them; and sell them to the sadlers and shoemakers, who used them to point their threads. That money we were allowed to buy our Christmas candy with.

As the concluding entry on hog bristles we shall quote from a letter Raymond E. Hollenbach wrote the author on December 10, 1956:

Regarding hog bristles I submit the following from the old day books of the William Krumm store at Jordan Valley [Lehigh County]. Krumm conducted a store at Jordan Valley for many years, and later as Lochland. In the first day books practically every farmer brought in hog bristles during the butchering season. For the season from Dec. 20, 1864 to February 29, the following brought in bristles. I give the whole list to show that these were brought in by different farmers:

John Miller	4½ ounces	14 cents
Gideon Peter	4½ ounces	13 cents
Gabriel Miller	3½ ounces	10 cents
Jacob Straub	11 ounces	34 cents
Aaron Smith	10 ounces	33 cents
Jonas Miller	10 ounces	30 cents
Nathan Gehry	10 ounces	33 cents
Jonas Sensinger	10½ ounces	38 cents
Nathan Fink	3 ounces	11 cents
David Krumm	3½ ounces	13 cents

You will notice the prices varied slightly, probably according to quality. The bristles had to be clean and tied in small bundles, several inches in diameter. The quantities shown above would seem to indicate that the 4½ ounces and 3½ ounces were probably the product of one hog, the 10 ounces from two hogs and the pound lots from a whole winter's butchering of three or four hogs.

My father bought hog bristles [in Saegersville, Lehigh County] as late as the early 1900's, but unfortunately the only day books I have saved of his are for the summer months, and hog bristles were brought in only during the butchering season. However, I also have some of the later books of William Krumm and in the one for the winter of 1884–1885 he bought hog bristles and the price was still the same, that is three cents an ounce or fifty cents a pound in larger quantities. However, in 1884–1885 the trade in bristles had already fallen off and instead of eighteen customers bringing in bristles [as in 1864–1865] I can find only three in Mrs. Krumm's book. William Krumm, however, kept his own book, so the number was probably twice that many.

Matzabaum, Moshey, and Bellyguts

Matzabaum, moshey, and bellyguts were Pennsylvania's candy specialties in the time of Open-Hearth Christmases. Matzabaum, a Christmas candy common to the Lancaster-York area, disappeared many, many years ago. Today only the matzabaum molds, which once impressed figures of animals and flowers thereon remain, most of them in the half-dozen famous Pennsylvania folk art collections in museums from New York to Winterthur. Bellyguts, a word of Scotch-Irish background, is little remembered any more. Of the three—matzabaum, moshey, and bellyguts—moshey alone survives, in the heartland of the Dutch Country.

First, we shall discuss these words etymologically, and then we shall proceed to present their usages chronologically.

MATZABAUM

Matzabaum derives from the German word *Marzipan* or marchpane, a candy made of pounded almonds. The "-pan" in Marzipan became "baum" or tree in Pennsylvania Dutch, folk-etymologically, because this candy was used specifically to decorate the Christmas tree.

To date, the earliest documentation for the word matzabaum is a reference in the Lancaster *Union* of December 27, 1836: "And when the Christmas trees have all been wondered at and matzebaum have lost their novelty and their paint, 'St. Claus' and his tiny chariot and horses will have ceased whirling through the brains of our little readers."

In the Lancaster *Weekly Intelligencer* of December 28, 1881, Simon Snyder Rathvon described the matzabaums:

These pseudo-confections were at one time extensively manufactured in Lancaster, and a patent was obtained as late as 1876 for a machine to make them. They were made of white dough, and at least two kinds: one containing sweetening and the other none; and they were either baked or dried. They were embellished with animals, trees, birds, flowers, bushes, men, women and children, pressed in a sort of "bold relief" upon the one side, and they were gaudily painted with red, yellow, green, blue, etc., and when the youngsters commenced sucking them, for the small quantity of sugar they contained, their hands and their faces from their mouths to their eyes presented a ludicrous aspect of commingled daubery.

Phebe Earle Gibbons in her folk-culturally important volume, *Pennsylvania Dutch* (1882 edition), page 415, wrote : "In Lancaster, at Christmas-time, is sold a cake called *Motzebom*, which is not seen in Eastern Pennsylvania."

The most illuminating article ever on this candy and Christmas tree decoration is from the pen of S. M. Sener, an early Lancaster folklorist. In the *Christian Culture* of January 1, 1892, pages 171–172, he wrote:

Years ago, about Christmas-time, there used to be manufactured in this community a cake or confection locally called "Matzabaum," and considerable discussion has arisen at divers times as to the origin or derivation of the name. The confection was of two kinds, those which could be eaten and those which had been made especially as a Christmas tree decoration.

The former were made out of flour, sugar, egg, spices and some variety of powdered nuts, such as peanuts or almonds, and when baked formed a delightful tidbit not unlike "macaroons!" The latter were made of starch and were of diverse designs, such as birds, fish, butterflies and the like, and were usually gorgeously painted. Both varieties were formed in clay or wooden moulds by pressing the plastic material into the design. There were quite a number of local manufacturers of these Christmas tree ornaments, but prominent among them was the father of the late Samuel J. Demuth, who lived on South Duke street.

As to the origin of the name it was supposed to have been derived from "Matza," a name applied by the Hebrews to unleavened bread, used in the feast of the "Passover." Evidently "Matzabaum" is a corruption of the German "Marzipane" (pronounced

Marr-tsee-pahn), or "Marcus-bread," a form of sweet bread (panis Marcius), probably in honor of the inventor, or some distinguished citizen of Venice. By the French it is called "masse pien," and in English "marchpane."

The second part of the word is evidently the Latin *panis*— bread. The first part has been identified by Professor Mahn [as] identical with the Latin *maza*, which Diez and M. Hayne approve of, and which means "mush."

The same idea is coincided in by Dr. Oswald Seidensticker, of Philadelphia, who further states that the name was in use in Germany during the XVIth Century, and in support thereof quotes *Grimm's Woerterbuch.* The English "marchpane," was evidently in use in England in the XVIth Century, also, as the following, quoted from Shakespeare shows: "Good, save me some march-pane!" It seems strange that such a delightful confection as the eatable variety is said to have been should have been called "mush-bread," by the Latins. A Christmas tree loaded down with the starchy varieties and illuminated with tapers, presented a very handsome sight. "Matzabaums" are unknown to the young folks of to-day, but the elder portion of the community remember them. Their manufacture ceased years ago, when the now common tinsel and paper Christmas tree ornaments came in vogue.

To raise money for the association, the YWCA of York in 1903 exhibited an old-fashioned Pennsylvania Dutch Christmas tree. The Hanover *Daily Record* of December 26th described it in detail; the account spoke of "quaint little objects known as matzebaums, which were made in moulds 100 years ago."

The late Cornelius Weygandt alluded to matzabaums five, six times in his half-dozen books on the Dutch Country, nowhere more pointedly, however, than in his *The Blue Hills* (New York, 1936), page 354, where he wrote:

We put the American turkey and Indian alongside the peacock and German Uhlan on our powder horns, and the stars and stripes and American eagles on our *matzebäume* alongside the pomegranates and storks we brought from the Rhine Valley.

MOSHEY

Mitford M. Mathews's *Dictionary of Americanisms* (University of Chicago Press, 1951) lists the words moshey and bellyguts as Pennsylvaniaisms, the former signifying unpulled taffy, the latter, pulled.

Moshey is a word still very much alive in certain parts of Pennsylvania, especially Berks County. Bel-

lyguts, though still known here and there, seems to have passed into the realm of the area's passive vocabulary altogether.

Professor Marcus Bachman Lambert, up to this moment the dialect's outstanding lexicographer, incorrectly assumed that moshey was a Pennsylvania Dutch word, for he lists it under the spelling *mooschi* in his 1924 *Dictionary of the Non-English Words of the Pennsylvania-German Dialect.* The authors of several regional cookbooks have followed suit, namely: the widely distributed Reading *Pennsylvania Dutch Cook Book* and Ruth Hutchison's 1948 *Pennsylvania Dutch Cook Book*, published by Harper's. Carl W. Drepperd, who up until his death a year or two ago, was the resident director of the Landis Valley Musuem, in a column in the Lancaster *New Era*[1] sought its origin in a French word *Moyeu*, meaning a sugar plum!

The most interesting conjecture to date as to the origin of the word moshey comes from Dr. Henry Young of the History Department of Dickinson College. Dr. Young informs the author that during his days as director of the Historical Society of York County, around 1935, a York lawyer, J. Edgar Small, now deceased, contended the word moshey derived from an ancestor of his by the name of Mosey, who, according to family tradition, was a famous York taffy maker. The family name Mosey—presumably French in origin—is, in fact, represented in York County as far back as the eighteenth century.

To date, the earliest reference to moshey is the 1849 entry in the *Dictionary of Americanisms*:

Mosey (sugar)—1849. W. DUANE *Lett. to Barlett* 22 Jan. (*MS*) *Sugar Mosey* or *Mosey Sugar,* the name of a cake made of sugar, for children, in Harrisburgh [*sic*] Pa.

Subsequent references are as follows: *Lippincott's Magazine* for March 1869, page 315 (in the section on Pennsylvaniaisms in Henry Reeves's article "Our Provincialisms"):

"Mosey sugars," molasses candy with the meat of nuts mixed with it. May it not have been originally "mosaic sugars," from *mosaic,* a species of inlaid-work which the candy, when cut, resembles? "Mosey," mealy, Gloucestershire dialect.

The July 28, 1870, issue of the *Nation*, in a very interesting contribution on Pennsylvaniaisms, says:

"Mosey-Sugar" was their great delicacy when they grew a little older and could take their pennies to the shops. It was a black molasses candy—not cake, as Barlett says—scalloped at the edges like our cake of maple-sugar.

Lee Grumbine, one of the early students of Pennsylvania provincialisms, lists the word "Moshy" in an article he wrote on the subject in the Lebanon *Daily Report* of April 13, 1892. Dr. Ezra Grumbine in an article "Folk-Lore and Superstitious Beliefs of Lebanon County" (*Lebanon County Historical Society Proceedings*, volume 3, number 9, 1905, page 256) has this to say:

Another Christmas goody was molasses candy. The best was made of black sugar-house molasses and contained a plentiful sprinkling of walnut kernels. It was cooled in miniature patty-pans with scalloped edges and was known as "Mozhey!"

In 1909 appeared C. H. Leeds's *Old Home Week Letters* about early Carlisle. The author refers thrice to moshey.

[Page 23:] Aunt Nancy also made a toothsome article of taffy or "mosey" on the cutest little tin dishes, about so big; don't you mind how she would tap on the bottom of the "patties" to loosen up the sweet stuff? [Page 32:] We must not forget the two oval-shaped waiters, one with round scalloped pans, about 3 inches in diameter, or "mosey sugar." [Page 57:] Do you mind old Miss Nancy Lougherty's inviting little cake shop on West Louther street. . . . Can you ever forget that delicious "Mosey?"

Thomas S. Stein in an article "Granny Forney's Cake and Beer Shop" (*Lebanon County Historical Society Proceedings*, volume 9, 1927, page 247) wrote:

"Moshy" is now known as molasses candy. But it may be made of sugar also. Molasses and butter are boiled to a certain consistency and then poured into small triangular or round, scalloped tins or "patty-pans." Frequently nut kernels were added. "Moshy" was one of the common confections of the day, when the stores were not flooded with innumerable kinds of candy and sweetmeats, as at present.

The word moshey is frequently heard today in the Dutch Country in two compounds—moshey apples and moshey pie, the latter a great delicacy that has been served annually at the Pennsylvania Dutch Folk Festival in Kutztown. Victor C. Dieffenbach of Bethel reports hearing, years ago, the terms moshey pan and moshey-seckel, the latter a dialect word used to describe someone who tries awfully hard to ingratiate himself.

BELLYGUTS

The word bellyguts—pulled taffy—is the most interesting of the three.

The contributor of the 1870 article on Pennsylvaniaisms in the *Nation* wrote:

The molasses candy which had been "worked" till it became white went by another name which we shall request permission to set down. "Belly-guts" was the name it bore—so unpolished was the Pennsylvanian of a former generation. Possibly he may have twisted the French *belles goutes* into this not very dainty term of his, but possibly too this derivation is an effort of the refined.

Bellyguts was an indelicate word to the Victorian era. In an article "Old Town Characters about 1830" in the November 23, 1860, Carlisle *Herald,* appears this characteristic sentence: "Then there was on the pavement, at the door, 'Granny Morrison,' with her long, yellow, flexible melting 'sticks' of molasses candy, called, not inaptly,—abdominal intestines!"

Commenting on the word bellyguts, D. W. Thompson of Carlisle wrote this author recently:

I can only suppose the name grew from a fancied resemblance between the belly guts of a butchered animal, with which every family would have been familiar, and the "long" and "flexible" dropping strands of taffy in the soft state, as when looped over a taffy hook. Every family would know that also. It seems to me that most of the kitchens I knew in boyhood had a taffy hook on the wall, on wooden door jamb or cupboard side. Neither latter word [belly or guts] was permissible in conversation in my time. I seem to recall that one of Judge Shute's books, *The Real Diary of a Real Boy,* or a sequel, tells how a young playmate shocked a Sunday School social merely by asking "What rhymes with jelly cake?"

To date the earliest use of the word bellyguts is from the *Hive*, a weekly literary journal published in Lancaster, Pennsylvania, from May to December, 1810, by schoolmaster Samuel Bacon (born in Sturbridge, Massachusetts, July 22, 1782, and died in Africa on May 3, 1820). In a humorous piece in the *Hive* there appears a description of a chance meeting with three Pennsylvania Dutch girls at the fair in Lancaster city:

I made my escape with all possible speed; but I had no sooner regained the street, than I was caught on three sides by as many strapping country girls, who brawled out in English *via Dutch,* for "fairings." Judge, Mr. Editor, of my consternation as well as of their disappointment when my three solitary "fifpennybits," (all the money I had, and of course all the ravenous wenches could get) were in an instant metamorphosed into—"belly-guts."

Indubitably the finest bit of bellyguts lore is a Pennsylvania Dutch-English poem entitled, "How to make Molasses Candy, vulgarly called Paley Cutts." The January 5, 1822, Paradise [Lancaster County] *Hornet*, which carried the poem, added this footnote: "On perusing an old file of the *Independent Balance*[3] [established in Philadelphia on April 16, 1817], I observed the following receipt which may be amusing to some of your readers." The macaronic poem, one of the earliest of this genre in Pennsylvania literature, runs as follows.

How to make Molasses Candy, vulgarly called Paley Cutts

Dake a pod or a kiddle,
Not doo pig nor doo liddle,
   Dey insite mit putter den schmear,
Bore molashes derein,
Alf way up do de prim,
   On de fire den blace him mit kare.
      Do mit a ri, ti, tiddle tum tay;
      Do mit a ri, ti, tiddle tum tay;
      Do mit a ri, ti tiddle tum,
        Ri ti tiddle tum,
        Do ri ti tiddle tum tay;
      Do mit a ri ti tiddle tay.

Den led him tsimmer and pile
Yust a liddle wile,
   Den tzuck in a spoon full of vlour;
Do mage de paley cutts ott,
Chincher pud in the pod
   And den led him pile alf an our.
      Do mit a ri, ti . . .

Den bore him oud in a blate or tish,
Or vat ever you vish,

Put mindt virst you rup him mit crease;
Mit lart, or mit putter
It ish not any madder,
   Unt you'll find him gum of mit creat ease.
      Do mit a ri, ti . . .

Den mit bulling and halling,
Unt vingring unt mawling,
   You'll hawl him into vight schticks;
Vich lay out in state,
On a port or a blate,
   Unt den de paley cutts will be quite vixt.
      Do mit a ri, ti . . .

The Lancaster *Journal* of April 12, 1822, in a letter from Harrisburg, reported: "In one corner you might see a crowd of sages closely wedged around a Huckster's table, bargaining for belly-guts and gingerbread."

In an article "Pennsylvania Idioms" by one T. S. in the Philadelphia *Press* of August 6, 1870, the author wrote: "'Belly-guts' still survives."

Perhaps the most informative articles that have ever been written on everyday things in the Pennsylvania Dutch country is a series by D. K. Noell, entitled "Seventy Years Ago," which appeared in the Sunday York *Gazette* in the 1890s. Noell wrote in the issue of August 19, 1895:

Belly-guts was molasses and a little flour boiled together, and drawn out into thin strips, then laid upon a salver, or waiter, and thus carried by boys and girls on battalion or fair days through the streets, for sale, seventy years ago.

That the word bellyguts was carried by Pennsylvania settlers early to other parts of the American continent becomes apparent from a letter (dated January 18, 1957) by David H. Gingrich of Grand Blanc, Michigan, to the author: "Making bellyguts was an annual affair in my boyhood in Waterloo, Ontario, but I had never seen the word in print before you used it."

CHRISTMAS DEW

For the past ten years we have been engaged full time in gathering data on the folk culture of Southeastern Pennsylvania. Roughly, half of this time has been spent in libraries, the other half in fieldwork, collecting the area's folklore. The material in this chapter, as the reader will soon realize, is primarily the fruit of field collecting. Folk beliefs are rarely come upon in printed sources, newspapers and periodicals.

Perhaps the best-known of all folk beliefs in Pennsylvania is that cattle in the barn can be heard to talk on Christmas Eve, between eleven and twelve o'clock. An interesting literary allusion to this belief appears in Henry L. Fisher's *Olden Times* (York, 1888), page 212:

I used to love and sit and watch
   The cobbler's cut and tailor's stitch;
To hear the learned arguments,
Between those learned disputants,
   Concerning elf, and ghost, and witch,
And whether they were black, or white,
Or, oxen talked on Christmas-night.

The old-timers will tell you that special gifts are required to understand what the cattle are saying. A person born on Christmas Eve, between eleven and midnight, is said to possess this gift.

Quite common is the folktale of the farmer who ventures out in the barn late on Christmas Eve. While there, he overhears one horse say to another: "Before many a day is past, we'll be driving our master to the cemetery." The farmer becomes struck with great fear, rushes back in the house, stumbles, and breaks a leg. And after suffering for a couple weeks death intervenes.

The choicest bit of lore along this line comes from Schuylkill County. An old-timer tells of hearing that anyone can acquire the gift of understanding animal talk Christmas Eve. One has merely to follow a certain set of rules: Sit down by lamplight at exactly eight o'clock on Christmas Eve and start reading the Bible from Genesis, in the very beginning, and continue reading three solid hours, without so much as looking up. Then at the stroke of eleven close the Holy Book, go and cut yourself a piece of bread (it must be from a rye loaf and a round one at that), sprinkle a goodly amount of salt on it, and eat it dry—without butter, that is. Having followed these instructions to the letter, you will be able to comprehend the tongue of all the beasts in the barn.

The dew which falls from heaven on the anniversary of the coming of the Christ Child is supposed to have beneficial effects. We personally know instances in Berks County where the mother of a family places a piece of bread (oftentimes the number is three) outside on Christmas Eve, away from cats and other animals. There it lies during Christmas night so that dew will fall on it. In the morning, the mother takes this piece of bread, breaks off a bit, and gives a piece to each member of the household to eat—all before breakfast is taken. Doing this, it is believed, will prevent fevers all year long until another Christmas rolls around.[1]

Likewise, the farmers used to go out in the barn Christmas Eve, where they set about throwing some hay down in the barnyard. There it lay all night long. In the morning, wet with Christmas dew, this hay was then fed to every horse and cow in the stables. Our own grandfather, so we are told, used to follow this practice on his Niss Hollow farm in Carbon County. The farmers believed if they did this none of their valuable animals would die between then and the following Christmas season.

In Lehigh County farmers used to hold to the belief that bees crawled about on the outside of the hive Christmas night, no matter how cold the weather, no matter whether it was mild or snowing.

A bit of general lore, of literary provenance probably, is the saying that on Christmas night water in wells is changed into wine for a brief moment. We came upon this lore in the Pittsburgh *Post* of December 25, 1858:

It was thought that during Christmas night all water was for a short time changed into wine, and that bread baked on this eve would never become mouldy. The fruit trees were "wassailed" to insure a good crop, and a great variety of similar simple, emblematic customs were observed.

In the field of the occult, there is John George Homan's famous formula from his *Long Lost Friend,* giving instructions on how to go about making a divining rod that works:

To make a wand for searching for iron, ore or water: On the first night of Christmas, between eleven and twelve o'clock, break off from any tree a young twig of one year's growth, in the three highest names (Father, Son and Holy Ghost); at the same time facing toward sunrise. Whenever you apply this wand in searching for anything, apply it three times. The twig must be forked, and each end of the fork must be held in one hand, so that the third and thickest part of it stands up, but do not hold it too tightly. Strike the ground with the thickest end, and that which you desire will appear immediately, if there is ought in the ground where you strike. The words to be spoken when the wand is thus applied are as follows: "Archangel Gabriel, I conjure thee in the name of God, the Almighty, to tell me, is there any water here or not? Do tell me!" If you are searching for iron or ore, you have to say the same, only mention the name of what you are searching for.

To catch a thief, go out to a crossroads over which a corpse has been taken in all four directions. You must do this Christmas Eve between eleven and twelve. Walk a circle and within it build a fire and melt a dime into a silver bullet. With this bullet the thief will be shot dead ere long.

Very widely known is the lore that a silver bullet, cast on a crossroads Christmas Eve at the right hour will, when loaded in a firepiece and fired, hit one's enemy wherever he may be. This bit of occult lore was tried by a Jonestown native during the Civil War; he tried, the Lebanon *Courier* of January 2, 1862, reports, to cast a magic bullet to end the life of Jeff Davis:

On Christmas eve, an individual who has great faith in supernatural agencies, undertook to cast a bullet that should kill Jeff Davis, at a crossroad, in the neighborhood of Jonestown. He made all his preparations, fixed his furnace, drew the magic circle, and was moving along "all right," when an explosion took place in his furnace as if powder had been concealed there; frightful creatures with horns and ghostly adornments gathered around his circle, spouting fire at him, and the whole scene seemed as if Pandemonium was on an earthly jubilee. The knees of our patriotic friend began to quake, his blood chilled, and not being able to withstand the terrors longer, he broke and ran for town, pursued for some distance by the fiery demons he seemed to have evoked. He arrived in Jonestown speechless and almost helpless, no doubt willing that Jeff should live rather than that he should undergo another such ordeal to get a bullet to kill him.

Christmas Eve, it is widely believed, is the time for looking into the future. Several years ago an elderly woman in northern Berks County told the author of a method she used, when a young girl, to find out whom she would one day marry. She said she set a pail of water out in the yard one Christmas night when the temperature was below freezing. She went to bed early; just before midnight she got up and dressed, took a lantern, lit it and went out in the yard to study the configuration in the ice that had formed in the pail. She said one was supposed to be able to figure out the tool, the trade in other words, of the man one was going to marry.

An open grave Christmas Day means an open grave throughout the year in the neighborhood cemetery, it was believed; also, it was said a green Christmas portended a full graveyard for the coming year.

On Christmas Eve any young lady, they said, had but to spread a handkerchief that had never been wet in the garden and leave it there until the mystic hour, when her future husband would bring her the handkerchief the very minute she stepped into the garden.

Any young man who washed his shirt in the evening and hung it up in the kitchen could, it was said, see his future bride turn the shirt on the line, if the young man waited in the kitchen between eleven and twelve o'clock on Christmas Eve.

No new tasks, it was believed, should be undertaken between Christmas and New Year's. A Bernville grandfather tells me when he was a hired hand on a nearby farm they were not allowed to take any manure out of the stable at this season of the year. If you did not obey, some of your cattle would be dragged out of the stable the next year on account of death, it was said.

Women were not supposed to sew or spin. Cloth spun between Christmas and New Year's, the old-timers believed, would not wear well.

And one was not to take a bath at this time, nor was one to change his underwear. If one did, it was thought, he would become full of boils.

Best-known item of all our folklore is the Pennsylvania weather lore concerning the Christmas season: If the ground is white on Christmas, it will be green on Easter; or if green on Christmas, then white on Easter.

One used to hear, too, if the ground thawed between Christmas and New Year's, it would also every month of the year. Put more concretely: If between Christmas and New Year the geese waddle in mud they will do so every single month of the following year.

And finally, the number of snowfalls, it was believed, could be foretold for the winter. This was indicated by the number of days from the first snowfall of the season until Christmas.

Ralph D. Dunkelberger has here fully captured the spirit of cookie baking in the days of Woodstove Christmases.

WOODSTOVE CHRISTMASES

Woodstove Christmases is, as indicated earlier in this volume, the name we have chosen to designate nineteenth- and early turn-of-the-century Christmas practices in Pennsylvania.

What recollections of bygone Christmases center around the old-time kitchen woodstove: boyhood's chore, keeping the ravenous wood chest filled; girlhood's stint, helping mother or grandmother with the week-long cookie baking; pre-Christmas pleasures nibbling on the broken cookies, brown horses with severed legs or missing tail, perhaps; and, finally, of a Christmas morning, what a myriad of mouthwatering aromas from the old woodstove!

The literary theme song we have chosen to head off this section on Woodstove Christmases is Benjamin Bausman's "An Old-time Christmas in a Country Home," which appeared originally in the January 1871 *Guardian*. The locale of the Bausman boyhood home, by the way, was a Lancaster County farmstead.

AN OLD-TIME CHRISTMAS
IN A COUNTRY HOME

By Benjamin Bausman

It was the week before Christmas. A busy week in the country home, for then "the butchering" had to be done. An ox and four hogs were slaughtered. The second day before Christmas the cooky-baking was done. Large tables in the bake-house were covered with cookies, in all manner of forms—birds, horses, hearts, lambs, stars, all carefully spread out on patty-pans. We children, meanwhile, watched the progress of events, burdening the bakers with many curious questions. A great mystery to my child-mind was the large bake-oven, which for a season seemed to devour all put into it. I peered into its glowing cavern, and watched with watering mouth the nut-brown cookies which it brought forth.

The day before Christmas was the "preparation day." The turkey had to be killed, and many other things provided for the Christmas dinner. The boys were sent in various directions, to practice "pure and undefiled religion." One wagon was closely packed with numerous baskets and packages, each containing a nicely arranged variety of gifts—meat, sausage, apples, cakes, and, perhaps, articles of clothing. Ere the boy started, the loving heart that had devised all these pleasure-giving packages, standing aside of the wagon, repeated her instructions: "Be careful you make no mistakes—this is for Mrs. Snow; yonder long basket for Mrs. Harris; that bag for Mrs. Weber, and this round basket for Mrs. Noble, etc." Mr. Noble was the pastor, whose basket contained, among other things, a large turkey. From house to house drove the boy, leaving the appropriate gift at each, and receiving in return, such a blessing from the fatherless and widows, as are worth more than gold and silver. The little old widow Weber rubbed her hands, and laughed like an overjoyed child. Indeed, she had reached her second childhood. The pastor—well, of course he had expected all, but was none the less grateful. Half the thankful messages sent to the parents by the receivers, the boy could not remember. Only this much, that they were made very happy.

Scarcely had this wagon left the house, when another of the boys, mounted on a grey pony, with large saddle-bags and a basket, tightly packed, was started on a visiting tour among country widows in the neighborhood. No less thankful were these than their poor sisters of the town. Indeed, to their dying day they remembered and blessed the boys that brought them gifts—which blessings some of the said boys, now that they are men, do greatly prize.

One of these Christmas visits to our pastor I distinctly remember. After the baskets had been emptied, the pastor invited the awkward country boy into the parlor. To my consternation, he introduced me to a gay-looking young gentleman, with a heavy gold chain at his vest, just arrived from Germany, whom he called Dr. Schaff. He took me kindly by the hand, and expressed himself pleased with my way of visiting my pastor. He was then on his way to Mercersburg for the first time.

It was a stormy Christmas Eve. The sleet rattled against the windows. Around the large "ten-plate" stove, filled with hickory logs, sat the family. The boys repeating their reports of their merciful errands to the widows; the parents telling the children how these pious poor people would, on this stormy night, pray the dear Christ-Child to bless them in their little beds. Then followed many questions from the little ones—whether Mrs. Harris had any little children, and whether the Christkindel would bring them anything that night.

There was no Christmas-tree. Then, as now, this tree was more of a town than country growth. The smaller children were still allowed to believe in a real bodily Christkindel. It would surely come that night. Where will mother set the baskets this time? In a dark front room—the parlor becomes the reception room of the kind heavenly visitor. Two bread baskets, with a clean white cloth spread in them, are placed on chairs. The little innocents, half-frightened, hold on to the mother's dress, as they follow her into the parlor, and watch the arranging of the baskets. Many puzzling little troubles they have. When will it come? Where will it get in? Ought not the front door be left open? Will the baskets be large enough? How heavenly this unsuspecting confiding trust!

What a fearful fuss the dogs are making! Watch runs barking about the house, as if he would tear some one to pieces.

Hist! Somebody's knocking.

"Come in," says father. And in they came; such as they are. A half dozen jovial fellows, led by a so-called Belsnickel.

"O ma!" scream a group of us smaller children, and seize hold of her dress, like an affrighted brood rush under the wings of the mother hen, when the hawk is after them. Belsnickel may either mean a fur-clad Nicholas, or a flogging Nicholas. In the wintry Christmas nights, he is usually robed in furs, and carries his whip with him.

Our Belsnickel is, most likely, some well-known neighbor friend. Under his ugly mask *(Schnarraffel-gesicht)* and an outlandish dress, such as no child ever saw mortal wear before, no one can tell who he is. We children tremble as in a presence of an unearthly being. Really, the Nickel tries to be pleasant, jabbers in some unknown tongue, and takes a few chestnuts and candies out of his vast bundle on his back, and throws them on the floor for the larger boys. One after another shyly picks up a gift. Among these older boys is a self-willed fellow, who sometimes behaves rudely. Whenever he picks up something, Nickel thwacks a long whip across his back—across his only. Whereupon the little ones scream and hold on to their mamma with a firm grip; and the older ones laugh aloud. The guilty boy puts his hand where the whip has made an impression. Again the unknown being puts his large working hand into the bag and scatters gifts, and again cracks his whip on the bad boy. How does this ugly man know who has been naughty?

Ere the little ones are tucked in bed, mother must repeat to them the story of Bethlehem. Then they kneel at her lap and pray

to the dear Christ-Child. Half-frightened they put their ears to the key-hole of the parlor door, to listen whether it is at work already at the baskets. Then they scamper off to their low beds, like lambs leaping into the fold. With their heads under the cover, they discuss the frightful visitor with the long whip, and the blessed Christ-Child, that carries no whip, and fall asleep over their talk. Visions of Paradise, where all good children will have baskets of cakes and candies, that will never be empty, cheer their dreams. Many a time during the night a little head is raised above the cover for a moment, to listen for the blessed visitor in the adjoining room; and quickly plunges into the invisible underworld again. "Can you hear it?" whispers a little neighbor.

Hours before dawn the little folks call the parents. They must see their baskets—shoeless, in their slips, they hopefully follow their mother to the full baskets—full of just the things they had been wishing for. Such a heaven on earth—a foretaste of the bliss above comes only to unsuspecting childhood.

A merry time we had on Christmas morning. All received presents. Father had a pleasant surprise for mother, and she a still better one for him; for woman's heart excels in this art. And the children's hearts were gladdened by many little gifts not found in the baskets. The hired girls merrily pack their gifts in their aprons, and shouting, bear them up-stairs to their rooms. And John— John Antweiler was his name—the hired man, must have his share. A great big German, with mighty limbs and a warm heart. No one could see him laugh without falling into a roar. When the spell would take him, he dropped his work, his eyes rolled and twinkled, his face becomes almost blood-red, with his brawny hands he would seize his thigh or side; his body seemed to heave with some internal tumult, giving him no rest till his haw haws turned into screams, and tears rolled over his flushed cheeks. He had a great story-telling talent. On many a cold winter's day, we little ones sat spell-bound in the stable, listening to his stories, while he was currying the cattle. And on long winter evenings, with well-nigh breathless attention, we drank his marvellous German tales, to which he gave his own coloring as he passed along. To our child-minds, John was a great man—interlarding his stories with an occasional whiff from his pipe, and a heartsome laugh—

Still we gazed, and still the wonder grew,
That one small head could carry all he knew.

That Christmas morning we climbed up the stalwart frame of our mirthful friend, and stuffed his pockets and his large heart with Christmas joy.

All the other members of the family, not needed to prepare the dinner, go to church. The pastor preaches about, and the congregation praises God for, the birth of our Saviour. Meanwhile, the whole house is redolent with the odor of the roasting, going on in the kitchen, and the little ones make merry over their stores of goods, and thankfully prattle about the happy birth-day of our Saviour.

It takes a large table, with much on it, for such a family. And the best that can be had is there—the best dinner of the year. All the children are taught to pray at table—but to pray silently. The father folds his hands on his down-turned plate, and all the children fold theirs in their laps, and all close their eyes, and offer a silent prayer, the father, in his earnestness, unconsciously prays in a whisper that can almost be heard.

Eating is a most exquisite enjoyment for a healthy child. No tongue can describe the pleasure it derives from it. Its appetite and palate enjoy food with the keenest relish. A Christmas dinner makes its heart glad a month before it comes. And as plate after plate is emptied, every nook and corner of its being is filled with joy. Fill the plate well, mother. The child's stomach is wonderfully elastic; like the boy's pockets, it can hold a little world of nuts, cakes, candies, turkey, sweet potatoes, celery, sausages, fassnachts, custard, apple pie, mince pie, etc. Look at it. The face blushes and beams with fatness, and the glad heart pumps like a well-oiled piston of a locomotive. It is a rich treat to see a child enjoying its Christmas dinner. All past grievances, all present and future tasks are forgotten under the charm of the gratified appetite. We enjoy our meals, in the fullest sense, but for one short period in life—in childhood. The palate of a Christian child is a religious organ, helping to understand and feel the power of Christ's birth and atonement.

It was then customary, and still is among German Christians, to observe the second day of Christmas. It was a holiday for all the hired people. The children could stay out of school, and enjoy themselves as on the day previous. On the following week came the poor for their share. With large baskets and bags came women and children. The butchering and baking had been done with an eye to these less favored people. And it might well be thus done. For it took quantities to give each one a gift. I can still see how patiently mother would leave her work, to wait on some of these beggars—sometimes three and four at a time. To be *sure,* some were the fault of their own poverty, people of lazy, thievish or drinking habits. And she, the kind soul, knew it all. But then, even bad people are to be pitied for being wicked and unhappy. Besides, she had an old-fashioned notion, that during the Christmas season we ought to be kind to everybody, good and bad. That as our Father in Heaven lets the rain fall on the just and the unjust, so ought our grateful hearts, by acts of universal kindness, teach others that the birth of our Saviour brings good news to all who come to Him to be saved.

CHRIST-KINDEL TO KRISS KRINGLE

The roots of the contemporary celebration of Christmas in the United States stretch back no farther than the first half of the nineteenth century. Largely devoid of folk roots, our Christmas is basically literature-inspired. In large part it is the accomplishment of three men, all three literary figures. The trio are Washington Irving, Clement Z. Moore, both from New York State, and a third author, an anonymous Pennsylvanian, the editor of *Kriss Kringle's Christmas Tree*, published initially in Philadelphia in 1845.

The purpose of this chapter is to show how the eighteenth-century Pennsylvania gift bringer, *Christkindel* or Christ Child, in the first half of the nineteenth century became Kriss Kringle, an old and bearded twin of Santa Claus.

What was the eighteenth-century folk concept of Protestant Dutch Pennsylvania in regard to the Christ Child? The author has been able to find but one major literary clue. It is a brief newspaper account in the Lancaster *Examiner* of December 30, 1887. A newspaper reporter, covering a Christmas Festival at Washington Borough, writes about what one Reverend A. W. Kauffman related to his audience, both adults and children, concerning his Christmas experience sixty-five years prior, when he was a seven-year-old hired "lad" on a Lancaster County farm. The reporter wrote:

He started out by saying that at that age he lived with an old farmer who on Christmas eve [about 1822] told him to set his basket as the Christ-kindel would come that night. He did as he was bade, but instead of a large plate or beautiful basket, he was given a large straw bread basket. He was also informed that he must put hay in the basket for Christ-kindel's mule; for says he, "Boys and girls, Christ-kindel was not as high toned as your Santa Claus now. Instead of a fine team of reindeer and fine sleigh and bells, he came on a mule—and an old gray one at

that. Now," continued the Rev. Kauffman, "boys and girls, what do you think I got in my basket?" There being no response he went on to relate, or rather enumerate the contents of his well-filled basket, viz.: "Walnuts, snits, choostets and starched gingerbread." The next morning, the old farmer said, "Well Abram, what did Christ-kindel bring you?" "Well," said Abram, "I guess Christ-kindel brought me the walnuts, snits and choostets, but Betzy brought me the gingerbread."

We shall now proceed to develop the two major facets of what we assume to have been the eighteenth-century Christ-kindel folk concept in Pennsylvania:

a) a gift bringer, who comes by night aback a mule or ass.
b) setting a basket to receive the presents brought by the gift bringer. (The hay in the basket is intended for the Christ Child's beast of burden.)

There is one bit of Christmas folklore in the Dutch Country which corroborates the mule as the Christ Child's beast of burden. The author's grandfather was a farmer in Carbon County. Each Christmas Eve, before retiring, he would go out to the barn and throw a pile of hay out in the barnyard. There it lay during the course of the night so that the Christmas dew might fall on it. In the morning he would feed this hay, heavy with dew, to his cattle in the conviction that by so doing, his livestock would prosper another twelve months. The folk mind gave this custom an interesting significance. Said the simple folk, "The hay is for the mule on which the Christ Child comes riding on Christmas Eve."

We shall now proceed to show how the eighteenth-century Christ-kindel became "old and bearded" Kriss Kringle by the 1840s. This was accomplished in two steps, one linguistic and the other literary, the former indigenous to Pennsylvania, the latter definitely not.

The first Kriss Kringle book in America, published by Thomas, Cowperthwait, & Co. in Philadelphia in 1842.

Pennsylvanians, originally Dutch in tongue, soon became bilingual. And once bilingual, intermarriage began to take place between the Pennsylvania Dutch and their "English" neighbors. The acculturation process—giving and taking between cultures—started to operate. Nineteenth-century scholars called what was going on "the brewing of the melting pot."

In the anglicization process, dialect Christ-kindel became Krist-kingle or Kriss-kingle. And Kriss-kingle, by virtue of a philological law known as progressive assimilation, was altered to Kriss Kringle. This charge was effected, however, not without considerable "cussing" and name-calling. The educated Pennsylvania Dutchman saw *red* whenever any writer "mutilated" Christ-kindel to Kriss Kringle. He could partly stomach Kriss-kingle but *not* Kriss Kringle. We now present the evidence:

From the Pottsville *Miners' Journal* of January 9, 1847. Letter to the editor: In conclusion, let me say to you, that I have lately seen a very frequent reference to the *Krist Kringle* and his frequent visits. Now my dear Sir, I beg leave to say to you that I am really astonished that a gentleman who possesses so much knowledge of German as I know you do, did not once discover that Krist Kringel is an unwarrantable change of the word *Christkindlein*, which is one of the beautiful compounds in which the German language abounds, meaning the "Little Child Jesus."

From the Reading *Gazette* of January 22, 1848. Kriss Kringle. The original word, which some Philadelphia book-publishers have corrupted into "Kriss Kringle," is *Christ-Kindlein,* or as it is commonly abbreviated *Christ-Kindle.* It means, literally, the Infant Christ; but by long usage it has become a familiar household word among Germans and their descendants, and is applied, particularly by children, to any gift made upon Christmas day. It would be as well, perhaps, for our big-city neighbors, to correct the orthography of the word, even though they may continue to pervert its meaning.

From the Reading *Gazette* of December 23, 1854. The Rev. A. B. Grosh, in a late number of the *Christian Ambassador,* notices in the following terms of merited condemnation, a meaningless corruption of a beautiful appellative of the Saviour, which has grown into such general use as almost to have displaced entirely the original word.

"'Kriss Kringle'—This is a horridly barbarous imitation of a German barbarism, into which an English ear has led many of our newspaper editors and writers. *Christ-kindlein,* or *Christ-kindchen,* is the German proper for *Christ-child,* or infant Christ. Many Germans have corrupted it into *Christ-kintle*—particularly in Pennsylvania. This is bad enough, but to corrupt it still more, and remove it utterly away from all semblance to the original is too bad. 'Kriss-Kringle,' as a name for the 'Babe of Bethlehem,' is neither English nor bad German, but a mere jargon or gibberish of the vilest kind—and when the facts are known, sounds like ribaldry. I hope that religious papers, at least, will cease from, and steadily discountenance such seeming profanity of the name of Christ. Use the German names—any of them—but avoid 'Kriss Kringle.'"

We are afraid Mr. Grosh has written to no purpose. We ventured, a few years ago, to correct our Philadelphia friends in the use of this barbarism, but all to no purpose. They stuck to "Kriss Kringle," and still stick to it, with the pertinacity which men usually exhibit when detected in a blunder of their own making—many of them probably, in their prejudice against everything "Dutch," preferring to use corrupt English rather than quote pure German.

From the Milford *Reformer und Pennsylvania Advertiser* of December 31, 1868. Kriss Kringle. Die englischen Blaetter sind wirklich gross in der Verdrehung deutscher Namen. Um die Weihnachtszeit spuckt der Ausdruck "Kriss Kringle" gar stark in ihren Spalten. Es ist aber schade, dass ein so schoenes Wort wie Christkindchen so jaemmerlich verhunzt wird.

[Kriss Kringle. The English papers are eminent in the distortion of German names. Around Christmastime the expression "Kriss Kringle" appears quite strongly in their columns. But it is a shame that such a beautiful word as *Christkindchen* is so deplorably mutilated.]

From the *Pennsylvania Dutchman* of January 1873. Kriss Kringel. This is neither Dutch nor German, but a perversion by uneducated newspaper editors. The German is *Christ-kindlein* (the Christ Child), and the Pennsylvania Dutch is Krisht Kintly, which is too good to be slaughtered by anything so harsh and uncivilized as a "Kriss Kringle."

From the Philadelphia *Weekly Press* of December 26, 1874. [A German correspondent writes:] Why is it that your native-born Americans spell this word in a way to make it not only lose its lovely sense, but even to make it entirely senseless? "Kriss-Kringle" you spell it, and if nobody checks you in this obnoxious orthography, a stupid, senseless word will receive the privilege of augmenting the English vocabulary, when, by a very little care, it could be enriched with a beautiful, friendly, and sensible expression. "Christ-Kindel" means the little child Christ; L'Enfant Jesus, as the French say.

From the Philadelphia *Lutheran* of December 22, 1881. Do not suffer this lovely picture [Christ Child] to be hidden by the hideous caricature of a Kriss-Kringle, that odious corruption of the German expression *Christkindchen,* or *Christkindle;* and do not substitute for the Babe of Bethlehem, the figure of a Santa Claus.

From the Philadelphia *Lutheran Observer* of December 21, 1883.
[From an article "The Heathenism of Christmas" by Germanicus:] Thus it was natural for them to combine the customs of the foreigners, the Dutch and the Germans; and Santa Claus and Kriss Kringle, as in their barbarous ignorance of the language they called the Christ-Child became hopelessly intermingled in the American mind.

From the Philadelphia *Lutheran* of December 23, 1897. The Germans taught their children that the Christ-child (Christkindchen, and in dialect, Christ-Kindle,) brought the Christmas gifts, and the English speaking people corrupted the same into the horrible "Kriss-Kringle," who is actually represented as the veritable Santa Claus. Santa Claus is the Dutch patron saint of Christmas, and "Kriss Kringle" is supposed to be the "Pennsylvania Dutch" form of the same jolly old saint. What a horrible perversion of the beautiful name "Christ-child."

AN EDITOR ANSWERS BACK
The only retort we have been able to locate to the furor we have just presented was made by a Pittsburgh newspaperman, in the Pittsburgh *Post* of December 25, 1868. (Perhaps he felt far enough away from the Dutch Country not to fear the area's barbs.) He wrote:

Kriss Kringle has come by this time, and has not missed many homes in this city. Some persons who are very stupid, say, we ought to say Krist Kinkle, and some who are very wise, say, we should say Christkindle, but we are used to plain, merry old Kriss Kringle, and shan't give him up.

CHRIST-KINDEL—A GIFT
In the Pennsylvania Dutch dialect the word "Grisht-kindel," besides designating the Christmas gift bringer, also means the Christmas gift. In contemporary usage a *Grisht-kindel* to many speakers of Dutch means only the gift anymore, no longer the gift bringer. An article on Kriss Kringle in the Lancaster *Weekly Examiner* of December 28, 1870, makes reference to the latter usage:

Among the "Pennsylvania Dutch" where we passed our boyhood, "Christ-Kindly" was applied to any gift made during the Christmas

Holidays; therefore a *Christ Kindly* among those people meant the same as a "Christmas Gift," or Christmas presents, among the English.

Dialect "Grisht-kindel" has one additional meaning. Farm folk use the word to describe an urban woman of farm background who puts on airs and dresses way beyond her station in life.

TERM KRISS KRINGLE BECOMES ESTABLISHED
The earliest printed use we have been able to find for the term "Christ-kindle" is from the York *Gazette* of December 23, 1823. In a humorous entry the Society of Bachelors of York announce their intention of "fixing a Krischtkintle Bauhm" which is to say a "Christ-kindle tree." From this time up to 1840 we have been able to locate *but* three additional instances of its use. John F. Watson in his 1830 *Annals of Philadelphia* writes: "Every father in his turn remembers the excitements of his youth in Belsh-nichel and Christ-kinkle nights." A reporter in the Germantown *Telegraph* of December 24, 1834, speaking of the anticipation of the child at Christmas, remarked: "How his eye sparkles, and his cheek flushes as he listens to the promises which his glorious friend Chryskingle is to realize." The third instance is from the *Gentleman's Magazine* of December 1837: "It [Christmas] is a day when 'wee responsibilities' rejoice in 'Christkingle's' visit."

With one fell swoop in 1842 and 1845 two Christmas books, published in Philadelphia, *created* Kriss Kringle as a competitor to Washington Irving's creation, Santa Claus.[1] The two volumes are: (1) *Kriss Kringle's Book* (Philadelphia: Thomas, Cowperthwait, & Co., 1842), and (2) *Kriss Kringle's Christmas Tree. A holliday* [sic] *present for boys and girls* (Philadelphia: E. Ferrett & Co., 101 Chestnut Street, 1845).

The editor or editors who created these two Kriss Kringle books did not utilize any phase of the Pennsylvania Dutch Christ-kindel folk concept we have described. Kriss Kringle was only another name for Santa Claus, the jolly old man who drove through the sky on Christmas Eve with sleigh and eight reindeer and who came down the chimney, a pack of gifts and goodies on his back. The only difference between the Kriss Kringle of the 1845 Philadelphia imprint and Santa Claus was that Kriss Kringle paid no attention whatsoever to stockings hanging by fireplaces: he deposited his gifts on the branches of the Pennsylvania Christmas tree.

In the introduction of the 1842 *Kriss Kringle's Book*, the editor introduces the children to Saint Nicholas or Kriss Kringle. The editor explains to his youthful readers that "Kriss Kringle is the name given by children to St. Nicholas." In describing Kriss Kringle to the children the editor says:

Now is not "Kriss Kingle" a nice, fat, good humored looking man. See how eagerly those little boys embrace him, hoping that he will give them some nice little present or other. Mr. "Kriss Kingle" loves good little boys and girls, and if they behave and mind what their parents tell them, they may rest assured that he will pay them a visit, and leave them something nice, as a reward for their good behaviour. [The reader will notice the dual use: Kriss Kringle and Kriss Kingle.]

Kriss Kringle's Christmas Tree appeared in two editions in Philadelphia, in 1845 and 1847, and in one New York edition, in 1846. In the 1847 Philadelphia edition, published by Grigg and Elliot, the anonymous editor writes:

Fashions change, and of late Christmas Trees are becoming more common than in former times. The practice of hanging up stocking in the chimney corner for Kriss Kringle to fill with toys, pretty books, bon-bons, &c., for good children, and rods for naughty children, is being superseded by that of placing a Christmas Tree on the table to await the annual visit of the worthy Santa Klaus. He has, with his usual good nature, accommodated himself to this change in the popular taste; and having desired a literary gentleman to prepare his favourite Christmas present in accordance with this state of things, the following volume is the result of the new arrangement, and all parents, guardians, uncles, aunts, and cousins, who are desirous to conform to the most approved fashion, will take care to hang one, two, or a dozen copies of the book on their Christmas Tree for 1847.

From 1845 on the American Christmas gift bringer bore three names: Santa Claus, Saint Nicholas, and Kriss Kringle, the latter, as we have shown, the creation of the anonymous Philadelphian who styled himself a "literary gentleman."

In the mid-nineteenth century Kriss Kringle was the most often used name for the Christmas gift bringer in Pennsylvania. The Pottsville *Miners Journal* of December 26, 1846, brings this to expression:

Who does not remember the days of his childhood, when the stockings were hung up by the fire-place and the good "Saint Nicholas," better known to most children as "Kriss Kringle," filled them up to the brim with the luxuries of childhood?

The Lancaster *Intelligencer* of December 23, 1849, put it this way:

Who among us does not remember the halcyon days of our childhood, when we hung up our stockings by the fire-place, and when the good St. Nicholas, more familiarly known as "Kriskingle" filled them with the nice things of the season?

A writer in the Philadelphia *Sunday Dispatch* of December 27, 1857, says that Kriss Kringle is the name of the gift bringer "in this latitude, while farther North he was known as Saint Nicholas, or Santa Claus."

Prominent stores in large Pennsylvania cities began to designate themselves in their newspaper advertising as "Kriss Kringle's Headquarters" beginning in 1846, J. W. Parkinson of Philadelphia taking the lead.

The earliest instance of a store in Pennsylvania employing someone to impersonate Kriss Kringle or Santa Claus was Parkinson in Philadelphia in 1841. The Philadelphia *North American* of December 25, 1841, reported:

Criscingle, or Santa Claus. Much as our young readers have heard and imagined of this worthy character as the bountiful patron of good children on Christmas Eve, they probably never expected to behold the real personage in the very act of descending a chimney, as our friend Parkinson has shown him over his well thronged shop door in Chestnut street. He was decidedly the attraction yesterday and last evening, and monopolized more than his share of the attention of the young folks, which is usually bestowed with undivided admiration on the bon bons in the windows.

In inland Pennsylvania the first city which had a live Santa Claus was Reading, in 1845. G. and A. M. Souders ran the following advertisement in the Reading *Gazette* of December 20:

I Santa Claus, hereby announce, I will be found at my *Depot des Confiseur*, No. 46, West Penn Street, a full and complete assortment of Christmas and New Year's Presents. The whole has been prepared and selected by me Santa Claus in person, and will be presented to the good burghers of Reading, by my own hand, this being the first visit I shall have ever made to this place. My only wish is that I may meet with a cordial reception by one and all of my juvenile subjects, so that I may not regret leaving the more populous cities, to pay this *pop* visit to the place where many natives of the Vaterland dwell, with my panniers well laden with all kinds of niceties. Signed, Santa Claus, or St. Nicholas.

The *Gazette* of December 27, 1845, reported on Santa Claus's first visit:

Old Santa Claus, in front of the Messrs. Souders' Confectionary, was the observed of all observers during the day. His *tout ensemble* was quite ingenious, and in our opinion, made a finer display than his prototype which attracted so much attention at Parkinson's in Philadelphia, a year or two ago.

By 1849, stores were employing people to impersonate Kriss Kringle. The Philadelphia *Sun* of December 24, 1849, reported:

A great sensation has been produced by McCurdy, at the corner of Thirteenth and Vine street. His representation of old Kriss Kringle, filling the stockings hanging above the fire-place, is said to be by the oldest inhabitant a very good likeness of the great original Kriss, who made his appearance in this country several centuries ago. He is the finest specimen of the old John that we have ever seen.

The earliest instance of a live Santa Claus appearing in a Sunday school Christmas celebration is documented in the Pittsburgh *Gazette* of December 28, 1869. A reporter, writing about the Christmas jubilee of the Sixth Avenue Presbyterian Sabbath school, says:

Hereupon the President, in order to vary the exercises, began to talk to the children of that mystic personage, the child's dear friend and patron saint, Santa Claus, when lo! from regions unknown, stepped forth on the platform a real, veritable Santa Claus, decked in all the fabled trappings of that mysterious personage. With his fairy whip he drove the superintendent from the platform, going through a series of other queer antics.

CONTAINERS FOR THE GIFT BRINGER

Before the introduction of the Christmas tree, the Christmas gift bringer traditionally deposited his gifts—frequently merely nuts, cookies and candies—in one of four different containers: straw bread baskets, hats, plates, or stockings.

In the whole of the eighteenth century there was but one Christmas gift bringer, Christ-kindel or the Christ Child, in Pennsylvania. The Christ-kindel as we have already indicated left his gifts in a straw bread basket. The custom of setting one's hat for Christ-kindel may have derived from the Easter practice of setting one's hat for the Easter Bunny to lay his eggs in. Setting one's plate at the table before going to bed Christmas Eve seems to be a nineteenth-century development, probably introduced by the wave of later German immigrants who started immigrating in

1830. Hanging up one's stocking by the fireplace or at the bottom of one's bed, a general American Christmas custom, is unclear in origin. One thing we are able to say, however, and that is that the practice of hanging up one's stocking at Christmas Eve was definitely not an *early* Pennsylvania Dutch practice.

STRAW BREAD BASKETS

The custom of setting a straw bread basket or just any sort of basket for the Christ-kindel is an eighteenth-century practice which continued in Dutch Pennsylvania well into the nineteenth century. The Easton *Democrat and Argus* of December 24, 1840, alludes to the custom of setting a basket:

It puts us in mind of younger and happier days, when the Beltznickle was our greatest terror, and the Christkindle our very, very best friend—when the basket was put under the table for [the Christkindel] to "make his deposits."

In an article "The Old Fashioned Christmas" in the *Messenger* for January 12, 1853, the author says: "Baskets, covered with clean white cloths, were set at a convenient place, into which the mysterious visitor could deposit his beautiful gifts." The Reverend Benjamin Bausman, in describing the Christmases of his childhood in Lancaster County, wrote in the *Guardian* of January 1871, page 15:

The smaller children were allowed to believe in a real bodily Christkindel. It would surely come that night [Christmas Eve]. Where will mother set the baskets this time? In a dark front room—the parlor became the reception room of the kind heavenly visitor. Two bread baskets, with a clean white cloth spread in them, are placed on chairs. The little innocents, half-frightened, hold on to the mother's dress, as they follow her into the parlor, and watch the arranging of the baskets. Many puzzling little troubles they have. When will it come? Where will it get in?[2] Ought not the front door be left open? Will the baskets be large enough? How heavenly this unsuspecting confiding trust!

The Richville correspondent of the Mount Joy *Star* wrote, under date of December 23, 1875:

Boys and girls, get your baskets ready until next Friday eve, place them on the table or any place you think proper in order for [Christ-kindel] to fill them for you. He will come around in the night while you are sound asleep, with a huge basket of presents on his back.

The cover of the most influential Christmas book in America. Twice reprinted, once in New York, it established Kriss Kringle as one of the triumvirate of Christmas gift bringers in this country.

A musical composition entitled "Kriss Kringle" from Godey's Lady's Book of December 1872.

The custom of setting the bread basket was carried by Pennsylvania settlers into other states as well, as becomes apparent in an article "The Pennsylvania-German in the Settlement of Maryland" by Dr. Daniel Wunderlich Nead in volume 25, 1914, of the *Proceedings of the Pennsylvania German Society*, page 72 (footnote): "In the childhood of the writer bread-baskets were used by the juvenile members of the family on Christmas Eve, being set in the chimney-corner, in anticipation of the visit of the Kris-kingle."

SETTING HATS

We have located but three references to setting a hat for Santa Claus in Pennsylvania. The Mifflintown *Tuscarora Register* of December 21, 1854, remarked: "We can remember how we used to 'set our hat' on the evening before Christmas, and how early we would rise the next morning to examine the contents." In an article on Christmas in the *Guardian* of January 1854, Henry Harbaugh wrote: "Then when it [Christmas] came, what a joyful fluttering of hearts as, the evening before, the hats, the baskets, and the stockings were ranged along the wall to receive the gifts of Christ-Kindlein." The Centerville correspondent of the Carlisle *American Volunteer* of January 1, 1880, wrote:

With the most buoyant hopes they retired early to their beds on Christmas-eve expecting Santa Claus to bring them rafts of presents and nice things, and leave them in their stockings, hats and plates, where they would find them the next morning.

Setting straw baskets and hats for Santa Claus or Kriss Kringle has completely vanished from the Pennsylvania scene; indeed, they never carried into the

KRISS KRINGLE'S

RARE SHOW,

FOR

GOOD BOYS AND GIRLS.

NEW YORK.
WM. H. MURPHY, Publisher and Printer,
354 Pearl Street, Franklin Book-Store.
1847.

Kriss Kringle books were published in New York from 1846 on.

present century. But Pennsylvania boys and girls still hang their stockings and set their plates.

PLATES

Pennsylvania children have been setting their plates at Christmas since at least the mid-nineteen-hundreds. The custom of setting one's plate at Christmas has survived, as far as we can tell, only among our Plain Pennsylvanians, Amish, Dunkards, and Mennonites. The reason that only the Plain Dutch any longer set plates at Christmas is that they do not put up Christmas trees and they do not tell their children about Santa Claus "because that would be lying." With no Christmas gift bringer and no Christmas tree to put the gifts under, they continue to resort to setting plates. On Christmas morning a little Amish boy or girl finds the gifts, from mom and pop, in a plate on the kitchen table.

We shall now proceed to list the references to setting plates at Christmas in Pennsylvania. The earliest one we have been able to find is in an article on Christmas at the Pittsburgh Infirmary in the *Lutheran Observer* of January 6, 1854:

On entering, the most prominent object that met our view was a "Christmas tree," about the centre of the room, ornamented with wreaths and various flowers and candied fruits, and illuminated with wax candles placed all around among the branches. About the room tables were set with plates upon which were some Christmas presents and a book for each of the patients.

In a description of the Christmas festival in the Germantown Home on January 3, 1861, we read: "The poor children . . . were led to their plates on the well-filled table, which contained a present for each child."

The Coatesville *Chester Valley Union* of December 24, 1870, describing Christmas Eve, states: "Supper is over, the plates placed, stockings suspended and the children all snugly in bed dreaming of tomorrow's joys." The Easton *Sunday Call* of December 23, 1894, on Christmas says:

Sometimes a plate is provided for each guest and child, which is in the first place half filled with nuts and confectionary. Then the presents are laid on top of those, with a card over all inscribed with the name of the intended recipient. Sometimes a number only is written on the card, which corresponds with the number attached to a card on the Christmas tree which bears the name both of the giver and the taker of the gift.

Henry C. Mercer's article on early Christmas trees in the *Bucks County Historical Society Proceedings*, volume 4, page 556, reads: "Miss Mary L. DuBois, representing one of the oldest families in Doylestown said they never had a Christmas tree in their family. They put out plates for their gifts."

In L. B. Henninger's *Recollections of the Old Chambersburg of Sixty Years Ago*, published in 1922, the author in describing Christmas (around 1862) mentions the custom of setting plates for the Christmas gift bringer (page 22):

We would set out little plates in different parts of the room and up to bed we would go, dressed in our nice, clean nightgown, and crawl in under an old time feather bed. We would lay and talk and laugh, when father or mother would holler up the steps, "You had better go to sleep or the 'Bell Snickel' won't come." Finally we would fall to sleep unconscious of what was going on down in the kitchen or sitting room below. The long looked for day came, and at the call of mother out of bed we would jump, down stairs in our nightgowns and bare feet and hunt for our little plates. It did not take us long to find them. Each plate was filled to its capacity with the old style dough horses, dough dogs, dough rabbits, dough birds, dough babies, a big apple, bunch of raisins, some stick candy, the old fashioned toys, some almonds, peanuts and the old style rag doll made by mother for the smaller ones of the family. The home was turned over to the little folks for the day.

Edward Hocker in an article on Christmas in early Montgomery County in the Norristown *Times-Herald* of December 20, 1929, wrote: "No stockings were hung up at the hearth, but there were plates upon the table, one for each child, and thereon they found their gifts in the morning."

John Rudy Mumaw in his 1932 dissertation at the University of Virginia, "Folklore among the Pennsylvania-Germans in Wayne County, Ohio," writes:

Many children in the "Pennsylvania Dutch" homes had no thought of hanging up stockings for Santa Claus. They were taught to set plates on the table instead. On these appeared candy, chestnuts, cakes and the other inexpensive eats. Their Santa Claus was called Grishkindli.

The *Country Gentleman* of December 1936 has an article by Ann Hark, entitled "O Little Town of Bethlehem." In it she describes Christmas in Bethlehem and refers to setting plates:

Another family custom that held a particular charm for us little ones was the filling of "plates" for the various members of the holiday company. Children and adults, teachers and students, servants and friends—all who spent Christmas beneath the old school's roof—were included in the hospitable practice. Under my mother's watchful eye, large old-fashioned soup plates were ranged on a white-clothed table, and while youthful mouths watered longingly, the process of filling them began. Nuts and raisins, popcorn and dates, figs and oranges, tangerines and grapes—one after another the various articles were doled out, and the matter of inserting the slip of paper on which my father had written the names of each recipient became a nice problem in engineering.

This account is slightly modified in the author's *Hex Marks the Spot* (Philadelphia, 1938), pages 182–183.

In a letter to the author, Mrs. Bertha Brophy of Reading wrote in 1950: "I was reared in the Oley Valley. Christmas eve before we children went to bed we set a large plate on the table. In the morning we had toys, popcorn, nuts, oranges in it—that was our Christmas."

The Winter 1951 issue of the *New York Folklore Quarterly,* pages 274–275, runs an article "Pennsylvania Yuletide" by Dorothy Krisher. She writes: "Half a century ago, Christmas time was to the Flack family of Lumberville, Bucks County, the favorite holiday of the year. On Christmas Eve Mother and her brothers and sisters 'set their plate.'"

E. Gordon Alderfer writes in his *Montgomery County Story* (Norristown, 1951), page 79: "Later in the night, when the children were sound asleep, came the invisible *Christ Kindlein* (the little Christ Child) who left a gift for each child on his plate at the table."

We have evidence of the custom of setting plates also from Lebanon County. In the fall of 1954 Mrs. Kathryn Richard of Fredericksburg told the author in a folklore interview that when she was a child they never put presents under a tree. Instead, small gifts were placed at one's habitual place at the kitchen table, under plates put there upside down.

Dr. Phil R. Jack in an article "Amusements in Rural Homes around the Big and Little Mahoning Creeks, 1870–1912" (*Pennsylvania Folklife,* Spring 1958), page 48, reports the custom of setting a plate for the holiday gift bringer in the area of northern Indiana County and southern Jefferson.

CHRISTMAS STOCKINGS

References to hanging up one's stockings on Christmas Eve are frequently come upon in our Pennsylvania Christmas literature after 1830. Whether this custom, like that of Santa Claus and his reindeer, is basically a literary-inspired one in this country we are unable to say, though we strongly surmise it.

To date the earliest pictorial representation of the Christmas stocking in this country appears in two engravings from *A New Year's Present,* a children's book printed in New York in 1821. The two verses below the engravings read:

Through many houses he [Santa Claus] has been,
And various beds and stockings seen;

Some, white as snow, and neatly mended,
Others, that seem'd for pigs intended.
       and
I left a long, black, birchen rod,
Such as the dread command of God
Directs a Parent's hand to use
When virtue's path his sons refuse.

The earliest reference in the newspaper press of Pennsylvania we were able to find to hanging up one's stockings at Christmas Eve is a literary piece which was often reprinted. The Philadelphia *Daily Chronicle* of February 5, 1830, which is one of the many papers which reprinted the item, states it originally appeared in the Baltimore *Minerva and Emerald*. In part it reads:

Then proceeding timidly to the fire-place, I hung up my stockings in the chimney beside those of my brothers, and crept softly into bed. My dreams were of the great Santa Claus, plum-cakes, sugar plums, comfits, toys, etc. At an early hour, I awakened my bedfellows, and eager to get our rewards, we all rushed towards the chimney. The stocking of one was loaded with luxuries; that of the other contained an orange and a beautiful edition of *Jack the giant killer;* tremblingly, I laid my hand upon mine; it was light—and my heart sunk within me—my elder brother seized it, and laughing while I wept, drew out a rod! How could Santa Claus have found out that I had *played truant* the day before? After that night I never ventured to hang up my stockings; "nothing stake, nothing lose," thought I, so I slept with my stockings on.

The Lancaster *Union* of December 27, 1836, speaks of hanging up one's stockings by the fireplace "according to custom." The *Pearl*, a Philadelphia Christmas annual for 1840, carries a short story by Mrs. Anne Bache of Gambier, Ohio, entitled "Christmas at Home." In it one of the children asks her mother, "Mother, it's such a beautiful day, and the Christkinkle has filled our stockings." The Pittsburgh *Daily Dispatch* of December 25, 1847, commented:

Old Kriss Kringle with his honest Dutch face has crawled down many a smoky chimney, and filled the stockings of good little boys and girls with miniature guns and soldiers, curly white dogs and pretty rosy cheeked and cherry lipped "doll babies."

A writer in the Philadelphia *Saturday Courier* of December 23, 1848, advises parents:

Let no stocking hang empty in the chimney corner; and even if Harry and Natty haven't been quite as good children as they ought to have been, don't disappoint them with a whip or an old rusty jewsharp by way of punishment.

This note of punishment appears also in *Kriss Kringle's Book for All Good Boys and Girls* (Philadelphia: C. G. Henderson & Co., 1852), pages 5–6:

If there should chance to be any idle, disobedient, bad-tempered boy or girl in the house, who neglects lessons, beats brothers and sisters, scratches faces, tells lies, breaks things, &c. &c., Saint Nicholas, instead of giving him toys, puts into his stockings a rattan rod, brought for that special purpose all the way from the East Indies. Such a child must feel very much chagrined, and look very silly the next morning when all the other children are laughing and clapping their hands at Kriss Kringle's presents.

Unquestionably, the best item on hanging up one's stockings at Christmas time comes from the Pottsville *Miners' Register* of December 24, 1853:

What a world of little stockings will be suspended, by cook-stoves and grates, in chimney corners and by old fashioned fire places, on that memorable twenty-fourth! Red, blue, black, and clouded; new, old, darned and tattered; ventilation stocking, every hole carefully tied up with towstrings, by the provident little owner, lest something should spill out of the expected treasures. Some hang by the frail tenure of a pin; others secured to a big nail, for who knows how much they may get? And, others again, fastened to the back of chairs, or swing from the bed-post.

Mention is made in the Doylestown *Bucks County Intelligencer* of December 27, 1859, that children's stockings were not filled with good things if the children had misbehaved just before Christmas: "However, we believe his [Santa's] keepsakes were generally very acceptable, except in some instances where he chanced to deposit a stick or corncob in place of the anticipated sweetmeats and toys."

The Pottsville *Miners' Journal* of December 23, 1865, has an apt description concerning Christmas stockings:

How fondly we look back to the days when we were easily persuaded to go to bed early, that "Kriss Kinkle" might more easily fill our stockings in the chimney corner. No man ever struck a "flowing well" of petroleum with more joy than did we grab our stockings on Christmas morns of yore.

A question in stylishness is raised by the Easton *Daily Express* of December 24, 1870:

Christmas card showing plates as the container for Christmas presents.

Is it more stylish to have Christmas trees for the children than to let the little creatures hang up their stockings as their grandmother did? No, no. We all do as we please in the matter. The high fashion authorities are silent here.

The Doylestown *Democrat* of December 26, 1871, writes:

We remember well the hanging of hose in the chimney corner on the eventful eve, the awakening long before the day-dawn, the scamper half-clad down the stairway, and then the rich store of sweetmeats and toys so gladsome to the eye, so toothsome to the taste. How sincerely we sympathized with the sorrow-stricken seniors whose stockings were stuffed with apples decayed or potatoes sprouting!

A writer in the Reading *Berks and Schuylkill Journal* of December 26, 1874, makes the assertion: "Christmas trees have ruled the hanging up of stockings out of order."

Reminiscing on experiences during the Civil War, a veteran wrote in the Philadelphia *Press* of December 26, 1886:

Another grim burlesque of old customs was to hang up stockings on Christmas Eve after taps. Most of us got snow, which was about all we

had to give each other, but a broken, used pack of cards, or an old pipe that had been "borrowed" six months before occasionally came back to the owner.

In his column "Observed and Noted" in the Lancaster *Examiner* of December 24, 1892, Robert Blair Risk wrote:

I never saw a Christmas tree in boyhood, but somehow the legend of Santa Claus was so far respected to be made welcome enough to pay respects to stockings hung in the old-fashioned fire-place. I think if the day came on Sunday no stockings could be hung up on Saturday night, and so Christmas did not come till after a verse in the catechism was memorized.

Fay Templeton in the Pittsburgh *Sun-Telegraph* of December 17, 1935, observed:

The saddest Christmas I recall, was when I was eight years old. I had committed some childish indiscretion, and for punishment, I found on Christmas morning the two stockings I had so hopefully hung on the mantle were empty. I have never forgotten the tragedy of that moment. As I sobbed my heart out I wondered what I had done to make Santa to forget me.

THE CHRISTMAS TREE IN PENNSYLVANIA

Scholars have been on the search for the first documented Christmas tree in America for the past forty years.[1] Their earliest well-authenticated date up to now is 1832.

We shall present evidence in this chapter to prove that Christmas trees were put up—though sporadically—as early as the 1820s throughout the Pennsylvania Dutch Country.

The earliest documented reference to a Christmas tree in the United States that we have succeeded in locating is 1821. In the diary[2] of Matthew Zahm, a resident of Lancaster, under date of Thursday, December 20, 1821, we read: "Sally & our Thos. & Wm. Hensel was out for Christmas trees, on the hill at Kendrick's saw mill."

In point of time, the next authenticated reference to a Christmas tree in this country is found in a humorous entry in the York *Gazette* of December 23, 1823:

Society of Bachelors. The Elections o'er, Old Gregg is beat, And Shulze has got the Chair of State. A meeting will be held at the Hall *Mud Island,* on second Christmas eve, the political Contest for Governor is at an end it is hoped that all will be unanimity with the members. The Old Maids have determined to present us with at least one Cart load of Gingercakes the society in turn therefore intend fixing a *Krischtkintle Bauhm* [literally Kriss Kringle Tree in Pennsylvania Dutch] for the amusement of such as may think proper to give them a call. Its decorations shall be superb, superfine, superfrostical, shnockagastical, double refined, mill' twill'd made of Dog's Wool, Swingling Tow, and Posnum fur; which cannot fail to gratify taste.

By Order B . . . . . . J . . . . . . president N.B. No smoking allowed in the Saloon, Admittance, Free gratis, for nothing at all.

Simon Snyder Rathvon, a well-known Lancaster County scientist and scholar, in an article on Christmas reminiscences in the Lancaster *Intelligencer* of December 24, 1881, wrote:

There are phantoms of humble little Christmas trees dancing through my mind that belong to periods from one to five years anterior to sixty years ago.

During the winter of 1822 and 1823 I was a member of a farmer's family in the township of Donegal, and then first participated in the erecting of a Christmas tree after the "country fashion" of that period—so far at least as that locality was concerned.

The tree on this occasion was a low cedar bush which "we boys" had "spotted" when we were out walnuting as early as the beginning of the previous November. The head of the family was of Irish descent, but had married into a family of "Pennsylvania Dutch," and had accommodated himself to their peculiar ways, and when necessary spoke their peculiar language. Only one of the elder boys, the housemaid and myself, in addition to the old folks, participated in the preparation of the tree.

The late Rudolf Hommel in his 1947 pamphlet "On the Trail of the First Christmas Tree" wrote:

We found . . . evidence which relates to Christmas celebration with a tree before 1826 in Harrisburg, Pa. It appears that the Rev. Mr. George Lochman (born in Philadelphia December 2, 1773) was the Lutheran minister at Zion's Church in Harrisburg from 1815 to 1826. His house was peopled with fifteen children, two from a first wife, and thirteen from his second.

The late Dr. William R. Dewitt, who was Presbyterian minister in Harrisburg since 1818, was a close friend of Dr. Lochman and furnished a sketch of him for Sprague's "Annals of the American Pulpit." He speaks feelingly of Dr. Lochman and vividly depicts some of the customs the latter observed during his incumbency, which terminated with his death in 1826.

"In those days," Dr. Dewitt relates, "Whitsuntide was a great day in Harrisburg, it was a high day. On that day all the youth of a certain age, of the Lutheran families, marched in procession through our streets, dressed in white, with plain white caps on their heads, to the Lutheran church. Easter, with its abundance of colored eggs, and Christmas, with its Christmas tree, all laden with Christmas presents, were institutions of those days in which the youth of our town greatly rejoiced, and whose joy no one was a

This is one of the earliest known drawings of a Christmas tree in America. It is by folk artist Lewis Miller (1796–1882) of York, Pennsylvania.

greater partaker than the good Lutheran pastor. On those occasions he seemed in his element—with a multitude of children around him, laboring to promote the joy of them all. But those days are past."

In a brief description of Christmas in Philadelphia the *Saturday Evening Post* of December 20, 1825, wrote:

There are visible trees [through windows] whose green boughs are laden with fruit, richer than the golden apples of the Hesperides, or the sparkling diamonds that clustered on the branches in the wonderful cave of Aladdin.

Among the persons whom Alfred F. Berlin interviewed in 1917 for his article "Introduction of the Christmas Tree in the United States" (*Bucks County*

Historical Society Proceedings, volume 4), pages 552–553, was a ninety-four-year-old Allentown woman who, according to Mr. Berlin, "remembers the custom since 1827."

THE DECADE OF THE 1830S

The earliest printed use of the term "Christmas tree" in America is in the year 1830. (The earliest entry quoted in the *Dictionary of Americanisms* in 1838.) The term Christmas tree appears in the York *Republican and Anti-Masonic Expositor* of December 14, 1830:

The Dorcas Society of York. This is an Association of Ladies, which was formed about ten or eleven years since, for the truly charitable purpose of clothing the poor widow and the friendless orphan.

The Society has therefore made preparation for a FAIR, which will be held in the front room of the house lately occupied by Genl. Spangler.

We are particularly requested to invite our country friends, as the goods will be sold low, and comprise the greatest variety of fancy articles, as well as the exhibition of a famous CHRISTMAS TREE. The fair will be open day before Christmas, closed on Christmas day, and open in the evening, and from thence until the articles are disposed of.

As far as is known, this 1830 York tree was the first public Christmas tree in this country. There was an admission of six and one-quarter cents to see this tree. The York *Republican* of December 21, 1830, wrote: "Tickets will be sold for 6¹/4 cts., which will admit the bearers to the 'Christmas tree!' during the time it remains for exhibition.

In an article "Dr. Constantin Hering" in *Mitteilungen des Deutschen Pionier-Vereins von Philadelphia* (volume 4, 1907), page 8, the author, a daughter of Dr. Hering's, describes how her father participated in setting up a Christmas tree in Philadelphia in 1834:

At the house of Mr. William Geisse he met Mr. Friedrich Knorr, who had come from Prussia a short time before this. He and Dr. Hering became most intimate friends, as also their wives and children. Together they crossed the Delaware and brought fir trees from Jersey, carrying them on their shoulders followed by shouting boys, for the first German Christmas trees in Philadelphia. The fame and curiosity of these wonders was spread abroad, so that by request evenings were appointed when the doctor's patients came to see the relighted trees, and thus this beautiful German custom was introduced here.

To date, the earliest known description of a Christmas tree in American literature is from Miss Sedgwick's "New Year's Day," which appeared in the *Token and Atlantic Souvenir* for 1836:

Lizzy Percival's maid Madeline, a German girl, had persuaded her young mistress to arrange the gifts after the fashion of her father land, and accordingly a fine tree of respectable growth had been purchased in market, and though when it entered the house it looked much like the theatrical representation of "Birnam woods coming to Duniane," [*sic*] the mistress and maid had continued, with infinite ingenuity, to elude the eyes of the young Arguses, and to plant it in the library, which adjoined the Drawing Room, without its being seen by one of them.

Never did Christmas tree bear more multifarious fruit; for St. Nicholas, that most benign of all the saints of the calendar, had through the hands of many a ministering priest and priestess, showered his gifts. The sturdiest branch drooped with its burden of book, chess men, puzzles, etc. for Julius, a stripling of 13, dolls, birds, beasts, and boxes were hung on the lesser limbs. A regiment of soldiers had alighted on one bough, and Noah's ark was anchored to another, and to all the slender branches were attached cherries, plumbs, strawberries and fine peaches, as tempting and at least as sweet as the fruits of paradise.

Nothing remained to be done, but to label each bough. Miss Percival was writing the names, and Madeline walking round and round the tree, her mind, as the smile on her lip and the tear in her eye indicated, divided between the present pleasures and the recollection of bygone festivals in the land of her home, when both were startled by the ringing of the bell.

There are two more references to Christmas trees in the 1830s, one in Lancaster and the other in Easton. The Lancaster *Union* of December 27, 1836, wrote:

The Holidays. Well, St. Nicholas has been before us—the old wag! Our young friends have already had the "Merry merry Christmas," and those of them who were caught napping, by our unfortunate omission to announce his Saintship's coming, but hung up their stockings, by the fire place, according to custom, are now revelling on the gingercakes, nuts, fruits and candies, which were so mysteriously put in them. Well, as there is an *end* to every stocking, so must there soon be to the stock in it;—and when the Christmas trees have all been wondered at and the matzebaums have lost their novelty and their paint, "St. Claus" and his tiny chariot and horses will have ceased whirling through the brains of our little readers, and we shall then wish them a Happy New Year, and *trunks* full of sweet things—which is more than the old fellow gave them.

An editorial in the Easton *Sentinel* of December 30, 1836, indicates that not everyone in that community was happy at Christmas time:

We have heard some matter of fact Misanthropes denounce the extraordinary dinners—the exchanging of presents—the passing of the compliments of the season and the indulgence and relaxation which every one feels privileged to enjoy, together with Christmas trees and New-Years firing, as idle and unmeaning ceremonies, fit only for children and even then without reason or meaning.

THE DECADE OF THE 1840S

In the 1840s the Christmas tree began to become more or less commonplace. Literary pieces, alluding to the custom of putting up trees at Christmas, began

An early engraving of a Christmas tree. It is the frontispiece of The Stranger's Gift, *edited by Herman Bokum and printed in Boston in 1836. Bokum was a Reformed clergyman in Pennsylvania in the 1840s. Deposed, he turned to teaching, for a time in Minersville, Schuylkill County. He died in 1878.*

to appear with some regularity each returning Christmas season. The very popular, and widely advertised, children's book, *Kriss Kringle's Christmas Tree*, published in 1845 in Philadelphia, brought a pictorial representation and knowledge of the Christmas tree and Kriss Kringle to children all over the nation. Trees started going up everywhere in the state, from Philadelphia to Pittsburgh.

Enterprising citizens were earning a pretty penny by exhibiting Christmas trees by 1840, and charging an admission. Rural swains, who traditionally brought their best girl to town on Second Christmas to see the sights, in addition to treating her to gingercakes, included the marvelous decorated Christmas trees as well.

By 1840 the Christmas tree had moved to the advertising columns of the local press. The York *Pennsylvania Republican* of December 16, 23, and 30, 1840, carries this advertisement:

Christmas Tree. For the amusement of the ladies and Gentlemen of York, and its vicinity, GOODRIDGE, will exhibit at his residence, in East Philadelphia Street, a CHRISRMAS [*sic*] TREE, the exhibition of which will commence on Christmas Eve, and continue, Sunday excepted, until New Year. Tickets to be had at his store.

The earliest instance of a Christmas tree being used in a school function is from Philadelphia. Theodore Ledyard Cuyler, a teacher in an unidentified boy's school in Philadelphia, writing his aunt Charlotte Morrell in New York under date of January 6, 1842, described the school's Christmas program as follows:

I promised to give you a description of the holy-day amusements. . . . On Thursday evening, we had our *annual soiree* at the school— the parents were invited. . . . Everything was genteel—the refreshments capital—(ice cream &) & I enjoyed myself amazingly. We had a large "Christmas tree" which was a great attraction, & novelty—it was decorated with the coat of arms of the boys—fanciful designs, & ribands & looked beautiful. [The original letter is in the New-York Historical Society Library.]

The Lancaster *Age and Gazette* of December 25, 1841, described Christmas Day: "Our good citizens have been busied in trimming churches with the green laurel, and as many more, erecting for the young of the household, ornamental trees, of a novel appearance indeed."

Two volumes appeared in Philadelphia in the 1840s with the words "Christmas tree" in the title, the one *Kriss Kringle's Christmas Tree* (already mentioned), the other *Voices in the Temple . . . The Christmas Tree*, printed by Joseph Rakestraw in 1848 for the Missionary and Book Society of the Evangelical Lutheran Church of St. John. The latter refers to the tree Charles Follen put up in Massachusetts in 1832.

In a description of Quaker City markets in the Philadelphia *Pennsylvanian* of December 25, 1848, there appears a reference to Christmas trees: "The markets have almost become impassable for the flocks of these little ones, purchasing a 'Christmas tree' whereon to hang their numerous Christmas presents."

The concluding year of the decade brings references to Christmas trees in Philadelphia and Pittsburgh, alike. The Philadelphia *Sunday Dispatch* of December 23, 1849, speaks of a "big Christmas tree, hung full of sugar toys and resplendent with its green branches and red berries."

A Lutheran clergyman, the Reverend W. A. Passavant, established an infirmary in the late 1840s in Pittsburgh for the aged and orphans of western Pennsylvania. In the church paper, the *Missionary*, of January 1850, he describes the institution's Christmas festival of December 1849:

A word before closing our Christmas Festival. According to the good old German custom, we had a "Christmas Tree" at the Infirmary on Christmas eve. I had often heard of the observance of the custom in the hospitals, asylums, and orphan houses of Europe, but had no idea before what happiness so simple an affair could produce. The tree was of spruce, and was erected in the Chapel of the Infirmary.

KRISS KRINGLE'S CHRISTMAS TREE

We shall restrict our references to the literary use of the Christmas tree theme in the 1840s—the material being rather too voluminous—to the most important Christmas publication ever issued from a Pennsylvania press: *Kriss Kringle's Christmas Tree*.

There were two editions of *Kriss Kringle's Christmas Tree* in Philadelphia, one in 1845, the other in 1847. There also was an 1846 New York edition.

The 1847 Philadelphia edition has this explanation (page v) concerning the Christmas tree:

Fashions change, and of late Christmas Trees are becoming more common than in former times. The practice of hanging up stockings in the chimney corner for Kriss Kringle to fill with toys, pretty books, bon-bons, &c., for good children, and rods for naughty children, is being superseded by that of placing a Christmas Tree on the table to await the annual visit of the worthy Santa Klaus. He has, with his usual good nature, accommodated himself to this change in the popular taste; and having desired a literary gentleman to prepare his favourite Christmas present in accordance with this state of things, the following volume is the result of the new arrangement, and all parents, guardians, uncles, aunts, and cousins, who are desirous to conform to the most approved fashion, will take care to hang one, two, or a dozen copies of the book on their Christmas Tree for 1847.

THE CHRISTMAS TREE COMES TO THE SUNDAY SCHOOL

The only phase of the history of the introduction of the Christmas tree in Pennsylvania not yet covered is its earliest use in the Sunday school Christmas festivals.[3]

The Christmas tree became an integral part of the Sunday school Christmas festival only after considerable opposition, much of it heated in character. For instance, parishioners of Dr. Clement Z. Weiser's church at New Goshenhoppen in Montgomery County denounced the early Christmas festivals with Christmas trees as a "puppet show."

In her book *How Christmas Came to Sunday-Schools* (New York, 1934), Katharine Lambert Richards tells us that it was in 1847 that Dr. William A. Muhlenberg initiated the Sunday school children of the Church of the Holy Communion in New York City into the joys of a Christmas tree. Dr. Edward Tiffany in his *History of the Protestant Episcopal Church* claims this as the first Sunday school Christmas tree in this country. Dr. Muhlenberg, a native of Reading, Pennsylvania, may possibly have carried the Pennsylvania Christmas tree idea to New York City.

The earliest Sunday school manual in Pennsylvania with Christmas pieces is *Familiar Dialogues*, published in Pottsville in 1848. On page 21 appears this Christmas dialogue:

Susan. Well, girls, how do you do? Where have you been? Elizabeth. We are just coming from Mr. . . . . Oh, I wish, Susan you could get a sight of the beautiful Christmas-tree they have at their house. S. Is it not beautiful? I was there last evening, and saw it. I am told that in Germany these Christmas-trees are prepared by almost every family, and that it is a very fine sight to see through almost every window, trees full of lights and gifts, and crowds of children playing and rejoicing around them.

In the Allentown *Welt-Bote* of December 24, 1872, the Reverend Jacob T. Vogelbach (born in Germany, July 25, 1814, and died in Philadelphia, November 20, 1880) claimed the honor of putting up the first Christmas tree in a Sunday school in this country—at Harrisburg, in 1851. Vogelbach wrote:

The first Christmas tree in a house of worship for use in a Sunday School Christmas festival was erected in St. Michael's Lutheran Church in Harrisburg on Christmas in the year 1851. Since that time it has become a common practice here in the East (what conditions are like in the West I have no way of knowing) to put up Christmas trees not only in our Lutheran churches and Sunday Schools, but in other denominations as well. But not a single person seems to know that it was a little German Lutheran church that started it all. The one who introduced the idea of putting up a Christmas tree in church is only too happy to see so many trees lit up in churches everywhere at Christmas time. After all, we merely helped introduce what is an old German custom.

Lindsay & Blakiston of Philadelphia published *Luther's Christmas Tree* by T. Stork in 1855. The Pittsburgh *Missionary* of December 1855, commenting on this forthcoming volume, said:

Permit me to announce to the Church at large, that we have in press, and will be ready for distribution early in December, a new work, designed for children and Sabbath Schools, entitled "Luther's Christ-

mas Tree," written at the request of the Board by Rev. Dr. Stork. This little volume, of about forty pages, will be published both in English and in German, and will be illustrated with *six large engravings,* representing important events in the life and times of Luther. 12½ per copy. It is hoped that this *first* publication of the Board [Lutheran Board of Publication] will meet with a favourable reception. Let every Lutheran Sabbath School aid in its circulation. A competent brother, Rev. G. A. Wenzel, has been engaged to translate Dr. Stork's "Christmas Tree" into German; it will be published at the same time and price as the English.

References to the use of Christmas trees in Sunday school Christmas celebrations are come upon but infrequently in the newspaper press, and not before 1858, in which year trees are reported for Bristol in Bucks and Lancaster City. A correspondent from Bristol, writing in the *Bucks County Intelligencer* of January 12, 1858, reported as follows on the St. James P. E. affair:

Their pastor, Rev. J. W. Pierson, and their teachers provided a gift for each child, and to this was added quite a number of other gifts by the friends of the school. These were all labelled with the name of the child and suspended to the branches of a large cedar tree provided for the purpose. On the tree was a large number of small wax candles. . . . After the address, the hundred candles on the tree were lighted and the gas lights extinguished, when they proceeded to take down the presents, read the names attached and handed them to the children.

Almost invariably an admission was charged to the early Christmas festivals, the purpose usually being to raise money to buy books and supplies for the Sunday school for the succeeding year. The Lancaster *Express* of December 24, 1858, reported:

A Beautiful Christmas Tree has been put up in St. Paul's (M. E.) Church, in South Queen st., by Mr. Wm. Hensel, which will be exhibited tomorrow, the price for admission (ten cents) to be appropriated towards aiding in extricating the church from its present financial troubles.

In 1862 the Reading *Daily Times* gives a somewhat detailed description of a dozen Christmas festivals. But *one* of the twelve churches described featured a Christmas tree, St. John's Lutheran.

Interesting from Civil War days is the following reporting in the Norristown *Herald and Free Press* of December 30, 1862. On Christmas night the Episcopal Church featured a festival at the Odd Fellows' Hall.

The title page of the most important Christmas book in the United States. Twice reprinted, once in New York in 1846, this juvenile established Kriss Kringle alongside of Santa Claus and Saint Nicholas as one of the three American gift bringers, and it introduced the Christmas tree concept to the youth of this nation.

In the centre of the room a cedar tree was planted reaching the ceiling. From every branch presents for the children were suspended, and from the top to the bottom it was illuminated by scores of colored lanterns. Around the tree the tables were spread, laden with the good things that were to be devoured. The children entered the room by classes and marched round the tree joining in the chorus of the "Christmas Tree." During the evening they sang several hymns and songs under direction of Mr. W. T. Koplin, and among them we were pleased to hear the stirring songs of "Rally round the Flag, boys!" notwithstanding the superintendent of the School objected to the song on the ground that it was not right to *mix politics with religion!* After the children had been feasted to their full, the Rector of the Church, Mr. Woart extended an invitation to all other children in the room to partake, and generous supplies of the fragments were handed around the Hall among the spectators. When the feast was over the work of disrobing the tree commenced. Each article bore the name of the scholar for whom it was intended, and as each name was announced, the eagerness and delight of the "little folks" was unbounded.

Generally, Sunday schools were introduced in rural areas somewhat later than in cities. In his autobiography, *Lebensbild aus dem Pennsylvanisch-Deutschen Predigerstand* (Allentown, 1906), page 328, the Reverend William A. Helffrich tells us: "On Christmas eve [1865] we celebrated the Christmas festival at Ziegel's Church. We had the very first Christmas tree in all that area."

A local note appears in the programming of Christmas festivals in the Pennsylvania Dutch Country: the reading of some entertaining bit of dialect verse. In Carlisle in 1873 at the Lutheran Church Sunday School Christmas celebration: "We cannot pass the occasion by without noticing the poem recited by John Treibler, composed by the late Dr. Harbaugh, of Lancaster, entitled the 'Kriss Kingle,' in the Pennsylvania Dutch." (This from the Carlisle *Herald* of January 1, 1874.) The Chambersburg *Valley Spirit* of January 1, 1880, reports that at the 1879 Grindstone Hill (Franklin County) Christmas festival next to a very large Christmas tree "the other important features of the exercises were the reading of *Das alt schul haus an der krick*, distribution of a treat, such as candies, oranges, etc." The Doylestown *Democrat* of January 2, 1883, reports that at the Chalfont (Bucks County) Lutheran Sunday School Christmas celebration, "James Cope read several selections in

'Pennsylvania Ditche' [*Deitsch*], which made the audience laugh heartily."

We shall include at this juncture a readable account concerning a Sunday school Christmas festival in Pittsburgh in 1818 (minus tree, of course!). It is from the Pittsburgh *Gazette* of December 25, 1867:

Christmas long ago. There are probably not many of our readers who can remember how Christmas was spent in the city of Pittsburgh so long ago as 1818. The people in those days do not seem to have been given to amusements, in a public way at least, for in looking over our files we see no mention made of any place of public amusement even during the holidays. We read, however, that a sermon was preached on the morning of Christmas day, to the Sunday School children by the Rev. Mr. Herron. On this occasion "several hundred children of both sexes, who had been rescued from idleness and vice," appeared with their teachers and deported themselves with exemplary propriety. The writer of the article from which we glean this, thought there was no place where such institutions were more needed than in this city, where the great mass of the population were careless of the morals of their children. He then laments over the bad influence exerted on them by the constant influx of strangers, and hoped that liberal persons would see that the "Sunday School Association did not expire." We are then told that the editors were particularly pleased to find what remarkable proficiency the pupils of the Messrs. Moody had attained, especially in grammar and geography, as evinced in the interesting exhibition the day before. We wonder if these were all the ways the people of those days had of publicly amusing themselves, and if they enjoyed themselves any less on that account. We wonder too if any of the boys who were so proficient in grammar and geography remember the interesting Christmas exhibition of 1818.

THE POST-1850 PERIOD

By the mid-eighteen-hundreds the Christmas tree had become the very core of the American Christmas celebration, not only in Pennsylvania but in other parts of the country as well. In an article "The Christmas Tree" in the December 25, 1852, issue of *Gleason's Pictorial*, the author wrote: "Already is the annual Christmas Tree established as one of the household gods of New England and a large portion of the States." In all of America there was no more important medium in spreading the Christmas tree in the decade 1850–60 than *Godey's Lady's Book*, published in Philadelphia.

This engraving appeared first in London Illustrated News *for December 1848, where it was entitled "Christmas Tree at Windsor Castle."* Godey's Lady's Book *reprinted it twice, once in 1850 and again in 1860, but made American citizens of the Royal couple, Queen Victoria without a coronet, and Prince Albert minus moustache.*

There have been no greater celebrators of Christmas throughout the entire history of the Commonwealth than the Moravians. They were among the very first to put up Christmas trees. In fact, in a taunting article in the Easton *Daily Express* of November 27, 1855, a writer thus describes their fame: "Its inhabitants [the inhabitants of Bethlehem, that is] are chiefly noted for their great taste they display in arranging Christmas Trees."

The *Lutheran Observer* of January 2, 1863, commenting on the popularity of Christmas trees in Lancaster, noted:

If a New Englander, who had never spent Christmas among the descendants of the Germans had visited our market during the last week, he would have been puzzled by the sight of the evergreens which made a forest of the public square, and lined the streets of the city. Hundreds, yea thousands, were required to supply the demand which the children made for Christmas trees.

Putting up Christmas trees had become a great fad in the 1870s, says the Carlisle *Herald* of December 27, 1877. Everybody caught the "Christmas tree fever." Noting pinpoints this quite so markedly as a statement in the *Herald* of a couple of years previously concerning a Mrs. Robert Allison of Carlisle who for the *first* time had "made" a Christmas tree—for her eleventh child. "The thought of dressing a tree never engaged Mrs. Allison's attention heretofore, but this season she was entirely carried away with the project," said the editor.

A sure sign that the Christmas tree had won on all fronts is the following item from the Philadelphia *Times* of December 26, 1877:

The Hebrew brethren did not keep aloof. Christmas trees bloomed in many of their homes and the little ones of Israel were as happy over them as Christian children. One of them said: "Oh, we have the trees because other people do."

No one put the importance the Christmas tree had assumed by 1877 quite as aptly as a writer in the Philadelphia *Weekly Press* of December 22, 1877: "As well might we dance without music, or attempt to write a poem without rhythm, as to keep Christmas without a Christmas tree."

Industrial Pennsylvania, too, was beginning to feel the glow of the Christmas tree. The Pottsville *Miners' Journal* of January 1, 1870, carried this item:

At 10 A.M. all the "Slate Pickers" of the Honeybrook Coal Co. were formed in line by the screen boss of each breaker, and marched to the residence of our Superintendent, who had fitted up a very handsome Christmas tree in the vestibule of his residence, and after viewing the tree each one as he left was presented with a new 25 cent note, as a Christmas present.

A new industry was a-borning: raising and selling Christmas trees. The *Bucks County Intelligencer* of December 29, 1874, says of the source of the trees: "Some of them come from the nurseries, but the bulk are brought from the Jersey wilderness, between the

This engraving of a beflagged Christmas tree is from Godey's Lady's Book *of December 1866.*

Delaware and the ocean, and from the slopes of the Pocono mountains, in Monroe county." Twenty years before, the same newspaper, under date of December 25, 1855, had written:

Parties of young people go out from the cities into the country, and procure large evergreen bushes, which they carry home with them for this purpose. In the Philadelphia market, the business of supplying evergreen bushes and wreaths for Christmas festivities is quite extensive, and the streets are lined with the wagons of the Jersey people, who strip their woods of their choicest and fairest trees for the purpose.

Any institution can be considered to be well established once when the public begins to think of it, or former aspects of it, as old-fashioned or traditional. Already in 1860, on December 25th, the Lancaster *Weekly Examiner* described the tree erected by the editor of the city's German-language newspaper, the *Democrat*, as an "old fashioned Christmas Tree." The Pittsburgh *Gazette* of December 24, 1866, commented:

We have noticed within the past few days, in our markets, good women, evidently in the most humble station of life—women who toil hard and long to keep the wolf from the door—carrying with them homewards, the *traditional* Christmas tree.

A similar note was struck in 1903. The Hanover *Daily Record* of December 26 wrote:

The Young Women's Christian Association of York realized several hundred dollars yesterday by charging admission to see an old-fashioned Pennsylvania Dutch Christmas tree, which was exhibited in the parlor of the association's building.

The tree was decorated with handsome ornaments, such as were used in making the Christmas trees a century ago, and many of the ornaments were handed down from that time. Not a modern article was to be seen upon the tree.

The decorations consisted of walnuts and hickory nuts, some dipped in flour, others painted in bright colors or covered with tinfoil.

Ears of yellow popcorn, strings of dried apples, or snits, as they are known among the Pennsylvania Dutch; horses and birds made of ginger cake dough and quaint little objects known as matze-baums, which were made in moulds 100 years old. Under the tree was a garden, in which clay sheep were grazing, and they were watched by Quakeresses made from hickory nuts and walnuts and by men made of the wishbones of turkeys.

At the top of the tree were suspended a beautiful wrought angel and shepherd, carved from wood a century ago by Louis Miller, the York artist.

The Christmas tree was decorated by the grandmothers of members of the association, and they also supplied most of the decorations, ransacking garrets and ancient chests for the purpose.

TWENTIETH-CENTURY DEVELOPMENTS

Since 1900 there have been three developments as far as the Christmas tree is concerned: decorating trees in private yards with electric lights; the community Christmas tree; and the burning of the greens ceremony.

The first community tree appeared in New York's Madison Square Park in 1912. The 1913 holiday season saw the spread of the idea to all parts of the United States. In Pennsylvania community Christmas trees were erected in 1913 in Altoona, Harrisburg, Philadelphia, and York. By 1914 other Pennsylvania cities followed suit: Allentown, Bradford, Jenkintown, Lancaster, Reading, Wilkes-Barre, and Williamsport. The Philadelphia *Record* of December 25, 1913, contains this interesting bit concerning Philadelphia's first community Christmas tree:

High above the crowd came a flash of light from an unexpected place. It was the cupola of the tower of Independence Hall, the place where the Liberty Bell first rang out the news of the signing of the Declaration of Independence. The oldest attendant at the hall could not remember a time when the cupola had been lighted before.

Into the lighted space stepped the six members of the celebrated trombone choir of the Moravian Church at Bethlehem, who welcome Christmas with the sounding of their instruments every year in their home town. They had been brought to Philadelphia for the first time to take part in the city's first municipal celebra-tion. Raising their long instruments to their lips, the trombonists sent forth a blast over the heads of the crowd. First they played "How Brightly Shines the Morning Star," then "From Heaven High to Earth I Come," and finally, very sweetly and in moderated tones, they sounded the notes of "All My Heart This Night Rejoices."

The ceremony of the burning of the greens in Pennsylvania dates back only to the early 1940s.

CHRISTMAS TREE ON CHRISTMAS MORNING

The editors of our early Pennsylvania newspapers and periodicals, from their very first allusions to the American Christmas tree, referred to it at frequent intervals as a German custom. But time and time again these same writers would call attention to the basic difference between the custom abroad and in this country: In Germany, they said, the children gathered around the Christmas tree on Christmas Eve for the distribution of gifts and in America on Christ-mas morning.[4] Or as someone writing in the Philadelphia *Sunday Dispatch* of December 30, 1866, put it:

The old German custom of dressing the tree and lighting the tapers upon it in the presence of the children on Christmas Eve is not followed in this country, nor in England. Here they are not permitted to see it till the festive morning.

The author of this volume, having given much thought to seeking an answer to how this happened, has come to the conclusion that the reason is to be found in the acculturation process. When the German custom was initially introduced into this country it had to adjust to an already firmly entrenched American Christmas tradition, namely: Santa Claus or Kriss Kringle coming down a chimney with a pack of gifts on his back *in the dead of night* to fill the stockings that the children had hung up by the fireplace before they were put to bed. When these two traditions, the German and the American, met, the thing that happened was that the American gift bringer, Santa Claus, continued to come, as before, *at night* with his sleigh driven by reindeer, but he no longer deposited his gifts exclusively in the stockings; he now frequently hung them in the German manner on the branches of the Christmas tree.

TRIMMING THE CHRISTMAS TREE

Shortly after the custom of putting up Christmas trees had become popular in Pennsylvania—around the mid-eighteen-hundreds—a Philadelphian, in commenting on the changes that the German-inspired tree was undergoing in this country, said that we were in the process of naturalizating it. And so we were, in actuality. To carry this thought one step further, one might even say that the Christmas tree received its American naturalization papers at the moment when someone—likely a mid-Westerner—first hung a strand of popcorn on its wax-tapered branches.

Before proceeding into our subject, we wish to say just a word about where the early trees were placed. The very first trees—true to the German manner of displaying them—were erected on tables in the center of the living room. These early trees were extremely modest affairs, a mere few feet in height. Somewhat later, however, when gilded paper decorations came into vogue, larger and larger trees were put up until finally the practice of putting up the tree on a table was altogether relinquished in favor of a ceiling-high tree, standing on the floor in the corner of a room.

The best account we know of on what happened to the Christmas tree idea—how it changed with time—is from an article by a nameless correspondent in the Lancaster *Daily New Era* of December 31, 1877:

What an infinite variety of Christmas decorations there are, and all are embraced in the common appellation of "trees." There is the round tree, the old-fashioned sort which stand in the centre of a table and is trimmed all around; there is the corner tree, hard to beat for beauty, if properly arranged; there is the "paper" tree, so called in distinction from other trees because its decorations are entirely of paper; there is the "glass" tree, so called because its ornaments are exclusively of glass; there is the bower, which is really no tree at all, but is none the less beautiful for that, for a better showing can be made on it than by placing the same amount

of material on a corner or a round tree; and there, too, is the "landscape," a succession of hill and dale, rustic bridge and charming rivulet. This last is rarest and prettiest of them all; rarest because few people have the proper room and requisite degree of artistic taste to form one, and prettiest because most like nature.

Many of our readers have no idea of the amount of interest felt in these Christmas decorations, the interest deepening and expanding with each succeeding year. As an illustration we may state that over one hundred persons called to see the writer's tree on Christmas, (an unpretentious tree, too) and that over one hundred persons on an average have called every day (Sunday excepted) since. These visitors were almost equally divided between women and children—the men forming a very small proportion. Squads of ladies—as high as ten in number—are to be seen daily going their rounds "among the trees." "It's a silly thing!" we hear some croaker say. It is not a silly thing—it is a good and useful thing, for it promotes social intercourse and leaves an impression on childhood's memory that can never be erased.

Of help, too, in assisting us to form a clear picture as to what happened to the Christmas tree in Pennsylvania in the first few decades after its introduction in the 1820s is an item in the Harrisburg *Daily State Journal* of December 24, 1872:

Some still retain the Christmas tree in its old form—that is, after the ornaments are on, space is left for the children's presents; others place all the family gifts on or under the tree, and, after those of the children are distributed, the little ones discover and present the gifts of the older members of the family; and others again make of their Christmas trees mere show pieces, on which to arrange artistically the glittering baubles, the stars, angels &c.

The earliest Christmas tree in America for which we have a description is the Donegal Township, Lancaster County tree of 1822 or 1823. Simon Snyder Rathvon, a scientist of note, gives us the following details concerning this tree in the Lancaster *Intelligencer* of December 24, 1881:

Luther's Family around the Christmas Tree, *painted in 1845 by Carl August Schwerdgeburth. This was reproduced a number of times in Pennsylvania periodicals.*

Our Christmas tree on this occasion [in the early eighteen-twenties] may have been four feet high (about the height of a boy of ten years old) and every available branch contained an article of some kind, and its base was garnished by the Christ-kindlies [Pennsylvania Dutch, meaning Christmas presents] of the children, which consisted of "henshing" or mittens, stockings, ear-warmers, shoes—usually Monroes—satchels, scissors, and thimbles, for the girls; cakes, nuts, raisins, apples, pears, and such like articles, all of domestic use. The tree was decorated with ginger bread cut in various grotesque forms, remote stars, hearts, sheep, goats—and even the "bad man"—diamonds, houses, rings, etc., and these were embellished with a mixture of starch and sugar, which gave them a frightful, it not a comic look. There were apples, here and there a bunch of raisins, or a "matzebaum," obtained from a town shop and brightly colored "rosettes," composed of scarlet, yellow and green flannel, made up the tout ensemble of the decorations of the Christmas tree of the country,

and even this was by no means universal for then, as perhaps now, there were large religious communities that never made any demonstration of this kind at all. They may have baked a special batch of sweet-cakes for their children, but nothing more except, perhaps, the usual religious service.

The custom, however, was more common in the towns, and there, too, being more accessible to the stores, other decorations were improvised such as glass beads, oranges or lemons, mint-drops—like rows of red and white buttons on slips of paper—toys and candies, according to the pecuniary circumstances of the host; but most of the toys, even, were homemade. Where pine, cedar or juniper could not be obtained, laurel was substituted for a tree. But no matter how little the tree was, it did not in the least diminish the general happiness of the festival. There, on a side table, too, stood the great mug of cider, with its accompanying glasses, flanked by dishes of apples and cakes, with baskets of walnuts, hickory nuts and chestnuts of all who came and the busy "chops" of the participants were actively exercised from early morn until late at night.

Although "us boys" by our participation in erecting and "trimming" the Christmas tree, were enabled to see "clear through" the deception of the Bells Nickel, and knew he was a sham, yet when his personator visited the house which he usually did early on Christmas Eve—we were terribly afraid of him, and with some reason too, for he could make himself painfully tangible if he chose.

Before listing the individual items that graced the early Christmas tree, we wish to present one additional overall description of a trimming scene. It is excerpted from an article "Grandfather's Christmas-Tree" by Henry Harbaugh in the January 1856 issue of the *Guardian*, page 13:

Although the children may not enter, we must take our readers into the dark parlor, and show them the mysterious growth of the Christmas tree. First, we take a rough box, paper it all over nicely, and fill it with earth. Then we take a nice round top of pine, or cedar, and plant it in the box. Then we cover the surface of the box with moss, which again we cover with little heaps of almonds, figs, raisins, and all kinds of nuts. Here and there we lay an orange, a cocoa-nut, and nice apples, to make it look rich. Then we take and hang all kinds of pleasant fruits upon the branches of the pine; branches of raisins, strings of almonds, little toy-baskets full of nuts. Then, all the little presents, for all the members of the family, are also hung on the branches. There hang handkerchiefs, collars, little red shoes, speckled stockings, little books, candy baskets, dolls, little men, and little horses, and little whips and wagons. See, there hangs a staff for grandpa, and a pair of spectacles for grandmother. See, I do say, if there isn't a Christmas sermon for the Pastor! Look, if it is not in his own handwriting. It is a chance if grandpa himself has not slipped it from the Pastor's study table, and hung it on the Christmas-tree. Now all is finished, but a number of wax candles must yet be tied in the tree, ready for being lit.

ORNAMENT ADVERTISEMENTS
Among the earliest newspaper advertisements offering Christmas tree ornaments for sale are the Easton *Express* of December 11, 1867, which, incidentally, is the earliest: "At Alcott's . . . ornaments for Christmas trees, wax candles"; the Pittsburgh *Post* of December 24, 1873: "Kinder Blair's Christmas Tree Ornaments"; and the Pottsville *Miners' Journal* of December 16, 1881: "So many charming little ornaments can now be bought ready to decorate Christmas trees that it seems almost a waste of time to make them at home."

From Pennsylvania newspapers and periodicals we have culled considerable material on the subject of early Christmas tree ornaments. We shall now present our findings in this area alphabetically. Under each rubric we shall lead off with the earliest instance located.

Apples
Der Evangelist of Tifflin, Ohio, of January 1, 1857, describes a tree, decorated with "vergoldeten Aepfeln" (gilded apples).

The Pittsburgh *Missionary* of December 29, 1859, describes a Christmas tree at the Zelienople Farm School: "and then those red cheeked apples."

Balls
The York *Democrat* of December 22, 1868: "a quantity of crimson balls representing ripe cherries."

The Philadelphia *Weekly Times* of December 28, 1878: "a score of venders with Christmas-tree balls."

Candy
The Philadelphia *North American* of December 25, 1874: "There are many new styles for trimming Christmas trees. Candies are very generally dispensed with, which has damaged the business of the confectioners."

The Philadelphia *Press* of December 24, 1891: "A new style of Christmas candy this year is made in the form of a chain and of different lengths, in necklace and bracelet form, by the yard, for trimming trees."

Cookies
The Baltimore *Lutheran Observer* of December 25, 1857: "The Christmas-tree, burdened with cakes and confectionary."

The York *True Democrat* of December 22, 1868: "Cakes of various forms and quality, droop from the different limbs, birds of paradise, humming birds, robins, peewees and a variety of others seem to twitter among the evergreens."

The *Guardian* of January 1872: "and good things of all shapes, from the gilded plums to the old-fashioned penny ginger cakes and pepper nuts."

The Philadelphia *Saturday Evening Post* of December 22, 1877: "rich in candies, ginger bread simulacra and cornucopia of choicest sweets."

Der schönste Baum.

Der Christbaum ist der schönste Baum,
Den wir auf Erden kennen;
Im Garten klein, im engsten Raum,
Wie lieblich blüht der Wunderbaum,
Wenn seine Blümchen brennen.

Denn sieh, in dieser Wundernacht
Ist einst der Herr geboren,
Der Heiland, der mich selig macht;
Hätt Er den Himmel nicht gebracht,
Wär alle Welt verloren.

Doch nun ist Freud und Seligkeit,
Ist jede Nacht voll Kerzen:
Auch dir, mein Kind, ist das bereit,
Dein Jesus schenkt dir Alles heut,
Gern wohnt er dir im Herzen.

O laß Ihn ein! Es ist kein Traum!
Er wählt dein Herz zum Garten;
Will pflanzen in dem engen Raum
Den allerschönsten Wunderbaum
Und seiner treulich warten.

So sang der Engel leis' und lind,
Ihr habt es nun vernommen;
Drum, wärst du gern ein Gotteskind,
Thu auf dein Herzchen, auf geschwind,
Und laß den Heiland kommen.

Ach, giebst du Ihm dein Herz noch heut,
Wie wird's der Engel loben,
Er sieht es, sieht es hocherfreut,
Schwebt selig in die Herrlichkeit
Und sagt's dem Vater droben.

Der hat dich dann auf immerdar
In's Herz, in's Herz genommen;
Sein Himmel steht dir offen gar,
Du darfst in jeglicher Gefahr
In Seine Arme kommen.

3

"The Loveliest Tree," a Christmas poem from Des Jugendfreundes Weihnachtsbüchlein für die lieben Kinder (The Jugendfreund's Christmas Booklet for Beloved Children, *Allentown, 1871). The* Jugendfreund *was a Lutheran children's paper for Pennsylvania Dutch families.*

Cotton

The earliest reference to wrapping the branches of a tree with cotton batting—a not uncommon practice in Berks County since at least 1900—comes from the Lancaster *Daily Examiner* of December 27, 1897. A fire is described in a home in Smithville, Indiana: "the Christmas tree was covered with cotton."

Cranberries

The *Moravian* of December 20, 1893: "Strings of cranberries."

Dolls

The York *True Democrat* of December 22, 1868: "its wax dolls and other toys, hanging to the limbs, or seated cozily in its shady looking recesses."

The *Guardian* of January 1872: "the doll-baby is exchanging furtive glances with the leaden soldiers."

Eggshells

For the earliest reference see page 74.

The Norristown *Register* of January 1, 1878: "The branches bear . . . eggs."

The *Moravian* of December 20, 1893: "empty eggshells adorned with decalcomania pictures."

Electric Lights

The Doylestown *Democrat* of December 29, 1885. Concerning a Sunday school Christmas festival at St. James Church: "A Christmas tree, lit up by electric lights, was to have been one of the principal spectacles, but owing to lack of time in its preparation, the exhibition was only partially successful."

The Reading *Weekly Eagle* of January 2, 1886:

Out at Cornwall today Christmas is being celebrated on a grand scale by big-hearted Robert H. Coleman and his many employees. A tree 25 feet in height has been erected in the centre of the large music hall, which will be illuminated by 220 two-candle power electric lamps, the electricity being supplied by a dynamo run by water-power in the basement of the building. The tree is loaded down with gifts of all kinds and gaily decorated.

Figs

The Lewisburg *Home Gazette* of December 24, 1857, mentions figs and oranges as decorations on a Christmas tree in the "front parlor."

Frosting

The Philadelphia *Record* of December 21, 1890: "Cotton-wool dipped in thin gum arabic and then in diamond dust makes a beautiful frosting."

Gas Jets

The Pittsburgh *Missionary* of January 5, 1859, describes a Christmas festival of the Sunday school of the English Lutheran Church of St. James in New York:

The great feature of the occasion, however, was the tree—the Christmas tree! It was a perfect gem in its way; and I verily believe it would have made your eyes dance with delight, connoisseur as you are in matters of this kind. The tree presented a new feature of this kind—a feature which, so far as I know—has never before been introduced into the Christmas tree. Instead of the usual tapers, it was lighted with gas. Nearly two hundred jets sparkled and glimmered through the branches upon which were suspended upwards of *six hundred* articles of various size and value, designed as presents for the children.

The Norristown *Herald and Free Press* of January 3, 1867, describes the Sunday school festival of the Lutheran Church of the Trinity: "A novel feature of the occasion was a tree lighted by more than two hundred jets of gas."

The West Chester *American Republican* of December 27, 1870, describes Christmas window decorations: "Mrs. L. A. W. Pyle has the most beautiful display in her window ever made in West Chester. . . . On either side is a tree from which scores of jets of burning gas light up the whole."

Gilt Paper

The Carlisle *American Volunteer* of December 31, 1874: "The tree itself loaded with an almost countless number of pretty ornaments, of the latest design, made of variegated cardboard, gold and silver and perforated paper." The same source describes a Ziegler tree: "It is trimmed with a large variety of handsome card-board ornaments, comprising banners, sleighs, gondolas, chariots, cornucopias, shoes, crosses, fairies, &c."

The Doylestown *Bucks County Intelligencer* of December 22, 1874:

In the country, where trees may be had for the cutting, a little ingenuity will enable any family to have a beautiful Christmas tree at very little expense. With a few sheets of bright colored paper, some pasteboard, some gay tarletan and a generous supply of popcorn, one may make cornucopias, gold fish, stars and balls, Christmas fairies, and graceful festoons enough to decorate a large tree very handsomely, with an outlay of less than one dollar.

The Norristown *Register* of January 1, 1878: "Boats, carriages, wagons, cornucopias, candy packets, eggs, oranges, lamps, sleighs drawn by deer, dolls of every shade and color, all this can be achieved in tinfoil and gilt paper."

The Doylestown *Bucks County Intelligencer* of December 23, 1882: "The recent rage for fancy paper and card ornaments has utterly died out, and sugar and crystal have taken their place, with small imitation silver and gold conceits of various designs to supply the glitter."

Lemons

The York *True Democrat* of December 22, 1868: "perhaps a huge lemon posted here and there to give tone and taste to the arrangement."

Nuts

The Pittsburgh *Missionary* of December 29, 1859: "the gilded nuts."

The *Moravian* of December 20, 1893: "nuts wrapped in tinfoil or gilt paper."

Oranges

The Lewisburg *Home Gazette* of December 24, 1857, mentions oranges as decorating a Christmas tree.

The York *True Democrat* of December 22, 1868:

In the meantime, old Santa Claus has paid a visit to the Christmas Tree, and now there is a rush in the direction to see what he has hung upon its branches. The first thing that attracts the attention (for the children always look to the top) is a number of oranges hung out in tempting array.

The Huntingdon *Globe* of January 5, 1875, describes a Christmas tree at Marklesburg: "and the oranges hanging so gracefully from the long arms of the beautiful hemlock spruce."

Paintings

The Philadelphia *Times* of December 27, 1881:

There has been a great change in late years in the application of decorative efforts to natural objects, and following in the wake of

Fir-cone Saint Nicholas doll with miniature Christmas tree from Godey's Lady's Book of December 1868. Note the use of pretzels as trimming.

painting sketches on oyster shells and crayonizing crabs has come the fashion of utilizing of recent inventive art to make Christmas trees prettier than they have ever been before.

Plums

The *Guardian* of January 1872: "golden nuts, candies, and nice and good things of all shapes, from the gilded plums to the old-fashioned penny ginger cakes and pepper nuts, are borne on the branches."

Popcorn

The *Western Missionary* of Dayton, Ohio, of January 18, 1866, describes a Sunday school festival in the German Reformed Church:

The first object claiming his attention was a large Christmas tree. Wonderful how that tree was carried into the church! It was beautifully ornamented. Pop corn was strung and hung in profusion over the far reaching branches; this is a new feature to him in ornamenting Christmas trees, but a good one.

The *Christian World* of Cincinnati, Ohio, of January 2, 1868: "The pop-corn was an emblem of abundance; plenty to satisfy our natural wants."

The Doylestown *Bucks County Intelligencer* of January 1, 1876: "With the aid of gilt paper, pop-corn and other cheap contrivances, we adorned the tree very prettily at trifling expense." The same paper under date of December 22, 1877, speaks of "strings of pop-corn."

The Chambersburg *Valley Spirit* of January 9, 1878: "The tree was handsomely decorated and the branches bent with candies, oranges, and popcorn balls.

The Hanover *Spectator* of December 25, 1884: "make festoons of pop-corn among the green of the tree. Will prove a pleasing sight to the little folks."

The *Moravian* of December 20, 1893, mentions "strings of pop-corn."

Pretzels

There are a number of references in the newspaper accounts of Christmas alluding to the use of pretzels in trimming the Christmas tree. At the time of the Civil War students of a Sunday school in Norristown were marched past a Christmas tree whose branches were hung with pretzels. As each child passed the tree he was given, among other items, a large pretzel. The pretzel was one of the decorations of the humorous tree put up in the Lebanon Valley Depot, according to the Harrisburg *Morning Patriot* of December 27, 1869: "The topmost branch, or apex, was crowned with a fresh pretzel of large dimensions." In a traditional Christmas wish in Pennsylvania Dutch sent the author in 1957 by Ira S. Hinnershitz of West Reading, the pretzel plays a role:

> Ich winsh eich en fraylichi weinachts-tsite
> Un en harrliches neies yawr,
> En bretzel so grose oss en shire-dawr
> Un en brote-warsht so dick oss en uffa-rawr.

(I wish you a merry Christmas time and a happy New Year, a pretzel as big as a barn door and a sausage as thick as a stove pipe.)

Raisins

Like cranberries, raisins were strung on strings and placed around the branches of Christmas trees. The earliest mention the author located to the use of raisins as a Christmas tree decoration is the Tiffin, Ohio, *Evangelist* of January 1, 1857.

Revolving Trees

The Philadelphia *Sunday Republic* of December 30, 1877, describes the Christmas tree of one Henry L. Taggert: "has a finely trimmed revolving tree in his parlor."

The Doylestown *Bucks County Intelligencer* of December 27, 1884, describes the Sunday school festival of St. John's Reformed Church of Riegelsville: "A novelty of the occasion was a very ingenuously arranged revolving Christmas tree."

Rosettes

The Allentown *Welt Bote* of December 15, 1869, carries this advertisement (translation):

Christmas rosettes. Rosettes are the loveliest decoration for a Christmas tree and are being used more and more each year. Two to three dozen suffice to do a rather large tree. They can be used year after year. The price is thirty cents the dozen. Siemon, Bro & Co, Fort Wayne, Indiana, and Hermann Albert, Allentown, Pa.

The same paper under date of December 20, 1871, and December 18, 1872, advertises rosettes for Christmas trees made by William Kaminsky, of Allentown, a bookbinder.

The Philadelphia *Times* of December 27, 1881:

The great gardens . . . seem to have pretty well gone out of fashion and in their stead has come the rage of plastering a lot of gorgeous rosettes and stars and fancy figures, all of the most artistic conception and execution.

Sand

The Philadelphia *Weekly Times* of December 28, 1878:

and finally a man with a great box of sand with a placard inscribed "Christmas Sand." The inquiring man will wait here a little, but his curiosity is satisfied as he hears the vender, in horse voice, cry out: "Her y'are; make yer Christmiss home beauterful at no money 'tall to speak of. Christmas sand does it for yer. Put her on yer Christmiss tree and make the little ones 'appy, cause it makes yer tree spa-arkle like dimings! Christmiss Sand."

Schnitz

Schnitz or snitz (the latter is the anglicized form) is a Pennsylvania Dutch word for quartered, dried apples. As a general rule sweet apples were dried unpeeled, sour apples peeled. At drying sulphur was frequently used to make the color of the schnitz very light. Schnitz were sometimes strung on strings to decorate the Christmas tree. The earliest reference we have to this practice is from the Harrisburg *Morning Patriot* of December 27, 1868: "Strings of apple snitz (unpared) drooped from the pendant limbs of the pretty holly."

Snow

The Philadelphia *Record* of December 21, 1890: "Another way to simulate snow is to sprinkle the tree with water and then with flour, afterwards dusting with diamond powder."

Soldiers

The *Guardian* of January 1872:

Face to face hangs the brave soldier of William I, with his proud French foe; the doll-baby is exchanging furtive glances with the leaden soldiers, surrounded with war vessels, cannon and all "the pride and circumstances of war."

Tapers

Tapers are mentioned, of course, from the very earliest references to Christmas trees. We are including an interesting item from a short story "The Christmas Tree" in the Chester *Valley Times* of December 21, 1867: "Meanwhile, upon the wick of each little taper the Doctor rubbed with his finger a drop of alcohol, to insure its lighting quickly."

Tinsel

The Philadelphia *Record* of December 21, 1890: "The sparkling *lamietta* (narrow strips of tinsel) may be piled on the tree in quantities."

Toys

Toys of all descriptions were used along with the early wax tapers in decorating Christmas trees from the time of the very first trees that were put up in this country. Names were attached to the toys and on Christmas morning Kriss Kringle's gifts were picked from the tree by some older member of the family,

ROUGHWOOD COLLECTION

Decorating the tabletop Christmas tree, from The Pictorial Scrap Book *(Philadelphia, 1860).*

and the name of the recipient was read off. This same practice was followed in the early Sunday school Christmas celebrations.

HUMOROUS CHRISTMAS TREES

It is only natural that such a popular institution as was the Christmas tree should have been burlesqued from time to time. In the newspaper press of Pennsylvania we located four such instances, which, because of their very great human interest value, we shall present as the concluding part of this chapter on decorating the Christmas tree.

The earliest humorous Christmas tree as far as we could determine was put up in Harrisburg in the

Lebanon Valley Depot. The Harrisburg *Morning Patriot* of December 27, 1869, described it as follows:

The tree in question was a good sized holly with bright red berries shining among the green leaves, forming a pleasing contrast to the foliage. The topmost branch, or apex, was crowned with a fresh pretzel of large dimensions. Festoons of raw peanuts, carefully strung on linen thread, were tastily arranged among the branches. Strings of apple snitz (unpared) drooped from the pendant limbs of the pretty holly, and squares of homemade gingerbread, prettily suspended, contrasted finely with a liberal supply of water crackers, hung up with white cotton thread. Tiny paper cases, filled with that choice confection, known as "mice dreklin" [little mice turds] among the Pennsylvania Dutch people, were interspersed with the bright holly leaves, while different kinds of well-fingered conductors' checks, ferry tickets, strips of blue paper, a "Wanamaker and Brown" calendar figure, printed in red ink, and a label ("hands off") finished the decorations of this splendid affair.

Next in time, among the humorous trees, is one erected on the steps in front of the residence of H. Seitz, Esq., in Easton, according to the *Daily Express* of December 26, 1871:

On opening the shutters of his residence yesterday morning, Mr. Seitz discovered the tree, which was a silver maple, poplar, ash, or something else of an equally leafless character, planted upon his steps, and hung with a great variety of pretzels, tin cans, empty segar boxes, and other equally beautiful and useful gifts.

No one it seems was exempt from having the trick of a humorous tree put up. The Philadelphia *Sunday Republic* of December 30, 1877, reported:

The keeper of the elephant at the Zoological Garden, thanks to the other employees, has one of the oddest Christmas trees ever seen. It was arranged in his bed room during his temporary absence, and such a collection of old boots, pieces of meat, dilapidated hats, and other relics, as hung from its branches, cannot well be imagined.

Finally, we have an "academic" humorous tree. The source is the Philadelphia *North American* of December 22, 1900:

In accordance with an old custom, the students in the University of Pennsylvania's Biological School presented a Christmas tree yesterday to their instructors. In its way, it was wonderful to behold. Long strings of vertebrae, arranged from an evolutionary standpoint, formed part of the decorations. Then on the branches were worms, crabs, bugs and beetles, while various kinds of fish hung near worms, to illustrate the inclination of one for the other. Twining in and out among the branches were specimens of reptiles, and near them birds' nests, full of eggs, and with the mother birds guarding them. The mammals were chiefly represented by stuffed monkeys.

Around the base of the tree were jawbones, old teeth, skulls and a pile of carpal and tarsal bones. Animal specimens in alcohol were so placed as to form a background for a collection of chickens, pigs and cats. Eggs of various ages filled in the interstices, and in addition there were various forms of fungi, while green mould, blue mould and slime appeared everywhere on old boots, green cheese and pieces of rotten logs.

AMONG THE CHRISTMAS TREES

In the period between 1850, when the Christmas tree began to become commonplace in Pennsylvania, and the year 1900, there is but one Pennsylvanian who left us a detailed description of early Christmas trees. He is an anonymous correspondent of the Lancaster *Express*. Each Christmas season, for four years, between 1873 and 1876, he sought out the most representative Christmas trees in Lancaster City. In great detail he described them for the public, hoping by doing so to improve the taste of the community. We reproduce the articles in toto with the same chapter heading he used: Among the Christmas Trees. We wish to make but one observation beforehand—there is an interesting mingling here of two traditions: the decorated Christmas tree and the Moravian putz, the latter being a subject to which we shall devote a full chapter later on in this volume.

From the Lancaster *Daily Evening Express* of December 30, 1873.

Never perhaps, in the history of Lancaster were so many Christmas trees erected, and they certainly never were more handsome. Men seemed to vie with each other in the struggle for the supremacy of their trees, while in almost every household, however humble, the modest branch or tree was raised, decorated with the pretty trinkets that Santa Claus brought to the good boys and girls of the family.

Having a great love for this good old German custom of putting up Christmas trees, (we never see one that we do not feel thankful to the German people for their good sense and good taste, and particularly to the Moravians, who, more than any other church people, have added to the cultivation and perpetuation of the custom in this country), the writer concluded to visit a few that had attracted more than usual attention. The first place visited was the residence of Mr. Peter Regennas, Lancaster's well known wood carver. On being ushered into the room, a scene of natural splendor met our vision that quite astonished us. It seemed as though we had just stepped into one of nature's loveliest, wildest scenes. On a table, adroitly concealed, that occupied fully one-half of the parlor, rose hills and mountains of real rock and earth five feet high, covered with real moss. At either end were fountains of water, sending their beauteous sprays high in the air, while from the mountain top a charming cascade of water trickled down the rocky ledges, and at last leaped into a lakelet below. Here, in the silvery little lake, were frogs and fishes, while in the barnyard close by, horses and cattle quenched their thirst at the tiniest running pump. In the rear of the pump, or near it, was the threshing machine, continually in motion and moved by an invisible power. To the extreme left stood the comfortable looking old-fashioned farm house, with its garden in the rear, and in that garden an arbor over which clambered an actual growing ivy plant, planted in real, good rich earth. In the mountain side we beheld a deep cavern, brightly illuminated, and in whose depths mystery seemed to swell. There, too, stood the old grist mill—barrels and all complete—run by water power, and looking a very thing of life. The background was a well-arranged moss of evergreens, looking like distant woodland. At either end of the scene hung a beautiful transparency, on one of which appeared the words, "On earth peace, good will toward men"; while at the other end appeared another scriptural quotation. In a word, the whole scene was nature in miniature—everything blending most harmoniously, and herein Mr. Regennas proves himself the artist and the genius. The mechanical contrivances are all of his own handiwork, and his reward lies in the gratification of having a Christmas tree that, for beauty and the harmony, cannot be excelled.

The next place visited was the residence of Mr. Frederick Wolf, (the well known Centre Square hair dresser). Here an equally beautiful, though entirely different scene, was presented. In the centre of which rose a lovely fine tree, fairly laden with fine and ingenious decorations. Glass pendants, doves, cupids, and what not hung upon the branches, while to the left, on another table, a succession of flying carriages, charging troopers, horsemen and horsewomen whirled giddily around in most rapid motion, the whole arrangement being impelled in most rapid motion. The whole arrangement was constructed by Mr. Wolf after much patient study and labor, and is decidedly the best of the kind we have ever seen. And now to the villages and mountains—for they are all here. Ranged around two sides of the good-sized room is a succession of villages—eight or nine in number—with the figure of almost every object imaginable upon them. They are all made of paper, and this is where the wonder comes in. Phaetons, buggies and all conceivable shapes of vehicles; one horse, two horse and four horse teams, with dogs capering on behind; men, ladies and children, with houses, churches, barns, shops, and industrial establishments of almost every description, while here and there a graceful church-spire rears its lofty head high over all. At one end of the chain is a modern three-story dwelling, with mansard roof and observatory—and from the latter the water runs down through a pipe and jets out of a beautiful little fountain in the front yard. At the other end of the chain of scenes we find a most natural looking mountain, with its jagged heights, rocky sides and natural steps of stone descending to its base. Over the big mountain top travels the sure footed mule, with a traveler upon its back, while *underneath* the mountain is a long tunnel, through which a locomotive wends its tortuous way, dragging after it a large train of cars. Days, weeks, yes months, at intervals, must have been consumed in constructing the villages and other arrangements of this extraordinary display. But it was worth the trouble after all, for it is truly a thing of beauty.

From the Lancaster *Daily Evening Express* of December 30, 1874.

Next to the pleasure of putting up a Christmas tree is that of *looking* at those put up by others. The writer of this article has enjoyed *both* pleasures during the season, and as we are not selfish we propose giving our readers the benefit of our observations "among the Christmas trees."

The first tree visited by us was that of Mr. J. M. Westhaeffer, who has been the first in this city to erect a tree the ornaments and decorations of which are almost exclusively of paper. Gold, silver, and all colors of the rainbow are embraced in the collection, the ornaments being made to represent angels, fairies, crosses, stars, blocks, baskets, etc., and the beautiful effect can hardly be intelligently described. The tree is literally covered with ingeniously constructed decorations, tastefully arranged.

Mr. Frederick Wolf, whose tree we referred to last Christmas, has made some very fine additions to his tree, among them a fountain which throws a stream at least four feet high. This is the best miniature fountain we have ever seen. The groundwork of the tree is arranged, this year, strictly in imitation of nature, somewhat in the style of the tree erected by Mr. Regennas, last year, but which (we regret to say) was not put up this year. In addition to Mr. Wolf's flying carriages, his French and German villages, all arranged with panoramic effect, the interest of the exhibition is enhanced by magnificent stereoptican views during each evening.

A corner tree from around 1900.

Mr. Hatz has a tree which rejoices in the possession of certain mechanical arrangements and effects which we have not seen elsewhere, they being the result of his own ingenuity. Among these is a fountain, (self-feeding and self-acting) which throws a powerful jet of water, caught below in a commodious basin. In the background are seen ranges of mountain tops, three to five feet high, in the narrow defiles of which march, in single file, three companies of soldiers, while in the distance, is a good-sized miniature church made by Mr. H. and fashioned after St. Joseph. From the inside of the church the subdued tones of an organ are continually heard, and the effect is remarkably fine.

Mr. H. C. Demuth, the well-known tobacconist, has a small, but very pretty tree, in his store. The novelty about this tree is that it is mounted upon a revolving pedestal, and it continues its revolutions for at least half an hour with one winding. Glittering with glass and other ornaments and continually revolving, as it does, it presents one of the prettiest sights we have yet seen in this line.

Mr. Andrew Eichholtz, in the Express building, has undoubtedly the greatest space of ground-work attached to his tree to be found in this city. The table cannot be less than ten feet by eight in its dimensions, and here, too, is a most perfectly working fountain. It cannot be properly called a tree, but rather a bower of evergreen; for the walls and ceiling are festooned with a close covering of evergreen, from every point of which hang glittering ornaments. A large cottage, completely furnished in every department, (the building and furniture being made by Mr. E. himself,) stands to the right, while not far off is an excellent miniature slave cabin, so familiar to all persons who have ever visited the Southern States. In front of it sit two "culled" individuals, the mother and father of the establishment, while around their feet are several "darky" babies, engaged in innocent play. Illuminated churches, natural looking horses with male and female riders, mechanical boats, which run on wheels, the tented field, with its soldiers, and a great collection of pretty toys, makes up a beautiful scene, reflecting great credit upon the good taste and patient perseverance of Mr. Eichholtz.

Last, but by no means least, we cannot refrain from saying a word about the tree of Hon. S. H. Reynolds. It is a beautiful pine, literally garlanded with wreaths of glass balls of every size and color, from the smallest to the largest size, and from the plainest to the brightest hues. They are arranged in festoons, in half circles, in perpendicular pendants, indeed in every conceivable shape, but all with perfect system of design, until the tree is literally borne down with its weight of glittering beauty. It must have taken a couple of good-sized toy shops to furnish the glass balls alone, to say nothing of the other ornaments and valuable toys. Beneath the graceful branches of the tree is a beautifully arranged garden, with a sparkling fountain in the centre, a menagerie to the right, and a duck pond in the rear. In the rear of the tree proper is a large table containing the gifts which Santa Claus gave to Mr. R.'s little folks, and we observed mechanical toys of such novelty of design and beauty of finish as to interest "children of a larger growth." Indeed the table could not contain half the gifts, the floor being strewn thick with them, showing that Christmas had been observed at this house.

We visited a great many other trees in the city, all of them beautiful, but much smaller than those mentioned. We have referred to the above because of their immense size, or by reason of some peculiar novelty of design, and if those who put up trees will take the hints thus given, they may be able to learn something that will assist them in improving their trees next year. We never saw a tree, in the whole course of our travels, however humble that tree might be, that we did not catch *some* one good idea or other, which we carried home and put into practice. We can always learn from others, and we can think of no pleasanter or more profitable study for parents than that of erecting Christmas trees. A pretty tree, at Christmas time, is of ines-

timable benefit to little folks. It attaches them to home, and they feel like staying there, because they believe no other place is prettier and pleasanter; and in after years the fond memory of those blessed Christmas times will cling to them. They may wander from the path of rectitude for a time, it is true, but we are a firm believer that the memory of those hallowed home joys will, in a great majority of cases, call them back. Herein consists the moral benefit of Christmas trees.

From the Lancaster *Daily Evening Express* of December 28, 1875.

Nothing, in our opinion, adds so much to the charm of Christmas as the traditional tree—particularly when there are children. It is not a matter of importance whether the tree be large or small, so that it exhibits the handiwork and ingenuity of the builder. Every tree *should* be an evidence of the taste and inventive ability of those who erected it, and taking this as an accepted fact, how various are the tastes and inclinations of the mind! The writer has seen hundreds of beautifully decorated trees, and never saw one that had not some peculiarity in which it differed from all the others. Nor is it necessary that much expense be entailed in the erection of a tree. Paper ornaments, (now the most fashionable) can be made of the most beautiful design, at trifling expense, if some one be "about the house" who has the "bumps of construction" well developed. A visit among friends revealed to us many very beautiful and ingenious trees, and we shall briefly describe some of them because it will be of interest to our readers—young and old.

Our readers will recollect our descriptions of several trees last year; the magnificent pine of S. H. Reynolds, Esq., which so glittered with rare and costly ornaments that we could readily comprehend Mr. R's brief explanation that he had "bought out a toy shop in Philadelphia"; the beautiful landscape of Mr. Peter Regennas with its fine mechanical contrivances; the proper villages and handsome fountain of Mr. Fred Wolf; the revolving tree in Mr. H. C. Demuth's tobacco store, (which has again been erected this year, with great improvements;) and the tasteful corner tree of Mr. J. M. Westhaeffer, literally covered with paper ornaments. All of these have been described, and last year's description would again answer if we add the remark that trees are larger and more elaborately trimmed than heretofore.

We have visited new fields this year, and we shall open with a brief mention of a charming tree at the elegant country residence of Mr. J. Fred. Sener, a short distance from the city. It is now properly a combination of trees—there being two of them, joined together by festoons of ornamental paper, and chains of bright-colored glass balls. The merit of this tree consists in its appropriate and natural groundwork, the rich blending of colors in the decorations on the foliage, and the further fact that, with the exception of the glass balls and a few toys, all the beautiful ornaments were made by the family—the paper decorations being the handiwork of Mrs. Sener. These consist of fairies, gondolas, boots, slippers, harps, musical lyres, baskets, stars, chains, and what not! and all of such good size and rich contrast of color as to make them the most attractive of this kind we have ever seen. The groundwork is the invention of Mr. Sener, ably assisted by his brother-in-law, Mr. John Keller, who lives on a neighboring farm. It consists of a fine miniature mansion, with a path strewn with marble chippings leading to it; a saw mill, run by clock-work with circular and upright saws buzzing in real earnest, and the figures of men bending to the work; a herd of live stock walking over a bridge in natural procession, also moved by clock-work; a neverfailing fountain of water, and many other attractive features which we have not space to mention in detail. Taking groundwork and tree decorations together, it is decidedly one of the most fascinating trees we have ever seen, and is well worth walking a mile to see.

Returning to the city we find another very attractive tree at the residence of Mr. Lemuel C. Eby. We were about to say, earlier in our article, that every tree has some distinctive feature—some one particular thing in which it excels. Mr. Eby's tree particularly excels in the excellent selection and fine construction of its paper buildings. The table is twelve feet in length, occupying fully one-half of the deep parlor. The foliage is arranged in festoons against the wall, and arching out over the ceiling to the centre of the room. The sky of green is dotted all over with fairies, gondolas, slippers, drums and other paper ornaments, (closely resembling those of Mr. Sener's) and all made by Mrs. Eby; while below, marble dust paths lead to lovely little villages, country churches, mountain forts, a large mansion (with mansard roof) and last, though not least, to a quiet, humble little stable representing "Christ in the manger." Above, on the canopy of green, are suspended egg-shaped glass balls of peculiar beauty purchased by Mr. Eby in Philadelphia, and the only ones of the kind (we believe) in this city. A very pretty fountain completes the beauty of the table, while graceful wreaths of evergreen which hang suspended in the centre of the room and around the pictures form a most enchanting scene.

And now we take a long walk . . . to visit a German citizen named Adam Mattern, a painter by trade. Here there is a very small tree, but an immense table, the distinctive feature of which lies in the display of mechanical skill. The table extends the entire length of the room, and at one end contains a Catholic chapel, the interior of which very much resembles St. Mary's church. Silver and golden candlesticks, with various sizes of wax tapers, adorn the altar, while a priest, in full robes, kneels at the altar in prayer, with his back to the audience. Figures of men, women, children, and all kinds of animals troop along the entire length of the table, moved by an ingenious crank, while away up on the mountain tops shep-

An early tree and a Schoenhut toy piano.

herds tend their flocks. At the base of the mountain is an excellent representation of "Christ in the Manger."

A few doors below this is the home of Mr. John Hatz, whose tree we described last year; but there is a vast improvement noticeable. Mr. H., though a factory boss, without trade, displays an amount of mechanical skill that would have made a fortune for him in almost any mechanical pursuit. Away up on a hill-top is a good-sized church, built after the style of St. Joseph's and within its painted walls we heard the rich tones of an organ, which will play for half an hour with one winding. By an ingenious clock-work arrangement, a boy and a girl play at "see-saw;" the same works turn a set of flying carriages, and, going on a short distance further, make a little rooster dip his head and drink from a fountain of water. The fountain plays a stream as high as the ceiling—being fed from a reservoir in an upstairs room, and empties its water into the cellar through a long pipe, thus doing away with the usual annoyance of carrying out the water of toy fountains. For mechanical skill, this table is hard to beat.

Leaving here we . . . visit the residence of Martin Blankemeyer. Here are mountains of natural designs, forts and fortresses, with full garrisons and drawbridges; troops of cavalry, infantry and artillery; paper villages; lakes of *real* water filled with boats; a fine fountain and much else that is beautiful; while across the way, at the residence of Mr. J. B. Matt is another novel tree—not so large as the former, but very pretty indeed, an abundance of paper buildings, also decorating it, together with "The Manger."

Going to East German street, at the residence of Mr. John H. Barnes, we find a very beautiful tree, with some features entirely different from any we have described. The wall is festooned with

Christmas in Easton, 1906.

evergreens, from the drooping branches of which depend a great variety of paper ornaments made by the family, while the table underneath is fairly laden with things curious and beautiful. A winter scene—a snow-capped dwelling, with snow-capped hills behind—adds much to the attractiveness of the scene; a small steam engine drives a set of flying horses and carriages; a good-sized locomotive engine (wound up like a clock) describes a circle around the table on a well-constructed track; and a self-feeding fountain adorns the centre of the table. Nor is this all; a mansion, with Mansard roof, a well-executed tunnel, and many other attractive features are noticeable, constituting one of the very prettiest trees in the city—although Mr. Barnes is too modest to admit it.

There are a great many other trees, which we should like to describe, but space forbids. Christian Sharp, confectioner, has a very pretty tree, the distinctive feature being a good-sized toy cou-

ple playing croquet; Dr. Pixton, dentist, has a three-story brick dwelling, with three apartments—parlor, bedroom and kitchen, each furnished complete with toy furniture whittled out of cigar boxes by the doctor, and of most perfect finish. Mr. Wm. Steigerwalt has a very little tree—his first attempt, and a very creditable one. Mr. John L. Binkley has a very fine tree, the original idea here being a cute representation of the babes in the woods.

From the Lancaster *Examiner and Express* of December 27, 1876.

Once more we find ourselves among the Christmas tress, and while we do not for a moment pretend to notice *all* the fine trees in the city, (for that were an impossible task) it is our aim: to particularly describe those that have some peculiar or distinctive feature, and by this means one person learns from another and there is no tree so perfect that an idea formed from some one else may not improve it in some particular or other.

In addition to the handsome private trees of S. H. Reynolds, J. M. Westhaeffer, Fred Wolf, Peter Regennas, and others described last year, we find some previously mentioned ones that are much improved. Mr. John H. Barnes, for instance, has added a mountain, tunnel, lake and admirable fountain to his groundwork, while a train of cars, drawn by a steam engine, run around an endless track, passing through a tunnel and presenting a most natural appearance. The tree has added to it a large number of the most exquisite paper ornaments, many of them being of patterns which we have never seen before, and Fort Hayes, an admirable, original arrangement, must be seen to be properly appreciated.

Mr. Lemuel C. Eaby [Eby] has also improved his handsome tree greatly, and Capt. George Erisman, hotel-keeper, excels all others in the extent and variety of his landscapes. As a gentleman remarked to us, he could not well add more to the view without taking off the roof or knocking out the end of his house.

Mrs. John B. Clements has added more ground to her tree, while the tree itself (a very large one) is literally covered with beautiful paper ornaments, many of which were made by her son Walter, a lad of 12 years, who also carved out a very neat fence. A barn in miniature, with everything pertaining to it, even to a running pump in the yard, is the handiwork of Mr. Clements, while turtles, snakes and toads, made out of putty by Mrs. Clements, are so lifelike in appearance that you imagine you must see them move. "Linwood," a romantic looking retreat, conceived and executed by Mrs. C. forms the background of the table scene, and "Washington Crossing the Delaware" completes the picture.

Mrs. Wm. H. Gorrecht has fairly outdone herself this year. Her tree (or more properly evergreen bower) completely covers three sides and the entire ceiling of the dining-room, and paper ornaments by hundreds and of almost every conceivable variety, hang from the tips of the evergreens. An evergreen pillor [*sic*] supports the centre of the bower, and a large mound, made of earth, is one of the most natural looking objects on the large and tastefully arranged table.

Mr. George W. Brown has also "caught the fever" pretty badly. This is not his first effort, a practice of three years having made him almost perfect. His tree is an importation from New Hampshire, and the foliage is rich and beautiful. Upon the tree may be seen many paper ornaments not common to this city, some of the choicest having come from Philadelphia, and the effect is heightened by the crowning piece—the Goddess of Liberty. The table extends the entire length of the room, and presents a variety of scenes. Mountains and (of course) valleys; lakes filled with live gold fish, a running stream, with "The Bridge of Sighs," and an admirable self-feeding fountain are among the notable features of this tree, while the fine German toy animals give a finish to it which makes it one of the most tasteful to be found anywhere.

Mr. John O'Breiter has a tree that exhibits a remarkable degree of patience and good taste in its arrangement. It is more properly an arbor, the posts and tops of which are festooned with evergreens, while the background consists of the words, in large evergreen letters, "on Earth Peace, Good Will Toward Men." The table, a large one, is filled with the choicest paper houses and other buildings. Here, among the rest, is a facsimile of the house in which Schiller was born, and another facsimile of the "Mouse Tower of the Rhine," the legend being that a wealthy nobleman, hoping to escape the demands made upon his purse for charitable objects, built this tower in the middle of the Rhine, fled to it, locked himself up and declared he would rather be eaten by rats than give of his means to the poor; and the story is that the rats swarmed in from the bed of the river and drove the poor wretch higher and higher in his tower until they overtook and drowned him. There is a natural mountain, with a tower; in the valley there is a windmill, while ancient monasteries and quaint old buildings of every kind meet your attention wherever you look. There is a fine large water-fall, resembling the cascade in Machinery Hall, a large fountain, with jets of water coming through rocks in the centre, and jets from the side, while metal gold fish frisk about in the water as though alive, because they are held by magnets in the bottom. A water course, several feet in length, meanders through hills, emptying into a pipe which carries it to the gutter in the back yard—the supply for the fountain being drawn from the hydrant. It is decidedly the best fountain and water arrangement generally that we have ever seen, and add to the whole scene a hundred or more natural looking trees, (a German production, made of feathers and known as feather-trees) and you have a pretty good idea of the picture.

Sparsely trimmed tree of about 1890.

Mr. William H. Roy, book binder, has also erected a very handsome tree, the most pleasant feature being the fountains and water courses. In one corner is a hill, from beneath the shaggy rocks of which flows a rippling stream of water, and as it trickles down the side the water falls on a water wheel which puts in motion a windmill and several other objects. It is well worth a visit to see.

The Moravians have an immense and very beautiful tree (or more properly a landscape) erected in their lecture room by Mr. Peter Regennas. We say immense, because a number of good sized store boxes, hundreds of bricks, bushels of stone have been consumed in its construction. The whole scene is true to nature, but further than this we shall attempt no description. It excels all private efforts in this city, but this is intended for public exhibition, an admission fee being charged. It must be seen to be appreciated.

Mr. John S. Rohrer has a tree of great height, (which the high ceiling of his handsome residence admits of) fairly laden with choice paper, glass and other ornaments, while on the table beneath is a natural pond, filled with live fishes, a farm-scene, bridges, mountains, water courses and much else that delights the eye. But while all this is beautiful, the most attractive object is on the other side of the room. It is a large table, upon which have been arranged perhaps a hundred moving figures; a cat swallowing a mouse, a monkey playing a hand-organ, a Chinaman swallowing a mouse, a comical looking fellow nodding his head, an entire orchestra of cats, all playing violins, a darkey playing a

Stereopticon card of an elaborate Pennsylvania Dutch Christmas tree from Schuylkill County, photographed by Bretz photography studio, Pottsville, circa 1875.

banjo, darkies dancing, a skating rink with innumerable figures (created by reflection of half a dozen figures in a mirror), a panorama, flying carriages, a couple playing at see-saw, a miniature saw-mill—all moved by a little engine, while the same power plays a hand-organ, making perpetual music. The nicety of arrangement in getting all the pulleys in place; (there being so many contrary and intricate motions) can only be appreciated by seeing this rare mechanical display, and to Mr. Rohrer belongs all the honor, for he erected it himself.

For an exquisite *little* tree we invite attention to that of Mr. Charles Brown. Every tip of every branch is adorned with some handsome paper ornament, hundreds of which hang from the branches. There are fairies, drums, cornucopias, satchels, shields, slippers, baskets and what not, and they are all made so prettily that we could not decide which was prettiest. It is Mr. B.'s first tree, and reflects great credit, while he has the satisfaction of knowing that every ornament which adorns it (with the exception of half a dozen sent from Philadelphia) was made by his wife.

Dr. B. F. W. Urban has also a handsome tree, the paper ornaments of which more closely resemble those of Mr. Barnes than any other. The table work exhibits the skill of a draughtsman, and the landscape is exceedingly fine. There is also a well arranged fountain, and in many respects this is one of the finest displays in the city.

There are of course dozens of other fine trees in the city, but those mentioned above are the only ones we have seen this season. Interchange of visits by those putting up trees gives new ideas, and whilst one may *borrow* an idea from his neighbor, it must be singular if that neighbor cannot give some other idea—just as good—in exchange. But our article has grown lengthy, and we must close for to-day.

From the Lancaster *Examiner and Express* of December 28, 1876.

We took another little stroll among the Christmas trees yesterday afternoon, and the first visited was that of Prof. W. H. Keffer, where we are free to say the finest scenic effect we have ever seen on a Christmas tree (save one) can be seen. That single exception is at Capt. George Erisman's Exchange Hotel, and the scenery is quite as fine as that of Prof. Keffer's. But to the latter tree. It is situated in the back parlor, the shutters of which are kept closed the entire day and the tree illuminated. The table occupies one-half of the room, and is surmounted by a beautiful bower, hung with rich paper ornaments made by Mrs. Keffer. The scene is Swiss—all the buildings save one being of Swiss design. That single exception is a "Centennial Inn," and that is where the quiet humor of the Professor (who made everything on the table) develops itself. There is a signboard outside bearing the inscription—"Centennial Inn, John Smith, proprietor"—and Mr. K. says this shrewd Yankee settled among the Swiss and opened a lager beer saloon. On the inside of the building are various little cards hung up, bearing inscriptions like these: "Lager Beer," "Smith's XXX ale," "Mishler's Bitters." Inside, the room being illuminated, is a bar, filled with tiny bottles, and a bar-tender behind. The smallest imaginable spittoons are scattered around, and the whole affair is complete. In the rear part of the building is a barber shop, and back of the "inn" is a livery stable. This is the humorous part of the scene; the grandeur lies in the natural looking mountains, the stone church and graveyard, with Sisters of Charity among the graves, an illuminated mansion with colored servant at the door and full-dress guests hastening to a party which is to be given, quaint old mills and windmills, Swiss cottage with thatched roof, old-fashioned draw-well with thatched roof, and in the distance the moon rising beautifully over the ruins of a castle. A prettier picture can hardly be imagined and the painting of the buildings (as well as their construction) stamps Prof. Keffer as an artist of no ordinary ability.

Mr. Philip Short has also a grand tree, but of altogether a different type from that of Mr. Keffer's. The bower, which is hung with a larger number of costly ornaments than any tree we have seen, covers the entire ceiling, and three sides of the room. The table is 13½ feet long and 7¾ feet in width, and is surrounded by a heavy green fence. Here is a large pond, in which are boats of several varieties, and very natural looking frogs; an immense fountain, which empties its water through a canal into a large lake, with a beautiful bridge over the canal. Cars run through a very large tunnel, fishermen lounge on the shores of the lake, and in the middle of the stream is the legendary "Mouse-Tower of the Rhine," described as one of the features of Mr. O'Breiter's tree. Taken altogether, it is one of the largest and handsomest trees in the city.

Peter Delzeit has also a large, curious and beautiful tree. The table is not less than 14 feet in length, and the grim humor of this display lies in the fact that many of the most prominent articles were made by inmates of the Lancaster County Prison, Mr. Delzeit having had an opportunity to see and secure them through his position as boss cigarmaker in the prison. One of these articles is a four feet high facsimile of the Centennial Art Gallery, or Memorial Hall. It is a wonderful piece of work. Here, too, is a facsimile of Gen. Lee's house, made by a prisoner, a large sailing vessel, full-masted, made by a prisoner, a curious fence, comical jumping jacks—all made by prisoners, and an entire set of household furniture, sofas, chairs, cradles, cribs, bedsteads, bureaus, cupboards,

all made by prisoners out of cigar boxes. A beautiful feature of this very odd tree is a canal 10 feet in length, running through a tunnel and filled with boats. Along side the canal is a railroad track, and cars also pass through the tunnel. It is a tree worth seeing, entirely different from any other in the city.

Capt. E. C. McMellen has a magnificent tree, the table of which is not less than 12 feet in length and about three feet in width. The bower is filled with choice paper ornaments, made by Mrs. McMellen, and the humor of this tree is found on the groundwork where "that same old coon" which was carried by the Third Ward Hayes and Wheeler Club during the late campaign sits as proud-looking as ever. Near by is a company of uniformed figures, and these the captain designates as the Third Ward Hayes and Wheeler Club. Besides these novel features there are houses on the table, with large sized, full-dressed figures of men and women going to a party at the large mansion which occupies a prominent position among the many pretty and attractive articles which constitute the groundwork.

Dr. M. L. Herr has a very large and very beautiful tree, upon which are over 60 eggs, of a variety of bright colors, all painted by the Doctor. They are the first ornaments of the kind we have seen, and we give this hint for the benefit of others. They are real egg shells. A small opening is made in one end of the egg, the contents are abstracted, and the shell is then dried and painted and hung up with a string. It makes a beautiful ornament. The Doctor has shown his constructive genius by making a four-horse team, harness and all, which looks exceedingly cute. The fountain arrangement is excellent, and the groundwork is filled with rare and costly toys.

We referred briefly to Capt. Erisman's tree, without having seen it this year. A visit yesterday afternoon fully repaid us. The tree is an immense affair and as tasteful as it is large. The table is 20 feet in length and 10 feet in width, and the Captain says the only reason that it is not longer is because the room is not larger. It is the largest private tree in the city, is in the Captain's private apartment, and is put up purely for the gratification of his children, no admission fee being charged. The hills are very natural, and the rocks are real—there being not less than half a ton of rocks on the table. The fairy grotto, or "Fairy Land," is indescribably pretty, and the sunrise and sunset scenes, with illuminated Paris in the distance, are given with true panoramic effect. The genius and patience exhibited by Capt. Erisman in the erection of this tree is something remarkable, and with this notice we close our rambles among the trees for the present.

BELSNICKLING

In the realm of the customs of the year in Pennsylvania, Quaker and Scotch-Irish settlers gradually came to adopt two practices from their Pennsylvania Dutch neighbors: the Easter Rabbit and Belsnickling.

The lore of the Easter Rabbit laying colored eggs (or as the "rationalists" put it: *bringing* them in a basket) was early introduced into this country by Pennsylvania Dutch settlers. Like the Christmas tree, which is first documented in America in Dutch Pennsylvania, the Easter Rabbit probably would not have won through as a general American custom had it not been for three factors: 1) the large migration of Germans into this country from 1830 on; 2) the English-language Christmas and Easter greeting cards imported by the millions from Germany from about 1850 on, popularizing the Christmas tree and the Easter Bunny; and 3) a simultaneous adopting by England, particularly by the Royal Family, of the German customs.

Of the two customs—the Easter Rabbit and Belsnickling—the latter is by far the more interesting: first, because Belsnickling was not influenced by nineteenth-century European influences, and secondly, for the reason that the custom of masquerading on Christmas Eve as it came to be practiced throughout Pennsylvania from about the beginning of the nineteenth century on was an acculturated custom, a mingling, that is, of English and German Christmas Eve traditions.

The reader will recall that we introduced this subject of the mingling of British and Continental Christmas Eve traditions in our introduction to the chapter on Christmas mummers. To repeat: Mumming, a custom practiced by eighteenth-century Philadelphians of Episcopalian background, consisted of groups of folk performers who went from house to house on Christmas Eve giving short traditional theatrical pieces with the expectation of being rewarded in return, with food or small coin. The rural Belsnickel, who customarily made his rounds alone, went from farmhouse to farmhouse rewarding good children and frightening and punishing the disobedient. When the two traditions, mumming and Belsnickling—met in Pennsylvania a new tradition evolved, one that continued in practice in inland cities of the commonwealth until the opening decades of the twentieth century: urban Belsnickling.

By urban Belsnickling we mean a group of masked youth who banded together on Christmas Eve and went from house to house entertaining on musical instruments and singing, all with the intent of being rewarded in return with Christmas goodies or small coins.

Throughout the nineteenth century, up to the discontinuance of the custom in the first two decades of the present century, *two* Belsnickling traditions existed side by side in Pennsylvania: the rural and the urban. The rural Belsnickel made his rounds usually alone, a bag of nuts and cookies in one hand and a switch in the other, to reward or to punish little children, depending on their behavior in the weeks immediately preceding Christmas; if they were well behaved the Belsnickel threw good things to eat on the floor for them to pick up and eat, or on the other hand if there was an ill-behaved youngster, boy or girl, a sharp switch of the whip was applied before the child was permitted to pick up the gifts.

Eventually, however, the urban Belsnickel also influenced the traditional rural one. Rural Belsnickels, too, began expecting a handout.

The Belsnickel tradition was carried wherever the Pennsylvanians migrated, into many parts of this country and Canada. Belsnickling, for instance, was practiced up until very recently in such distant places as North Carolina, Virginia, and Nova Scotia.

The earliest reference we have been able to locate to the Pennsylvania Belsnickel is from the York *Gazette* of December 23, 1823: "'Belsnickles' are warned to keep within the limits of the Hall."

Ralph D. Dunkelberger drew this Belsnickel for the original 1959 edition of this book. Note the Belsnickel's switch and bag for nuts and candies.

Storekeepers in Dutchland used to sell more masks at Christmas time than at Halloween. The Allentown *Daily News* of December 23, 1871, commenting on Christmas provisions in a local store, wrote: "Piles of candies, heaps of cakes and congregations of grinning masks are there to delight the youngsters."

In the accounts that follow the reader will learn of our two Pennsylvania Christmas Eve traditions: rural and urban Belsnickling.

From the Philadelphia *United States Gazette* of December 24, 1825.
Mr. Grigg, in Fourth street, has food for the mind of the young, as well as the old, at his usual low prices, so that when "the stocking is hung up," as of course it will be in all well regulated families, it is probable that the *bellsnicker* [*sic*], will fill it in part, with more lasting *sweets* than those which the confectioner serves out—the latter, however, should by no means be omitted.

From the Pottstown *LaFayette Aurora* of December 21, 1826.
Bellsnickel. This is a mischievous hobgoblin that makes his presence known to the people once a year by his cunning tricks of fairyism. Christmas is the time for his sporting revelry, and he then gives full scope to his permitted privileges in every shape that his roving imagination can suggest. Pottstown has had a full share of his presence this season if I am to judge from the wreck of lumber that is strewed through our streets and blockading the doors generally every morning, which indicates the work of a mighty marauder. A few mornings since a little before sunrise, as I was wending my way past your office, I beheld a complete bridge built across the street, principally composed of old barrels, hogsheads, grocery boxes, wheelbarrows, harrows, plows, wagon and cart wheels. It is reported that he nearly demolished a poor woman's house in one of the back streets a few nights ago. He performs these tricks *incog,* or otherwise he would be arrested long since by the public authorities, who are on the alert; but it will take a swift foot and a strong arm to apprehend him while he is in full power of his bellsnickelship, as he then can evade mortal ken. He has the appearance of a man of 50, and is about 4 feet high, red round face, curly black hair, with a long beard hanging perpendicular from his chin, and his upper lip finely graced with a pair of horned mustachios, of which a Turk would be proud; he is remarkably thick being made in a puncheon style, and is constantly laughing, which occasions his chunky frame to be in perpetual shake; he carries a great budget frame on his back, filled with all the dainties common to the season—he cracks his nuts amongst the people as well as his jokes without their perceiving him. His antique clothing cannot pass unnoticed, as a description of its comical fashion may

excite some ambition amongst the dandies, who are always on the look-out for something flashy and neat, beyond what an honest, industrious, plain mechanic wears, to correspondent [*sic*] their mode of dress with his, whose costume is entirely novel to the present generation; besides the French and English fashions are completely exhausted and have become obsolete; therefore, a description of his grotesque raiment I presume will be acceptable.

This genus [*sic*] of the night winds and storms is, when at a distance, entirely a nondescript; but when he approaches his uncouth magnitude diminishes, and you can accurately survey his puncheon frame from top to toe. His cap, a queer one indeed, is made out of a black bearskin, fringed round or rather stuck round with porcupine quills painted a fiery red, and having two folds at each side, with which he at pleasure covers his neck and part of his funny face, giving sufficient scope for his keen eye to penetrate on both sides when he is on his exploits of night-errantry. His outer garment, like Joseph's of old, is of many colors, made in the Adamitish mode, hanging straight down from his shoulders to his heels, with a tightening belt attached to the waist—the buttons seem to be manufactured entirely in an ancient style—out of the shells of hickory nuts, with an eye of whalebone ingeniously fixed in each,—when he runs the tail of his long coat flies out behind, which gives an opportunity to behold his little short red plush breeches, with brass kneebuckles attached to their extremities, the size of a full moon. His stockings are composed of green buckram, finely polished. His moccasins are the same as those worn by the Chippawa nation. He carries a bow with a sheaf of arrows thrown across his miscellaneous budget, thus equipt, he sallies forth in the dark of night, with a few tinkling bells attached to his bearskin cap and the tail of his long coat, and makes as much noise as mischief through our town, while the peaceable inhabitants are quietly reposing under the influence of Morpheus.

From the Philadelphia *Pennsylvania Gazette* of December 29, 1827.
Of all the religious festivities, none are so religiously observed, and kept in the interior of our State, especially in the German districts, as Christmas. It is the thanksgiving day of New England. Every one that can so time it, "kills" before the holydays, and a general sweep is made among pigs and poultry, cakes and mince pies. Christmas Eve, too, is an important era, especially to the young urchins, and has its appropriate ceremonies, of which hanging up the stocking is not the least momentous. "Bellschniggle," "Christkindle" or "St. Nicholas," punctually perform their rounds, and bestow rewards and punishments as occasion may require.

Our readers are perhaps aware this Mr. Bellschniggle is a visible personage—Ebony in appearance, but Topaz in spirit. He is the precursor of the jolly old elf "Christkindle," or "St. Nicholas," and makes his personal appearance, dressed in skins or old clothes, his face black, a bell, a whip, and a pocket full of cakes or nuts; and either the cakes or the whip are bestowed upon those around, as may seem meet to his sable majesty. It is no sooner dark than the Bellschniggle's bell is heard flitting from house to house, accompanied by the screams and laughter of those to whom he is paying his respects. With the history of this deity we are not acquainted, but his ceremonious visit is punctually performed in all the German towns every Christmas Eve. Christkindle, or St. Nicholas, is never seen. He slips down the chimney, at the fairy hour of midnight, and deposits his presents quietly in the prepared stocking.

We need not remark that Bellschniggle is nothing more than an individual dressed for the occasion.

From the Norristown *Herald* of January 13, 1830. This issue of the Herald speaks of "those abominable bell schnickels."

From John F. Watson's 1830 *Annals of Philadelphia*. The "Belsh Nichel" and St. Nicholas has been a time of Christmas amusement from time immemorial among us; brought in, it is supposed, among the sportive frolics of the Germans. It is the same also observed in New York, under the Dutch name of St. Claes. "Belsh Nichel," in high German, expresses "Nicholas in his fur" or sheep-skin clothing. He is always supposed to bring good things at night to good children and a rod for those who are bad. Every father in his turn remembers the excitement of his youth in Belshnichel and Christ-kinkle nights. . . .

From the unpublished diary of James L. Morris, of Morgantown, in the library of the Berks County Historical Society in Reading.
December 24, 1831: Christmas Eve—saw two krisskintle's tonight—the first I have seen these many years. They were horrid frightful looking objects.

December 24, 1842: Christmas Eve—a few "belsnickels" or "kriskinckles" were prowling about this evening frightening the women and children, with their uncouth appearance—made up of cast-off garments made parti-colored with patches, a false face, a shaggy head of tow, or rather wig, falling profusely over the shoulders and finished out by a most patriarchal beard of whatsoever foreign [material] that could be possibly pressed into such service.

December 24, 1844: This evening being Christmas Eve, we had the Kriskingle's annual visit. Some 4 or 5 hideous and frightful looking mortals came into the store dressed out in fantastic rags and horrid faces.

From the York *Pennsylvania Republican* of January 8, 1840.

In a lecture on Christmas delivered by Thomas E. Cochran before the Columbia Lyceum on December 25, 1839, Cochran said: "The school-boys . . . hail it [Christmas] with a faint anticipation of the bounty of St. Nicholas, dashed with a terror of the horrid 'Belschnikkels'—a word so foreign to the festivity of generous antiquity, as it is strange to English orthography and excruciating to sensitive ears."

From the Philadelphia *Saturday Courier* of December 25, 1847.
Among the other candidates for the capital of Peltznickledom, are Henrion and Chevan's, Isaac Newton's, etc.

From the Easton *Whig* of December 24, 1851.
The occasion [Christmas] is celebrated by all in ways too various to be mentioned; all, at the same time however, contriving to make it the merriest part of the year. And the children! What a season for them! Such a planning, and talking, and conjecturing as there is among them on the eve of Christmas, and New Year especially. I was staying at a friend's house during the holidays of '46. The father purposed to the older ones of the family, that he should be quote "Santa Claus," or "Bellsnickle," as the children termed him. Accordingly, they were sent to bed quite early in the evening. Nothing occurred to disturb their visions of overflowing stockings, trees bending beneath their burdens, and so on, until nearly daybreak, when they were startled by a loud knocking at the head of the staircase. Everyone was awakened by the noise, and the first impression was the "Bellsnickle." Hastily dressing themselves they met at the landing, when a consultation was held between them who should go down first. This was not so easily settled, and they proceeded to go down, carefully searching every corner for fear he might still be lurking in some secret place. Arriving in the parlor, each one proceeded to lay hold on what he considered his own, when a loud thumping in [an] adjoining room sent them bounding upstairs in double quick time. Nor could they be prevailed upon to come down again until the sun was high in the heavens.

From the Norristown *Herald and Free Press* of December 31, 1851.
Christmas Eve was celebrated with processions of "Kriss Kringles," arrayed in all their fantastic costumes, who paid their annual visit to the shopkeepers and citizens, soliciting the "good things" and rendering an equivalent in caricaturing the sable sons of our soil.

From the Reading *Berks and Schuylkill Journal*.
December 27, 1851: Parents, within doors, were making all sorts of purchases for distribution on the morrow—while juvenile harlequins were running from house to house, scattering nuts, confections, consternation and amusement in their way.

A Paul R. Wieand Christmas card, utilizing the Belsnickel theme.

December 30, 1854: It is customary in these parts to associate Krisskingle with the grim monster, who frightened children, and whips them for amusement.

From the Harrisburg *Morning Herald* of December 26, 1853.
Bellsneekling. The annual recurring practice of representing Santa Claus was fully carried out in this place on Saturday night last. Masks were in demand, and white bed sheets were constantly flitting to and fro in the darkness like grim spectres from the phantom world.

From the Norristown *Olive Branch* of December 31, 1853.
Silly children parade the streets dressed in hideous masks, to look unlike themselves.

From the Easton *Daily Express* of December 27, 1858.
The "bell-snickels" were also a most attractive feature on the streets—indeed, more so than they have been for several years—as there seemed to be a general feeling among the juveniles this time to participate and not "take turns," as on previous occasions of the kind.

From the York *Gazette* of December 31, 1861.
On Christmas eve and Christmas night, quite a number of grotesquely attired "Peltz-Nickels" paraded the streets and visited private houses, affording great amusement to both themselves and to those who witnessed their ludicrous costumes and performances.

From the Easton *Daily Express* of December 26, 1866.
Men and boys dressed in most fantastic garbs paraded the streets in numbers and caused considerable merriment to those who were fortunate enough to witness their amusing costumes and fantastic tricks.

From the Wrightsville York *Star* of December 28, 1866.
The prominent feature of the evening was the appearance on the streets and in many of the dwellings, of the largest lot of "Bellsnickles" we have ever seen together, numbering thirteen, six males and seven females, dressed in appropriate costumes. These costumes were decidedly rich and exceedingly well gotten up, of their kind. One of the characters represented the aborigenes [*sic*] of our country, being clad in a complete suit of Indian uniform and trappings, sent here some time since from the frontier, by a young man from this place. Other countries were also represented, Africa having two or three sable hued phiz's in the troupe. The troupe visited many dwellings.

From an article by P. E. Gibbons on the Pennsylvania Dutch in the *Atlantic Monthly* for October 1869, page 484.
I was sitting alone, one Christmas time, when the door opened and there entered some half-dozen youths or men, who frightened me so that I slipped out at the door. They, being thus alone, and not intending further harm, at once left. These, I suppose, were Christmas mummers, though I heard them called "Bell-schnickel."

At another time, as I was sitting with my little boy, Aunt Sally came in smiling and mysterious, and took her place by the stove. Immediately after, there entered a man in disguise, who very much alarmed my little Dan.

The stranger threw down nuts and cakes, and when some one offered to pick them up, struck at him with a rod. This was the real Bell-schnickel, personated by the farmer. I presume that he ought to throw down his store of nice things for the good children, and strike the bad ones with his whip. Pelznickel is the bearded Nicholas, who punishes bad ones; whereas Krisskringle is the Christkindlein, who rewards good children.

From the Allentown *Daily News* of December 28, 1869.
The occasional appearance of a bells-nickel on Friday evening gave evidence of the near approach of the festive day, but still not

in the spirit as in the days when we went bells-nickeling, and year after year that old usage seems to be growing less and ere many years more will be obsolete.

From the York *Gazette* of December 28, 1869.
The streets were remarkably lively on Christmas Eve, and several troupes of masqueraders or "Peltznickles," paraded the streets, adding much to the interest and amusement of the occasion.

From the Lancaster *Weekly Intelligencer* of December 28, 1870.
What a dread we had of the "Pelz-Nickel" when we were a child, notwithstanding our desire that he would quietly enter the house, during our sleep, and fill our stockings, or the "Christmas boxes" we had set apart for him. We dreaded him because his hideous representative was always fearfully masked, and was accompanied by a long whip and a bell. This bell, was perhaps the origin of the corruptions of "Bells-Nickel" or "Bell-Snickel." But this is not the origin of the term *Pelznickel*. It comes from *pelz*—fur; because St. Nicholas was represented disguised in a huge fur cap, and strange fur-trimmed apparel, with a capacious bag flung over his shoulders, from which he distributed his gifts among the little folks, and especially if they had been good children.

From an article "An Old-Time Christmas in a Country Home" by the Reverend B. Bausman in the *Guardian* of January 1871, pages 15–16.
What a fearful fuss the dogs are making! Watch runs barking about the house, as if he would tear some one to pieces.

Hist! Somebody's knocking.

"Come in," says father. And in they come; such as they are. A half dozen jovial fellows, led by a so-called Belsnickel.

"O ma!" scream a group of us smaller children, and seize hold of her dress, like an affrighted brood rush under the wings of the mother hen, when the hawk is after them. Belsnickel may either mean a fur-clad Nicholas, or a flogging Nicholas. In the wintry nights, he is usually robed in furs, and carries his whip with him.

Our Belsnickel is most likely some well-known neighbor friend. Under his ugly mask *(Schnarraffelgesicht),* and an outlandish dress, such as no child ever saw mortal wear before, no on can tell who he is. We children tremble as in the presence of an unearthly being. Really, the Nickel tries to be pleasant, jabbers in some unknown tongue, and takes a few chestnuts and candies out of his vast bundle on his back, and throws them on the floor for the larger boys. One after another shyly picks up a gift. Among these older boys is a self-willed fellow, who sometimes behaves rudely. Whenever he picks up something, Nickel thwacks a long whip across his back—across his only. Whereupon the little ones scream and hold on to their mamma

with a firm grip; and the older ones laugh aloud. The guilty boy puts his hand where the whip has made an impression. Again the unknown being puts his large working hand into the bag and scatters gifts, and again cracks his whip on the bad boy. How does this ugly man know who has been naughty?

From the York *Daily* of December 25, 1871.
When we were a child . . . we dreaded him [the Belsnickel] because his hideous representative was always fearfully marked [masked] and was accompanied by a long whip and a bell.

From *Pennsylvania Dutch*, S. S. Haldeman (London, 1872), page 58.
Bellsnickle. A masked and hideously disguised person, who goes from house to house on Christmas eve, beating (or pretending to beat) the children and servants, and throwing down nuts and cakes before leaving. A noisy party accompanies him, often with a *bell,* which has influenced the English name.

From the Lancaster *Examiner* of January 1, 1873.
Christmas at Manheim: The evening before Christmas was a most jolly time, especially for the young folks, and even old ones enjoyed the comical sights which were to be seen. The exercises consisted of a repetition of what has always characterized this evening, mainly acting "Belsnickel." Quite a number of our boys and young men by various fantastical fixings tried to personify various characters, and endeavored to appear ridiculous, succeeding most admirably in the latter at least.

From the Carlisle *Herald* of January 2, 1873.
There were numbers of bell-snickles going from house to house in quest of cakes, wine, apples, or whatever else the good housewife might place at their disposal, large boys and small boys, and it was not a good time for bell-snickling. The costumes were as varied as the colors of the rainbow and were gotten up regardless of appearance, though each one seemed to vie with the other in burlesquing the ruling fashions among the ladies.

From the Lancaster *Daily Evening Express* of December 26, 1873.
The old custom of playing "Bellsnickle" was renewed in our midst, and we heard of perhaps a dozen parties, dressed in hideous disguise, going about on Christmas eve from house to house, and entering without so much as "by your leave," greatly to the amusement of adult persons, and somewhat to the consternation of the juveniles.

From the Pottstown *Ledger* of December 26, 1873.
Pottstown was full of "bell-snickles" on Christmas Eve, young chaps with their faces blacked, with masks, and dressed in all kinds of outlandish styles. These fellows, with their ugly mugs, visited the

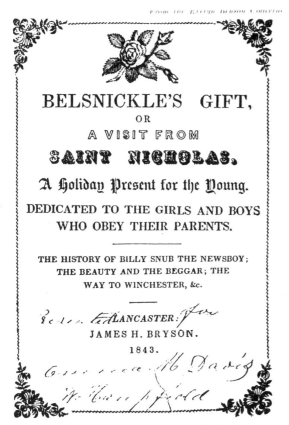

The title page of an 1843 Christmas gift book showing the Pennsylvania impress. It sold at the time for six and one-quarter cents.

hotels, stores, shops, and in many instances private dwellings, and went through their monkeyish grimaces, and annoyed people with their horrible attempts at singing, making themselves odious throughout the town generally. This "bell-snickle" business, which is becoming more of a rough and rowdyish observance of the Christmas season each year, might as well be omitted altogether

From the Carlisle *Herald* of January 1, 1874.

When we penned the two-line squib, announcing that the "Beltz-snickles would be out in force to-night," and which appeared in last week's paper, we never for a single moment entertained the thought that there would be such a large demonstration as our citizens witnessed. We cannot account for it, but our mansion was visited by at least 60 of these characters, embracing persons of all ages, sizes, colors, wealth and custom. Anticipating an ovation of this sort, we had previously fortified ourselves with at least a bushel

of fine cakes, a half a bushel of choice apples and a peck of shell-barks. When the last individual departed, we gazed upon the refreshments and could find but 4 apples, a small piece of cake and a handful of shellbarks. The first of them appeared shortly after 7 o'clock in the evening, and continued coming until ten p.m. The Beltz-snickles were dressed in all sorts of disguises imaginable representing clowns, Indians, harlequins and women, rendering them completely unrecognizable. It was not confined to the "bhoys" exclusively, for we chanced to see a group of fine ladies, and only recognized them by their walk and conversation.

Several of these crowds had musical instruments with which they discoursed "sweet notes!" One party representing the "Eleventh Pioneer Band" were dressed in handsome red costume, and elicited much admiration. The members each played on a musical instrument, embracing a hand organ, violin, guitar, trombone and triangle. They were the "observed of all observers," and received numberless invitations to visit the residences of many of our citizens, but the brief time necessarily precluded them from doing so. One beltz-snickle enjoyed himself walking up and down Main street ringing a small dinner bell.

From the Reading *Gazette* of January 3, 1874.

Hamburg: A certain family have a boy of about thirteen years of age, who sometimes is rather unruly. Two "bellsnickels" were determined to frighten this young chap, and proceeded to the above family. They plagued the boy in a way that was really ludicrous in the extreme. First they made him whistle "Yankee doodle on a hornpipe," and then made him dance, and finally they made him repeat the Lord's prayer, which he did without hesitation. He is thankful that Christmas comes but once a year.

From the Carlisle *American Volunteer* of December 24, 1874.

Masqueraders. Such of our country friends as may wish to enjoy a spell of fun should make it convenient to come to town this evening (Christmas Eve) and witness the parade of masqueraders. The display cannot but afford much amusement, and will be well worth seeing. There will be a large turnout of the Mystic Krew of Komus, who will be ably commanded by Hamlet's Ghost, mounted on a Danish mule (uneducated). The music will be furnished by a full band of silver horns made of tin. (This will account for the recent brisk spell among our tinners.) The procession will parade through our streets, stopping now and then to give an opportunity to the Krew to take a peep into certain houses to see that the children have said their prayers and gone to bed early. They will also have one eye open on Christmas trees, while with the other they will be looking around for refreshments. Of course, our local option laws will forbid anything stronger than cider; but there will be no serious objection if a concealed trap-door suddenly flops up and they are landed into the boudoir of the "crathur." After having marched through the town, distributed alms to the deserving poor and toys and candies to good and obedient children, the Krew will be marched to the market-house, where they will all join in a festive dance. The clerk of the market will see that all the lamps are properly lighted, and all obstructions—such as meat blocks, big rats, and bummers—are carefully removed, so that the jolly Krew will have a fair shake of their feet. The dance will continue until 12 o'clock, then, as soon as the last stroke of that hour had died away, Prof. I-can-spiel, leader of the "silver band" and orchestra, will give three blasts through his horn, which will be the signal of the Krew to immediately bunch around their beloved commander and sing a Christmas hymn, written for the occasion by a son of the man in the moon; after which the Krew will be divided into squads and sent out to spread the glad tidings of the dawn of another Merry Christmas.

From a short story "Krist Kindle" by Dr. Hermann in the Doylestown *Bucks County Intelligencer* of December 23, 1874.
"Papa, at what o'clock do you think he [Krist Kindle] will come?" inquired Eddie.

"'Tis hard to say. At any time between now and morning; therefore you should get asleep as soon as possible," he returned.

"I feel quite certain that Krist Kindle will be here at eleven o'clock, precisely," said his mother. "And from what I have learned I am afraid that *Belsnickle* will accompany him."

We all knew who Belsnickle was, so we were not surprised to hear father ask who it was that had been naughty.

"Perhaps no one has been really naughty," answered mother, "but something tells me that Krist Kindle is not well pleased. Why, Eddie, what is the matter with you?"

Eddie was choking over his tea. I knew what was the matter. My efforts to undermine his faith had been fruitless; his curiosity had been aroused, but his belief was as firm as ever. He felt guilty, and when mother spoke of Belsnickle the "tea went down the wrong way."

After supper we spent half an hour in the kitchen with Aunt Barbara. "Belsnickle will have plenty to do this year," she remarked, "I hope that he has no account to settle with any of you."

"Oh, dear, I hope not!" exclaimed Eva. "Does he always go along with Krist Kindle?"

"Yes, he is always with his master, whom he assists in many ways. He carries the black book, the birchen rods, and the 'bad filling' for naughty children's stockings. It is his duty to deal with the bad children and who knows but what he may be on his way to *this* house at this very minute? Be off to bed with you, one and all!" exclaimed Aunt Barbara in a loud voice, as she turned to the pantry for a fresh supply of raisins.

From the Easton *Morning Dispatch* of December 25, 1874.
The "Belsnickles" were out in full force last night, with banjos and bones. This is an old and wide-spread custom among the boys. In North Britain the boys are known as "guisers," from the various displays worn.

The braying of multitudinous horns on the streets last evening, the presence of troops of fantastically arranged marchers and the generally festive appearance of the streets were sufficient indication to those "frouzy bachelors" who had no children of their own to remind them of the fact, that Christmas Eve was present.

From the Easton *Express* of December 26, 1874.
The "pelznickles" were numerous, many of them being very elaborately gotten up as clowns, Indians, negro minstrels, and others.

From the Lancaster *Examiner* of December 30, 1874.
Manheim news item: The evening before Christmas was an unusually merry one. Bellsnickels were out in large numbers, and in an endless variety of fantastic costumes. About a half dozen were out in full Indian style, and attracted much attention. Four others formed an impromptu string band, and gave delightful music.

From the Reading *Daily Times* of December 25, 1875.
Reminiscences of one E. B. W. of Brooklyn, N.Y., a native of Reading: Another old custom prevailed in your city which was amusing. There used to be on Christmas Eve a weird-looking hobgoblin, that went round where there were children, particularly, dressed most fantastically, all sorts of colors of ribbons, flowers, laces, regardless of taste, or style, and withal frightful enough to scare the infantile portion into convulsions. A bell announced her coming, followed by a loud tap at the door with the knuckles, accompanied with the question, "Are there any children living here?" "Yes, walk in, take a seat." "Yes, thank you, I am tired of going round after the little folks." In the meantime all the juveniles of very small growth had huddled round their mother, characteristic of course when danger was apprehended, they waiting to see what kind of antics this "Bellsnickle" was going to perform. Belsnickle! I am of the opinion that the lexicographer has not furnished us with any such word; it may be found in Germany, very probably, among some of their old dusty tomes. But I digress.

I left the children at their mother's side, and when this nondescript personage had recruited, she flourished a whip she had concealed under her cloak, and hobbled round the room and then commenced her long string of interrogatories: "Do you obey your parents, attend church, repeat your catechism, say your prayers when you go to bed, go to school, and do every thing which constitutes good and dutiful children?" "Yes, marm!" very meekly responded all of them with a unanimous voice. So they were all thoroughly canvassed and their general behaviour found to be satisfactory, notwithstanding the old Adam was hidden away for some future time.

Then the Ogre was changed into a lovely fairy, and she took her basket from her arm and strewed the carpet with cakes, nuts, raisins, apples, candy, toys of various kinds, and then what a scrabbling there was. Each one tried to get more than his fellow-men and women in miniature, all for self. Then the good lady disappeared, and was not seen again until next Christmas, but after her exit she was soon transformed into a good grandmother that did not live more than a hundred miles from the house. I am inclined to think that the custom has died out, nevertheless it was a pleasant thing for the young ones, and it had better be revived again to please the youngsters, as they will always bear it in remembrance in after years.

From the Lancaster *Examiner* of December 29, 1875.
Manheim news item: Notwithstanding the continued rain, the merry scenes which characterized the evening before Christmas were carried on in their wonted vigor. Bellsnickels were out in full force, and in every variety of fantastic costumes. These persons, by means of masks, devices, etc., resembled birds, animals, Indians, etc., and by their odd performances afforded intense delight to old and young. These performances have been one of the features of Christmas for many years, and everybody enjoys them, and to those persons who are fond of antiquity, they afford a beautiful train of historic thought as to their manner in which these customs have come down to us through the ages.

From the Harrisburg *Patriot* of December 25, 1876.
The description of Momus—the fun and mischief loving portion of our population—were also "about" dressed in the costumes of "Beltznickels," clowns, harlequins, Indian chiefs, rag-a-muffins, girls of the period, negro performers, and in masquerade suits of every imaginable cut, shape and color, making night hideous with horn music (?), kettle-drums, trumpets, penny whistles, etc. This latter class were given all the license they needed to carry out the time-honored old custom of merry making on Christmas eve, and in not a single instance that came under our observation, were they molested or interfered with. At many private residences the masqueraders were invited to enter and receive Christmas "treats." The scene and the occasion revived memories of the past, when many of our old, substantial citizens were boys and did exactly the same thing. In point of numbers the harlequinade of Saturday night exceeded that of former years to a considerable extent. The streets had much the appearance of Venice on a carnival night and everybody and their friends appeared to enjoy the scene and the occasion.

From the Lancaster *Daily New Era* of December 26, 1878.
"Beltznickle bands" were to be seen in all directions; there were dozens of them on the march.

From the Lancaster *Daily New Era* of December 27, 1878.
Marietta new[s] item: The streets of Marietta were enlivened on Christmas eve by various bands of "Belsnickles" dressed in style to suit the occasion.

From the Lancaster *Intelligencer* of January 2, 1878.
The "bellsnickles" were out in force in every imaginable grotesque attire. Indian warriors and bandit chiefs, devils and demons, darkeys and every species of nondescript were out in surprising numbers, frightening the wits out of the small boy, for whom, despite their terrifying aspect, they seemed to have the old-time proverbial fascination, and who, despite the numerous repulses received at the hands of these terrible creatures, continued to follow them around and manifest the greatest glee at their antics and absurdities. No instances of any special misbehavior on the part of the bellsnickles have come to our notice, though perhaps some of them visited too many beer saloons, and got unduly noisy as the evening wore on.

From the Mount Joy *Star* of January 14, 1878.
But there is an old custom in vogue which I think should be entirely condemned and suppressed. It is the practice of disfiguring the person with old clothes and a false face, and going around to neighbors' houses frightening the children. I once saw a family of children frightened almost into convulsions at one of these nuisances, and I hope the time is not far distant, when our boys will be taught better manners, for such proceedings are entirely too far behind the enlightened age of the nineteenth century.

From the Harrisburg *Telegraph* of December 26, 1879.
Bellsnickles in the most outlandish costumes were out in droves. They infested the stores and played on antique musical instruments as a prelude to passing around the hat, and generally departed with a parting salute on their tin horns. Some were quite proficient as musicians and handled the violin, cornet, bones and tamborine in a lively manner, but the majority were simply frightful. Glee clubs, attired in quaint costumes, the singers with blackened faces, made the air hideous with their alleged warbling. We regret to say that some of them were the worse for liquor, unscrupulous dealers having given even boys under age "something to drink" when called on.

From the Reading *News* of December 25, 1880.
Parties of grotesques were to be seen edging their way among the crowds upon the sidewalk and good-naturedly jostling their neighbors. Some amusing characters could be seen among these merry

masqueraders, but that of the Ethiopian seemed to be the most popular, and it was no uncommon sight to see an exaggerated specimen of this race escorting a wondrously contrived representative of the noble red man. The besieged residents of Jericho never had the delicate tympanum of their ears more severely bombarded by the unearthly sounds proceeding from the goat-horns of Joshua's army, than did the traveller last evening, who accidentally fell in with these fantastics.

From the Doylestown *Democrat* of December 27, 1881. Springtown correspondent: In "ye olden times" chestnuts were invariably saved until Christmas, for the purpose of going out to "Bells-nickle," as they termed it. Parties started out on Christmas Eve in couples, masked, and arrayed in phantom or any other fantastic costumes, ("scare-crow" style, very often,) representing male and female; the one with bells attached to the garments, or else a strap or sleigh bells secreted in some way was christened "Bells-nickle," while the other, provided with a bag full of chestnuts, or else shellbarks, and a handful of twigs, was Kris-Kingle. Going from house to house, they spent nearly the entire night carrying out their nonsensical sport. The first intimation the inmates had of their presence was a rattling of the twigs on the window panes from the outside. After a lapse of several minutes, the door opened, slowly and softly, but only on a crack, and presently a handful of nuts went rattling over the floor, as an inducement to the children, who were, as a matter of course, frightened at the strange manoeuvres, although not suspecting any danger. In a few minutes more the door opened a little wider, and some more nuts scattered. By this time, the youngsters having mustered up a little courage, advanced, endeavoring to gather up the tempting nuts, when, quick as a flash, the masqueraders bounded in on them, and "crack," they received a stinging rap across the knuckles, were seized, and pretended threats of violence made in case the little innocents offered any resistance. This sudden transformation scene almost made their hair stand on ends, and begging for mercy, were induced to do almost anything asked of them, dance, sing, stand on their heads, etc. so as not to be molested any further; others, more venturesome, attacked the intruders and unmasked them, when, sometimes to their utter astonishment, they turned out to be members of their own family, who started away immediately after supper, pretending to have some business "down town." This contemptible practice has lately been entirely blotted out of existence, and thanks to goodness that such is the case, for surely, there was no benefit derived from it; many a child was almost driven into convulsions with fright; while the parents apparently enjoyed the joke, being not aware of any danger.

From an article by Simon Rathvon in the Lancaster *Intelligencer* of December 24, 1881. (The information applies to Donegal Township about 1822 or 1823.)

In this engraving, a child plays the role of the Belsnickel with beard and whip. The younger children are terrified, but the older brother is simply amused.

All the others were the victims of the harmless little ruse which parents saw fit to resort to once a year, in order to furnish an agreeable surprise and pleasure to their little ones, whose boxes, hats, caps and stockings occupied different nooks and corners to receive the gifts of the "Bells-Nickel" to good little boys and girls, and somehow all claimed to be good on that occasion at least. But when the Bells-Nickel appeared in his proper person on Christmas eve, with his hideous visage, his bag of nuts, and his long whip, jingling his bells withal, and speaking in a dialect that seemed to have been brought from the confusion of Babel, the children were not quite so sure of their goodness, if they did not fly in terror from his presence and hide themselves under the remotest corner of their beds. The name of Santa Claus, as far as I can remember, had then no currency in the rural districts of our county. It was the Bells-Nickel that rewarded good children and punished bad ones, and it was he who filled the stocking legs, the hats, caps and boxes on Christmas night. These gifts to children, and indeed all gifts passing between the young and the old were severally termed a "Christ-kindly," but as little was heard and known of Kriss-Kingle as of Santa Claus.

From an article by Rev. I. K. Loos in the *Messenger* of December 19, 1883. (The information applies to Tulpehocken of 40–50 years earlier.)

"In the Olden Time" we celebrated also the day succeeding Christmas, called *Second Christmas*. It was spent mainly as a social holiday—in talking, visiting, sleigh-riding, games in the house and barn, and by youths and maidens in tender love. The close of this day brought the evening for the *"Pels-nichol,"* perhaps one side of the present *St. Nicholaus*, clothed in *pels* or furs. But in the eyes of the children in the Olden Time, *Pels-nichol* was a personification of the principle of punishment of the bad, though this also had its good side. He was a rough, strong, fur-clad individual, with long, stout rods in his hand. His bells and heavy boots announced his coming, and his rude entrance struck terror into the hearts of the smaller children. The whole family was on hand; the smallest in mother's arm, the next on father's knee, safe from the rude blows which *Pels-nichol* administered to the boys, men and women, as he shed his coarser fare of walnuts and shellbarks on the floor, and compelled them to pick them up under the rod. With a bound and a yell he was out of the house, and striding in long steps towards a neighbor's house, where the rod and nuts were in like way dealt out.

When quiet was restored in the house and we stepped out, we could hear in various directions, the yells of *Pels-nichols,* or the shouts of sleighing parties on the turnpike, as one of these wild, uncouth figures rushed by them.

From W. J. Buck's chapter "Manners and Customs" in the 1884 *History of Montgomery County*.

Our intention here is only to mention briefly such customs as were associated with it [*Christmas*] the night before, upon the outside of the church. It was at this time that children would be induced to set plates on the tables or windows with the expectation that, if they would be good, the "Christ-kindlein" would bring them something nice, and, if naughty or disobedient, then the "Belznickel" whom they greatly feared, would come to correct them. They were made to believe that these could enter through fastened windows, locked doors or down the chimneys. The presents would generally consist of candy, toys, and cakes expressly baked for this occasion. The Belznickel was some disguised person who generally carried a rod, and the children that would promise him to reform from certain habits mentioned he would not chastise, but would give presents; but if they did not make their promise good in mending their ways by the next Christmas, they would then receive the merited punishment. Instances have been known of the children banding together when the Belznickel attempted to correct them and ejecting him from the houses, or of his being worsted by them. Sometimes he would go from house to house with a protecting company, who would enter the house first and report. Of course, on all such occasions he would be so disguised that it would be impossible to recognize him unless divested of some of his habiliments. If he happened to get into any tussle, this would be the great object. Where all would pass off well, on leaving the door he would sometimes remove his mask or a portion of his raiment, to leave room for conjecture as to whom he might be.

From the Lancaster *Daily Examiner* of December 30, 1886.

Reamstown news item: The "belsnickle" did not show up last Christmas eve; consequently no children were frightened. For this all praises. It requires a straight-down fool to put on a hideous looking mask and act the lunatic's part, anyhow.

From the *Christian World* of December 24, 1891.

Peltznickel. This fellow belongs to the world of ridicule and perversion, and should have nothing to do with our Christmas celebrations, but we have to suffer the wicked world still in their abuse of that which is good and sacred. Peltznickel used to come on Christmas eve to the children's houses. They could hear his coming which was terrible in heinous noises, rattling of chains, etc. His appearance was still more frightful, wrapped in furs or skins like a huge animal. No wonder the children hid and sometimes fell into fits when they saw him. Some parents did not permit him to come into their homes, but others take delight in seeing the children in fear. He carried a large bag in which he had some nuts and candies, and when the children had made good promises he would throw a few on the floor. Woe to the child who would attempt to pick some up while he was near, for he also carried a limber stick. The children did not like him and we hope they do not like his semblance now—worldliness.

From the Philadelphia *Public Ledger* of December 24, 1891.

From an article by the Stony Run, Berks County, correspondent on Christmas customs among the Pennsylvania Dutch of long ago: In the evening of Christmas Day the children would gather around the old-fashioned fire-places, anxiously awaiting a visit from a Belsnickle—a personage similar to Santa Claus.

The Belsnickles were generally young men of the neighborhood dressed in fantastic garbs, and wearing masks, with bags of candies and nuts slung over their shoulders. They always received a hearty welcome from parents and children, and travelled from house to house, distributing their gifts. Often they would scatter them over the floor, while there would be a lively scampering among the children to get them, the visitors at the same time applying to their bodies long thin switches, which was considered great fun in those days.

From an article by Frank Brown in the Reading *Weekly Eagle* of December 31, 1892.

In some part of Berks, the "belsnickel" parties have ceased making their annual visits, but in most sections they are still keeping up the old custom and having lots of fun, too. In the northern part of the county parties of this kind are especially large.

At six o'clock on Christmas eve unusual bustle broke the customary quiet of the big kitchen of a certain farmhouse near the Blue mountains. There were fourteen boys, ranging in age from fourteen to twenty years, in the kitchen, and seven or eight more were on the porch outside. The kitchen and porch were noisy with the continuous passing in and out and the laughing and rompings of the boys.

On the wood chest, behind the big woodstove in the kitchen, sat a short but very stout man, aged about sixty-five, and by his side sat his wife, a woman of medium weight, but a few years older than her husband. The marks left by years of hard work could be plainly seen on both. The old man couldn't talk for laughing. The old lady, however, was busy chatting with the young people around her. Around a table near the center of the room sat six girls, two of whom are daughters of the house. All the girls were laughing and chatting with the boys. Two of the sons went round and spoke hurriedly to the others, giving instructions.

At half past six o'clock the six girls, the two old people and the two sons went into an adjoining room, where there was a big heap of old clothes, including Shaker bonnets, which were worn so extensively by women forty years ago, hoop skirts, piccadilly collars, linen dusters, high silk hats of ancient fashion, etc.

On one of the window sills there were a lot of masks, such as are sold in the Reading variety stores. Soon four of the boys in the kitchen were also called into the side room, where each of them was turned into a Santa Claus, or belsnickel. The girls dressed two of the boys in women's clothes, as grotesquely as possible. The two brothers helped the two others dress ludicrously in men's clothes. Next the face of each boy was blacked with burned cork, so that nobody could discover their identity in case the masks should give way, as sometimes happens.

In this way fourteen young people were rigged up as full fledged belsnickels. The old people and the girls laughed heartily. The two brothers were the last to assume disguise. Shortly before eight o'clock the party was ready to start out. Some had peanuts, some candy, others dried apples or pears, others nuts, and still others popcorn. Before they left the old lady gave them a bag containing about a peck of dried pears. When outside the house each took a hickory "gad" they had brought along from home with the rest of their paraphernalia the evening before.

When the party had gone and the girls were in another room the old man, who had but a short time before laughed so heartily, said, with tears in his eyes: "This makes me think of the time when I was young. How we used to have fun on Christmas eve. That time we had larger parties than the one that just left. Those dear old times are right before me tonight. I haven't been so happy in a year as now, but still, when I think of the fact that all those who used to travel with me from farm house to farm house the night before Christmas are now dead, I cannot keep back the tears. These boys that just left our house have brought back to me memories that couldn't be awakened in any other way. I can't see why some people are so foolish nowadays as to not to allow their children to 'act belsnickel.' It is only innocent fun. I like to see young people happy. It makes me happy to see them happy."

The Santa Claus party that left this farmer's house, visited farm house after farm house. They gave the children chestnuts, popcorn, dried apples, candy, etc., and the obstreperous ones they whipped a little. Many of the farmers gave the party apples and cider. At about midnight they ate a hearty dinner at a farmhouse about four miles from the place from which they started. They said they would make a trip of about ten miles, and arrive home about six o'clock the next morning. The average party wasn't as large as this one and didn't make as large a trip.

From the reminiscences of Matthias Mengel, then 65, in the Reading *Weekly Eagle* of December 28, 1895. (The information applies to Caernarvon about 1845.)

Particularly vivid in my memory is a Christmas eve when I was one of three or four lads who started out to act the "Belsnickel." Well, each of us boys carried a switch in his hand. We dressed in the clothing we could find at home, tied handkerchiefs over our faces and filled our pockets with chestnuts and hickorynuts. We went to the house of a neighbor where there were children, and expected to have some fun by frightening the children by our singular appearance, throwing the nuts on the floor, and belsing the children if they should pick up any of the nuts. We tinkled our bells, entered the house and began jumping about and throwing nuts, when the head of the family, who was an old Amish, said very sternly, "I don't believe in such foolishness, clear out!" and we cleared. You see that was an English and Amish neighborhood. The English did not observe the German customs of Christmas and the Amish were a very plain people like the Quakers and had no festive occasions as had the Germans of other denominations in other sections of Berks, where Christmas especially was a season of feasting, merriment and general rejoicing. We knew nothing of Santa Claus, rosy and plump, with twinkling eyes and furry dress making his aerial visitations in a sleigh drawn by reindeers at dead of night and silently, expecting the tinkling of his bells, which the children could only hear if they were awake when Santa appeared, but the children are never awake at that time, for he comes only when they are asleep.

From an article by Daniel Miller in the Reading *Reformed Church Record* of December 21, 1899. (Miller hailed from near Lebanon.)

In the days of the writer's boyhood Santa Claus was not known, at least in our neighborhood, but another personage filled the office now occupied by him. His name was "Belsnickel." He was not as rich as Santa Claus, but the children were thankful for his gifts. Weeks before Christmas the children were told that if they behaved well they might expect a visit from Belsnickel. That had a good influence upon the young folks. Well do we remember the first visit of the friend of children of those days. It was Christmas eve. Every now and then the question was asked, "Is he coming?" And frequently the children would lift the curtain at the window and peep into the darkness. Time passed and it looked as if we would be disappointed. Suddenly we heard the noise of sleigh bells on the porch, and the next moment Belsnickel was in the room. He looked very much like our Santa Claus, with a long rod in his hand. While giving expression to Christmas greetings he took a lot of gifts from his huge bag and threw them on the floor. These gifts consisted of cakes, chestnuts, small pieces of sausage, etc., and while the children stooped to pick up the gifts, Belsnickel laid his rod on their backs and explained, "Will you pray? Will you pray?" This threw the children into a state of fear and excitement, and by the time they had recovered therefrom Belsnickel had disappeared. Only his heavy footsteps and the jingling of his bells were heard as he went away. It was a wonderful experience. The same questions arose in the minds of the children then as now: "Where does Belsnickel live? What does this mean anyhow?" Some had painful cuts on their hands, but Belsnickel's gifts were relished by the children, and his visit was the subject of the family talk for weeks.

From the Hanover *Weekly Record* of December 28, 1900.

Bandana news item: A number of young sports, disguised as "pelznickels," made things lively about town on Christmas eve and tormented some persons sorely. One man called to his wife to bring his pistol, and the masqueraders decamped in a hurry. The joke of it was that there was nothing like a shooting iron in that particular household.

From the *Lutheran* (Philadelphia) of December 20, 1900.

In the days gone by (that is, when you and I were younger) we used to go out "Peltznickling." We then believed in frightening children into good behavior; and the poor timid creatures used to find a sort of delight and exhilaration in the very fright they experienced when the ominous birch of the "Peltznickel" brushed against the window panes or shutters. Now that would be considered cruel, and very detrimental to the nerves of a wiser but weaker generation. It would not accord with the more modern kindergarten ideas of nursing and protecting the darlings. Though cases of infant hysteria were few and far between—perhaps much rarer than now, when under far less provocation the little ones are ready to become disembodied spirits—yet times and customs change, and we must now adapt ourselves to a method of celebration not half so spontaneous and delightful as were the Christmas pranks and antics of our younger days.

From the Lancaster *Examiner* of December 26, 1902. Manheim news item: The Christmas festival was ushered in at Manheim with unusual demonstrations by the "Bellsnickels," as in bygone days. The streets presented a lively appearance on Christmas eve and scores of young men marched to and fro attired in costumes that struck terror to the young and caused much sport for the older persons. As usual, these bands gathered in front of George H. Danner & Co.'s store, on Market Square, where they played and sang and performed all sorts of antics before several hundred spectators. There was much merriment and jollity and the demonstrations continued until midnight.

From an article "Folk-Lore and Superstitious Beliefs of Lebanon County" by Dr. Ezra Grumbine in volume 3, number 9, 1905, of the *Lebanon County Historical Society Proceedings*.

"The night before Christmas" often bro't a wonderful personage clothed in an outlandish raiment of animal skins and old clothes. A home-make [*sic*] mask concealed his face, and he carried in one hand a bag or a basket and a long switch in the other. His name was "Belsnickle," which means Nicholas in pelts, or skins. Unlike his English prototype, the mythical Santa-Claus, who rides in a sleigh drawn by reindeer and who enters dwellings on Christmas eve by way of the house-top and chimney, our "Belsnickle" was of flesh and blood, generally the wag of the neighborhood, and entered the house at the door. In his basket he carried apples, nuts, cakes and sometimes candy. These he threw upon the floor, and when the half-scared youngsters went to pick them up he would sometimes lay to with his stick, making them promise to be good and obedient children. The writer remembers one case in which a child was frightened into the nervous disease called St. Vitus's dance by a "Belsnickle's" performances.

From the York *Sunday Gazette* of December 24, 1905. The presence of a few youngsters on the street last evening playing "bellsnickle" recalled to the memories of the older persons how suddenly that harmless and once almost universal pastime on Christmas Eve has fallen into decay and without any apparent reason.

There were more in evidence last night than for some years and some of them were gorgeous or ridiculous, as their tastes varied. But they were not the real old-fashioned kind. Groups of them attracted much attention on the streets. Most of them were children, but some were artistic and gave stunts that greatly amused. They reaped a harvest of pennies, nickles [*sic*] and dimes from the good-natured Christmas shoppers.

Less than a decade ago if from twenty-five to fifty "bellsnickles" did not visit the homes of each prosperous farmer, something was wrong and the owner of the fireside thought himself slighted and felt as if he had not lived at peace with his neighbors. It has all changed now. Not a real bellsnickle is to be seen. A few boys occasionally "dress up" and visit a home or two, but they are not the bellsnickles of old and the amusement and fun of the past is dead.

A veteran of the three-score years variety commenting on the situation yesterday said:

"It is strange how suddenly the bellsnickle passed away when once it started to decline. It is less than twenty years ago when every musician in the country blackened up and joined a crowd to visit the homes for a good time on Christmas Eve. Now a person scarcely hears of a bellsnickle and in another decade the children will only know what bellsnickles were by reading about them.

"When I lived on the farm ten or fifteen years ago, each farmer's wife made great preparations for the coming of the bellsnickles. There was cake and mince pie and fastnachts, apples, hard cider and they were all dispensed with a bounteous hand.

"The young fellows and even men of forty would blacken up, and with fiddles, jewsharps, mouth organs and banjos, make the rounds of the best homes in each neighborhood. They would play and sing and dance and after each set as they called it, the mince pie and cake and apples and hard cider would be passed around.

"The bellsnickles shined up too, and don't you forget it. No patent affairs that was guaranteed not to harm the skin, but common stove black or shoe blacking was rubbed on the face and hands and then a brush was used until the face shone and until the bellsnickle had the real appearance of the darky minstrel.

"How did the bellsnickling originate? Well, that is a hard one, but it has been in vogue ever since I can remember—about 1845. I have often heard it said that it was following out a custom established in the south when slaves would appear before their masters on Christmas Eve and there dance and sing and play the banjo for the master and guests' entertainment and after each number the slaves would be treated to the best in the house, the one occasion of the year.

"And I guess that's how it originated. The bellsnickles of a generation ago were the country minstrels who were to carry good cheer and Christmas carols to the homes of the big farmers of the country and they in turn got the best the land could afford.

"Bellsnickling began to deteriorate about the time the present generation of young men began to bloom. They would not blacken up and they insisted on buying cheap black false faces. That never took, because one of the real ideas of bellsnickling was to "shine up" so that the bellsnickle would not be known even by his own friends and neighbors. With the coming of the false face the young ladies would make a descent on the owner of a false face and by the time the melee was over the false face had been torn to pieces and there was no bellsnickle. That I believe led to the decay of bellsnickling and the dispensing of good cheer on Christmas Eve to the country boys."

From the reminiscences of W. W. Davis in the New Holland *Clarion* of 1909–10.

Permit me to drop a tear to the memory of Belsnickel. The dear old fellow must have passed away about the time we left the East [1850s], for I never heard of him here. How faithful he was to me year after year. No matter how cold or snowy he never failed to fill my stocking. There is a Santa Claus in the West, but I doubt his existence, as I have never had a glimpse of the chap and he certainly does nothing for me. Belsnickel, requiescat in peace!

From the Reading *Eagle* of December 21, 1913.

Rev. Dr. Jacob Fry, who was the pastor of Trinity Lutheran Church for many years, said that when he was a boy in the village of Trappe, Montgomery County, the Belsnickel with mask and costume made his rounds and threw nuts and confections on the floor, and when the children attempted to pick them up he rapped them over the knuckles with his switch.

Robert Reber, aged 63 years, who has been living in Reading for 15 years, said that when he was a lad living in Manheim Township, Schuylkill County, Belsnickels dressed in women's old clothes and wearing big hats which nearly covered their faces, came to the house the evening before Christmas and threw walnuts, hickory nuts and chestnuts on the floor. When the children attempted to pick them up they were struck on the hands, arms and backs with switches.

From the Philadelphia *North American* of December 21, 1913.

A century ago, and even later, the children used to see him [Santa Claus], talk with him, get their presents from his hands, and even get their spankings from those hands, too. But then his name wasn't Santa Claus. It was the Beltznickel. They have the Peltznickel still—his name softened by time to the gentler initial and, it may be hoped, his hand gentler as well—in the good Pennsylvania town of Emaus. But this city's kids have never so much as heard of him.

It was he who, in living flesh and blood, a great sheepskin coat covering him and an immense white beard bushing his stern old face, appeared on Christmas eve in the old town and gave the children their Christmas gifts, unless they had been very, very naughty. If they had, it was he who switched them for it, or applied to them the hard palm of punishment in default of switches.

From the Philadelphia *North American* of December 28, 1913.

Reminiscences of 98-year-old Mrs. Anna Faddis, who lived in Lansdale in the formative years of her life: At this time of the year we children didn't know of Santa Claus. He is just a new-fangled Christmas saint. We had the old Beltznickel, who used to come right in on Christmas eve and look as if he was going to whip us, but always gave us candy instead. Some of our neighbors had Kris Kringle, who wasn't so stern as the Beltznickel at first, and couldn't be any jollier afterward.

From the reminiscences of John B. Brendel of Reinholds, submitted to the author in 1948.

Christmas Eve, along about 8 o'clock, one would hear a sharp knock on the door and one of the parents would open up. There in the doorway stood some of the weirdest characters that one ever had the occasion to behold. Belsnickels they were, masked and carrying a peeled willow whip or a buggy whip. Then the kids would get a work-out. A Belsnickel demanded to hear their "Grischdawgs Schtick" (a poem memorized for presentation at the Sunday School Christmas festival) or the latest poem that was learned at school. After this devilment was indulged in for awhile, there began to appear from the folds of the Belsnickel's garments chestnuts, walnuts, peanuts and pretzels. These were tossed in front of the children and when they tried to pick them up, they were whipped around the legs with the willows or buggy whip. After a few moments, however, the kids were allowed to pick up what had been thrown on the floor for them.

Then came the host's time to act. The woman of the house would bring "Grischdawgs Kichlin" (Christmas cookies) and apples. The man of the house went to the cellar for a pitcher of "Schdeefens Schdofft" (hard cider) or a jug of homemade wine, or both. Well, you can imagine what happened to the Belsnickel along about the fifth stop. I can pity those kids today that were the victims of one of the later stops. Those lashes of the whip stung. I know.

From a Franklin and Marshall 1950 folklore term paper by Robert F. Fehr. (The informant was Mrs. Cora Sandt of Nazareth.)

Two or three boys of the community where she lived, would dress up in the oldest rags they could find on Christmas Eve. They would also blacken their faces, get a big stick or whip, and then with their pockets full of nuts and candy they would roam from house to house in the community on Christmas Eve. They were the terror of all the children and the neighbor dogs and cats, and their trouble making was not always appreciated in all households. Their unannounced calls were made in a rude manner at times, and many a mad housewife would brush them out with a broom or stick at times. This was fun for the boys, unless at times they were hit a little bit too hard with the broom. The houses they did enter they would reach into their pockets for the nuts and candy they had there, and throw some on the floor for the children to reach for. As soon as the children would reach for them the Belsnickel would hit him over the hand with the whip or stick he was carrying. The children would either cry or look annoyed. Then the Belsnickel would laugh, and throw upon the floor twice as many nuts and candy as were already there, and with a last crack of the whip, this time not on the children's hand, would leave the house to roam on for some more mischief.

I, myself, remember all too well the Belsnickel that came into our house in Tatamy when I was a small child. He had a weird mask on when he got there, and I was really scared. I was just playing with one of my early gotten toys when he got there, and I was speechless. He hit me over the hands once when I went for the candy, and then he handed me a whole handful of candy corn. It was a great experience, and one which I will never forget.

From an article "Christmas Customs of the Perkiomen Valley" by Andrew S. Berky in the *Dutchman* of December 1952.

Two and three generations ago, the most important event for the children in rural farm areas, on Christmas Eve, was the arrival of "Der Belsnickel." This awesome personage was usually garbed in old clothes and it always concealed its face behind some crude mask. In one hand it carried a bag of walnuts or candy, while the other hand maintained a firm grip on a large whip or switch. After this strange individual had ascertained to its satisfaction that the children of the household had behaved quite satisfactory during the past year, it threw the candy and walnuts on the floor. As the eager children grasped for these favors, however, they were often whipped smartly across the knuckles and many of the more timid youngsters were quite frightened by this stern individual. Sooner or later, the strange visitor would depart from the scene and the children were then free to gather the tid-bits left behind. Only the more discerning youngsters saw any resemblance between "Der Belsnickel" and a neighbor or member of the very same family.

This, then, was the general pattern for Christmas Eve, but there were many variations. The recollections of some of the older inhabitants of the Perkiomen Valley vividly reconstruct the scene as it appeared many years ago.

Miss Emma Stauffer of Sassamansville remembered that "Der Belsnickel" came to her mother's store in Corntown for many years. He always wore an old overcoat and covered his head with an old stocking which had holes cut out for his eyes.

Mrs. Mabel S. Berky recalls that as a girl she was always deathly afraid of "Der Belsnickel," who always came to her house with several companions. It was her practice to keep the dining room table between herself and the strange arrivals.

Dr. E. J. Johnson said that "Der Belsnickel" always ran around the outside of their home, making queer noises and tapping at the windows with a stick. He fondly recalled that on one particularly dark Christmas Eve, two men who had come to his home to play "Belsnickel," tripped and fell into an uncovered water trough behind the house.

Mr. Jacob Reiff, formerly of Skippack, declared that his mother was accustomed to dress-up as "Der Belsnickel" on Christmas Eve and "bedarned we didn't know her." Mr. Reiff said it was a common practice for small groups of older people in his area to go around "Belsnickeling" on Christmas Eve. These groups would then receive food and drink at the various farmhouses which they had visited.

Mrs. Geneva S. Reiff, who had no personal recollections of "Der Belsnickel," said that her mother hated Christmas Eve for many years, because the visitor to her home was particularly mean. This "Belsnickel" would put plates of candy in front of the children as they sat around the table, but, as soon as one of the children would try to touch his candy, he would whip them on the arm.

Miss Ella Schultz said that "Der Belsnickel" never frequented her home, but the neighboring children informed her that he came to their house and always covered his face with a handkerchief.

Mrs. Charles Conway remembered that she was several times forced to dance in front of "Der Belsnickel."

Mrs. Rebecca Pfrommer said that "Der Belsnickel" always rattled the windows and doors before making an entrance. He always made the children recite poems and say prayers before they were given candy and little cakes.

CARNIVAL OF HORNS

Pennsylvania came forth, as far as we have been able to determine, with but one indigenous contribution to the American celebration of Christmas: the Philadelphia Carnival of Horns. Too bad—though pandemonium must have reigned in central Philadelphia—that the Quaker City fathers banned this Christmas Eve custom, first in 1868 and finally in 1881.

Philadelphia's Carnival of Horns saw its heyday from about 1860 to 1868. Every youngster within a radius of many miles of the Quaker City foregathered in central Philadelphia on Christmas Eve, armed with every noisemaking instrument imaginable, ranging all the way from a penny horn to a horse fiddle.

Though we commiserate with all the old ladies of the time with weak nerves—and one gathers from the press of the day that their number was not one whit smaller than nowadays—we nonetheless regret that so unique an institution as was the Carnival of Horns should have been outlawed by old-fogeyism.

As far as the literature goes on the subject, the youthful tooters subjected themselves to but one possible physical injury. The Philadelphia *Times* of December 28, 1878, warned all youth: "Small boys, in tooting Christmas horns, should know that the buccinator muscle is often destroyed entirely when strained too heavily." Reader, can you imagine the all-American boy of 1878 worrying about straining his buccinator muscle on Christmas Eve?

The Carnival of Horns was twice banned by the Philadelphia municipal authorities, the first time in 1868. Though the ban was effective for a number of years, the custom revived and continued in full vigor until 1881, when Mayor King dealt it a second and final deathblow.

One can follow the first outlawing of the Carnival of Horns in the Philadelphia *North American*, which chronicled the matter as follows:

[December 28, 1868:] Everybody on Saturday blessed the order that rendered illegal on the previous night the customary din of horns and horse-fiddles. Such a Christmas night was never before known in Philadelphia. [December 27, 1869:] In conformity with the orders issued by Mayor Fox for the prevention of masquerading and the tin horn nuisance, the police made 185 arrests in the several districts. [December 25, 1871:] There were but few horns heard, and none of that rowdyism was displayed on Eighth street which has marred Christmas eve so many years. [And finally December 25, 1872:] Christmas Eve. It has been customary in this city for many years to celebrate Christmas Eve with great hilarity. Eighth and Second streets have heretofore been crowded with masqueraders, particularly the former street, but last night both were remarkably quiet. *Not* a horn was blown on Eighth street, and but comparatively few persons were on the streets.

In four years' time every vestige of the Carnival of Horns had been wiped out. Nonetheless, it somehow revived. The custom, however, as stated was struck a second deathblow, its interdiction by Mayor King in 1881, from which it never revived. The Philadelphia *Saturday Dispatch* of December 25, 1881, reported: "Mayor King's order prohibiting the blowing of horns was not a dead letter last night. The streets were never so quiet upon any previous Christmas eve, not even a toot being heard in any quarter of the city."

We shall now present the literature, chronologically, on Philadelphia's Carnival of Horns. Let each reader, having read the chapter, pass on whether the custom should have been outlawed or not.

From the Philadelphia *Daily Chronicle* of December 26, 1833.
Throughout almost the whole of Tuesday night—Christmas Eve—riot, noise, and uproar prevailed, uncontrolled and uninterrupted in many of our central and most orderly streets. Gangs of boys and young men howled and shouted as if possessed by the demon of disorder. Some of the watchmen occasionally sounded their rattles; but seemed only to add another ingredient to the horrible discord that

murdered sleep. It is undoubtedly in the power of our city police to prevent slumbering citizens from being disturbed by the mad roars of such revelers.

From the Philadelphia *Public Ledger* of December 25, 1844.
Some, more fantastic in their taste, and extravagant in the expression of their pleasure, were tricked out in burlesque garb and whimsical costume, and excited much amusement in the crowd, while musical instruments, from the trumpet to the penny whistle, enlivened the air with sound, if not with melody or harmony.

From the Philadelphia *Public Ledger* of December 25, 1851.
Numerous parties of half-grown boys paraded the streets with horns and other hideous instruments, so that no one could mistake the close proximity to some great holiday.

From the Philadelphia *Evening Bulletin* of December 27, 1853.
On Saturday night a band of young men, dressed in fantastic mock military equipment, paraded through the streets, but conducted themselves quietly.

From the Philadelphia *Evening Bulletin* of December 26, 1854.
Several parties of young fellows made exhibitions of themselves by parading the streets in fantastical costume, and they generally succeeded in convincing judicious spectators that "the fools were not all dead yet."

From the Philadelphia *Evening Bulletin* of December 26, 1855.
Gangs of young fellows paraded, clad in fantastical costumes, and accompanied by Calathumpian bands, which discoursed most discordant strains on penny trumpets, tin horns and iron pans.

From the Philadelphia *Public Ledger* of December 25, 1857.
Boys paraded the streets with drums and fifes; something of the old custom of dressing in fantasticals was revived, and there was no lack of joyousness manifested.

From the Philadelphia *Sunday Dispatch* of December 26, 1858.
The birds, in a more modern signification of the phrase, were "about" early, and staid "about" until it was early again, and they not only sang all night, but they shouted and they yelled, and clattered upon sleigh bells, and they blew tin horns and penny whistles, and they made night hideous with their cries and noise generally.

The quietly disposed, who preferred sleep to roystering, bestowed left-handed blessings upon the roysterers, and endeavored to console themselves with the reflection that these calathumpian doings, rowdy as they are, come in direct descent from the freaks of those Christmas observers of Queen Elizabeth's time, who had their "Lords of Misrule," their "Christmas Princes," and their "Abbots of Unreason" and who kept up the frolic from Christmas eve until the grand culminating point of the festival at "Twelfth Night."

There were a number of persons about on Christmas eve dressed in fantasticals, who attracted attention, not only for their appearance, but in consequence of their rowdy conduct. Among these mummers was a man dressed in female attire, who figured in a crowd in Eighth street, above Market, and who received a mauling from the good-natured crowd which he will remember for a while.

From the Philadelphia *North American* of December 27, 1858.
The gala of Christmas eve was prolonged until a very late hour. People of steady habits, as a general thing, vacated the streets before midnight, or when the places of amusement were closed for the night, and spent the remaining hours in venting drowsy imprecation upon the rollicking multitude outside, who "wouldn't go home until morning," and who made night hideous with Calathumpian doings. Such roystering as was kept up all that night, would have done honor to the good old times of Queen Bess. Everybody appeared to be indulging with an entire abandon. Groups of hobbledehoys with strings of sleigh-bells and fish horns, vented their glee in abominable discords, and goaded the sleepless city into unwilling vigils. People who had remained to take "just one glass more," careened along the streets, indulging in popular but incoherent refrains; while occasionally a policeman would be seen with a wheelbarrow, trundling along some unlucky wight, whose imbibitions had led to helplessness, and that peculiar state of bliss experienced by Mr. Pickwick under similar circumstances. It was not until the east began to purple that the revellers were quieted, and the hush properly belonging to midnight fell upon the Quaker city.

From the Philadelphia *Daily Evening Bulletin* of December 27, 1859.
Troops of young men, in fantastic dresses and masks, marched through the streets ringing bells, blowing tin horns, squeaking upon six-penny trumpets, clattering upon tin kettles and making just as much noise and discord as possible.

From the Philadelphia *North American* of December 25, 1861.
Christmas Eve. The like of it in Eighth street, especially, was never before seen. The carnival commenced at about eight o'clock, and by

LITTLE FOLKS' CHRISTMAS MARCH.

COMPOSED BY T. C. O'KANE.

Noisemaking on Christmas naturally included the children too. Here is the "Little Folks' Christmas March," by Philadelphia composer T. C. O'Kane, from the December 1873 issue of Schoolday Magazine *(Philadelphia).*

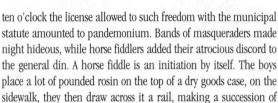

ten o'clock the license allowed to such freedom with the municipal statute amounted to pandemonium. Bands of masqueraders made night hideous, while horse fiddlers added their atrocious discord to the general din. A horse fiddle is an initiation by itself. The boys place a lot of pounded rosin on the top of a dry goods case, on the sidewalk, they then draw across it a rail, making a succession of sounds that take all the honors for the biggest saw filer's shop in the whole country. Troops of youngsters and oldsters, with tin horns, made satanic music all along Eighth and Chestnut streets, while others lacking the horns, yelled "Gideon's band" in a style that

> Cracked the voice of melody
> And broke the legs of time!

To induce infants to slumber must have required paregoric by the bottle full.

Two-thirds of the pedestrians were women, who suffered smashed in bonnets and crushed crinoline to a serious extent. The opposite sex, in many cases, behaved with desperate freedom. The women being unable to resist were wantonly kissed by young men, who ducked their heads after the operation, and squeezed away through the crowd. We saw one lady rolled in the gutter by a fellow whose coat collar the next moment was in the grasp of a policeman.

From the *Moravian* of January 1, 1863.

From our Philadelphia correspondent: The thoroughfares during the day preceding Christmas are thronged with pedestrians; and as evening advances, a dense mass of humanity is packed almost immovably in the more frequented streets; and a perfect saturnalia is held far into the night, and scenes are enacted which are far from creditable to those engaged in them. All kinds of musical instruments are brought into requisition from a penny-trumpet to the noisy boatman's horn; numerous Calathumpian Bands vie with each other to make night hideous; the police meanwhile appearing to be quite oblivious until some serious outbreak compels them to interfere.

From the Philadelphia *Sunday Dispatch* of December 25, 1864.

Last evening was a carnival of tin trumpets, penny whistles and deviltry generally. Crowds of roystering blades passed through the principal street, blowing tin horns and penny whistles, and making night hideous with their discordant music. In some cases the bands of Calathumpians were clad in fantastic dresses, and with smutted faces, wigs, false beards, and ridiculous costumes, generally, they cut a queer figure. Eighth street from Walnut street to Race, was the grand centre to which the tin-horn carnival tended, and the scene there beggared description. The street was jammed with legitimate shoppers and sight-seers; but in addition to them

there were crowds of masqueraders who marched in procession, making, meanwhile, all sorts of diabolical noises. Tin horns of every calibre, and almost all other sorts of noise-producing contrivances, were brought in play, and the racket which prevailed was ear-splitting and distracting. About four-fifths of the persons on the street were armed with squeaking instruments of ear-torture, and the Christmas "Lords of Misrule" and "Abbots of Unreason," so unctiously described by Scott, had their matches last night among the rollickers upon Eighth street.

As usual, there was a good deal of rowdyish pushing and pulling in the crowd, and several young men who were engaged in this work were overhauled by the police and afforded the opportunity of spending the remainder of the night in the station house. Such events as that of last evening tend to damage the business of the streets that are the scenes of them. Decent females dare not venture into the streets for fear of insult, and quiet persons of the sterner sex have no taste for such scenes of confusion. The masquerading and deviltry are fine fun for those who indulge in them, but the game is death to the storekeepers, whose business is ruined by such rough "carryings on."

From the Philadelphia *North American* of December 26, 1864.

Horse-fiddles and horns sent their din upon the stilly air. A club, who style themselves the "Bengal Tigers," marched through Chestnut street and blowed horns the while, making night supernaturally hideous with the uproar.

From the Philadelphia *Press* of December 26, 1864.

On one night in the year the strict authority of the law relaxes with the kindly influence of the time, and Christmas Eve is allowed a night of uproar and riotous mirth. Last Saturday night exhibited this custom, not to such a great extent as we have seen it, yet so full that Eighth and Chestnut streets seemed then pandemoniums and not earthly places. From early dusk, when, by the questionable music of horns, which custom has adopted to make this of all nights hideous, till midnight passed and ushered in the happy Christmas Day . . . the braying of trumpets and horns, all combined to make the scene a vast Babel.

From the Philadelphia *Sunday Dispatch* of January 1, 1865.

About Horns. We mean tin horns, such horns as made night hideous on Christmas eve, and that kept up an incessant squawking during several days and nights that immediately followed that festival. Well, these horns became a first-class nuisance, and last week Mayor Henry, commiserating the condition of the people who have weak nerves, or who are sick, or who think they have a right to a reasonable share of the quiet they pay for in the way of police taxes, issued an order to his Knights of the Star to put a stop to the tooting, and to hold all offenders for fine or such other pains and penalties as they may have incurred.

There is an old ordinance against the blowing of horns, which was adopted in 1830. It was the result of the indulgence of the musical tastes of a peripatetic vendor of carbon, who was familiarly known as "Jemmy Charcoal." This smut-faced and smock-frocked Gabriel used to go about town armed with a tin horn about ten feet in length. He would sing improvised verses appropriate to the trades followed in the stores he was passing with his wagon. When Jemmy ran out of rhymes he would resort to his horn, and he would blow blasts thereon that would have caused him to be considered a first-class risk in any office where lives were to be insured against diseases of the lungs.

Jemmy had imitators in the horn line, and the music they made was either so bad, or the appreciation of the city fathers was so poor, that the horn music was voted a nuisance, and an ordinance was passed making the amusement liable to fine, and if repeated too often subjecting the offender to imprisonment. Jemmy Charcoal defied the law, and he brought up in limbo; the other hawkers of the Jersey staple, taking the hint, dropped their long horns and took to hand-bells, and thus arose the practice of heralding the approach of a coal wagon by the clattering of a bell. It is under the horn ordinance begat of Jemmy Charcoal that Mayor Henry and Chief Ruggles now utter threats and denunciations against horn-blowers in general and Christmas masquerading calathumpians in particular.

From the Philadelphia *North American* of December 25, 1866.

Last evening presented one of those scenes that Christmas eve alone presents. The general jollity, indeed, was of a character that on no other night would be tolerated. Not that the scene was one of disorder, but that the boisterous jocundity manifested by the people in the streets was such as on any other occasion would have been out of place. Calathumpian bands and masqueraders were moving about during the whole evening, and the clock struck twelve considerably before the streets were quiet.

From the Philadelphia *Press* of December 25, 1867.

At about seven P.M. the usual gay party who seek Chestnut street made their appearance, and tested their lungs on tin horns, penny whistles, and all manner of wind instruments calculated to create discord. The masqueraders were also out in full feather, and all the costumes of Indians that could be obtained were brought into requisition. The police closed their ears to noise, and did not interfere with the capers of those disposed to enjoy themselves, unless they proceeded too far beyond the bound of propriety.

From the Lebanon *Courier* of January 9, 1868.

From a Philadelphia correspondent: We left the billiard players and wended our way towards Eighth Street. Here it seemed as if all Pandemonianism had been let loose. Parties of hideous looking "belsnickles" now paraded the street, many of whom had tin horns which they were continually blowing, making a noise like the braying of a thousand country brass-bands! These were mostly boys dressed in various costumes, some, like Indians with large rings in their ears and noses, "war paint" on their cheeks, and tomahawks in their hands; others had their faces blackened, while a red shirt, white trousers and a straw hat composed their dresses; others again wore hideous masks upon their faces, and immense hats on their heads. Still others had turned their coats and pantaloons inside out, while most of them had instruments with which to make noise. Some were beating drums, others carried pans or old kettles, others again played the bones, while many were blowing trumpets, and those who had none of these made use of their lungs and yelled as though for dear life. One party were singing "Marching through Georgia," and these were met by another who did their utmost to let the admiring multitude know that they had made up their minds "not to go home till morning!" Though everybody was running against everybody and appeared to be in everybody's way, everybody seemed to be in an excellent humor, and was smiling and laughing. A great portion of the fair ones in the crowd had been wise and left their hoop-skirts at home, and were thus enabled to pass through the throng with greater facility. We elbowed our way along until we were heartily tired and then sought our room. As I closed my eyes I still heard the noise in the distance, and in my dreams I saw repeated the scenes which I witnessed on Eighth Street.

From the Philadelphia *Sunday Dispatch* of December 30, 1877.

The Tin-Horn Fiends. Does anybody know who introduced the custom of blowing tin-horns to celebrate Christmas, New Year day, and the Fourth of July? Is there any one living who can trace this nuisance to its origin, and point to the man who first instructed the Small Boy in the art of making life miserable for days at a time, at certain seasons in the year? There are a few hundred thousand citizens of this land who would like to see the tin-horn inventor about now, and congratulate him upon the successful manner in which he has enlisted the youth of America in his cause— which if results are any consequence, is to drive people with nerves to the verge of distraction of holidays.

There is a legend, we believe, that his Satanic Majesty was seen in a blind alley, one Saturday morning, selling a Small Boy with a dirty face a tin-horn, and instructing him how to get the most discord out of it. But as this has never been traced to any authentic source, it is only believed by crusty old bachelors, and unmarried ladies with a weakness for cats and tea. The rest of the world—or rather that part of it which thinks of the matter at all—believes that the tin-horn is the invention of some hater of his fellow-men, who put it in the hands of the Small Boy to torment Mankind with. That his experiment has been a grand success, nobody can doubt.

It is wonderful with what satisfaction the horn-blowers perform their part in the "drama of life." Their work is a "labor of love" to them. If half the wind and strength they waste through the horns could be utilized in some useful labor, after two Christmases and a Fourth of July they could retire with a fortune. It takes about a cubic foot of breath every twenty seconds to properly manipulate a tin-horn, and we know some boys who have been engaged in this occupation on an average of eight hours a day for ten days. That would make fourteen thousand four hundred cubic feet of air these youngsters have wasted through tin-horns this Christmas. Double this amount, and add five days blowing for the Fourth of July, and you will see that thirty-six thousand cubic feet of breath has been blown into the horns. Now we leave it to any fair-minded man if this amount of vitality, expended in any useful way, would not be sufficient to earn a fortune. But you could no more make the Small Boy believe this than you could use Cleopatra's Needle for a toothpick. He would blow his interior mechanism through the horn before he would listen to you, and ten chances to one, when you tried to explain the matter to him, he would call his "crowd," and you would be tooted home by the gang. There is only one kind of argument that has any weight with the tin-horn fiends, and that is a policeman with a club. Even this sometimes fails to convince the tooter that it is not a duty he owes to himself to toot.

There is a wonderful similarity between the Small Boy and his horn. Both of them are erratic, and both are governed by no known laws. It makes no difference who the Small Boy's father and mother are, nor what influences are brought to bear upon him; he is liable to fly off at a tangent at any time without a minute's warning. The tin-horn is the same way. Nobody knows what is going to be the effect of a blast blown on it. It may resemble the shriek of a locomotive, or the bray of an ass; or it may make a sound of which the civilized world had before been in blissful ignorance. The most expert tooters themselves have no more idea of what particular discord a new horn is going to make than you have of who will be our next President. But no matter what new combination of ear-splitting sounds may be produced, the performer is happy; and the worse the discord, the happier is the Small Boy.

The horn-fiends wander about the streets alone or in gangs; and the very houses seem to tremble when they blow, while the people put their hands to their ears and exclaim: "Oh! those horrid horns!" if the hearers be ladies. If they be of the opposite sex, the exclamation is made more forcible by the substitution of another word for "horrid." But this has no effect upon the blowers. They toot as vigorously as ever, as they go along gaily on their way, waking babies, and causing old men who never swore before to display a proficiency in the pastime which they never dreamed they possessed. For ten days they maintain their supremacy, and the joy of Christmas is marred. Then the parents of the horn-blowers spank them, and take away the horns; the streetcars and wagons run over others; the policeman's argument prevails with the rest, and the city is again happy.

From the Philadelphia *Times* of December 25, 1878. Masqueraders were wonderfully new and woefully subdued. The feathered Indians were too cold to shriek, and the wind offered no inducements even to the silliest to prance through the streets acting the clown to life in a pair of last summer's linen pants and the customary bells and other "fixins" of course.

From the Philadelphia *Press* of December 25, 1879. The time-honored custom of horn blowing was indulged in to the full, with as much zest as ever, and about every other person on the street had one either at his lips, in his hand or concealed somewhere about him. A quiet, staid father going home with his pockets full of bonbons for the little ones would suddenly hear alongside of him, the sound going through him like an electric current, an unearthly squeak from one of these abominations, and as he turned to see the author of the music, would be saluted on the other side with half a dozen more, each giving out a different sound and none of them having the slightest relation to musical tone. The peculiarity about the horn-blowers was that they never played this trick except where they noticed a party was annoyed by the deafening din. The toot of the torturing implement was not only heard down town; it spread all the way out to the suburbs the boys taking it up where the men left off. At times eighteen or twenty "mummers" dressed in fantastic costumes would come sweeping through the crowd in soldier order, each armed with a horn, his cheeks puffed out like a balloon, and with the full force of his lungs each and every one would give a solid blow, lasting sometimes for squares, as fast as they could catch their breath. As a rule these parties were given as much room as possible, for the passer-by could not depend very far on the police as a guard against a blast close to his ear; but the people as a rule have become so used to the recurrence of this practice, heathenish as it is, that the great majority do not seem to mind it; to those of weak nerves, however, it is especially distasteful and harrowing.

Masquerade troupers were fewer than usual, and those who did appear in carnival costumes were generally going it on their own hook, and there was a countless variety of them. One squad from down town was made up of parties clad as Indians, and the unearthly yells which they gave vent to occasionally would have been no discredit to the wild Pintos, and the costumes they wore would have been a delight in their dirty appearance to Mexican Diggers. Scattered about, the pedestrians would come upon a chap clad in red and white bunting with some stars in the middle of his back, called by sufferance "young America," and clowns with piebald suits, harlequins and columbines were making themselves ridiculous along with the great crowd of nondescripts always to be found on Christmas eve. With the exception of pushing and crowding and the blowing of the horns (a nuisance in itself which all efforts have failed to suppress) there was no disorder on the streets which called for police interference.

From the Philadelphia *Times* of December 25, 1879. There was no end to the noise in the streets last night. Ten thousand tin horns with ten thousand boys behind them broke loose as early as 6 o'clock in the evening and swooped down on the ears of inoffensive and law-abiding citizens to a degree that was maddening. At 10 o'clock the din and uproar had attained the fury of a pestilence and, being reinforced by old tin kettles and horse-fiddles and bells, peace fled utterly from the streets and the very walls of substantial buildings seemed to shudder. Boys, in the interest of horn-dealers, paced the crowded sidewalks with basketsful of horns strung from their necks, loudly proclaiming: "A few more left yet—only five cents!" and found buyers right and left. These buyers would instantly rush off to join the already numerous band of horn-blowers. No necessity of any introduction; the horn was a bond of union between man and man and boy and boy. Anybody who had a horn had the protection of the whole family of horn-blowers. The police recognized them and merely looked in a noncommittal sort of way as the horn-blowers rushed past as though they would intimate that they might keep the business up all night for all they cared, so they stirred up no fights. These horns were of every conceivable description. Everyone seemed to have a different tone. The noise increased as night advanced. There was nothing it could be compared to. "Oh! my glory!" exclaimed honest servant girls as the chorus would be thrust into their ears on Eighth and Chestnut streets while they were innocently taking in the shop windows. Grown men as well as boys were blowing the horns. Girls, too, on the arms of their boys were doing their share in the same direction. A ceaseless din and racket; an awful prolonged groan; a terrible ear-swelling, blood-curdling shriek—those were the kinds of sounds that entered into the general uproar and made it impossible for the throng of promenaders to hear their own voices.

The horn-blowing would rise and fall, grow faint and then burst out at its loudest, like the noise of breakers or the roaring and

changing of the wind. Sometimes it would stop utterly, but only for a moment. Just as the afflicted citizens would be congratulating themselves that all was over, there would be a sudden toot! That would be the signal. Then, like the outburst of a volcano would come the rest, a great avalanche of hideous sounds that would seem to drive everything else to the remotest corners of the earth and leave them in possession forever. "Too-oo-oo-oot-oot-oot!" "Squee-ee-ee-eek-eek!" "Squi-e-u! Squi-e-u!" These may give a faint idea of what it was like. Imagine, amid this, yells and shouts and exclamations from platoons of excited individuals moving up and down the sidewalks. The city was like an immense bee-hive. The horns were the bees. Till a late hour in the night the racket was kept up. The ears of the remotest corner of the city were pierced by them. People who thought themselves secure and retired and beyond the reach of the street-cars and steam-cars' racket were driven nearly crazy by the awful sounds that penetrated their homes. "It's terrible!" "It's awful!" "Isn't that deafening?" "Gracious Heavens, this is fearful!" These were some of the exclamations that burst from agonized pedestrians' lips as, wedged in by horns, they turned in every direction to escape, only to be confronted by cow-bells and horse-fiddles. Where horns were lacking, everything that would make a noise appeared to be in league with the horns, and altogether they succeeded in entertaining Christmas Eve with every bit as much stir and bustle as the city when it entertained Grant.

From the Philadelphia *Press* of December 25, 1880. As usual, both sexes participated in the noise, and the girls apparently enjoyed it more than the boys. There were a few masqueraders here and there, but it was evident that most of the revelers were waiting until a week later. Eight boys, dressed in a costume of reversed coats and decorated trousers and having the words "The Big Eight" painted on their backs, scattered themselves among the crowd when the theatres let out and a mock band paraded, creating pandemonium along their route.

From the Philadelphia *Press* of December 25, 1880. Urchins armed with hoarse-sounding tin horns vied with each other in making the air resound with a confused din, which forever rose above the merry laugh of the jostling throng. About 10:30 o'clock the masqueraders began to appear, and by 11 o'clock crowds of small boys wearing grotesque masks and young men in character costumes paraded through the streets blowing tin horns in a chorus to the sound of the drum. The sight of a score or more of young men thus arrayed recalled to mind side-scenes of the Mardi Gras and provoked unlimited amusement to all who witnessed it. The streets were crowded and the din of the tin horns was hideous until midnight, at which hour many returned home to hang up their stockings before old Santa Claus appeared.

From the Philadelphia *Inquirer* of December 26, 1881. Christmas eve was the quietest known for many a year on the principal thoroughfares. The order interdicting the tin horn was rigidly enforced, or would have been had there been any provocation. It seemed to be a foregone conclusion among the boys, old and young, who usually need a tin horn to enliven their enjoyment of the festival, that they would get into trouble by such indulgence, and they refrained accordingly. During Saturday evening a score or more of young men bearing huge tin horns over their shoulders, each horn decked with crepe, trudged along Chestnut, Eighth and other streets headed by a drum major, whose occupation was gone, for not a single toot came from a single horn. A number of young men, however, managed to mystify and annoy the officers on Chestnut street by blowing a little device which could be readily concealed in their vest pockets, but which produced a sound not unlike the ordinary tin-horn.

From the Philadelphia *Inquirer* of December 25, 1883. The horn blowing nuisance was effectually suppressed last night. In a lengthy stroll of the streets a diligent reporter found only one case. A party of young men walked almost the length of South street, blowing small horns and otherwise delighting their own childish natures. No arrests were made for this species of disorderly conduct, for none was necessary. There was some masquerading, but it was not a conspicuous feature of the evening.

From the Philadelphia *Press* of December 25, 1885. The old-time noises of Christmas Eve, when tin horns were blown and Calathumpian bands filled the street with discord, were hushed by order of the Mayor. It was only four or five years ago when the street revels of that joyous time became so excessively boisterous as to cause disorder and spoil the enjoyment of those more placidly inclined. Mayor King was the first to forbid the bands, the masqueraders, and horn-blowing, and they have never since been permitted.

OF COOKIES AND
COOKIE CUTTERS

No phase of Pennsylvania folk culture is as deserving of scholarly attention as is its regional cookery. There have been cookbooks galore, particularly of recent years on the Pennsylvania Dutch cuisine; Pennsylvania newspapers, the bigger ones, all have food editors who run daily cooking columns; radio and television stations feature cooking demonstrations, morning upon morning. The concern, however, of each single one of these media is with recipes and little else.

Now recipes, needless to say, are but a small part of an area's culinary culture. It would seem to this observer at least that the time has come to approach cookery on an overall folk-cultural basis. And no more interesting beginning could possibly be made than on the subject of Christmas cookies and cookie cutters.

What of Christmas cookies in Pennsylvania?

Since the Pennsylvania Quakers and Scotch-Irish to a man were staunchly opposed to celebrating Christmas, early that is, it becomes immediately obvious that Christmas cookies were originally the concern of the only other numerically important element in the commonwealth: the Pennsylvania Dutch. "Concern" is a mild word though to use in connection with Christmas cookie baking in Dutch Pennsylvania; a much more appropriate terminology would be "orgy," for this is exactly what cookie baking has always been—an orgy—in the valleys of the Lehigh, the Schuylkill, and the Susquehanna.

In the days of Woodstove Christmases cookie baking started literally weeks before Christmas in the Dutch Country. The tin cutters—in the form of every animal almost in Noah's Ark—were brought down from the attic, where they had been stored for safekeeping since the Christmas of a year before. Because of their intriguing shapes, scrubbing them prior to their use was never considered a chore by youthful Keturah or Maggie, who otherwise did not take too kindly to the threefold daily duty of dishwashing.

Quantity was always the very keystone of Christmas cookie baking in Pennsylvania. "By-the-washbasket-full"—this was always the standard of measurement, in Dutch Pennsylvania. A grandmother complained to the author a Christmas or two ago: "People don't bake Christmas cookies like they used to. When I was a child we baked several washbaskets full. And people don't bake the dunking kind either anymore, as we did. Why ours used to be great big cookies, perhaps six or eight inches across the middle. Today people bake apees and sand tarts, but such small ones!" If, by some miracle, our grandfathers of old should be able to return to earth for a brief Christmas stay, how they would despise our wafer-thin butter cookies of today!

A note of explanation is in order why mothers in Dutch Pennsylvania baked Christmas cookies in such profusion. The answer is plainly, they needed them and for many purposes. You needed many, many, to begin with, to appease the appetite of some forty or fifty Belsnickels who came a-begging Christmas Eve; some went into the basket mother prepared for the poor, old widow, who lived down the road a piece; then you needed a good many dozen to trim the Christmas tree with; the children took some of the nicest to display in the windows of the front room facing the road to serve as a sort of Christmas greeting to passersby; and mother, of course, simply had to dole out two, three dozen to the lady from across the valley who lent her a couple of animals she didn't happen to have among her own cookie-cutter flock, a deer or an exotic elephant, perhaps.

From among our Pennsylvania Christmas cookie literature, we have culled a half dozen or so of the best pieces, which follow.

From a "Christmas-Eve Reverie" by N. A. M. E. in the *Lutheran and Missionary* of December 22, 1864. Standing upon tip-toe, we peep over the broad cake-board and, with real wonder, watch to see how mother compels dogs, horses, long-eared rabbits, armless babies, and great and little hearts come, as though by magic, from out of the tin moulders.

From an article "Folk-Lore of Lebanon County" by Dr. Ezra Grumbine in the *Lebanon County Historical Society Proceedings*, volume 3, 1905, page 256.

And there were cakes, too—Christmas cakes, *par excellence*. The Christmas cake was a cake *sui generis*. It was a cookie cut in the shape of birds of the air, beasts of the field and fish of the sea. It was of two kinds, a dark and a light. The darker kind contained molasses as the sweetening ingredient; the lighter variety, white sugar. When the cakes were to be especially fine they were ornamented in white with figures resembling commas and semicolons and interrogation marks and other hieroglyphics made with starch water by means of a pointed stick. On Christmas morning it was the custom of the children to display them in rows in the windows of the living room.

From an article "Descriptive and Historical Memorials of Heilman Dale" by Rev. U. Henry Heilman in the *Lebanon County Historical Society Proceedings*, volume 4, 1906, page 247.

During the Christmas . . . holidays the cheery housewives were not satisfied with less than a bushel or more of the best molasses and sugar cakes, some of them being moulded in the form of horses, rabbits, stars, dolls, stags and others, and these with apples or cider were freely offered to every caller, whether friend or foe. There is no baker living who can make cakes to equal those made by somebody's grandmother. They were unusually big, had a raisin set into the centre, and were most eagerly sought by her children, grandchildren, and others in the neighborhood. These cakes were suggested by a loving heart, distributed by willing hands and accompanied with a smiling countenance, and they were so toothsome because they had been sweetened with a gentle spirit of the maker. There always was much hurrying to and fro on Christmas mornings to secure some of grandmother's famous cakes, and the child esteemed itself very happy whose feet could outrun those of the other children. They were coveted not only by the children, but were equally sought and enjoyed by the elders.

From an article "How Christmas Was Observed in Olden Times" in the Reading *Weekly Eagle* of December 21, 1913.

A woman over eighty years old, said: "When I was a girl, living at Kutztown, a large party assembled at the home of a friend on Christ-mas eve, when the Belsnickel suddenly appeared with a basket full of molasses cakes, each baked in the shape of a baby, and he laid a cake on the lap of every woman. This caused great merriment."

A woman who lived in Orwigsburg when she was a little girl said: "I recollect that fifty years and longer ago my mother had many tin cake cutters and baked cakes representing babies, horses, pigs, rabbits and birds, and these were covered with icing and ornamented with sugar of different colors. Neighbors loaned cake cutters to each other before Christmas and gave cakes in return for their use."

LEB-CAKES

In colonial and post-colonial days, when all rural baking was carried on in outdoor bake ovens, there was not the great variety of Christmas cookies we associate with the Christmas holidays nowadays.

Extant accounts which mention early Christmas cookies—and their number is slim indeed—do not reach farther back than about 1830. In a manuscript in the Berks County Historical Society, the reminiscences of an old wandering umbrella mender, we read: "About the only Christmas cake there was around in those days was 'Leb-Kucha.'" The old man continued:

I know yet well the time when I first heard of the woman who baked two kinds of Christmas cookies. My, but all the people did talk about such a big notioned people. They said such a thing must make almost any man break up. Then when red, yellow and blue colored sugar first came out and the women did begin to put that on their cookies the children did think it was wonderful.

The German-language York *Gazette* of June 10, 1796, has a humorous entry concerning a female character called "Big Mary" and her rapacious appetite for leb-cakes:

Today was the pleasant day of our local fair. Many lovely things were to be seen and there were enough leb-cakes in the beginning. Annagreth, Lovis, Lisle and Annelle had Stophel, Hans and enough other beaus. Breeches could be seen on all corners of the streets. A marvel that excelled all others was that of Big Mary, who sat on her lover's lap on a butcher block in the market and ate 39 leb-cakes. She bit through seven leb-cakes all at one time in a wager for a kiss from her sweetheart.

Leb-cake is the partly anglicized localism in the Dutch Country for *lebkucha*, which appears as gingerbread in translation, though it should be observed

ROBACKER COLLECTION

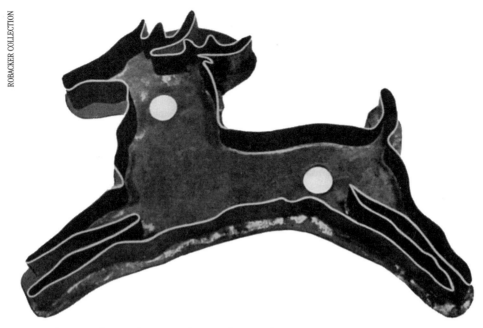

A foot-long reindeer cookie cutter. Sizes as large as this are rare.

that our old-time Pennsylvania recipes for leb-cakes seldom call for ginger.

Popular in the opening decades of the nineteenth century, all over Dutch Pennsylvania, were gingerbread horses, made of extremely large tin cookie cutters.

There are two interesting allusions to the gingerbread horses in early sources. The earlier is a humorous entry in the York *Gazette* of December 31, 1822, in which a Society of Bachelors published the minutes of their society:

It was resolved that a committee of two be appointed, to return the large Gingercake Horse, presented by Miss Clara Snubnose, and inform her that whilst the society appreciate her motives, they condemn the practice of Baking Cakes, in commemoration of the Birth of Our Saviour, and henceforth would recommend the women, to appropriate the money so insipidly expended to some charitable purposes.

The other account is a description of Second Christmas Day in Abraham Ritter's *History of the Moravian Church in Philadelphia* (Philadelphia, 1857), pages 131–132:

Two male and two female chapel servants, bearing trays of half-pint cups, evaporating savory fumes of chocolate, and two baskets, redolent of the odor of light cake, were soon relieved of their burden as they kissed the lips that greeted their issues, whilst unplied hands awaited the return of the palatable supply of their share. This course was followed by a gingerbread horse, or infant-shaped, to each child, and with it a book, of some eight or ten pages, with mottled pasteboard cover, not a cheap book, but of duodecimo size, containing hymns touching the Nativity, and after this a printed half sheet, with a special hymn or ode, to be said, or sung, on the next ensuing Christmas.

The *Independent Balance*, a humorous Philadelphia weekly, in the issue of December 6, 1820, gives the "experiences" of a New England lad in the Quaker City. The youth is made to say: "Wonder they don't have more gingerbread here—'spose they like sourcrout better."

In some undated newspaper clippings at the Lancaster County Historical Society there appear the reminiscences of Susquehanna rafters, written up by someone who signed his name Grantellus. The writer observed:

We have known some of them who would work hard from "early dawn to dewy eve," earning perhaps a dollar, and then sitting down in an oyster shop, and eating nearly the whole amount out in oysters, peanuts and gingerbread.

Christmas cookie cutters from the Robacker Collection.

The Lancaster *Journal* of April 12, 1822, in a letter from Harrisburg, remarked: "In one corner you might see a crowd of sages closely wedged around a Huckster's table, bargaining for belly-guts and gingerbread." Among the goodies on Battalion Day, the Sunbury *American* of May 15, 1847, wrote: "Besides, there will be plenty of extras on the ground, in the shape of pretty girls, ginger cakes, small beer, peanuts, and molasses candy."

Quaker Phebe Earle Gibbons in her article "Pennsylvania Dutch" in the *Atlantic Monthly* for October 1869 describes how her little son came home from school, where he learned to pronounce words the Dutchified way. "For a while I would hear him repeating such expressions as . . . 'I don't like chinchpread.'"

In 1878 the New York *Tribune,* in an article on the Dutch Country, described a couple of rural lovers coming to town: "It is a common sight to see a young and timid Hans escorting a beautiful Gretchen to one of the stands where slabs of gingerbread can be had for a cent and home-made beer for two cents a glass."

C. H. Leeds in his *Old Home Week Letters* (Carlisle, 1909), page 23, reminisced:

A few steps farther east was the home of old Aunt Nancy McNaughton (pronounced McNattan), who kept her little shop where you could buy the best home-made beer, mead and old-fashioned gingerbread. It was a daily afternoon occurrence of us boys, on our way down to the Garrison "swimming hole" to stop there and frequently buy her out.

In fine, we wish to note the oft-repeated anecdote of the penurious Dutchman who one day came to New Holland. He had his two young sons with him, aged seven and nine respectively. The youths, seeing some delectable leb-cakes, pestered their father until he agreed to buy them each one. Now they sold for a penny apiece. As the miserly farmer drew two pennies from the bottom of his money bag, he remarked: "Des reisst avver ins geld." (This is going to eat a hole in my bank account.)

APEES

Among cookies, the apee used to be *the* Christmas cookie in large parts of Pennsylvania. In Woodstove Christmas days, that is. It is still a favorite in families that hold to the old ways.

The word *apees* has been puzzling scholars ever since 1830, in which year J. F. Watson wrote in his *Annals of Philadelphia:*

Philadelphia has long enjoyed the reputation of a peculiar cake called the apee. . . . Ann Page, still alive . . . first made them, many years ago, under the common name of cakes. . . . On her cakes she impressed the letters A.P., the letters of her name.

The earliest literary reference to apees is in the June 29, 1844, issue of the Reading *Berks and Schuylkill Journal.* A local poet indited a poetic picnic wish, containing these lines:

We wish to all, nor rain, nor burning sun,
But fleecy clouds, and cool refreshing breezes
And may two thousand pair of sparkling eyes
Grow brighter, at the sight of mighty stores
Of pound cake, jumbles, apees, gingerbread.

In Dr. Preston A. Barba's "Eck" in the Allentown *Morning Call* of December 12, 1936, Raymond E. Kiebach, a Berks Countian, presented this query:

I wonder whether you or some reader of the "Eck" could give me the correct name for the "Apiece" cookies that are still baked in many of the Pennsylvania German households. This cooky is made of a sweet dough, rolled out, and sprinkled with sugar. It can not be classed as a particular dainty, but to youngsters with an ever unsatisfied appetite it proved very welcome. We nicknamed it "hardtack" but have never heard any other name for it from the usual "die Apiece Kuche" of my grandmother. The cake is most excellent for dunking with coffee.

Dr. Barba answered the Kiebach query as follows:

Some of our readers may be able to shed more light upon this somewhat obscure word for the well-known Christmas cookies. The word is variously spelled. It has been pointed out that the name is really "A.P.'s," named for a beautiful Baltimore belle by the name of Ann Page. But it seems to be a cooky identified largely with the Pennsylvania Germans. The fact that we find it spelled in some of the old Pennsylvania German cookbooks as "Apiece" leads us to concur with Professor Lambert. In his *Dictionary of the Non-English Words of the Pennsylvania German Dialect*, the word is spelled EEPIES, and defined as a "cooky, Christmas cooky (frequently cut in the shape of animals)." He deduces it from the French EPICE (pain d'epice, gingerbread).

Although the cooky known by that name among the Pennsylvania Germans does not contain spices, it is not unlikely that it was a general name for cookies in earlier times and only later given a specific application.

In the October–December 1953 *Historical Review of Berks County*, Professor Paul Schach of the German Department of the University of Nebraska discusses apees in his article entitled "The Pennsylvania-German Contribution to the American Vocabulary." Professor Schach writes:

Since the excellence of the Pennsylvania-German cuisine has become almost legendary, we would expect at least some food names to be adopted along with the dishes themselves. Among those listed in the *Dictionary of Americanisms* we find *Apee (cake)*. . . .

The word *apee cake* is a partial translation of Pennsylvania-German *eepikuche*, which in turn is derived from French *pain d'epice*. The French word, which means literally "spice bread" or "spice loaf," is generally explained as "gingerbread" in bilingual dictionaries. Actually, however, this word denotes a popular honey-flavored cake for which Dijon is as famous as Nürnberg is for *Lebkuchen*. Lambert lists only the form *eepies* (with correct etymology) in the sense of "cooky, Christmas cooky (frequently cut in the shape of animals)." How did this French word get to Pennsylvania via Germany? Unable to find the word in any German dialect dictionary, I recently wrote to Professor Walter Mitzka of the University of Marburg for information. Professor Mitzka, director of the *Deutscher Sprachatlas* and editor of the *Zeitschrift für Mundartforschung*, forwarded my request to Professor Ernst Christmann of Kaiserslautern, who is one of the greatest living experts on the Palatine dialects. Professor Christmann assured me that the word *eepikuche* is not known in the Palatinate, and requested information regarding its appearance and manner of preparation. The French origin of the word plus its present geographic spread permit one to hazard the guess that the word was brought to America by the German-speaking Huguenots; for while *eepikuche* and its English form *apee cake* are current in and around the Oley Valley, they seem to be virtually unknown in the western part of the Pennsylvania-German area. Indeed, these dry breakfast cakes similar to shoefly cakes are there called *Dutch Cakes*. It might be added here that popular etymology has connected this French-German-American word with *A.P. (Ann Page) cakes!*

Why these scholars failed to cast a single look at the overall Pennsylvania culinary culture before launching upon the wide sea of speculation is not easily apparent. The slightest checking of Pennsylvania cookbooks on their part would have shown that the recipe for apees was circulated in fifty-six printings by 1856 in the Leslie cookbooks, alone.

The earliest use of the apees recipe is from Eliza Leslie's *Seventy-five receipts for pastry, cakes, and sweetmeats*, printed in Boston in 1828. The apee recipe appears also in the many printings of Miss Leslie's *Directions for Cookery*, the first edition of which appeared in Philadelphia in 1837.

1828 Leslie Apees Recipe

A pound of flour, sifted.

Half a pound of butter.

A glass of wine, and a tablespoonful of rose-water, mixed.

Half a pound of powdered white sugar.

A nutmeg, grated.

A teaspoonful of beaten cinnamon and mace.

Three tablespoonfuls of caraway seeds.

Sift the flour into a broad pan, and cut up the butter in it. Add the caraways, sugar, and spices, and pour in the liquor by degrees, mixing it well with a knife. If the liquor is not sufficient to wet it thoroughly, add enough of cold water to make it a stiff dough. Spread some flour on your paste-board, take out the dough, and knead it very well with your hands. Put it into small pieces, and knead each separately, then put them all together, and knead the whole in one lump. Roll it out in a sheet about a quarter of an inch thick. Cut it out in round cakes, with the edge of a tumbler, or a tin of that size. Butter an iron pan, and lay the cakes in it, not too close together. Bake them a few minutes in a moderate oven, till they are very slightly coloured, but not brown. If too much baked, they will entirely lose their flavour. Do not roll them out too thin.

Lest any Pennsylvania reader become suspicious that this apees recipe might not be the forerunner of the one currently in use in the Dutch Country—because of all the spices included—we append the following bit of instruction in the introduction of the Leslie cookbooks:

Where economy is expedient, a portion of the seasoning, that is, the spice, wine, brandy, rose-water, essence of lemon, etc., may be omitted without any essential deviation of flavour, or difference of appearance; retaining, however, the given proportions of eggs, butter, sugar, and flour.

Peterson's Magazine of March 1858 contains a recipe for apees, as does *Godey's Lady's Book* for January 1859. Another Pennsylvania magazine, the *Caterer* of June 1886, page 319, has two recipes for "A.P.'s."

SAND TARTS

Without a doubt, apees and sand tarts were the favorite cookies in the time of Woodstove Christmases. They are still great favorites, though, substantively, they have undergone a great change: grandfather liked his quite thick—for dunking, while we today prefer ours wafer thin.

The earliest documentation we have been able to locate for the use of the word "sand tart" is in the Philadelphia *Evening Bulletin* of December 24, 1858.

A description of Christmas in Dutch Pennsylvania in the Philadelphia *Inquirer* of December 26, 1897, mentions sand tarts:

A great custom among all classes of the people is the laying in of profuse quantities of a cake indigenous to the German settlements and adopted by their neighbors known as "sand tarts." They are very rich in composition. They get their name from a top glazing of raw egg, white and yolk mixed, over which is sprinkled a little granulated sugar and one or two kernels of hickory nuts carefully adjusted when the cakes are spread out to dry. The most humble of the people feel as if they were not doing honor to the religious festival if they did not turn out at least a "wash basket" full of "sand tarts."

Mrs. Anna B. Scott's cooking column in the Philadelphia *North American* of December 19, 1920, turned the attention of Quaker City women to sand tarts:

Those with a penchant for finding symbolic meaning behind every folk art object, whether cooky cutter bird or A-B-C book distelfinks, are saying the name "sand tart" was early "sand hearts" and earlier still "saint's heart."

DOUGHNUTS

In early Pennsylvania the doughnut was considered, along with gingerbread and mince pie, as a Christmas specialty. In the reminiscences of an 85-year-old Berks Countian, recorded in the Reading *Weekly Eagle* of December 28, 1895, we learn that school children in 1815 carried a Christmas cake in their lunch boxes, which—to use the words of the old man—"we now call doughnuts."

An unusual early cookie cutter in the Geesey Collection.

William J. Buck in his *History of Bucks County*, published in 1855, writes: "Doughnuts were considered such a rarity as to be eaten only on Christmas."

Doughnuts are mentioned in connection with the Moravian celebration of Christmas in an article in the Easton *Daily Express* of November 27, 1855:

[The inhabitants of Bethlehem] are chiefly noted for their great taste they display in arranging Christmas Trees, for the skill they display in baking a cake called Doughnuts, which they serve up with coffee to make a dish they name *bruckel*.

The Philadelphia correspondent of the Pottsville *Miners' Journal* in the issue of December 31, 1853, in describing the Quaker City Christmas, speaks of "huge piles of gingerbread and dough-nuts."

In York County the name of the doughnut served at Christmas time was "krentzlen" or "grenslin." The Wrightsville *York County Star* of December 31, 1857, alludes to this cake: "The way the juveniles made the sweetmeats, gingerbread, krentzlen, &c. fly, was not

only a caution to the old folks, but must have been a great discomfort to the stomach of the young ones." In February 1953, the author interviewed a Mrs. William E. Werner of Jefferson, York County, then an 81-year-old woman. She mentioned that thereabouts Shrove Tuesday *fasnachts* were always raised. The unraised "fat cakes" she said were locally called *grenslin*.

Christmas doughnuts in early Pennsylvania were probably what we call crullers today. In shape they were likely anything but round. Prof. J. A. Grier in an article on early holiday observances in the Pittsburgh *Workman* of December 21, 1893, writes of "a gingerbread elephant or a doughnut rabbit . . . sometimes there were doughnut men, who looked for all the world like star fish."

DUTCH CAKE

From the 1830s to the time of the Civil War, Philadelphia and Norristown confectioners advertised three kinds of cakes at Christmas time: fruit cakes, plum cakes, and Dutch cakes. The cake bakers tried to outdo one another in making the largest cake each year, sometimes advertising fruit cakes as large as a "wagon wheel" or weighing "over a thousand" pounds. Stock of the trade were valuables baked into the mammoth cakes. These were all carefully listed in the advertisements. Actually, these large cakes were a baker's lottery, in a time when everyone was running lotteries, churches, schools, and bridge companies.

Our concern here is with the Dutch cake. Incidentally, the recent University of Chicago *Dictionary of Americanism* fails to list this term. Pennsylvania newspapers between 1830–50 list Dutch cake literally scores of times. The Philadelphia *Public Ledger* of December 23, 1837, carries the following advertisement: "Come and See! Fresh Dutch Cake, for Christmas and New Year." The same newspaper advertises December 25, 1846: "Superior Dutch Cakes, equal to Fruit Cake, may be had fresh every day, in 6, 12, 25, and 50 cents loaves"; December 25, 1847: "Very Superior Dutch Cake, made of the best materials, with a large quantity of Fruit."

The first literary piece on Christmas in *Godey's Lady's Book*, "Christmas Presents" by T. S. Arthur (December 1848, page 370) alludes to Dutch cake: "A large chicken for a Christmas dinner, and some loaves of a fresh Dutch cake for the children, had not been forgotten." It is also mentioned in a poem, "A Merry Christmas," in the Norristown *National Defender* of December 20, 1864:

> Thy board with good things spread,
>   (The turkey in the middle)
> Dutch cake, and home-made bread—
>   Then strike up the fiddle.

The *Reformed Church Messenger* for July 8, 1868, published the following recipe for Dutch cake: "One pint of sour milk, one quart of sots, three-quarters of a pound of butter, six eggs, one pound of sugar, one pound of currants, one pound of raisins, and one nutmeg."

CHRISTMAS DAY

Descriptions of Christmas Day are legion in number, most of them prosaic, some few original. None, however, in all of our Pennsylvania literature, can quite match the originality of someone, likely the editor, writing in the [Lebanon] *Pennsylvanian* in 1856: "Christmas Day has come. The lump of sugar in the coffee-cup of life, the *sauce piquant* to the mutton-chops of existence, the spiced wine to the pudding of being."

From the first Open-Hearth Christmas in Pennsylvania to now, Christmas, next to its religious implications, has always meant two things above all else: a fond remembering of childhood Christmases in the old home and a day when the scattered members of one's family were all reunited "at home" around a festive table, more bounteously spread than on any other day in the whole year. More recently, since 1850 or thereabouts, Christmas has come to mean one thing more—the Christmas tree and the exchanging of gaily wrapped gifts from Kriss Kringle or Santa Claus.

Many Pennsylvanians of literary bent have written on the meaning of Christmas to themselves, none more poignantly, however, than Henry Harbaugh. "Exiled" in a theological seminary in a Scotch-Irish community in south-central Pennsylvania, among Presbyterians who paid no heed whatsoever to holy days, Professor Harbaugh in 1867 wrote:

Christmas Day! What a beautiful thought. Here where I am living—in the westerning Pennsylvania hills—the people are of English extraction. They want to hear nothing of Christmas. They spend the day working on this holiday as on any other day. Their children grow up, knowing nothing of brightly lit Christmas trees, nor of Christmas presents. God have mercy on these Presbyterians—these pagans.

And I have to live out here. Often, in the pre-Christmas season, I get homesick for the good old time I knew as a youth in Dutch Pennsylvania. What a pleasure Christmas was then. People did not work on Christmas Day; instead, in the morning, church bells used to peal forth an invitation over field and wood to all within hearing to come to God's House for the Christmas service. One saw old men, smiling through their beards. Grandmothers had faces as bright as the full moon. And children! Children shouted for joy!

And a week or two before Christmas, what an endless baking of cookies—horses, rabbits, stars, hearts, birds and many shapes more. How richly this *Christ-kindel* rewarded the children. Then it was truly a pleasure to be a child. Would that I could be one, once again! I tell you, a childhood without Christmas is like an evening sky without stars, yes, like a world without a Saviour.

We shall not devote any space here telling of Christmas Day morning, for this has already been done—in the chapter treating of Christmas stockings and straw breadbaskets. Nor will the reader be hearing here of Christmas dinners with turkey and chestnut filling and all the "fixins." As for dessert at Christmas dinner, there of course was mince pie, always, and if we can trust the many literary accounts in the press, plum pudding betimes, at least in urban centers around the time of the 1840s. We admit to liking particularly the eighteenth-century name our early Pennsylvanians applied to mince pie: Christmas pie. Would only that this name had persisted! There are but two things more we wish to say about Christmas dinner before we pass on to another subject. Back in the days of the Civil War, though there was no USO then, the military, the soldiers and sailors, fared just as well from the hand of the women folk, every inch as well as did the servicemen in the Second World War. A number of Massachusetts sailors who happened to be quartered in Philadelphia at Christmas time the year before the Battle of Gettysburg were invited to a Christmas dinner by some Quaker City ladies. One of the sailors from the Tar State, in writing his folks at home afterwards about the "bird" he was called on to carve, remarked: "The table before me was occupied by a turkey so large that the breast bone could be used for a boat keel, and the wishbone was about the size of a hay fork."

The second item we wish to insert at this point is a humorous letter in Pennsylvania Dutch-English[1] by one "Yawcup de Schleeber" in the Philadelphia *Balance* of January 31, 1821.

Ellendown, Lie-hei Kounty
Chennuwerry de 27endt, 1821

Oaldt Freindt,

Ah, ha! I had sitch a nise Krissmass tinner, und dit soe winsch dat you, mein friendt, vas hier zu helb me to ead it—dere vas one tisch, a kreat bick one es vas too, full mit schweet schmelling sourkrout, and a fein fett schmoakt koose rite on de dop of de tisch; at de onder endt of de dabel vas a goot flitch of pacon, amoast kiverd all ofer mit schweet schnitz, barsnips and tumplings—dont it maik yure mout wader ven you readts dis ledter—I know mein does ven I only dinks apoudt it. Vell, I did eadt und dit eadt, bis, als mein sohn Beeder dells me, I fallt fasdt aschleeb, mit one of de vings of de koose in mein mout.

Sauerkraut, judging from the frequent references in the press of the period of 1840–60, was commonly served on Christmas in public places in southeastern and central Pennsylvania. We understand that turkey and sauerkraut was long the favorite Christmas and New Year dinner combination in the York–Adams–Western Maryland section. In a humorous piece in the York *Gazette* of December 31, 1822, the Society of Bachelors "Resolved that we celebrate Christmas in social meditation, feast upon 'Gnepp Dompfknoodle, Oyer unt Schnitzs,' and not like every inconsiderate fool involve ourselves in difficulty to obtain 'Turkey and Sourcraut.'" The Chambersburg *Valley Spirit* of January 23, 1856, carried this news item: "We dined on Sunday last with M. W. Houser, 'mine host' of the Hagerstown Hotel, on 'sauer krout' and Turkey." The earliest reference found to date to serving the turkey and sauerkraut combination at Christmas is a humorous Dutch-English piece in the Carlisle *Spirit of the Times* of January 19, 1819: "When him and de qwack toctor Mealy kame back from eating roast durkies and sourkrout on krismas dey made a bargin."

This chapter is concerned not with the good things there were to eat on Christmas Day, but with the manner in which some of our Pennsylvania fore-

fathers spent Christmas afternoon. If the day was cold and ice had formed on lake and river, there was skating, of course. No need here, however, to say more about this winter sport, for have not most of us experienced its exhilaration! Rather, we want to tell of potato picking contests, pig races, fantastic parades, and Trilby socials.

Down Yardley way, the *Bucks County Intelligencer* of January 3, 1890, tells us, the folks went in for contests:

A potato picking contest took place here on Christmas. Fifty potatoes were placed on the ground, one yard apart, and the contestants strove to see who could pick up the potatoes, one at a time, and deposit them in a basket at the starting place in the shortest time. Several young men entered the race. John Harman, a colored youth, was the winner; time about 12 minutes. Another contest took place on New Year's Day with 100 potatoes.

Nothing ever, though, for sheer spectator enjoyment, quite approached the greased pig catching contest in popularity. This is the way they enjoyed the sport in the Quaker City a century ago, according to the Philadelphia *Press* of December 27, 1858:

At Sixteenth and Christian streets, a pig-chase came off. The spectators of this unique affair numbered not less than a thousand people, the rag-tag of the vicinity. A shoat pig was the object of the chase. He was a long, lanky animal—weighing, perhaps, two hundred and fifty pounds. He was first shaved closely all over his body, and then lubricated with lard. He was led out in advance of his pursuers—who had paid for the privilege, at the rate of a dollar each—and at a given signal the crowd started, the four-legged hog far in advance of the others. He ran for several squares, the foremost of the crowd grasping his slippery limbs, only to lose their grip, amid the jeers and merriment of the multitude, until some fellow, with his hand full of cinders, seized the caudal appendage of the animal, and retained his hold.

Some years later there was a greased pig chase in the state capital. The *State Journal* of December 27, 1872, described the event thus:

The pig race was also a gratis arrangement, and at least one hundred competitors joined in the chase. The porker, with tail shaved and greased, was started on Foster street, and had a busy time to get clear of the fleet footed runners who gave chase to his pig-ship. The lucky individual who managed to hold on to the nicely shaven and artistically greased narrative of the pig, was one John Pierce, a native of the Emerald Isle, who got a secure tail-hold of the flying porker; and, after getting astride of the squealing game, and asserting his right to the captured animal, according to the rules of the turf, toted the pig off to his home.

CHRISTMAS FANTASTICALS

Fantasticals, or fantastics, were grotesquely clad men— young men usually, who paraded the streets on horseback, in wagons and sleighs or on foot in a noisy fashion on certain festival days, primarily on New Year's morning and on First and Second Christmas Day.

Research indicates that the fantastical parades were held sporadically in all parts of Pennsylvania, most commonly in Central Pennsylvania, least often in the Bucks-Montgomery-Chester County section. Not every community had a fantastical parade by any means; they were scattered, seemingly much like the Battalion Days of former times.

The fantasticals were either the whole show—as on New Year's Day or First and Second Christmas; or they were incorporated as parts of a bigger parade—as on the Fourth of July, Battalion Day, or on Washington's birthday.

How old the custom is and whence its origin are both unknown quantities as of now. The name fantasticals or fantastics (the term fantasticals is used more commonly in Pennsylvania than fantastics, the ratio of use being three to one)—the name itself strongly suggests British Isles roots. The earliest evidence to date for fantastical parades in Pennsylvania is for the year 1829.

From the Pottsville *Miners' Journal* of December 29, 1855.
Fantastical Parade. On Christmas day, amid the peltings of a pitiless storm, some twenty individuals belonging to Port Clinton, entered and paraded through the streets of our Borough. They were arrayed in every imaginable burlesque costume, and wore tiles apparently manufactured from damaged hardware, and discarded hats reduced to a shocking bad state. The captain wielded with herculean grasp a long wooden scimitar, and manoeuvred his men with a military skill to the music of a well soaked fife and drum, operated by well soaked performers. A member of the company bore upon a fragile stick a piece of not the whitest muslin we ever saw, upon which was inscribed "Santa Anna Life Guards—0, git out." The Falstaffian army created much amusement, and if the weather had been pleasant, the array on the part of the Guards would, we presume, have been more formidable, in point of numbers.

From the *Miners' Journal* of January 2, 1858.
Christmas was celebrated in Cressona with the usual destruction of turkeys and gingerbread common to the day. But the sports were principally in-doors, out-doors being very quiet. The day succeeding Christmas was rather more lively out-doors. The prominent feature of the day was a burlesque, by some of the "fast men" of the place. With but few exceptions the horses looked as though a peck of oats would be an extremely welcome luxury. The riders did not look very warlike, but everybody thought they were "funny." By means of paint and *outre* clothing, most of them were beyond recognition. The regimentals embraced all sorts of style and all kinds of colors. The hats were of very original shapes. In some cases, the head, "the palace of the soul," was surmounted by a steeple, hideous enough to be the residence of a Hindoo Idol. The music consisted of the stentorian voice of the Lieutenant, tin horns and ten penny whistles.

From the Pittsburgh *Gazette* of December 27, 1866.
Two or three troops of "Fantastics," dressed in grotesque unseemliness and accompanied by execrable din, paraded in the early morning the streets of Pittsburgh and Allegheny, and men and boys were out from early till late, celebrating the peaceful advent of the Christmas Festival with the anomalous uproar of fire arms.

From the Lebanon *Courier* of January 3, 1877.
Fredericksburg news item: On "Second Christmas" some young men gave a street entertainment by dressing themselves in their parents' old clothes and marching down through town in the noble capacity of "Fantasticals."

From the Carlisle *American Volunteer* of January 1, 1880.
Centerville news item: Some of the Penn boys celebrated Christmas with a fantastic parade through the streets of Centerville. The way the different nationalities and races were counterfeited and burlesqued was ludicrous and laughable in the extreme.

From the Pottsville *Evening Chronicle* of December 29, 1886.
Mauch Chunk news item: On Christmas afternoon a special train on the Central Railroad of New Jersey rushed into Mauch Chunk, and brought with it Santa Claus and an escort of 30 fantastics. The train's arrival was announced by the explosion of 50 railroad torpedoes, the locomotive's whistle blowing all the way up, and the ringing of all the church bells in town. The train stopped at the Mansion House depot where old Santa was met by a procession of 400 fantastics.

From an account written for the Folklore Center by Victor C. Dieffenbach in the early 1950s.

I remember as a kid I went to Millersburg [the former name for Bethel, Berks County] on the day after Christmas to see the fantastic riders that could always be seen at the various hotels. There might have been fifty riders, from different places, assembled in the square, vying with each other with their comic regalia and occasionally some well accoutred steed. A big lout of a fellow from Hamburg was up on an immense mule, fully eighteen hands high, and he was what today, in army parlance, is called the "Big Brass." Every inch of harness was full of bright brass spots, and that mule glittered so one could hardly bear to look at him. This "Beau Brummel" was now in the hotel, having himself a good time. Along came a kid and looked at that mule, all bedazzled, and as he walked around him his eyes were taking in every detail of the shiny outfit. Finally, to satisfy his childish curiosity, he lifted up the mule's tail, looked under, and silently shook his head. Undoubtedly he was disappointed in not finding any more brass hidden, and so he gave the mule's tail a yank. And did that kid roll—clean across the square! He got up and went into the barroom. He told that big fellow, "You better move your big shiny old mule out there. I looked at him and I fell over." This remark so pleased the crowd that the kid had more ice cream and candy than he could eat. Luckily, having been so close to the mule, he was not injured but keeled over, and badly scared.

CHRISTMAS TRILBIES

Trilby socials were much in vogue around the turn of the century in Berks County according to the Reading *Eagle* of December 22, 1895:

Invitations are sent to an equal number of young ladies and gentlemen, so there would be equal numbers of couples to make the affair a success. At the rear end of the room a large sheet was fastened from one side of the wall to the other, behind which the young ladies were to sit later in the evening. After the guests have arrived, the young ladies retire to the next room and remove the shoes while the young men remain patiently waiting. One of the young ladies enters as "manager" and gives instructions to the "boys," after which she notifies the young ladies that everything is in readiness. Unobserved by the boys, they enter the room and take their places behind the screen. The boys are then ready for action. Suddenly the girls stick their feet out from under the screen. All kinds of stockings are in view—woolen, cotton, silk, etc. and of different colors. The young lady manager acts as doorkeeper, and at the request of one of the girls, calls out the name of one of the boys. This is done in an undertone. The young man called arises

and goes forth to the screen to examine the feet. The ones he thinks the daintiest, he must catch hold of while the doorkeeper announces the lady's name. The two then retire to the back room where he must put on her shoes, and she is his partner for the balance of the evening. After all have secured a partner, the ladies again sit behind the screen, and a committee of three of the gentlemen is appointed to decide upon the girl having the daintiest foot. The lucky one secures a prize in the shape of a Trilby Heart. The screen is then taken down and dancing and games are indulged in, after which a collation is served when the young folks depart for home. In some cases the young men must show their feet.

CHRISTMAS FAIRS

A popular institution in Pennsylvania cities from about 1830 to the time of the Civil War was the Christmas Fair, also called the Ladies Fair or Fancy Fair.

The Christmas Fairs were sponsored by women's groups to raise funds for charitable causes, churches, orphanages, and other non-profit organizations. These fairs usually opened a day or two before Christmas and continued through Christmas Day. The women solicited donations of goods to sell in the community, and they themselves supplied needlework and food.

Many people spent part of Christmas Day in visiting one or the other of these fairs.

The earliest evidence of these fairs comes from the Philadelphia *Democratic Press* of December 26, 1828, which commented:

The mode of collecting contributions by means of Fairs is a happy one, and at this season of gifts, the purchaser while he aids those who really want, may provide himself wherewithal to gratify his young friends and pay the substantial compliments of the season.

Objections were occasionally voiced in the press to these fairs on the part of city merchants and women who made a living sewing. The Philadelphia *Inquirer* of December 25, 1833, noted: "These Fairs are, no doubt, designed for the most benevolent purposes, but the store keepers complain of them, and say that they greatly injure business." The Columbia *Spy* of January 4, 1834, carried an item on the subject:

A poor woman, who has a family of children to maintain, came to a house a few days ago, where she was known, and where every one knew she was entitled to credit. "Formerly," she said, "I was able to maintain myself and my family by fine needle work. But now, I can dispose of nothing—every one buys at the fairs. And at this

*Watchmen in Philadelphia distributed a broadside verse, called "The Watchman's Address,"
each Christmas season to the families they served, expecting a gift in return.*

season of general festivity, when, from a little extra demand, I could distinguish Christmas day by rather a better dinner, I am threatened even with the want of bread, for this is the very season chosen for the fairs."

The sponsors of the Young Misses Fair held in Philadelphia struck a unique note in 1832 according to the *Daily Chronicle* of December 26, 1832: "It is expected that one table will be furnished with various articles manufactured from the *Anthracite Coal.*"

In the diary of R. M. McKnight in the library of the Western Pennsylvania Historical Society we get a personal reaction to the Christmas Fairs in Pittsburgh. Under date of December 24, 1845, Judge McKnight entered:

Fairs. We just dropped in, at that of 2nd Pres. church where we surveyed, something were quite pretty but we purchased nothing but some good icecream. . . . Called in at the 5th Pres. church one on Smithfield st. where were few customers—got a couple of pen wipers—while every thing was tossed toys, all the lady managers seeming to know us & calling our name—concluded we must purchase something so we sat down to the refreshment table, where we got bad coffee, worse pickles, worst pies, & very execrable Ham. Merely tasted & jested. On attempting to withdraw we were hemmed in by the ladies who diligently pressed their wares upon us.

Opposition, particularly on part of the clergy, seems to have been responsible for the discontinuance of the Christmas Fairs. An article, which follows, from the Reading *Gazette* of January 3, 1846, presents the position of the opponents to these fairs:

Reading is at present the theatre in which is acted the play of Fancy Fairs—the world being its encouragers, and professedly religious persons its actors, most of whom, too, are found to be from the ranks of the fair sex. It is felt that no sufficient reasons, or any sufficient results flowing from any pretended reasons, can justify the existence of what may be termed *Religious farces.*

Is it right—morally—religiously right—to institute Fairs, as they now exist? Here is the test by which their expediency must be tried.

But the money is to be applied to the benefit of Churches—to the support of the Poor; in fine, altogether to spiritual purposes. Very well. All this is right enough in its place.

However, the days have gone by, when men acted on the Jesuitical principle that "the end justifies the means." Theatres have been engaged in building Colleges, Lotteries, too, have been pressed into the service of Benevolence, but do such applications

change at all their nature, or establish their right? A Theatre remains a Theatre, full of abomination; a Lottery remains a Lottery, dealing out ruin to its devoted victims; and a Fair remains a Fair, to whatever worthy purpose made subservient. Besides, are we bound to degrade the nature of Benevolence, so as to secure its end by unworthy means?

There are several objections to Fancy Fairs—Bazaars, or with what name soever titled. It is expected, and facts prove its truth, that those who delight in them, generally speaking, are altogether worldly-dispensed, whose liberality arises not so much from a spirit of charity, as from the pleasure and amusement they expect to enjoy. A Fair, then, is of a worldly nature. In this respect, it cannot be distinguished *in principle* from a Ball, or a Dancing Party. Let facts speak for themselves. Is the success of such an undertaking based on any appeal to the understanding, or any benevolent feeling? On the contrary, are not the humors—the passions of worldlings played upon and pampered, as much as possible? Is it not trumpeted forth before it happens that, at such and such a time, in such and such a place, a Fair will be held—held in an *orderly* manner—a needed apology, rather suspicious at the same time. Besides, Eatables, such as Cold Turkey, Venison, Roast Beef, Ice Cream, Floating Island, Pound Cake, etc., are held out as inducements. Do the feelings of Benevolence rest in the *stomach,* for such appeals to our appetites go on that supposition? Here, however, lie the principal attractions—the very essence of the whole entertainment—stript of the idea of pleasure, they would surely vanish. And yet we are told that the object is charity. Strange it is that many really good persons—that Churches—Protestant Churches countenance such acts. Can the ladies, Dorcas-like, take to themselves, rightfully, the pleasing consciousness of doing good, as they say, call upon the world to give, from religious motives— what will be the result? Put it to the test. Ah! a mere subscription list is something too dry—there must be some spice—some variety—something to excite.

Then the way of obtaining money presents rather an objectionable feature. Some few years ago at a Fair in Boston, a lady took in, as it is termed, $45,000 by selling "secret packages," which, when opened, contained a couple of *dusters* for the eyes. But this is nothing, because applied to Religious purposes; hence it is true that "the end justifies the means," and Religion, which has its end in itself, becomes the tool of mere worldly policy! Are the friends of Fairs prepared to endorse?

Then were must be, necessarily, an *improper exposure* of those engaged in the business itself. Policy forbids the gentlemen to take it in hands, for under their management a complete failure would ensue. The Ladies must be engaged. Accordingly, arrayed in all species of finery—bedecked with all the tinsel of Art—in their

THE
SPRING GARDEN
WATCHMAN'S ADDRESS,
ON THE RETURN OF
CHRISTMAS DAY, 1848.

Once more doth peace her pinions spread
O'er the fair land where freemen tread ;
The harvest hymn's been sung, and now
Stern Winter comes with ruffled brow ;
Yet in its train the season brings
Some joys upon its icy wings :
Among them to delight appear,
Glad CHRISTMAS and the New-born year.

And Jack Frost will you surpass,
Sketching rich landscapes on the glass,—
Not Fancy's, Natures sketches bold;
So beautiful, and yet so cold.
And all will shun old frosty Jack,
To his bleak breath all turn their back ;
Tho' out of doors all now would place him,
Your Watchman thro' the storm must face him.

The sweet domestic joys of life
Are yours, nor do you fear the strife
Of elements when raging high,
For you in calmest slumbers lie ;
And dreams of pleasure or of gain
Now o'er your sweetest slumbers reign,
While faithful Watchmen are awake,
To see no ills those slumbers break.

Or, if you have a sleepless night,
How pleasant is the torches' light
Gleaming along your chamber clear,
To tell a watchful friend is near.
Your friend when you repose in bed,
The vagrant's fear—the robber's dread,—
And when the night would threaten harm,
His rattle springs the loud alarm.

'Tis this that makes your slumbers sound,
Your Watchman goes his wakeful round,
To guard your homes from ev'ry ill,—
Tho' often slandered, faithful still.
Then midst the gaiety and mirth
That circles round the Christmas hearth,
Remember him in your delight,
Who guards your happy homes at night.

Oh while your hearts with pleasure beat,
May be a Christmas Welcome meet,
And with the greeting leave your door,
Smiling, as he has oft before.
Then while the Old Year bids farewell,
Oh may the New your bosoms swell
With happiness, and bless your board
With all the comforts life affords.

WATCHMAN'S CALENDAR, FOR 1849.

	Sunday.	Monday.	Tuesday.	Wednesday.	Thursday.	Friday.	Saturday.		Sunday.	Monday.	Tuesday.	Wednesday.	Thursday.	Friday.	Saturday.		Sunday.	Monday.	Tuesday.	Wednesday.	Thursday.	Friday.	Saturday.
Jan.		1	2	3	4	5	6	**May**			1	2	3	4	5	**Sept.**							1
	7	8	9	10	11	12	13		6	7	8	9	10	11	12		2	3	4	5	6	7	8
	14	15	16	17	18	19	20		13	14	15	16	17	18	19		9	10	11	12	13	14	15
	21	22	23	24	25	26	27		20	21	22	23	24	25	26		16	17	18	19	20	21	22
	28	29	30	31					27	28	29	30	31				23	24	25	26	27	28	29
Feb.					1	2	3	**June.**						1	2		30						
	4	5	6	7	8	9	10		3	4	5	6	7	8	9	**Octr.**		1	2	3	4	5	6
	11	12	13	14	15	16	17		10	11	12	13	14	15	16		7	8	9	10	11	12	13
	18	19	20	21	22	23	24		17	18	19	20	21	22	23		14	15	16	17	18	19	20
	25	26	27	28					24	25	26	27	28	29	30		21	22	23	24	25	26	27
Mar.					1	2	3	**July.**	1	2	3	4	5	6	7		28	29	30	31			
	4	5	6	7	8	9	10		8	9	10	11	12	13	14	**Nov.**					1	2	3
	11	12	13	14	15	16	17		15	16	17	18	19	20	21		4	5	6	7	8	9	10
	18	19	20	21	22	23	24		22	23	24	25	26	27	28		11	12	13	14	15	16	17
	25	26	27	28	29	30	31		29	30	31						18	19	20	21	22	23	24
April.	1	2	3	4	5	6	7	**Aug.**				1	2	3	4		25	26	27	28	29	30	
	8	9	10	11	12	13	14		5	6	7	8	9	10	11	**Dec.**							1
	15	16	17	18	19	20	21		12	13	14	15	16	17	18		2	3	4	5	6	7	8
	22	23	24	25	26	27	28		19	20	21	22	23	24	25		9	10	11	12	13	14	15
	29	30							26	27	28	29	30	31			16	17	18	19	20	21	22
																	23	24	25	26	27	28	29
																	30	31					

A MERRY CHRISTMAS AND A HAPPY NEW YEAR.

"The Spring Garden Watchman's Address" from Philadelphia, 1848.

gauze—their silks—their everything, only to please the senses, without any reference to the solid and the lasting, they open their Battery and, as was expected, obtain a bloodless victory. Having framed a vocabulary of light and airy—rather ethereal words, they throw them out, mechanically put into sentences; to which must be added, in many cases, a feigned pleasantry—an affected gracefulness—all of which are well calculated to *draw* on visitors; and the more a young Lady "takes in," the better claim has she to the name "Sister of Charity." At the same time, it must be confessed that while the Ladies attack with lips *fair,* they are very liable to be attacked in return with lips *foul*—they are subject to the notice of every star-gazer—to the remarks of every flippant tongue.

A crowning objection comes in on the score of *Morality.* A low estimate of Morality must they have, who think to increase Charity by outward pomp and show—who, while they attend to any excitement intended to develop it, neglect the very source of it. What a picture is presented, when the Church, forgetting her high vocation, condescends to cater to public taste, in order to promote her pecuniary welfare! It is not meant to cast any unjust reflections upon the Episcopal or Lutheran denominations, or any which may hereafter set up Sales—it is meant to protest against the *thing* itself, injurious, as subversive of the end it is designed to reach. Fairs, as now held, cannot be defended in theory, much less in practice; for the latter, in its results, has been before our eyes whilst the former generally escapes observation.

WATCHMAN'S ADDRESSES

In addition to its Carnival of Horns, Philadelphia seems to have developed a second unique Christmas institution in this country: the annual Watchman's Address, a broadside, which the city watchmen took from house to house on Christmas Day, expecting a dole in return.

We have been able to locate but six of these Watchman's Addresses, the earliest one for the year 1818. The other years located are between 1825 and 1864. In part, the 1849 Address reads:

> And if the Watchman now should pause
> This season at your door,
> Your pleasures will reveal the cause,
> 'Tis Christmas once more.
>
> You know his duty, and you know
> His ancient custom too,
> To guard your home the long year thro'
> And Christmas call on you.
>
> The custom is of ancient date,
> The oldest people say,
> The Watchman with his verse to wait
> On you this sacred day.
>
> And now kind patrons all adieu
> May you continue gay;
> Until the Watchman calls on you—
> Upon next Christmas Day

CHRISTMAS NIGHT

One stray figure runs through our mind when we contemplate Christmas night. A non-Pennsylvanian, Christmas to him was no different than any other day. The Pottsville *Miners' Journal* of December 29, 1855, tells us of him and his activity Christmas night:

Places of business nearly all closed during the afternoon, and in the evening, the only person we observed worshipping the almighty dollar at the altar of Mammon, was the Yankee traveling book peddler, who held an auction with a slim attendance. We pity that man who cannot set apart a few hours aloof from business, on Christmas, for congenial communings and heart-felt thankfulness to God for favors past and present.

SECOND CHRISTMAS

econd Christmas, the custom of celebrating the day after Christmas as the "secular" holiday, is of Continental origin. Up to about the turn of the century Dutch Pennsylvania continued to celebrate a second secular day on *all* traditional church holidays: Easter Monday, Whit-Monday, and Second Christmas.

The Quakers and Scotch-Irish, who rejected all church festival days up until the middle of the last century, of course never accepted any part of the "second" holiday.

The German-language *Volksfreund* of Lancaster on December 27, 1808, alludes to a debate of a couple weeks earlier in which a Mr. Spangler observed before the legislative body that since the Pennsylvania Dutch customarily observed Second Christmas as a holiday no business could, therefore, be transacted before that body on that day, because the Pennsylvania Dutch constituents would absent themselves.

Someone fifty years later—quite palpably a Quaker—in an article "One Christmas Not Enough" in the *Bucks County Intelligencer* remarked that the Pennsylvania Dutch element in the county were not satisfied with just one day of Christmas holidaying, but that "when others have concluded their festivities *they* just order up the day following, which they term "Second Christmas."

Second Christmas was always a gala day in old Dutch Pennsylvania. After our county seats had grown to attractive proportions, the chief recreation of rural youth on this holiday was a trip, more often than not by train, to Reading, Lancaster, or York "to see the sights." The accommodating innkeepers customarily staged a dance on the occasion, one that commenced ordinarily in the afternoon and continued well into the night. Confectionery stores did a land-office business. And many a farm youth sat for his photograph on this day.

In the country, shooting and hustle or raffle matches and somewhat later wheelbarrow matches were the order of the day at crossroad taverns on Second Christmas. Here, too, the township bullies would all foregather and would pit their strength, the one against the other. However, it must be said, the bullies much preferred to stage their exhibitions of brute strength on the semiannual Battalion Days.

SHOOTING MATCHES

Shooting matches are so commonplace, even today, that we shall restrict ourselves to presenting a folk theme one encounters every now and then in early Pennsylvania newspapers: the illiterate schoolmaster. Typical of this type of thing is the following account from the Lebanon *Advertiser* of December 26, 1849:

We opine that the people of Reamstown, Lancaster County, are blessed with schoolmasters, who are more fond of attending shooting matches and "deanses" [dances] than poring over the pages of Webster or Walker. The following *verbatim ac litteratim* we received too late for last week's paper, and this week would be of no use in publishing as an advertisement, as the time will have gone by when our subscribers in that neighborhood receive the paper, but for sake of literature we give it here as a genuine specimen of the impure.

MARKS Men Take Notis

that on the SackK Kentday of Crismes on Wansdday the 26th of December, 1849 there will Be a Shooting Match in Reamstown Lancester Coty at the publick House of Isaac Reber for a Hog weiing .3.25 lb. with Rifler Distance 100 yards, marks men are all in withet to attain for and Ner. There will Be a pardy or a deans [dance] in the sam Evening all young man & ladis are in withet to attant.

RAFFLING OR HUSTLING

"To raffle" or "to hustle" are words interchangeably in Pennsylvania to denote a game[1] of chance common at holiday seasons in which seven old-time pennies are thrown from a hat or, more recently, a leather

"Shooting for the Turkey," an F. O. C. Darley print, circa 1850. Shooting matches for turkeys, fat hogs, and steers were popular holiday activities at country inns on Thanksgiving Day, Christmas Day, Second Christmas, and New Year's Day.

box. Heads are counted and each player gets to throw the container three times. The player who throws the largest number of heads wins the prize. The highest score possible is twenty-one. Second prize is awarded to the player who throws the lowest score.

In times gone by raffle or hustle matches were carried on in country taverns after the shooting match of the day ended. The purpose was to attract the shooters into the barroom, where liquor was being sold. In recent years the locale where the hustle matches used to be held, the crossroads tavern, has changed to local fire or community halls, where the form of gambling any longer is carried on solely by club members.

Of the two words, "hustle" or "raffle," the former seems to be the earlier usage in Pennsylvania. Today the word "hustle" is restricted in usage geographically. The word "raffle" is the one now commonly used. Sometimes "hussle-cap" was used instead of "hustle."

The earliest documentation for this game of chance in Pennsylvania is from a rare imprint, "The Dying Confession of Charles Cunningham, aged about 19 years, who was executed at York-town (Penn.) on the 19th, of September 1805, for the murder of Joseph Rothrock." On page seven: "On the evening of that fatal day [May 16], Joseph Rothrock came to Mr. Dinkle's pavement, and bantered me to play at husslecap."

A year later appeared the "Trial of James Jameson and James M'Gowan in Dauphin Courts Dec. 1806 for the murder of Jacob Eshelman, on the night of the 28th August, 1806." In this imprint we read: "The hat with which they hustled was mine."

Samuel S. Haldeman in his pioneer linguistic study, *Pennsylvania Dutch* (London, 1872), page 59, among provincialisms lists: "Hussling-, or Hustling-match, PG. hossel-maetsch (with English *match*), a raffle. From the root of *hustle*, the game being conducted by shaking coins in a hat and counting the resulting heads."

In the Philadelphia *North American* of December 25, 1862, there is a reference to raffling: "These raffling people, by the way, buy the largest and best poultry. Up in the morning early, they cull the offerings of the hucksters."

The Reading *Gazette* of January 2, 1875, gives us a good sketch of raffling:

Hustling is the favorite method of raffling. It is done with seven old copper cents. The cents are put into a hat, and each raffler is entitled to three throws. The person who throws the most heads up, in the three throws, takes the prize. A regular committee is chosen to conduct the raffle. They receive tickets, check off names, count the heads and handle the pennies. As each raffler throws, his number is put opposite his name. The winning numbers run from sixteen to eighteen, and sometimes as high as nineteen and twenty. The latter throws are rare. If two or more tie each other they can decide it among themselves by throwing off or sharing the proceeds.

A fuller account of raffles appeared in the Lebanon *Daily Times* of February 4, 1876: "Mr. Adam Black . . . threw 18 heads and won a 2,500 pound steer." Four drew seventeen heads and divided seventy-three dollars among themselves; twelve threw thirteen heads each and after a contest the highest score was thirteen heads and the winner won seven dollars; Mr. Philip Strebly of Sheridan threw twenty-one tails and received a cooking stove, being the lowest.

The Pottsville *Miners' Journal* of December 15, 1882, described a raffling match at Womelsdorf in Berks County:

The customary old hat used to place the pennies in is not in use here. They have had made a leather box with handles at the sides. There is a loose fitting lid to the box. The judges place the pennies in the box and put the lid on it. The raffler seizes the handles of the box, places his thumbs on the lid, and shakes the pennies. He then places the box, cover down, and when the judge raises the box, the pennies remain in the lid on the table. The heads are counted and recorded, the pennies put back into the box and the raffler finishes his throwing. The person who has the highest number of heads thrown is allowed to remain in the room where the raffling is conducted, and when his throw is exceeded, he must give way to the fortunate raffler. There are two judges and two clerks to a match.

WHEELBARROW MATCHES

From the Wrightsville York County *Star* of December 13, 1857.

One of the funny features of the day [on Second Christmas] was a wheelbarrow match with a wheelbarrow for the prize of a fat hog valued at $16, which came off in the afternoon, in a field adjoining the Borough. A post was planted in the field as a target; at a starting point, eighty yards distant from the post, was a wheelbarrow, and any one paying fifty cents was entitled to one chance to win the prize, which was to be done by the person being blindfolded, and in this condition wheeling the barrow to or nearest the target. There were thirty-three persons made trial of their skill or luck, a number of whom in their efforts to do the *straight* thing, veered so much from the track as almost to describe a circle, and none came nearer than fifteen feet from the post, excepting Louis Haines, who took the prize by running the wheelbarrow against the post.

From the Norristown *Montgomery Ledger* of December 25, 1866.

Wheeling matches are taking the place of raffles in some parts of Chester and Berks counties. While we cannot endorse the legality or morality of either, we cannot help but think there is far more fun in the wheeling matches. All the contestants for the prize are required to be blindfolded in turn, take hold of the handles of a wheelbarrow, turn three times around, and then wheel towards a stake, the one approaching the nearest being the winner. When completely blindfolded, the mark is pretty difficult to hit, and in many cases persons will wheel very far off, or perhaps in an entirely different direction, which is of course very amusing to the spectators, if not very profitable to the "wheeler."

From the West Chester *Village Record* of December 28, 1869.

Among the excitements on Christmas day, probably one of the most laughable, was the Wheeling Match, which took place in the afternoon, on the farm owned by Joshua Darlington, on the pike, below West Chester. The prize offered was a turkey, to be given to the person, who, after being blind-folded, would wheel a wheelbarrow the nearest to a certain point at a distance of 70 yards. Each competitor for the prize was taxed 25 cents, and some sixteen entered themselves for the contest.

From the Lebanon *Courier* of January 18, 1872.

The "wheelbarrow match" in Annville, for a horse "worth $160," came off the other day. The contest lasted until "dewy eve," with varying fortunes—some striking the stake and others "cutting a circle," and attended all the time with interested spectators. John Thomas, who *propelled* the barrow for John Thomas, won the prize, coming within half an inch of the middle of the stake.

From the Reading *Weekly Eagle* of January 5, 1895.

Fleetwood news item: Two wheelbarrow matches came off on the farm of Martin Schaeffer. The first wheelbarrow match was won by Daniel Deisher, and the second by O. C. G. Lentz. Each received a turkey as a prize. The former came within $7\frac{1}{2}$ feet, and the latter within $2\frac{1}{2}$ feet of the poles. These 2 matches were very amusing. In the first 15 participated and in the second 25. Each participant was blindfolded, and, after being led about in a circle several times, set out with the wheelbarrow for a pole 300 feet from the starting point. Some made several circuits of the field, coming almost to the starting point. Morris Kelchner missed the pole by 232 feet.

From a letter by H. A. Showalter of Lancaster to the author.

Wheelbarrow matches were quite common in Eastern Lancaster County about sixty years ago.

Frequently on Sunday afternoons we boys from the village went out to visit our school companions who lived on farms. There we played hide and seek, coaly up, hat ball, corner ball and occasionally had a wheelbarrow match. All simply for fun. One of the more energetic boys staged a barrow match to pick up a little spending money for Christmas. The prize was a live duck. The privilege to push the barrow cost ten cents. I was there but did not have the coveted dime but I got a big kick out of watching the other fellows come far wide of the stake.

I saw the same stunt pulled off several times at shooting matches with groups participating. It always evoked a lot of merriment.

Some twenty-five or possibly thirty years ago the Amusement Committee at one of our family reunions revived this sport, staging events for youth and adults. Everybody got a big bang out of it, even men and women up in the eighties. Of course, the latter did not participate.

There is a drawback to these blindfolded games. It is a difficult matter to keep the crowd quiet behind the starting line. The further the performer gets away from his goal the more the onlookers giggle. This gives the contestant a tip that he or she is going wrong.

OF PYRAMIDS AND PUTZES

The Moravians made more of Christmas than any other religious denomination in this country—from colonial times on. But since this study of Christmas in Pennsylvania is a strictly folk-cultural one, we shall not attempt a description of their colorful Christmas Eve vigils, there having been two in early days, one for the children at dusk and a later one for the adults. Nor is it in the province of this study to enter upon a discussion of the Christmas music of the Unitas Fratrum.

Instead, we shall concern ourselves with Moravian Christmas pyramids and putzes, and with a description by contemporaries of what life was like at Christmas time in the early 1800s in Bethlehem and Lititz, both closed Moravian communities at that time.

However, before proceeding with the subjects we have just enumerated, there is one statement about Moravian life and culture that we shall have to make. It is this: As Pennsylvanians they belonged neither to the plain groups nor to the gay. Though the Moravian immigrants were German-speaking, they never considered themselves Pennsylvania Dutch. In other words, they were a group quite apart. For this reason we have thought it best to treat them separately in this study.

Christmas pyramids were four-sided frame structures (pyramid-shaped, as the name correctly implies), some two to three feet in height. Placed on tables, they served as a Christmas decoration, being loaded down with cookies, candies, and all sorts of fruit. Christmas pyramids, incidentally, have a long history in northern and eastern Germany.

We have documentary proof that the Moravians introduced Christmas pyramids into this country as early as 1748. In the *Bethlehem Diary* of December 25, 1748 (old style), the scribe wrote concerning the community's Christmas celebration:

Quite early, the little children enjoyed a delightful festal occasion. Their brethren had decorated various pyramids with candles, apples, and hymn stanzas and, also, drawn a picture in which the children were represented as presenting their Ave to the Christ-Child, all of which Brother Johannes (de Watteville) explained to them in a child-like manner, so that the love-feast conducted for them at the same time had a very blessed effect upon them as well as upon all the brethren and sisters present.

This English translation of the German original was made by the late Moravian archivist, Dr. William N. Schwarze, in "Transcription of Items from the Bethlehem Diary Relating to Early Celebrations of Christmas in Bethlehem, Pennsylvania," published in volume 6 of the *Proceedings of the Pennsylvania German Folklore Society*, page 14.

In the translation of the first twenty years of the *Bethlehem Diary*, this is the only reference to the Christmas pyramid. We do not encounter this custom again in our Pennsylvania Christmas literature until almost a century and a half later, in the *Reformirter Hausfreund* of January 14, 1875: "A golden pyramid was built by using oranges, though it was not nearly so large and impressive as the ones of former times."

THE OLD HOUSE OF BETHLEHEM

The Reading *Gazette* of January 6, 1849, carries an article "The Old House of Bethlehem." Lifted from the New York *Mirror*, it presents the reminiscences of an alumna of the Bethlehem Female Seminary, founded in 1785. The author, who remains anonymous, presents a very revealing, as well as a most human picture of Christmas in Moravian Bethlehem circa 1800.

For a month before Christmas, we commenced saving our pocket-money; a dollar a month was the allowance. Happy they were whose friends remembered them in time to send a remittance. I must premise, by saying that we of the Old House, being the younger portion of the school, were in three divisions, inhabiting separate rooms during the day, and separated by connected dormitories during the night. The two younger rooms, containing from twenty to thirty girls a piece, enjoyed the full romance of "Santa Claus," "Chryskinkle," or whomsoever the tutelar saint may be. On the morning of Christmas-eve, we of the younger rooms were gathered round the closet in the wall, wherein were deposited our little money-boxes, to receive a portion of their contents. Away we flew to the "Sisters' House," to make our purchases. A dollar went a great way in those days. Behold us returning across the corner of the green, hands and aprons full!

Let me see what you have there? Gingerbread, wafers, doughnuts, a bunch of small wax-candles, exquisitely moulded wax figures of a cat, deer, sheep, and *apropos* to the time, a cradle with its little occupant imbedded in moss; bundles of candy, dried fruits, and branches of fragrant box! We gather round dear Sister Caroline Shubb, and to her confide our treasures.

Out into the play-ground we hasten, our comfortable and spacious room is too circumscribed in limit for the exuberance of our spirits; a game at snow-balls, and then, with or without gloves, no mittens, we Philadelphians and New Yorkers begin to build snow cities in different corners of the yard. Drawing a circle we pile up a wall, in the centre a mound, on which we plant a flag; round this we rally, and then, as boys say at marbles, the "hardest fend off." Incessantly fly the balls, until one or the other fort is destroyed, the victors proclaiming their city preeminent in every excellence. With glowing cheeks and stinging hands we assemble at the sound of the dinner-bell; in procession the three rooms move on to the refectory, the youngest in each room leading. Silently we stand in our places, on either side of the three tables; a word is spoken, and a handful [of] youthful voices chant forth praise to the Giver of all Good, and implore his blessing on their food. The meal is taken in silence; in order we move back to our rooms, to prepare for the evening service in church.

At early twilight the bell tolls, the large centre-door of the Old House is thrown open, hand in hand the youngest girls in the school lead the way. Two sisters have charge of each room. As the sisters of the youngest room pass ours, the second follows in the same order, and so on to the third, fourth, fifth, sixth; the three latter occupying what was called the "New House," a building on the opposite extremity of the play-ground, but within the enclosures of the school. The young ladies in the three last rooms were from fifteen to twenty years of age. Two-and-two, in our simple caps and pink ribbons, we walk beneath the dark arched passage to the church. Two rows of long, low-backed benches occupy the centre of the building. We enter at a door on one side of the pulpit, the youngest children leading the way, and, taking their seats at the end of the first bench nearest the middle aisle, the sisters of the

room at the other end, the second room is seated on the next bench, and so on to the end. Two hundred fair girls are here assembled, themselves the unconscious centre of attraction to all eyes, flirtation and coquetry out of the question.

On the opposite side of the middle aisle are seated the male part of the congregation; on a bench the whole length of the church, on either side, are seated the strangers. On the female side this bench is occupied by what were called the "great-girls," that is, girls of an age between childhood and womanhood; they were distinguished by having their caps tied with the same flat-bow of ribbon, but of a bright cherry color. The married women tied their caps with blue, and widows with white ribbon; not a bonnet was seen. On a platform, raised one or two steps from the floor, and extending from door to door, were placed two benches, one on either side of the pulpit, and on these sat the oldest men and the oldest women in the village.

I forget the order of the evening service, but the music was ravishing; instrumental music of every description, together with vocal. After the benediction had been pronounced, women bearing trays, on which were small white mugs of delicious coffee, passed through the church, distributing to every individual; they were followed by others, bearing large baskets filled with small loaf-cakes [streislers] by name; these, in like manner were distributed. The ceremony was called the "Love Feast." The mugs being retaken, the sisters again appeared, each one bearing a separate tray, filled with small wax-candles, inserted in a small square of wood painted green. Each person in the church took one—all were burning.

And now commenced the return. The congregation stood in silence to witness the procession of children, the youngest again leading, with their tapers burning. It was not through a darkened archway that we now passed—a glorious illumination of wax-candles, brilliant eyes, and joyous faces cheered the hearts of all beholders, and as the graceful forms of the older girls vanished from sight, a "Merry Christmas," and "God bless you," were the aspiration of every heart.

At the earliest dawn, the morning-bell roused us from our blissful dream. Descending the entries leading to our respective rooms, we stood in the dim twilight on either side of the closed door; at a given signal, the Christmas Hymn arose, triumphantly proclaiming "Glory to God in the highest, and on earth peace and good-will to men." The door is opened, our eyes are dazzled with sudden brilliancy. Hundreds of wax-tapers, arranged in lines of light, mark out the portion of the long table allotted to each girl— within these bright enclosures our purchases of the previous day are fancifully displayed. Beneath the tiny box-tree reposes, on a diminutive bed of moss, the speckled deer; in an opposite corner, a

Members of the Lititz Moravian Congregation in the 1950s, dressed in period garb, depict an early Christmas Love Feast. Buns, called streisslers, *and mugs of coffee are served, and, later in the service, special beeswax candles are distributed to worshipers by women servers, called* dienerinnen.

PENNSYLVANIA FOLKLIFE SOCIETY COLLECTION

little, old-fashioned shepherd tends his patient flock; a portly Dutch doll watches over the safety of the Lilliputian cradle. Bundles of tapers are in readiness to continue the illumination through the day; for, until the appearance of to-morrow's sun, our shutters remained unopened. Walls of gingerbread impart a substantial look to each little domain, while raisins, almonds, sugarplums, and an endless variety of cake, promise full employment to every happy proprietor. Our kindhearted sisters have decorated the walls with wreaths of evergreen and bright winter-berries. The delicious Christmas breakfast, who can forget the triangular piece of Moravian sugar-cake,[1] a feast for an epicure.

Happy days! happy days! The orphan found kind friends in the dear Old House—where are ye now?

BUSHWHACKER CHRISTMAS

The following account of Christmas in Moravian Lititz in the opening decades of the nineteenth century was written by James N. Beck (1828–1885), a Lititz native. It is from the Philadelphia *Evening Bulletin* of December 24, 1858. To fully understand the author's highly illuminating description, the reader must keep two things in mind: First, the Moravians, living in closed religious communities as they did in Pennsylvania for generations, developed a "ghetto" mentality; secondly, the outsiders did make a nuisance of themselves during the Christmas Eve vigils, comparable to the current situation in Lancaster County, where tourists walk into Mennonite meetinghouses in shorts.

We shall quote two items from the *Moravian* of January 2, 1862, which shed light on the disturbances during the early Christmas Eve vigils:

Bethlehem—As usual, there were numbers who flocked in from the surrounding country. There is a very noticeable improvement from year to year in the character and respectful deportment of these crowds. Well we do remember from our childhood, how the uncultivated yeomanry and their buxom dames and lasses thronged these assemblies, disturbing the sincere worshippers by their unseemly behaviour. But a better day has dawned, that speaks well for the increasing intelligence and culture of our country people; and seldom does anything occur nowadays that indicates irreverence or mockery.

Lititz—The multitude from the country, commonly present on that evening, again appeared, but behaved in a very becoming and devout manner, and as they occupied the galleries and the vestibule, the body of the church was left principally to the members and the children.

On the 24th of Dec. 18.., all the lanes, highways and paths leading to the peaceful, lovely Moravian village of Lititz, in Lancaster county, presented an unusually animated appearance, about the time when the sun, gliding majestically beneath the western horizon, threw a flood of golden light upon the tops of the more elevated objects of the landscape.

It was Christmas Eve; and the Bushwhackers for miles around, following a time-honored custom, were flocking en masse along the roads, and over the fields, to attend the interesting and festive ceremonies of the season, which preeminently characterize the observance of the great religious anniversary amid the Moravian brethren.

An intelligent and finished writer, whose purity of style, correctness of diction and gracefully constructed phrases, merit the highest encomiums, in a recent work entitled the "Bethlehem Souvenir," thus graphically and truthfully alludes to the impressive, interesting, and cheerful observance of Christmas amid this zealous body of Christians:

If the remembrance of any one of the great festivals of the Christian Church, as celebrated by the Brethren, is fixed on the minds of those who have been pupils of the Seminary at

Bethlehem, (or sojourners in any Moravian congregation), it is unquestionably that of Christmas. The season is one of pleasing and impressive religious and social festivities, many of them peculiar, and all designed to afford a lively conception of the great event which is the subject of commemoration.

The minds and hearts, especially of the young, are addressed by truthful illustration, and their grateful love called forth in view of the incarnation of the Son of God. The shepherds watching their flocks by night—the song of the celestial heralds—the babe in the manger—the adoration of the wise men, furnish them for discourse in the house of God, and subjects for the exercise of unpretending yet earnest art in the homes of even the lowliest. There is not a house without its room, in which a corner is set apart for the pictorial representation of events in connection with the Saviour's birth. The parent delights to deck the consecrated spot with wreaths of spruce, and boughs of shining laurel—fit garniture of scenes which are destined to bloom with unfading beauty and be forever green in the memory of the child. In the afternoon of the 24th of December, there is a special service for the children, on which they celebrate the vigils of Christmas Eve. The boys and girls, in their respective schools, occupy the seats immediately before the minister, in accordance with a usage by which the Church intends to signify her care for the little ones of the flock, to whom she would assign even the choicest place in the sanctuary, and nearest to him who is to testify to them of the love of the Good Shepherd. Mothers also bring their helpless babes, desirous that their tender offspring may participate in the joyful occasion. The gospel narrative of the Saviour's birth, which is read on the opening of the services, furnishes the minister with matter of discourse, in which he strives to impress the hearts of his hearers with the love and condescension of God in the incarnation of his Son. The children raise their voices in the Christmas hymns which they were taught in the schools, or unite them with those of the choir in anthems of gladness and praise; and when, near the close, Christ is being sung as the "Light of the World and Sun of Righteousness," the doors of the hall are thrown open, and hundreds of burning wax tapers illumine the uncertain light of declining day, words cannot express the delight beaming in the countenances of the happy gathering of little ones.

Festivities thus peculiar and impressive, annually congregated into Moravian towns immense herds of country farmers with their sons and daughters, attracted partly by the ceremonies inside the church;—but furthermore, by a desire to pass around into the various private houses, in order to behold the really beautiful and oft

Getting ready for the annual Moravian Christmas service in Lititz in the 1950s.

times highly ingenious Christmas decorations—or, to employ a trite German name of these, the PUTZES. At an early hour of the afternoon had the stream of corduroy, linsey-woolsey, flannel, and beaver-hats commenced to flow into the quiet street of Lititz, upon the particular Christmas Eve now under consideration; but it reached its culmination about the hour of sunset, when, as has been shown above, the highways and lanes of the vicinity seemed filled to repletion with hurrying throngs of vehicles and pedestrians. The spacious hotel at the entrance of the village became rapidly filled, and its floors and passage ways, howbeit thoroughly rinsed and cleaned in the morning, now bore filthy traces of field and roadside mud, plastered over the boards in fantastic, heel-shaped trails. Friends and neighbors jostled one another, shook hands roysteringly, and jocularly demanded a "Christ kindel" (literally a Christ Child, but intended in its ordinary acceptation to denote a Christmas present).

Long lines of burly boys and ruddy girls streamed along the neat, well-ordered street, alternating between the hotel and a cake-shop and confectionery, famous throughout the entire region for its spongy, delicate, copiously sugared "streislers"—its crisp, brittle, highly seasoned "pretzels"—its so-called "sand tarts," "shrewsburys," and other gastronomic peculiarities for which the cara-

vanserai under consideration stands unrivalled. Here then gathered, in tumultuous force, the enthusiastic Bushwhackers, loading their pockets and even their wide chapeaus, until these sate uneasily upon their heads, with the various condiments of the season; ogling girls, and presenting these with gingerbread cakes, moulded into artistically shaped men, pigs, cows, rabbits, and other devices, and exclaiming, as they handed them into the broad palms of the expectant belles, *"Sukey, doe hoscht du dei Christ Kindel,"* (Sukey, here you have your Christmas gift) or, if the cake chanced to possess the shape of a man, *"Doe due wid gaern heire; hoscht yetz a mon."* (Here, you wish to marry; you have a husband now!) Or, perchance, the rustic cavalier might purchase a handful of so-called "love letters" (secrets) and essay to decipher, if he possessed a slight smattering of the fundamental laws of grammar, the sentimental mottos attached to those. —And, as each one had concluded his purchases, he would elbow for himself an exit from the contracted shop in the street, and after exchanging salutations with newly arrived friends without, he would hook his little finger into that of his inamorata, and make another peregrination to the hotel, leering upon his companion, swinging her arm fit to wrench the same from its socket, and affording the intelligent inmates of the various houses, as these sate by their windows, an infinite quota of innocent amusement.

These uncultivated Christmas visitors to the enlightened village of Lititz, furthermore, made incursions into private domicils, without sufficient knowledge of ordinary etiquette to ring the door bell, or rap the brass knocker. It was no uncommon occurrence for the pater familias, or the tidy housewife, to find their entries or parlors suddenly crowded with shad shoals of blunt Bushwhackers, who, without removing their hats, or wiping the dirt from their heavy plough boots, would stand huddled together, and staring, in meaningless silence until their wishes were demanded from them; when, perchance, the foremost might reply, *"Mer welle die 'Putz' sehne."* (We wish to see the "Putz," or Christmas decoration.) Moreover, the sounds of a piano infallibly brought with them suchlike abrupt incursions. Dared a lady open her music book, and commence her favorite cavatina or fantasia, her parlor soon filled up with wondering faces, unasked and undesired. The impressions produced by the music invariably called for an interchange of lucid opinions from man to man.

"Denk shpiele ish net so hort, wen mer's amole kon." (Think playing is not so hard, when you once understand it!) quoth one.

"Woss for a dish ish sell?" (What kind of a table is that?) added another, referring to the piano.

"Konsht shoulder's joy shpiele?" (Can you play the soldier's joy?) might be the request of a third; and so on, until the performer, wearied of her unabashed, illiterate audience, bethought her best course to close the lid of the instrument—a mode of pro-

cedure which forthwith cleared the apartment, and brought into requisition the services of the hired domestic, who always found a complete hour's toil to remove all the muddy traces of the rude incursion.

Amid the pressing throng which crowded around the portals of the antique stone church, which looms prominently from behind the lovely square in the lower portion of Lititz, at its primary summons to the religious vigils of the Christmas Eve in question, stood Betsy Dieffenbach, from the Furnace Hills.

Never surely has there appeared amid the enlightened influences of the present age, a specimen of the genus homo, so simple-hearted, totally ignorant, or so naturally dull as was the Betsy under consideration. Not an hour's schooling had ever illumined her benighted intellect with a single ray from the gladdening, beaming, enlightening radiations of education.

To her was the busy, teeming world beyond the circumscribed landscape which spread its fertile fields, scraggy tracts of woodland, and dotting farm houses—beneath her native Furnace Hills,—the great outside world, with its dizzy whirl of progressive enterprises, commercial, mechanical and intellectual,—with its mighty pulsations of invention and intelligence—a closely sealed book. Never before had the simple girl ventured further from her humble cot than, perchance, to a neighboring country church on Sundays, where she comprehended but a tithe of the words and doctrines which fell from the minister's lips. Thus, to speak the truth plainly, Betsy Dieffenbach differed, intellectually, in marvelously few points from the most uncivilized denizens of the South Sea Isles.

When the doors of the Lititz church had been thrown wide, and the waiting crowd tramped into its galleries, Betsy followed the current, and soon found herself seated in a position which commanded an entire view of the neat little auditorium. Presently the rich, gushing tones of the organ, moulded into devotional harmonies by a well-skilled student of the solid German choral style, pealed solemnly through the edifice; and from the keynote at the close of the voluntary, proceeded a classic symphony, in which a full orchestra combined with the instrument to enhance the general effect. And after the symphonic prelude, the choir, numbering many well-trained voices, arose, and vocalized an anthem replete with love and gratitude—glorifying the incarnation of a world's Saviour in strains of joyous and heavenly harmony. What a novel sensation must these imposing effects needs have produced upon the mind of the illiterate Betsy Dieffenbach, who had never before listened to any music but that of nature's grand symphony as improvised by the warbling birds in her native woods. The sentiment and purport of the glorious anthem fell upon her ears meaningless as might have a Sanscrit oration; but the deeper, more mysterious, spiritual influ-

ences of the music pervaded her unsophisticated heart, and infused therein a new-born yearning for information.

Attentively pricked she her ears, when the minister continued the festive services by reading the gospel narrative of the Saviour's birth. Hitherto had Betsy Dieffenbach possessed vague, garbled ideas of Christmas—impressions founded upon the narratives of others, who had celebrated its festivities as a time of worldly merry making and carnal pleasure, and calculated to convey to her simple mind an analogy between this great Christian anniversary and the worldly celebrations of great political and civil memorabilia. Without the ability to read for her own edification, and comprehending but a limited quota of that which she heard from the pulpit, she had thus far even lacked a well-defined knowledge of the events attendant upon the Saviour's birth. But when the officiating clergyman had read the narrative from the gospel according to St. Luke, and had associated therewith an apposite, practical discourse, clothed in the plainest Saxon vernacular and appealing directly to the heterogeneous capacities of his audience, a new light began to dawn within the benighted intellect of the heroine of this sketch. And when, finally, the burning wax tapers were handed to the band of children, arrayed upon the front benches, and a flood of mellow light flickered over the scene, Betsy's very face glowed with the force of emotions thrilling inwardly, such as she had never experienced during the entire course of her career. The fitting emblem of the "Sun of Righteousness" here wrought a hallowed effect; for, howbeit unconscious of its true purport, the illiterate subject of this sketch first wondered within herself in what manner the radiant scene before her could be associated with the foregoing ceremonies—and then inquired of her neighbor, a colossal plough-boy, in the following whispered conversation:—
"Woss maynt sell ol? Sis schoensht woss ich sei loewe g'say hob!" (What does this all mean? It is the handsomest thing I have ever seen in my life!)

"Denk soll youscht a licht gewe, weils Chrishtog ish." (I think it is merely intended as an illumination, because it is Christmas) was the rather ambiguous and unsatisfactory reply.

So Betsy held her peace; and with the conclusion of the services, trudged she forth into the street, silently wondering at the things she had both witnessed and heard. Suddenly she encountered a bevy of country folk, in whose circle proved to be several acquaintances from her own vicinity.

These announced their intention to make a circuit of the village, for the avowed purpose of visiting the various private decorations in the individual houses, and entreated Betsy to accompany them upon the interesting tour. Accordingly, the entire party started into the nearest front door, sans ceremonie, and soon mingled with a crowd of faces beaming with delight upon an unusually large, elaborate, and ingeniously wrought Christmas tree. Amid the boughs of spruce, which hung in graceful and thickly netted wreaths and festoons, forming a verdant alcove, shone high above the fanciful imitations of landscape features,—mills in active operation, ponds alive with toy ducks, steadily sailing with the motion of an unseen magnet, flocks of sheep, and squadrons of grazing cattle,—over these was suspended a large, brilliantly illuminated transparency, portraying with vivid effect the infant Saviour, in his rude manger, surrounded by the brute denizens of the stable. The Bushwhackers all stared with overt symptoms of delight at the scene before them, rendered brilliant to a fascinating degree by the beaming effects of multitudinous wax candles, which caused the newly painted toys on the landscape and the angels pendant amid the festoons to shine with unwonted lustre, and so to throw a fairylike charm over the entire scene. Delighted children of the village, their faces beaming with innocent mirth and youthful enthusiasm, stood around, enjoying moments such as they might well sigh for in after life; and one of the crude country boys called out with a chuckle, *"Ess beet, by jucks, em Lindsy sei show!"* (This beats Lindsay's show, by jucks!)

As for Betsy Dieffenbach, her entire interest seemed centered in the brilliant transparency, heretofore alluded to; for in its well-conceived groupings, she perceived a beauteous illustration of the scenes which her attendance at the church-service had, to some extent, unfolded to her mind.

Suddenly there appeared at her side a man, whose suit of black, white cravat, and benevolent countenance unmistakably betokened his position in life, and who, having remarked her wrapt observance of the picture inquired whether she felt specially interested in its contemplation.

Betsy shrunk back with feelings of mingled confusion and reverence, when she recognized in the individual who addressed her the clergyman of the evening's religious services.

"Yoh," replied she, *"Sell plaesirt mich gar ewig: ich hob schu uft dofon kaert, awer ich habs niemmy so recht vershtonne."* (Yes, that pleases me most eternally: I have often heard about it, but never rightly understood it.)

Astounded beyond measure to discover an immortal soul, existing as it had been almost within the sound of his church's bell, thus untutored in the most familiar feature of the Christian religion, the worthy pastor drew the uncivilized Bushwhacker girl to one side, and through the medium of ordinary conversation unfolded to her simple mind the inestimable value of a Saviour's incarnation to a fallen world, and added thereto a plain narrative of the final sufferings and deaths, upon the bloody cross, of the same "God manifest in the flesh,"—to all whereof his companion gave ear with silent eagerness and wonderment.

Some months thereafter, it fell to the lot of Betsy Dieffenbach to remove to Lititz, where she had been engaged by a worthy tradesman to occupy, in his house, the position of cook and domestic.

The events of her first Christmas Eve had made a lasting impression upon her simple heart, it would appear; for no one in the peaceful little community occupied a seat in the village church with more scrupulous regularity than the veritable Betsy of this rapid sketch. And thus, even though the seeds of temporal education had never been sown within her bosom, and she remained uncouth and illiterate, she acquired convictions which made her wise unto salvation.

Many readers of the foregoing cursory sketch may deem the above delineation of extreme ignorance, as depicted in the person of the imaginary Betsy Dieffenbach, grossly overdrawn and exaggerated. To such, the writer would address a few casual remarks in conclusion. The Bushwhacker, as portrayed in these articles, the scenes of which are invariably represented as having transpired some years anterior to the present time—only exists here and there in certain localities at this day. The progressive spirit of the age has shed its influences, to a marked degree, over the German counties, and the worthy yeomanry have exchanged their former mistrust of schools for a fair appreciation of the blessings of education. The English language, too, finds more favor, and better circulation among the hardy knights of the ploughshare, and many of our popular boarding schools number within their flocks, young scions of the wealthy farmers, of both sexes, who aspire to branches beyond the rudimental, primary basis. The Bushwhacker of fifteen years ago, therefore, by no means occupies the entire territory of the inner German counties now, howbeit there are still numerous dark spots and clouded districts, into which the cheering rays of education and refinement have thus far vainly striven to pierce. At that time, however, such cases of extreme mental inanition as the writer has ventured to depict herein, were by no means uncommon; and although the imaginary character of Betsy Dieffenbach has had its birth in the desire to present to the readers of the *Bulletin,* a rural Christmas scene among the Moravians, there actually once strayed into the town of Bethlehem, during the solemn Easter services, on Good Friday, a country wight, who, after being accosted with a query as to where he had been, from a resident of the place, who had joined him on his way home, replied, in the patois of his class:—*"In die Kaerch; un sie hen fom a kerl gesproche, dern sie uf a bohm g'negeld hen, un hen em negel in die feess un hend nei g'schloge; awer ich glob kay wort d'von."* (Literally: In Church; there they spoke of a fellow whom they nailed upon a tree, and into whose hands and feet they drove nails; and I don't believe a word of it.)

A Christmas putz of a Moravian family in Lititz.

Let the reader pause, and reflect upon the foregoing, which is well-attested fact, before he shall finally decide the case of Betsy Dieffenbach to be exaggerated.

MORAVIAN CHRISTMAS PUTZ

Among Moravians the word *putz* means a crèche or a landscape which is erected in churches and homes during the Christmas holidays. It is the German word *Putz*, which means ornamentation or decoration. (A facetious etymology, of recent vintage, derives the word from the English verb "to put": because in building a putz one *puts* a piece here and one *puts* one there.)

The principal student of the Moravian Christmas putz was the late Elizabeth Myers of Bethlehem. In her book, *A Century of Moravian Sisters*, Mrs. Myers ably describes the Moravian custom:

The "putz" is so distinctive of a Moravian Christmas that it merits a special word. It was, and is, an elaborate miniature landscape built under and around the Christmas tree, and telling the Christmas story, from the appearance of the angelic choir to the shepherds where they were tending their sheep, to the manger with its Holy Family, and the adoration of the Magi! This was brilliantly lighted with the beeswax candles in tin holders, in greater or lesser degree. Much ingenuity was shown and beautiful effects obtained. The modern putz is the same thing, greatly elaborated with electric lighting effects, painted backgrounds and even victrolas hidden under the moss and playing the Christmas songs.

Everyone was glad to show the results of their labor, so "putz parties" became popular. They called it "going to see the putzes" and probably this first brought the boys and girls together. Before the town "opened up" in 1844, the sexes did not mingle at all in this way, but after that the bars were let down somewhat, and although very strict rules were made the boys did go out with the girls. They would help drive the cows home, and on Sunday go to see the wax works together, and walk down Bartow's path along the canal, for wild flowers. But the putzes provided the entering wedge.

One of the chief decorations of the putz was the shepherd scene, and plenty of white sheep were always placed upon the green moss, on a miniature hillside or in a tiny meadow. These sheep were also made in the Sisters' House, by one Benigna Ettwein, familiarly known as Benel. Kindly, big-hearted Benel, whose fate it is to bring a laugh whenever her name is mentioned! But a laugh may be a very eloquent epitaph and so it is for her. Benel's sheep were wonderful to behold! They were shaped out of clay, then cotton was wrapped around them, four matches were stuck in to represent legs, and a splash of Chinese vermilion was daubed on the end where the nose belonged. She also made chickens out of tow and glued chicken feathers on them, and both chickens and sheep appeared on the putzes of her friends.

Building putzes in Moravian communities is a custom that reaches back into the eighteenth century. Mrs. Myers, writing in the Bethlehem *Globe-Times* of December 19, 1923, says:

The earliest family putz of which we have definite knowledge, though doubtless there were earlier ones, was that of Peter Fetter, in 1782. In that year Mr. Fetter carved a cow from a piece of wood for the Nativity set on his putz. The cow is still in existence, having been used on the putzes of successive generations in the Fetter family ever since.

One more bit of evidence regarding the antiquity of the putz is to be found in the *Moravian* for December 1867:

How far back they date we are not prepared to say. They were in the full tide of their glory when we were a boy, twenty-five years ago, when we were sufficient advanced to lend a helping hand, and *then* the great *Putz*-makers were men well advanced in years, so that it is fair to presume that *Putz* making is amongst the ancient institutions of this venerable town. The taste and ingenuity displayed in these decorations was often very considerable. We use the word "decoration" for the want of a better, though it does not convey a correct idea of the *Putz,* which is not a festooning of the rooms with garlands and wreaths, but a miniature representation of some scene in nature, imaginary or real. As we have said, the art displayed in these mimic scenes was frequently very creditable. Mountains and valleys, tumbling waterfalls and peaceful fields, lakes and villages, in the bright green of summer, or the delicate snow covering of winter, were represented with a faithful minuteness of detail, and in really artistic groupings. Many evenings, until late in the night, were devoted to the making of them. Who will say that it was labor thrown away? Now-a-days, we fear, you could scarcely gather together a dozen men who would be willing to devote themselves to the preparation of one of these grand *Putzes* of the olden time, just because they loved to do this sort of thing, and the time is now to them so precious a thing for business, that they cannot spare it for the purpose of pure and innocent amusement. Are we any the happier or better now? Are boys any more frank and innocent, or the girls any more loveable and modest than they were then? When, even on a Christmas Eve, the great *Putz*-seeing evening, they came home at nine o'clock, and were thankful for the privilege of being allowed to go, and to be an hour later than usual.

Besides these *Putzes* which were made on a grand scale, there were smaller ones in abundance; the humblest home having its little table, covered with a white cloth, and backed by branches of evergreens, from which were suspended glittering stars, wax angels, bright colored candies, &c., in pretty confusion, illuminated by many burning candles. Who, that ever saw or played at them, will forget those bright Christmas scenes? The cave from which issued the monster bear or lion, the looking-glass lake, on which ducks and geese of various sizes sat in motionless propriety, the silver-sanded road, on which was ranged the contents of a Noah's Ark, with the patriarch and his family walking first, and the animals following two by two in solemn procession; the little village with its church and rows of stiff poplar trees; the pleasant minglings of bird and beast and fish, all in perfect peace with one another, as became them at Christmas time; the stable where the "blessed child" was born; the mill hoisting up its bags and letting them down again, as long as the hidden machinery remained in working order, whilst the miller smoked his pipe, and his dog kept up a very energetic, if somewhat methodical jumping at his feet; all these, and a thousand other recollections, rise before the memory, and force us to the conclusion that *Putzes* are a great institution, and ought not to be allowed to die out. And there are other memories associated with them, some of which are of too sentimental a character to be mentioned. The expeditions in search of moss, the pleasant preparation for the great *Putz,* the mysterious darkened and carefully locked up room, the anxious suspense, the joyous surprise, the happy hearts and smiling faces, the sweet interchange of precious presents between the juveniles, not of the same family or sex, the fortunate and often repeated meetings whilst going the rounds of visiting the many *Putzes,* which it was necessary to see. We wonder whether the young ones enjoy Christmas as thoroughly and innocently as they used to do when Bethlehem was only a little village, and the outer world was quite shut out.

The Moravian custom of building a Christmas putz seldom caught on in non-Moravian areas. Occasionally between 1860 and 1885 one reads in the press of cities like Allentown and Reading that so-and-so built a putz "in the Moravian fashion." Essentially the putz was an in-group affair. But one important exception has come to the fore.

The Philadelphia *Press* of December 21, 1867, describes an exhibition of a Christmas putz in Philadelphia, sponsored by the Bethlehem YMCA to raise money for their building fund:

The Moravian "Putz." From time immemorial the sterling but unobtrusive denomination of Christians known as "Moravians" or United Brethren have observed the Christmas festival with peculiar emphasis and preparation. To this day our principal Moravian settlements make the Christmas holidays a season of free, joyous, social intercourse, such as no other denomination attempts, and the great, essential features of every well regulated home is the Christmas "Putz"—a German word which means to decorate or embellish, and, in Moravian usage, has come to signify specifically a large Christmas decoration. It usually consists of a miniature imitation of some real scene. All Christendom adopts the Christmas tree, but the Moravians improvise an entire in-door landscape. Some of these are arranged with genuine artistic skill, and the most beautiful "Putz" in a Moravian town will be talked about approvingly by old and young through the entire year. The Young Men's Christian Association of Bethlehem, which is erecting a large hall for its use, has now arranged—for the double purpose of gratifying public curiosity and raising funds for their building—a superb specimen of the Moravian "Putz," at National Hall, Market street, above Twelfth, where it will remain on exhibition from Monday next until after New Year. The committee in charge have produced this pleasing spectacle of active country life on a magnificent scale. Several car loads of rocks, stumps, mosses, and ever-

greens, brought from the Lehigh Valley, were used in its construction; and under the artistic management of Mr. William Yohe, the builder-in-chief, assisted by Messrs. F. Krause and C. F. Oestereicher, all of Bethlehem, a scene has been produced which will not only repay every admirer of the beautiful, but will familiarize our citizens with a most interesting Christmas custom, and give them new ideas in rendering our great annual holiday a household happiness. The scene represents mountains, gorges, meandering streams, with water flowing rapidly; undulating farms, houses, barns, mills, lakes, carriage roads, and, in short, everything to make up a perfect landscape on a small scale. The fidelity to nature is double assured by the materials employed being all natural. The entire room is an arbor of evergreens.

The custom of building putzes among Moravians today is very much alive. In the larger Moravian churches in Bethlehem and Lancaster men of the congregation labor for weeks in the evening in putting up a larger putz than in the preceding year. It is interesting to note that the first television program ever to emanate from the Lehigh Valley was on the Bethlehem Christmas putz.

In fine, we wish to cite two more references to the Christmas putz, both out of the twentieth century. Rev. Charles D. Kreider, writing in the *Moravian* of December 18, 1907, said:

The Christmas "putz" must be admired and enjoyed: played with, in fact. For every genuine "putz" should have its foreground of sand in which the children can make Noah and his family travel once more in procession to the ark or in which treasures can be buried to be dug up again to the wonder and enjoyment of every one.

We like particularly the simile from the Philadelphia *Record* of December 22, 1907: "What the husking bee is to the farmer lad and lassie, the arranging of the Christmas putz was to the Bethlehemite years ago, and is still, in a large measure."

FIRECRACKER CHRISTMASES

Nowhere in Pennsylvania has the influence of the South been so great as it has been in the southwestern tier of the state. The first scholar to document this influence, along folk-cultural lines, was Samuel P. Bayard. His *Hill Country Tunes* of a few years back, a study of the folk music of the area, points to this Southern impress, again and again.

This study of Christmas in Pennsylvania—like Bayard's a folk-cultural one—shows that Pittsburgh's celebration, and that of the other western counties as well, was characterized, traditionally, by the discharge of firecrackers, the same as in, say, North or South Carolina.

This is a plate, one of eight, in The Children's Friend, *a juvenile book published in New York in 1821. In some of the plates Santa Claus is depicted distributing his gifts. The caption under the plate here reproduced reads:*

> *To some I gave a pretty doll,*
> *To some a peg-top, or a ball;*
> *No crackers, cannons, squibs, or rockets,*
> *To blow their eyes up, or their pockets.*

Two accounts shall suffice to demonstrate the custom of setting off firecrackers—in the Carolinas. One is from the North Carolina Wilmington *Daily Journal* for December 23, 1851:

John Barleycorn retained his usual spirit . . . and our town authorities on Christmas generally let the boys have their way so far as mere noise is concerned. There was therefore much firing of crackers, rockets, serpents, etc. and good deal of cheering and shouting, but nothing worse and as the night wore on even these ceased and the town slept.

Peterson's Magazine of December 1858, in describing Christmas customs in the United States as a whole, says about the holiday in South Carolina: "In Charleston, it is welcomed, by the negroes, with the discharge of Chinese crackers, and all the uproar which distinguishes the Fourth of July at the North."

FIRECRACKERS IN PITTSBURGH

The earliest documentary evidence[1] for the custom of shooting off firecrackers at Christmas in western Pennsylvania is from an advertisement in the Pittsburgh *Gazette* of December 24, 1846: "Fire Crackers! Fire Crackers! Decidedly the best ever imported; the report is like that of a pistol, loud and clear—wholesale and retail at the Eagle Bakery, 42 Diamond Alley, and the Saloon, Wood street."

The Pittsburgh *Daily Commercial Journal* of December 27, 1848, gives us the most interesting description of a Firecracker Christmas in the City of Steel we possess:

We are in the midst (not of a revolution, but) of the Holidays. . . . "Juvenile artillerists" shake the streets with small thunder; and fire crackers emulate the sputtering of musketry, while the screams of alarmed ladies, as some young rogue discharges his fire crackers at their feet, would prove annoying, were it not for the peals of merry laughter that invariably follow the fright.

Wretched is now the youngster who cannot raise powder; and proud, indeed, is the warlike owner of a pistol—Christmas is a

Firecrackers for Christmas advertisement from the Pittsburgh Daily Commercial Journal *of December 17, 1846.*

Firecracker-fireworks advertisement from the Pittsburgh Daily Commercial Journal *of December 10, 1849.*

great teacher of the "young idea how to shoot"—and the venerable holiday has most apt pupils.

At mid-century the Pittsburgh *Daily Dispatch* (December 24, 1850) carried a Christmas advertisement regarding firecrackers:

Toys! Toys! Toys! Storekeepers and others are informed that I have received a large stock of Toys, Fire Crackers, and fancy articles, for Christmas, which will be sold very low, at the sign of the Gilt-Comb, No. 72 Wood street. Simpson Horner, Successor to G. W. Kuhn.

On Christmas Day 1875, the Pittsburgh *Post* had this to say of the holiday:

Christmas was ushered in by the ringing of Trinity chimes, and here and there by the explosion of fire-crackers.

Half the joy of the Christmas time for the young in the cities, is to go out among the streets the day and night before Christmas and revel in the wonderful wealth of the show windows, decked out with such reckless magnificence. It is the one great treat of the year to them to walk the principal thoroughfares, under the glimmer of the gaslight, and look upon the wonders of the show windows.

Like Philadelphia's Carnival of Horns, Pittsburgh's Firecracker Christmases seem to have been outlawed in the 1880s by the municipal authorities. A *Digest of the Acts of Assembly Relating to, and the General Ordinances of the City of Pittsburgh from 1804 to Sept. 1, 1886,* by W. W. Thomson (Harrisburg, 1887) contains the following ordinance:

If any person shall throw, cast or fire any squib, rocket or other fireworks in or into any of the streets, lanes or alleys of this city, every such person shall forfeit and pay for every such offense a sum not exceeding five dollars.

That fireworks were a part of Pittsburgh's Christmas celebration as early as 1831 we learn from an advertisement in the Pennsylvania Museum in the *Gazette* of December 23, 1831: "A Band of Music is engaged to play during the day and evening, and the splendid exhibits of Artificial Fireworks and Phantasmagoria will be given several times during the day and evening."

Abolishing fireworks in Pittsburgh and other municipalities in the area was not accomplished until the 1930s. The *Sun-Telegram* of December 4, 1934, wrote: "Five more municipalities of Allegheny County joined the City of Pittsburgh last night in taking action toward abolishing the sale and use of fireworks in a wide-spread anti-fireworks campaign."

With the abolishing of the custom of setting off firecrackers on Christmas in Western Pennsylvania in the latter part of the last century, this area's only distinctive manner of celebrating Christmas in the state disappeared. One cannot help but side with the editorial in the Pittsburgh *Post* of December 25, 1874:

We find a great many people of the straight-laced kind who are inclined to make the Christmas holiday a gloomy season. We have but little faith in the acceptability of that piety which would to-day, or in fact on any day, praise God with sighs and groans and gloomy countenances.

Conclusion to the First Edition

The reader, if he has come the whole way without too much skipping, probably will have reacted much the same way as the author: How regrettable that not more of so rich a Christmas folk tradition as we have presented in this volume, how regrettable, we repeat, that not more of it is incorporated in our present-day celebration of Christmas in Pennsylvania.

One fact has continually come to the fore in this study—the "de-folking" of Christmas, which is a natural, though unfortunate, concomitant of the whole Americanization process, the melting pot concept. Symbolic of the "de-folking" process is the fate that befell the early Pennsylvania gift bringer, Christkindel or the Christ Child: the Babe of Bethlehem was secularized—to use a non-folk expression—into Kriss Kringle, a jolly, old fellow devoid of every religious meaning.

As of this writing, American scholars of many disciplines are just beginning to face up to a pressing national problem: religious pluralism. This volume on Christmas in Pennsylvania—though a study of but an isolated phase of Pennsylvania folk-cultural pluralism—poses one important question: What ends may one unwittingly be serving by lending his support to such contemporary programs as ecumenicity in American Protestantism or One-Worldism in the political sphere? There is a danger that the ends may be mere religious and political "Kriss Kringles."

Afterword

And so ends Dr. Shoemaker's study of Christmas in Pennsylvania. At this point I would like to summarize some recent research on Christmas and touch on some other folk-cultural aspects of the holiday. First, however, I offer my own perspective on Christmas, which comes from my childhood Christmases—partially modern, partially traditional—as celebrated in a Protestant community in the Allegheny Mountains of Central Pennsylvania.

The traditional elements included the annual Christmas tree, which brought the woods and its fragrance into our house at midwinter; a plate set with cookies for Santa Claus that was mysteriously emptied during the night and found in the morning filled with little gifts for my sister and me; Christmas carols sung both at home and in the cold winter air as we tramped in the snow to the neighbors' houses; Christmas gift giving; Christmas dinner, with special foods and delights; and of course, the joyous church and Sunday school services. Among the "modern" aspects of our Christmas was the setting up of my Lionel O-gauge electric train on its platform with stations, switches, mountain tunnels, and villages—my equivalent of the Christmas putz! And as we grew older, my sister and I searched the closets before Christmas looking for presents, which we pretended not to recognize when we got them on Christmas morning.

When I asked my father, a native of a Pennsylvania Dutch–speaking valley of Schuylkill County in Eastern Pennsylvania, how he remembered celebrating Christmas as a boy on the farm in the 1880s and 1890s, I learned to my shock that there had been no Santa Claus. There was in his place a curious and semifrightening figure known as the Belsnickel. This was usually the father of the family, who masked and dressed in rough clothing and tapped on the window

to be let into the house. He carried a switch and a bag with candies and nuts, which he scattered on the floor. When the children scrambled to retrieve them, he gave them a token switching, to the fright of the younger and the amusement of the older children.

My father informed me also that in his boyhood days Christmas gifts were few and far between. An orange at Christmas was a precious gift, rarely seen at other times of the year. Feasting on Christmas and a week later, on New Year's Day, involved large festival meals, with sauerkraut for New Year's to bring good luck and prosperity throughout the coming year. And I learned also that often on Christmas Eve, and usually on Second Christmas (December 26), and again on New Year's Day, masked troops of belsnickels—not the fathers this time but teenagers—whooped it up in the neighborhood and in the nearby towns.

How different it all had been, and yet my father's Christmas memories were part of my Christmas heritage too. Hence it was in researching the lengthy introduction for *Christmas in Pennsylvania* that I learned there were throughout the eighteenth and nineteenth centuries Pennsylvania Dutch and English groups who actually refused to join in the folk celebration of Christmas—poor things! This "anti-Christmas faction," as I called them, included the Quakers, Methodists, Baptists, Presbyterians, Mennonites, Amish, Brethren, and a few other groups. The Christmas celebrators, who went all out in both the religious and folk customs of the festival, were the Lutherans, Reformed, Moravians, Episcopalians, and, of course, Catholics.

At any rate, perspectives on Christmas celebration do involve changing historical paradigms, weakening or reinterpreting of folk traditions in favor of popular culture, and the adaptation of all ethnic groups to overarching American patterns of culture.

FORTY YEARS OF CHRISTMAS BOOKS

In the forty years since this book was first issued, research on Christmas has multiplied on both sides of the Atlantic. Out of a multitude of possible choices, let me comment briefly on three German and three American studies.

The absolute top level of Christmas research is Ingeborg Weber-Kellermann's *Das Weihnachtsfest: Eine Kultur- und Sozialgeschichte* (The Christmas Festival: A Cultural and Social History), published in 1978. Its ten chapters are History of the Christmas Calendar; Advent; Song and Play; Gift-Giving; The Christmas Tree; Christmas Folk Art; Cooking and Baking; Silvester and New Year; The Festival of the Three Kings; and Christmas and the Nations. The author was Professor Adolf Spamer's student and successor at the University of Berlin, and later professor of European ethnology at the University of Marburg, where she made two series of documentary films, one on German, the other on Hessian folk culture, that have never been excelled. Her Christmas book, which deserves translation in an English edition, is illustrated with rare prints, photos, paintings, and magazine and book illustrations from her own vast collection of Christmas memorabilia.

A different sort of book is Oskar Bischoff's *Das Pfälzische Weihnachtsbuch* (The Palatine Christmas Book), published in 1970. Essentially a Christmas reader from the pens of popular writers from the Rhenish Palatinate—the area that produced a significant proportion of the Pennsylvania Dutch population—it deals with the entire Christmas cycle of festive events from Advent to Epiphany. Several items deal with the "Belznickel," Christmas Butchering and *Metzelsupp*, and the Christmas Tree in the Palatinate. There are even several Pennsylvania-oriented items. These include Ralph Charles Wood's translation into Pennsylvania Dutch of the second chapter of Matthew; a description of "Shooting in the New Year in Pennsylvania" (from *The Pennsylvania Dutchman*); and a charming fraktur Christmas card designed by the Pennsylvania Dutch artist and playwright Paul R. Wieand.

Another German regional study of Christmas stems from the area known as Westfalia. It is entitled *Weihnachten in Westfalen um 1900* (Christmas in Westfalia around 1900), edited by Dietmar Sauermann (1976). Much of the book is made up of written ethnographic reports giving the Christmas memories of twenty-five Westfalians of various classes, from ministers and teachers to farmers, born between the years 1877 and 1925. The reports, which if they had been recorded instead of written would be called "oral history," were written down by the informants themselves from the 1950s to the 1970s. The originals are preserved in the *Archiv für westfälische Volkskunde* (Archives of Westfalian Folk-Culture) at the University of Münster.

This book is an excellent example of the European practice of regional ethnology (folklife studies) in recording the memory culture of persons living today recalling Christmas customs from around the turn of the century. This is essentially the approach taken by Dr. Shoemaker in *Christmas in Pennsylvania* in those sections of the book based on interviews with various Pennsylvania Dutch individuals. But Europe is still far ahead of American scholarship in such ethnographic studies of the past. Many of the universities in Scandinavia and Central Europe have huge archives of historical and ethnographic data on the traditional cultures of their areas.

Of recent Christmas studies by British and American scholars, William Sansom's *A Book of Christmas* (1968) is a readable treatment of the English and American Christmas celebration, with some comparative data on continental European Christmas customs. The book is written in a pleasant essay style that is a pleasure to read, and the illustrations are in many cases new and rare indeed.

Tristram P. Coffin has written an equally attractive introduction, *The Book of Christmas Folklore* (1973). It is especially good on the literary aspects of Christmas, carols and plays, Christmas ballads, and descriptions of Christmas from the pens of major British and American writers. Unfortunately, in his brief section on Kriss Kringle, he quotes Alfred Shoemaker but confuses him with Henry W. Shoemaker.

The most recent general description of the American Christmas and its multiple backgrounds is Penne L. Restad's *Christmas in America: A History* (1995). This book is certainly the most thorough explanation of the American Christmas celebration, how it was pieced together in regional Christmases from European elements imported in the colonial period, and

Print of St. Nicholas, with two reindeer and Yankee sleigh, from an 1841 American periodical.

how a national Christmas in a sense was "invented" in the second half of the nineteenth century to unite diverse America in a truly national holiday focus. The author has searched out much of the available historical documentation about various aspects of Christmas from biographies, diaries, popular magazines, short stories, and other sources, the same range of material that Alfred Shoemaker drew upon for *Christmas in Pennsylvania*. She is particularly good in summarizing the place of Christmas in the slave culture of the antebellum South, and the complex development of the American Santa Claus. And she uses quotations from *Christmas in Pennsylvania* dozens of times!

SAINT NICHOLAS AND SANTA CLAUS

St. Nicholas has been thoroughly researched by various European and American scholars who have written about the ecclesiastical career of Bishop Nicholas of Myra in Asia Minor (now Turkey) and the fantastic corpus of legends that grew up around him. By the high Middle Ages the cult of Nicholas had spread over both Mediterranean and Northern Europe. Nicholas became the patron saint of Holland, of Russia, and of countless parish churches in the German-speaking sections of Central Europe. In recent centuries he became (via the Holland Dutch influences on the Hudson Valley) the American "Santa Claus," who has continued to develop an American persona.

Despite the fact that the Second Vatican Council removed his day (December 6) from the universal calendar of the Roman Catholic Church, St. Nicholas has continued to the present day to be among the most popular, if not the most popular, male saint in the Catholic catalogue of saints. His popularity extends over both the Roman Catholic and the Eastern Christian worlds. And despite the fact that Protestantism exscinded the invocation of saints from its world, and downgraded St. Nicholas as Christmas gift bringer in favor of the Christ Child, Nicholas won out in the end. What would American Protestants of today do without Santa Claus?

In looking at the European studies of the Christmas saint, we can start with Colette Méchin's *Saint Nicolas: Fêtes et traditions populaires d'hier et d'aujourd'hui* (Saint Nicholas: Festivals and Folk Traditions Yesterday and Today) published in 1978. In addition to presenting very readably the life and legends of the saint, and offering rare Christmas prints not often seen in this country, the book is an ethnographic study of the present-day Christmas customs in the town of Saint-Nicolas-de-Port in Lorraine, with plenty of current photographs showing the Christmas celebration there. Much comparative material is presented also on the Nicholas cult in adjoining sectors of Alsace. Since St. Nicholas has the function of being the protector and patron of mariners—among other groups in society—in the area under study he was looked upon as protector of river boatmen, canal boatmen, and even of raftsmen taking logs from the Vosges Mountains down the rivers to the sawmills. This is a charming book that would do well in English translation.

Santa Claus at the chimney, filling a Christmas stocking, an illustration from The Pictorial Scrap Book *(Philadelphia, 1860).*

FOR FURNITURE
OF EVERY DESCRIPTION
—GO TO—
Dorney, Berkemeyer & Co.

Allentown trade card for Dorney, Berkmeyer & Co., circa 1880. Trade cards were given out to schoolchildren as Christmas tokens and as advertisement for their parents.

IVAN HOYT

Among contemporary artists using the Belnickling theme, Ivan Hoyt of Wapwallopen, Pennsylvania, is outstanding. His work captures the spirit of the old-time Pennsylvania Dutch Christmas festivity.

Of the studies of the Nicholas cult by American scholars, the most detailed treatment is by Charles W. Jones, *Saint Nicholas of Myra, Bari, and Manhattan* (1978). It traces both ancient and medieval Nicholas legendry, and what the author calls the saint's "second childhood" in America as the Knickerbocker "Santa Claus" of Manhattan as well as his ramifications in modern American culture. There are a thirty-three-page bibliography of works cited and eighty-six pages of footnotes. But, good as the book is as a general introduction, it is weak on Pennsylvania traditions and, alas, fails to mention or cite *Christmas in Pennsylvania*.

BELSNICKEL RESEARCH

It is with the Christmas figures associated with the Nicholas cult that much European scholarship has concerned itself. In the Netherlands, and originally in the Holland Dutch settlements of New York and New Jersey, Nicholas, dressed as a bishop and riding a horse, did not travel alone. He was accompanied by a black figure of frightening aspect, *Zwarte Piet* (Black Pete), who represented the dark side of life, punished evildoers, and terrified children.

Among the Pennsylvania Dutch, Nicholas as such was absent from the Christmas scenario, but aspects of both the saint and his dark associate were embodied in the Belsnickel. This fascinating and distinctive Christmas figure was imported by our eighteenth-century emigrant ancestors. The name derives from the Ger-

man *Pelznickel*, or Nicholas dressed in furs. Apart from the minimal gift bringing of the Belsnickel, the figure has more consonance with *Zwarte Piet* and countless European pagan parallels than he does with Nicholas.

The Belsnickel did bring gifts of nuts and candy, which he threw on the floor so that he could give a token switching to the children scrambling for them. The real Christmas gift bringer in the Pennsylvania Dutch Christmas was the *Grischtkindel* (German *Christkindel* or Little Christ Child), who did not normally appear but left his gifts during the night hours when children were supposedly asleep. In the Pennsylvania Dutch Christmas vocabulary, the word *Grischtkindel* means both the Little Christ Child who brings the gifts, and the gifts themselves. The word was also the source of the curious Americanism "Kriss Kringle," which has nothing at all to do with the Christ Child but is rather a synonym for Santa Claus.

Actually the Christ Child as gift giver is a Protestant development. The Protestant Reformation of the sixteenth century and its further enfoldment in the seventeenth and eighteenth centuries opposed and exscinded the Catholic cult of the saints, including Nicholas, and replaced the invocation of the saints with direct prayers to God and/or Christ. Because Nicholas was theologically taboo to the Protestant ministry, the attempt was made to outlaw Nicholas from the Protestant Christmas celebration and replace him as gift giver by Christ in the form of the Christ

Child, whose birth after all led to the ecclesiastical holiday called Christmas. In attempting, however, to divest Christmas of its ancient folk accretions, including the St. Nicholas cult, the Protestant ministry fought a losing battle. The Christ Child was brought to Pennsylvania as the legitimate Protestant Christmas gift giver, but along with him came the incorrigible Belsnickel with all that he represented of the world of darkness, evil, and terror.

The Christmas feast of the birth of Christ was, after all, grafted onto the midwinter solstice festival of our pagan European ancestors. In Europe, the pagan "associates" of Nicholas in the Christmas holiday cycle have been researched for their connection with and derivation from prehistoric demonic figures in the midwinter cults of the Germanic and Celtic religions that dominated Scandinavia and Central Europe before the Christian missionaries came across the Alps from the Mediterranean cities. (Some areas in Europe, Russia and Scandinavia, for example, were not Christianized until the tenth or eleventh centuries. Hence the pagan elements of what Philadelphia folklorist Charles Godfrey Leland called the "old religion" were able to survive among people as lore, folk belief, and folk custom long after Christianity took over.)

These masked figures, sometimes wearing animal masks and horns and clad in furs, represented, according to various theories, the forces of evil and darkness in opposition to the forces of light; the spirits of the dead who both frightened and blessed the living during their midwinter visitations on earth; and the forces of fertility.

The midwinter spirits had different names in different parts of German-speaking Central Europe: *Berchten, Wilde Leute, Butzemänner, Nachtrabe, Nachtgrapp, Roggenmuhme, Böögg.* Even the names are frightening, and of course parents used them to frighten children into good behavior. There was also the *Wilde Heer,* the wild horde of mounted spirits that fly at night through the storms of midwinter, around the time of what became Christmas. There were forest spirits and water spirits, and spirits of the grain. And curiously enough, there were several demonic figures that bear names beginning with *Pelz* ("fur"), including our Belsnickel, but also *Pelzmärtel,* Martin in furs; the *Pelzbock,* the buck or he-goat in furs; and even, through folk etymology, *Beelzebub.*

These frightening figures were originally demons who had to be propitiated with offerings to ensure a bounteous harvest and full flocks and herds during the coming year. In Christian times these masked figures, whatever they represented, were associated with the entire December–January Christmas cycle of holidays, from St. Nicholas Day (December 6) and the winter solstice until Twelfth Night or Epiphany (January 6).

I have never forgotten the delightful surprise I had in my graduate school days at the University of Chicago, reading *Medieval Handbooks of Penance* by one of my professors, John Thomas McNeill. The book is a collection of manuals designed for Catholic priests in dealing with human transgressions, and it gives the penances required for a whole range of "sins," which are listed in detail. The book included the *Corrector* of Burkhard, Bishop of Worms, who in the eleventh century cautioned his priests against the people's custom of wearing animal skins and masks on the calends of January (i.e., January 1). Here indeed is one of the earliest references to a practice that found expression in the Belsnickel custom of the Pennsylvania Dutch culture.

The Pennsylvania Dutch custom of masking and dressing up in bizarre clothing, both to frighten and reward children on Christmas Eve and to whoop it up on Second Christmas (the day after Christmas) and New Year's Day, can also be traced to the medieval Shrove Tuesday Fastnacht or carnival customs that are still featured in the Catholic areas of Central Europe and a few Protestant centers such as Basel in Switzerland. Costuming and masking for Fastnacht largely disappeared in Protestant areas but were transferred to the Christmas and New Year holidays and, of course, the masking of children on Halloween.

The only remnants of the Fastnacht holiday customs among the Pennsylvania Dutch today are the massive baking of *Fastnachtkuchen,* called in English "fastnacht cakes" or simply "fastnachts," and the custom of calling the last person in a household to get up out of bed on Shrove Tuesday morning the "lazy fastnacht." And although Belsnickling is a thing of the past in Pennsylvania Dutch culture, except for its sporadic revival by historical societies or "Belsnickel Days" at museums, we still have the elaborate Philadelphia Mummers Parade on New Year's Day, the urban development related to the rural Belsnickling of the nineteenth century.

Masked carnival revelers from Black Forest villages in Baden, Germany. They parade at Fastnacht, before Lent begins in spring. They are one source of Pennsylvania's Belsnickel tradition.

In 1950, on my first visit to Germany, I had the good fortune to meet Dr. Johannes Künzig of Freiburg, who founded and directed for many years a research institute for the study of the folk culture of the German Diaspora settlements of Eastern Europe. At the time, he gave me a copy of his book, published that year, entitled *Die alemannisch-schwäbische FASNET*. The book describes the Alemannic-Swabian carnival celebration in the villages and towns of Southwest Germany. Freiburg is often called the gateway to the Black Forest, and many towns in the area, in both Baden and Württemberg, carry on elaborate masking and costuming for Fastnacht. Carving wooden masks representing grotesque human, witch, and animal faces is in fact a major folk craft in the area, as it is in the Tyrol and other parts of Austria.

Since the publication of the first edition of *Christmas in Pennsylvania*, "Belsnickel research" has progressed on both sides of the Atlantic. On this side of the ocean, the pioneering article by Richard Bauman of the University of Texas at Austin, "Belsnickling in a Nova Scotia Island Community," appeared in *Western Folklore* in 1972. Professor Bauman makes two crucial points. First, he turns away from the earlier "survivalist" approach that traced Belsnickling to fertility cults, midwinter saturnalia, and spirits of the dead revisiting the earth, all in "dim antiquity," to the ethnographic study analyzing the "social and symbolic significance of the institution where it may still be studied as a living tradition." Secondly, he focuses his research on one particular community, the La Have Islands, off the coast of Lunenburg County, Nova Scotia. Lunenburg County was settled in part by German-speaking emigrants in the eighteenth century, who came from the same Rhineland areas in Europe as the Pennsylvania Dutch.

Bauman reports three types of Belsnickel disguises in the community he studied. The most common was "a wild, disheveled, grotesque, but essentially anthropomorphic figure," achieved by "dressing in torn, tattered clothes hanging in shreds and turned inside out to hinder recognition still further." The masks were made of painted canvas, stockings, or other cloth, with holes cut for eyes and mouth. Usually a long nose of canvas was added, and hair and beard of rope or wool. A tall, pointed hat capped the costume, so that the wearer actually had to stoop to get through the doorway. The second disguise featured a more animal-like mask, with horns attached. Cowbells were often hung around the Belsnickel's neck, as noisemakers. The third type of disguise involved sex reversal, where males dressed as women, with skirts and padding in appropriate places, and masks painted with women's features. (These practices can, of course, be traced, as survivalists do, to ancient or prehistoric customs associated with midwinter rites.)

The Nova Scotian Belsnickels were usually teenage boys or young unmarried men who went about in groups after dark on Christmas Eve, visiting the houses of their communities in turn, ringing bells, blowing horns, and in general making noise. At each house, they knocked on a door or window and asked formally for permission to enter. Inside the house, they went through various performances, acting up, step-dancing exaggeratedly, singing, and playing harmonicas. Part of the performance was the attempt of the visited family to guess the identity of the disguised Belsnickels, who even altered their voices to preserve their new persona.

Since one of the time-honored purposes of the Belsnickels was to frighten children, they acted as inquisitors of the terrified smaller children, calling them forward and asking if they had been good that year. With the unanimous affirmative replies, the children were rewarded with gifts of candy. In return, the Belsnickels were given treats, which they did not eat there but carried away in a basket to the end of their rounds, where they ate at a Belsnickel party later that night.

Following his excellent ethnographic description, Professor Bauman finally asks the question, "What can we say of the symbolic structure of belsnickling, its meaning as a ritual of social relations within the La Have Island community?"

The teenagers or young unmarried men who roamed as Belsnickels were in a transitional status in society—no longer children and yet not married with households of their own. Bauman's view is that Belsnickling represents "a symbolic and ritual manipulation of the transitional position of the belsnicklers." They are in a sense on a threshold, with childhood behind them and married life ahead. In disguising themselves, they symbolically placed themselves outside the social order, "becoming variously animals, women, or lumpish and infrahuman creatures." Their ambiguous position between childhood and complete adulthood enabled them on the one hand to exploit the children's fears, which they well remembered from their own childhood, while in their inquisitional role they served as "an agency of social order."

But the Belsnickels interacted also with the adults in a household. In this context, it was the adults who represented social order; the Belsnickels were outsiders. Hence the visitors could violate "the everyday rules of adult decorum" by carousing, making noise, exercising sexual license, and "resisting adult attempts to pin them down in their true social identities."

Bauman's explanations of the function of Belsnickling in Nova Scotia are suggestive and can help us to understand some of the now forgotten underlying meanings that our ancestors once saw in their Belsnickels. There seems to have been in Nova Scotia a lingering feeling that somehow, although the adults realized that their visitors were, after all, members of their own communities disguised, the Belsnickels represented visitors from the supernatural realm. In ancient folk belief, the world outside the house was the world of darkness and danger to mankind, where supernatural demonic figures, including the spirits of the dead, circulated at certain times of the year, especially at night and midwinter. On the other hand, the house, which sheltered the family, was looked upon as sacred and therefore safe. But on Christmas Eve the world of danger and darkness invaded the house, in the visit of the Belsnickels.

Finally, a word on Christmas mumming. Herbert Halpert, folklorist at the Memorial University of Newfoundland, at St. John's, places Belsnickling in a wide spectrum of related holiday customs, which he gathers together under the label of "mumming." He defines mumming as masking or costuming for fun, or for making the rounds of houses in the Christmas season. In the book he edited with G. M. Story, *Christmas Mumming in Newfoundland* (1969), he offers a listing of "mumming activities in the English-speaking world, whether British, Irish, or North American, as well as related European traditions." His typology includes "such contemporary phenomena as the Philadelphia Mummers Parade, the New Orleans Mardi Gras, the North of England Sword Dance, the St. Stephen's Day Wren-boys, the Shetland 'skaklers,' the 'belsnickles' from German tradition in Nova Scotia, Pennsylvania, Virginia, and West Virginia, mediaeval and renaissance pageants, the court masque of England, the *perchtenlauf* of Austria, and the folk plays of Thrace." Originally the roving bands of mummers presented a play at the houses they visited, but most of the forms of mumming listed above represent home-visiting without the presentation of a play.

Belsnickels today? Alas, the classic age of Belsnickling is over. It is still possible to record from older Pennsylvania Dutchmen their vivid memories of the Belsnickling they witnessed in the early part of this century. Rarely, too, photographs have surfaced showing troops of Belsnickels, masked and dressed in fantastic costume, occasionally mounted on horseback to

THE PERRY HISTORIANS

THE PERRY HISTORIANS

These rare photographs reveal the strong remnants of the Pennsylvania Dutch custom of Belsnickling in groups, on holidays, west of the Susquehanna River in Perry County. Note the beards, masks, cross-dressing, mounted figures, and fantastic headgear. Both shots were taken in Liverpool, the one above in 1910 and the other below on January 1, 1912.

ride into the neighboring towns to whoop it up on Second Christmas or New Year's Day. Perry County, west of the Susquehanna River in Central Pennsylvania, where many older customs linger, is one area where local photographers had the good sense to record Belsnickling on film. Let us hope for future research that additional examples will come to light.

While the classic traditional Belsnickel is no more, at the present time Belsnickling has modestly been revived by local organizations, museums, and historical societies. For one example, the Landis Valley Museum in Lancaster County has recently sponsored "Days of the Belsnickel" at Christmastime.

THE MORAVIAN CHRISTMAS PUTZ AND ITS ORIGINS

There is no doubt that among all the Pennsylvania Dutch denominations, our Moravians were (and are) the most enthusiastic celebrators of Christmas in Pennsylvania. Their array of Christmas customs, both on the elite and folk levels, is elaborate indeed.

The Christmas putz of the Moravian settlements in Eastern Pennsylvania and elsewhere is, through a long migration into Central Europe, derived from the medieval Franciscan *presepio* or three-dimensional depiction of the birth of Christ. The word *Putz* is derived from the German verb *putzen* meaning "to decorate." The French name for it is a *crèche*, or crib, and the common English term is manger scene, usually associated with the Christmas tree. The usual German term is *Krippe* (crib) or *Weihnachtskrippe* (Christmas crib). Originally put up as Christmas decorations in churches, these seasonal displays of devotion eventually moved into the Moravian home, where they became a major part of the family celebration of the festival.

Essentially the putz is a three-dimensional, graphic reconstruction of the story of Christ's birth, but if the putz maker feels really adventuresome, he or she could extend the story presented beyond the Christmas cycle to the entire life of Jesus, with scenes also from the Old Testament as prefigurations of the coming of the Savior. The most elaborate putzes in Pennsylvania's Moravian towns, like those of the most renowned of all putz makers, Jennie C. Trein of Nazareth, covered whole walls of the living room, and presented the entire history of man's salvation. Very often the background

"landscape" was painted, and moving toward the foreground, one saw three-dimensional mountains, Biblical cities, and usually in the center, a rock grotto or cave with the Holy Family including the Infant Jesus. Shepherds tended flocks of sheep on the hills, a dove (representing the Holy Spirit) flew over the display, and angels sang (silently) their "peace on earth, good will toward men."

During her long and active life of ninety-six years, Jennie Trein constructed over sixty putzes. For many years she also built a midyear Putz for the Pennsylvania Dutch Folk Festival at Kutztown and, clad in authentic Moravian costume, explained it to visitors from all over the United States. During the year she collected stray bits of scrap wood, colored paper, and other materials that she fashioned into figures, houses, and other constituent elements of her putz displays. She even made, especially for me, a six-pointed Moravian Christmas star covered with Palestinian buildings— representing the town of Bethlehem as a miniature putz in itself—which is still treasured and brought out every Christmas.

Where did all this come from? In the last decades German scholars in particular have issued thorough treatments of the history and lineage of the Christmas crib. One of the best of these is by Josef Lanz, *Krippenkunst in Schlesien* (The Art of the Christmas Crib in Silesia), published at Marburg in 1981. The Eastern European area of Silesia, now chiefly in Poland and the Czech Republic, was once a major center of German mysticism, both Catholic and Protestant, and the home area of our Pennsylvania Dutch Schwenkfelders. Our Moravians also had settlements in Silesia.

In carefully researched cultural maps, and a thoroughly documented text, the book traces the spread of the Christmas crib from the Mediterranean cultures, Italy in particular, across the Alps and Danube to Prague, where the first Christmas crib north of the Danube was documented in 1562. From there it spread to Breslau in Silesia (1581), and thence into Saxony, Prussia, and other areas.

The Jesuits, the most active missionary foundation of the Catholic Counter-Reformation, were responsible for introducing the custom into Prague. They had elaborate Christmas agendas including Christmas plays (also known in the Middle Ages), and Christmas dialogues and eclogues recited in the churches. They

Jennie C. Trein of Nazareth, Pennsylvania, in front of her fifty-second putz, which she built in her home at the age of eighty-two in 1960.

the sacrificial nature of Christ in calling him the *Lämmlein* (the Little Lamb); even the logo of the Moravian Church pictured the Conquering Lamb bearing its banner of salvation.

Curiously enough, the worship of God as Divine Child is found in other world religions. In Hinduism the god Krishna is the focus of a widespread devotional cult. An essay by Charles S. J. White in the journal *History of Religions* for 1970 gives details on the origins of the cult and its spread. In dealing with the origins of the cult of Krishna as Divine Child, scholars have found Buddhist, and supposedly even Christian, influences. Similarities with the story of the Christ Child include special honors paid to Krishna's mother, Krishna's birth in a stable, a star announcing the birth, the foster father of Krishna fleeing with his infant son, the evil king massacring male children, a baptism, and so on. The subject is controversial, with scholars taking dramatically opposing sides of acceptance and refutation. But the similarities in the Krishna and Christ Child legends are striking indeed.

The Moravian Christmas putz has received much scholarly treatment in America as well. The sixth volume of the *Publications of the Pennsylvania German Folklore Society*, for the year 1941, is dedicated entirely to the Pennsylvania Dutch Christmas. It offers George E. Nitzsche's "The Christmas Putz of the Pennsylvania Germans"; Charles H. Rominger's "Early Christmases in Bethlehem, Pennsylvania (1742–1756)"; and Richard E. Myers's "The Moravian Christmas Putz." This is one of the few volumes offering photographs of the twentieth-century Moravian putz displays. Finally, the essay by Sue Samuelson, "Nativity Scenes: Description and Analysis," in *Folklore and Mythology Studies* for Spring 1979, includes the Moravian putz in her discussion.

Because of the enthusiastic promotion of their traditional Christmas customs by the Moravians, Bethlehem, Pennsylvania, has become widely known as the "Christmas City." The friendly custom of "putzing"—making the rounds of the neighbors' houses to see and discuss their putz displays—still goes on there. And at Christmastime the city of Bethlehem has even added to its presentations a *Christkindelmarkt*, an open-air Christmas market with booths of Christmas toys and confections, modeled on similar markets found at Christmas in all the major German cities.

had a definite sense of theater, as did Roman Catholicism in the baroque era, and as part of their missionary thrust they in a sense acted out the Christmas story. In fact, we can point to the Catholic customs of the Counter-Reformation era in the seventeenth and eighteenth centuries as the principal origin of our Moravian Christmas emphases. The Moravian stress on the worship of the *Jesulein*, the Little Jesus, or Baby Jesus, is found in both the cult of the *Bambino Gesu* (Baby Jesus) in Italian Catholic spirituality and in the Central European devotion to the Infant of Prague.

The Moravian theology taught in Pennsylvania's Moravian settlements in the eighteenth century also reveals strong Catholic influences. One example is Zinzendorf's "Blood and Wounds" theology, which emphasized (and some would say overemphasized) Christ's Passion. Another is the Moravian focus on

CHRISTMAS FOODS AND FEASTING

In the past forty years much has been written about the foods associated with Christmas in Pennsylvania and the family feasting customs that form a culinary high in the Pennsylvania Dutch year. The most original and solid research on this subject has been done recently by leading American food historian William Woys Weaver in two books entitled *The Christmas Cook: Three Centuries of American Yuletide Sweets* (1990) and *Pennsylvania Dutch Country Cooking* (1993).

The Christmas Cook is much more than a festival cookbook, although it does offer dozens of rare American recipes from dated historical sources, some of them Pennsylvania Dutch. The book offers fascinating insights into the history of the American Christmas. The chapter "Martin Luther's Christmas Tree" presents a concise history of the Pennsylvania Dutch Christmas. Of course, Martin Luther never had a Christmas tree, but once Christmas trees made their appearance in homes, they were frequently decorated with edibles—culinary folk art, one can call them—in the form of cookies, candies, and stamped and painted gingerbread cakes. The tree stood up until January 6 (Twelfth Night), when it was shaken and the children collected the goodies.

Among the German and Pennsylvania Dutch recipes included in *The Christmas Cook* are Chocolate Apeas (1904), Dutch Cake (1824), Gingerbread (1833), Honey Cake, or *Lebkuchen* (1859), Kringles (1846), Marzipan (1804), Mrs. Crecelius's Springer Cake (1874), North German Christmas Cookies (1905), *Oblatgebackenes*, or Rolled Wafers (1778), *Speculatius* (1839), Sweet Pretzels (1914), and Waffles, or Iron Cakes (1660).

Pennsylvania Dutch Country Cooking, also by William Woys Weaver, was published in 1993 and selected by the Pennsylvania German Society as its annual volume for that year. Chapter 6, "The Masks of Midwinter: Foods for Holiday Feasting," traces Christmas in Pennsylvania in its major features and offers many unusual Christmas recipes. These include Christmas Gingerbread Men, or *Mummeli*; Kutztown Jumbles; Mice (*Meisli*); St. Martin's Horns; Mahantongo Diamond Doughnuts; Brother Johannes's Flaxseed Fastnachts; Mifflinburg Rose Soup; Ginger Kraut; Red Cabbage with Quince; and Sweet-and-

The Christ Child and St. Nicholas are still competing as Christmas gift bringers in Germany. These two Lebkuchen (Christmas gingerbreads) were for sale at the Christmas Fair at Frankfurt in 1990. One says, "From the Christ Child," and the other says, "From Nicholas."

Sour Stuffing. All recipes are given with metric as well as traditional American measurements.

THE FOLK ART OF CHRISTMAS

Folk art with the theme of Christmas is somewhat of a rarity in the Dutch Country. The folk artist concerned himself more, it seems, with rites of passage—birth and baptism, confirmation, marriage, and death—than with special days in the Dutchman's calendar and the customs associated with them.

The folk art that celebrates Christmas involves several types of early Americana, manuscript (fraktur) as well as printed (broadside) documents. Most of the examples here come from the upstate Dutch counties, with a few broadsides from Philadelphia.

Christmas Addresses

Throughout the nineteenth century, newspapers, businesses, and groups of public servants in the cities issued broadsides either at Christmas or New Year's, distributing them as Christmas or New Year presents among their patrons. It was good public relations and good advertising, and a tip from the patrons was usually forthcoming. The most common of these broad-

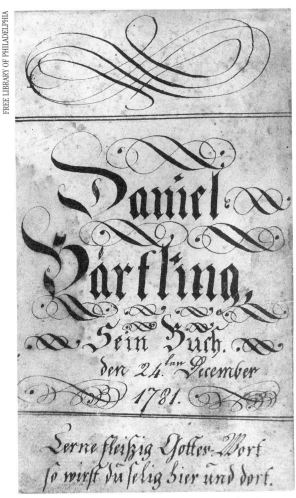

A Christmas bookplate from 1781. It is translated to read: "Daniel Hartling, his book, the 24th of December, 1781. Diligently study God's Word, so shalt thou be saved here and in eternity."

sides was the New Year's address given to patrons by the carriers of the town and city newspapers. These were usually published as separate broadsides, but at times they were printed as part of the New Year's issue of the paper itself.

Two Christmas addresses by the night watchmen of Philadelphia are included in this book. The first of these is the attractive *N.E. City Watchman's Address, For Christmas Day, December 25, 1835* (see page 111).

Pictured on it are vignettes of the American eagle, two ships a-sailing, a bespectacled Dr. Franklin, the coat of arms of the Commonwealth of Pennsylvania (with the motto "Virtue, Liberty, and Independence"), and a woodcut of a cloaked watchman with lamp and ladder leaving his octagonal watch box for a tour of duty. At the bottom appears the calendar for 1836. The second example is *The Spring Garden Watchman's Address, On the Return of Christmas Day, 1848* (see page 113).

Christmas Bookplates

Of Christmas bookplates there are many examples in the public collections of fraktur. We include one from the Free Library Collection, from a book given to Daniel Härtling on December 24, 1781, with an admonition to study God's Word in order to be saved on earth and in heaven (see left).

Dutch Madonnas

Very rarely did a fraktur artist try his hand at the Christmas theme of the Madonna. The Dutch Madonna included here (see page xviii) portrays a somewhat unfolkish Madonna, obviously copied from a print of a Renaissance painting, flanked by two cherubs, and lighted by stars that would have made excellent Dutch Country "hex signs." The hymn at the bottom, *"Gelobet seyst du, Jesu Christ"* (Praise Be to Thee, O Jesus Christ), was a favorite German hymn for the season of Advent, dealing with the Incarnation. It appears in most of the early Pennsylvania Lutheran and Reformed hymnals.

It is interesting to compare this Pennsylvania Christmas item with the Gustav S. Peters engraving of the Madonna and Child, published at Harrisburg about 1845 (see page xv).

Fraktur Christmas Texts

Two additional items from the Dutch Country are undated fraktur texts from the first half of the nineteenth century. They seem to have been done by the same artist, thus forming a pair with Christmas themes. Were they given as gifts, as were the more elaborate *Vorschrift* pieces awarded by country schoolmasters to good pupils in the German schools of the Dutch Country? Possibly so.

A pair of Christmas fraktur sketches from the early nineteenth century, reflecting themes of the Incarnation and the Cult of the Infant Christ.

One of the pair (see page 146, top) has the verse "O Jesu Christ! *Dein Kripplein ist Mein Paradies, da meine Seele weidet*" ("O Jesus Christ, Thy little crib is my paradise, where my soul feedeth"). In identifying its source, one thinks immediately of the Pennsylvania Moravian tradition, with its mystic cult of the *Jesulein*—the Baby Jesus—and its elaborate Putz tradition. On the reverse side is written the name, in crude German script, "Joseph Xander."

The companion piece (see page 146, bottom) deals with the more conventional Christmas theme of the Incarnation. The German verse, evidently from a favorite Christmas hymn, reads:

Der selge Schöpfer aller Ding
Zog an ein's Knechtes Leib gering,
Dass Er das Fleisch mit Fleisch erwürb
Und sein Geschöpf nicht all's verdürb.

This can be translated: "The blessed Creator of all things took upon himself a servant's humble body, that he might win flesh with flesh, and that his creation might not ever be destroyed."

Christmas Cards

Although our present-day custom of the Christmas card stems from Victorian England, occasionally Christmas broadsides turn up that might be claimed as isolated forerunners of the American Christmas card.

One such is the rare Ephrata broadside Christmas greeting printed by the Brotherhood on the cloister press in 1769 (see page xxviii). It begins with the scripture verse: "And she shall bear a son, whose name shall be Jesus, because He shall save His people from their sins" (Matthew 1:21), and a German hymn verse that can be translated: "No name is so beautiful as the name of my Jesus, because in German he is called Savior. This child is also the true seed of the woman, which alone shows us the way to eternal life. His name I will bury deep in my heart, and have it on my lips in my last hour." At the bottom are printed the words: "For the Holy Festival of Christmas 1769."

CHRISTMAS IN MULTICULTURAL AMERICA

In the century that is closing, a national American Christmas has taken shape, submerging for the most part the regional Christmases including the colorful Pennsylvania Dutch customs that are detailed in this book. Gone are the Belsnickel and the *Grischtkindel*, and in their place is the ho-ho-hoing Santa Claus. Commercialization has so secularized Christmas that conservative religious groups occasionally sound the cry, "Put Christ back into Christmas." Perhaps they do not realize that the Christmas holiday complex is historically vaster and more ancient than the story of Christ's birth, and that in a very real sense Christ was grafted onto the Mediterranean and Northern European midwinter festival, the pagan holiday that stressed propitiation and sacrifice, life and death, gift giving and feasting.

With the recognition of the multicultural nature of American society, however, Christmas now shares the stage with the Jewish Festival of Lights, Hanukkah, and the new tradition of Kwanzaa, based on African harvest festivals, which provides African-Americans with an end-of-year holiday. The literature on both of these holidays is increasing by leaps and bounds. Will Herberg, in his book *Protestant, Catholic, Jew* (1960), makes the statement that Hanukkah, which was an ancient Palestinian celebration of the Jewish victory of the Maccabees over Syrian tyranny, was in fact a minor Jewish holiday in Europe, but here it has achieved major importance in competition with Christmas. It has even attracted to itself some outward aspects of Christmas, including Hanukkah cards and even Hanukkah bushes to rival the Christmas tree.

Some groups in present-day America have remade the Christmas holiday to suit their own beliefs. At the far left are the "solstice people," neopagans, self-styled atheists, modern-day deists, agnostics, and others who reject organized religion. This group celebrates the Winter Solstice in December, when the sun begins to gather strength once again as winter heads toward spring. Nevertheless, their celebration of the solstice is similar to Christmas. They express their seasonal joy by decorating "solstice trees," singing "Jingle Bells," and exchanging gifts. As one of the leaders of the solstice movement, quoted in the Philadelphia *Inquirer* in 1984, put it, "We have a hell of a good time. We have a time of merrymaking, a time of giving presents because nature has given man the ultimate present. Nature has given man a sun." And the president of the Freedom from Religion Foundation, cited in the same source, went on record with this statement: "My contention is that the Christians stole Christmas. We're happy to share it, but we pagans would like a little credit."

Taking the long historical view, these arguments, extreme as they may seem to some, have unquestioned validity. December 25 on the Roman calendar was the birthday of the Invincible Sun (*Sol Invictus*). The pagan Midwinter Festival was celebrated all over Europe, but as Christianity spread, the day metamorphosed into Christ's birthday. Attempts to Christianize the pagan elements of the festival have never been a complete success, and in most cases the pagan aspects were simply carried along and syncretized with the properly Christian, ecclesiastical elements. All this is conclusively proved in dozens of scholarly books investigating the complex origins and development of this intricate and fascinating festival.

Attempts by various American Protestant groups, including some Lutherans, to "Christianize" the Christmas tree are also in evidence at present. A curious movement centered in a Lutheran Church at Danville, Virginia (a congregation peppered with Pennsylvania Dutch surnames like Shaver, Swicegood, and Stirewalt), has issued instructions for depaganizing the Christmas tree by changing it into the "Chrismon tree." So instead of "pagan" ornaments, only Christian symbols called "Chrismons" are promoted. The word was coined as a combination of "Christ" and "monogram." Hence in some Pennsylvania homes one now sees trees decorated with crosses, anchors, chalices, shells, scrolls, descending doves, circles, censers, grapes on the vine, the hand from the cloud, the lamb with banner of victory, roses, the phoenix, five-, six-, seven-, and eight-point stars, and even shamrocks and triangles (representing the Trinity).

And finally, in the last forty years, criticism of Christmas anxieties has surfaced in psychological, medical, and pastoral counseling journals. In recognition of the recurring demands placed by Christmas upon its celebrants, American psychologists have issued reports with such titles as "Christmas and Suicide" (1953), "Christmas Neurosis" (1955), "The Holiday Syndrome" (1955), "Seasonal Gloom" (1962), "Infantile Crises Associated with Christmas" (1968), "The Gift Game" (1971), "Christmas Blues" (1976), and even "Cornered at Christmas" (1978). All of these are commented upon by one of my former graduate students, Sue Samuelson, in her useful book, *Christmas: An Annotated Bibliography* (1982). Her own Ph.D. dissertation at the University of Pennsylvania was on the subject of "Christmas Malaise." And we can be sure that since her book came out, this series of articles with their intriguing titles has continued to multiply. Have a look at the Internet for the post-1982 evidence.

Obviously, for some Americans, Christmas is an effort and a burden year after year. Yet the holiday continues to charm and draw most of us into its many-layered festivities, constructed as they were from pagan and Christian, secular and ecclesiastical, folk and elite building blocks in the cultures of the Near East, Mediterranean and Northern Europe, and quintessentially for Americans, Pennsylvania. And so the majority of Americans continue to savor Christmas as the high point of their personal and family year.

May the music, the fantasy, the hope, the love, the sharing, and the joy that Christmas has meant for so many people in the past continue to flourish and spread its message of "peace on earth, good will toward men" into the new millennium.

DON YODER
THREE KINGS DAY
JANUARY 6, 1999

Notes

INTRODUCTION

1. Typical is Henry Ward Beecher's Statement:

To me Christmas is a foreign day, and I shall die so. When I was a boy I wondered what Christmas was. I knew there was such a time, because we had an Episcopal church in our town, and I saw them dressing it with evergreens, and wondered what they were taking the woods in church for; but I got no satisfactory explanation. A little later I understood it was a Romish institution, kept up by the Romish Church. Brought up in the strictest State of New England, brought up in the most literal style of worship, brought up where they would not read the Bible in church because the Episcopalians read it so much, I passed all my youth without any knowledge of Christmas, and so I have no associations with the day. Where the Christmas revel ought to be, I have nothing. It is Christmas day, that is all. (*Pittsburgh Gazette*, December 26, 1874)

For New England's attitudes on Christmas, see the novels of Harriet Beecher Stowe (*Oldtown Folks, Poganuc People*, and others) and the recent treatment of them by Charles H. Foster, *The Rungless Ladder: Harriet Beecher Stowe and New England Puritanism* (Durham, N.C.: Duke University Press, 1954).

2. Puritans in England had all sorts of reasons for neglecting Christmas. They were biblicists, sabbatarians, sparers of time and substance, believers in a simplified version of Christianity which left out the outward Catholic elements of church year and festivals. The Presbyterian, Baptist, and Quaker groups came generally out of the larger Puritan movement in the British Isles and shared its attitudes on some, though not on all, points. The Quakers, for instance, while intensely Puritan in morality and restraint of manners, were not sabbatarians, believing that all days are equally holy and refusing to pay exaggerated attention to the "sabbath" or Lord's Day. The nineteenth-century revivalist groups in America were likewise Puritan in morality and in their preference for a simplified Christianity. These included the Methodists and their Dutch Country satellites, the United Brethren, the Evangelicals, and others. The Plain Dutch (Mennonites, Amish, and Brethren), while having no historical connection with British Isles Puritanism direct or indirect, showed a "puritan" spirit on many points of interpretation. Hence my use of the term Puritanism in the wider sense; cf. James Hastings Nichols, *Democracy and the Churches* (Philadelphia: The Westminster Press, 1951), pages 10–11.

3. For a recent analysis of the confusion of tongues and cultures that was Colonial Pennsylvania, see Frederick B. Tolles, "The Culture of Early Pennsylvania," *The Pennsylvania Magazine of History and Biography*, volume 81 (1957), pages 119–137.

4. Typical of the austere Methodist attitude to Christmas, as late as 1886–87, is the statement published in the *Christian Advocate* for that year and reprinted approvingly by the *Friend* (Philadelphia): Christmas—"a purely Roman Catholic day, on which more sin and sacrilege and pagan foolishness is committed than on any day in the year."

5. This story is told in full detail in Katharine Lambert Richards, *How Christmas Came to the Sunday-Schools* (New York, 1934).

6. The growing Catholic influence on the celebration of Christmas in the nineteenth century was recognized in an article in the Harrisburg *Patriot*, December 23, 1875, quoting *Harper's* for January 1875:

The Puritan element in this country long held old Christmas at bay. But as the Puritan rigor relaxed, and the national influence of the great Irish and German immigration began to be felt, a more festal spirit was developed, a more evident fondness for pleasure and enjoyment appeared.

And again, from the Pittsburgh *Gazette*, December 25, 1856:

The neglect to celebrate this festival among the early fathers of New England, sprung from their hatred of anything 'popish'; among the children of Penn, all show or form, or formal celebration was discarded. In those portions of the Republic where the Catholic first fixed their abode the day is held in greater regard than elsewhere.

7. "The Christmas of Our Forefathers," *North American*, Philadelphia, December 15, 1907.

8. David McClure, *Diary* (New York, 1899), pages 105, 107, quoted in Elizabeth Hawthorn Buck, "Social Life in Western Pennsylvania as Seen by Early Travelers," *Western Pennsylvania Historical Magazine*, XVIII (1935), 130–131.

9. William Duane, Jr., ed., *Extracts from the Diary of Christopher Marshall* (Albany: Joel Munsell, 1877), page 151; actual quotation from original at Historical Society of Pennsylvania.

10. "The Christmas of Our Forefathers," *North American*, Philadelphia, December 15, 1907. On the relation of New York and Philadelphia to the chief holidays of the year, the New York correspondent of the Philadelphia *Sun* for December 25, 1851, writes: "Philadelphia in its celebration of Christmas, is far ahead of New York, but when it comes to celebrating New Year's Day, 'we're thar!'" It would seem that the great festival of the year was, for Boston, Thanksgiving; for New York, New Year's Day, with its survival of Dutch New Year's visiting customs; for Philadelphia, Christmas.

11. H. D. Biddle, ed., *Extracts from the Journal of Elizabeth Drinker, 1759–1807* (Philadelphia: J. B. Lippincott, 1889), passim; quotations given as found in original at Historical Society of Pennsylvania.

12. The Quaker portions of this chapter were done as part of my work in connection with a grant from the American Philosophical Society, 1957–1958, to study Pennsylvania's plain cultures and their interrelation.

13. A writer in the Philadelphia *Sunday Dispatch*, December 27, 1857, thought that Quaker resistance to Christmas had made no converts:

Pennsylvanians are naturally spirited Christmas observers. The early settlers were English and German; and if ever Christmas flourished heartily, it was in the countries from which our early ancestors hailed. The Quaker element amount to but little in this State, for, although the disciples of William Penn refused to keep vain holidays, they made no active opposition to their being kept by the "world's people," and their silent disapproval amounted to nothing.

14. One senses Quaker influence also in reading the secular newspapers in Pennsylvania Quaker communities in the nineteenth century. Was Freas, editor of the Germantown *Telegraph*, a Quaker? At least his paper is almost completely lacking in references to Christmas. Cf. December 31, 1856:

It is not often that we write about Christmas or any other holiday, for the reason that we believe them all to operate disadvantageously against the morals and well-being of the people. We have seen enough in our short life to convince us of this fact, and we defy any contradiction of it.

15. On the question of sabbath observance, Quakers differed from the other Puritan-influenced groups. Puritans proper celebrated the Sabbath as a divinely appointed day of rest and worship, holier than other days. When the nineteenth-century sabbatarians—which by 1840 included the Methodists and other revivalist groups—began their campaign to keep the canal boats, trains, horsecars, and mails from running on "the Sabbath," Quakers dissented and, true to their Inner Light doctrine, let it be known that to them "Firstday" was not holier than other days, and as a day of rest it was a civil rather than a religious institution.

16. General Christmas customs invaded the Quaker "Firstday School" as early as 1876. Cf. Edward Hocker in the Norristown *Times-Herald*, December 22, 1944: "On December 27, 1876 the Firstday School of the Norristown Friends' Meeting for the first time undertook to have a Christmas festival—closed with lighting of a Christmas tree.

17. J. D., "Deceiving Children, Causing Them to Believe and Tell Falsehoods," *Friend*, 1904, page 214. J. D.'s article is dated Fernwood, Pennsylvania, Twelfth Month 31, 1903.

18. Another excellent caricature appeared in the Lancaster *Intelligencer*, December 26, 1866:

In this country Christmas has never been fully observed, except in the South. The self-righteous Puritans who settled New England thought it a sin to be glad; and they established Thanksgiving day, with long sermons in unadorned churches, as their annual holiday. When Jedediah drove the wagon in which he had been peddling ligneous hams and wooden nutmegs back to the old barn yard, Jerusha Jane came home with her children and the whole family sat down with long faces to feed on pumpkin pie. The Dutch settlers of New Amsterdam made New Year's day the great annual holiday of New Year. In Pennsylvania Christmas has always been honored; but it was never celebrated with an approach to old English heartiness except at the South.

19. Robert Blair Risk, "Observed and Noted," *Lancaster Daily Examiner*, December 22, 1888.

20. The article "Christmas Memories," by Charles A. Smith, D.D., which appeared in the *American Presbyterian* in 1869 and was reprinted in the *Reformed Church Messenger* for February 10, 1869, suggests a similar combination of Pennsylvania Dutch and Presbyterian elements. Smith, in describing his boyhood Christ-

mas, says that the cooking at Christmas was "thoroughly German," Christmas breakfast including sausage, fricasseed chicken, and apple sauce (he means "apple butter" and tells of the laborious process required to make it). There was a Christmas tree, with gifts hung upon it, and *Christ-Kindlein* was the giver.

21. Robert Blair Risk, "Observed and Noted," Lancaster *Daily Examiner*, December 21, 1912.

22. An amusing theory about church decoration is set forth in the *Church Register* (1827) in an article entitled "Christmas Evergreens" (reprinted from the *Pulpit Magazine*): Tradition says that the first church in Britain was built of boughs. Christmas came at the same time as the feast of Saturn, which was held under the oaks, in December. "[A]nd as the oaks were then without leaves, the monks obliged the people to bring in boughs and sprigs of evergreens. . . ." Which shows that even in 1827 the popular and romantic explanations of Christmas customs were beginning to spread through the fashionable church world.

23. In the nineteenth-century periodicals of the Lutheran and Reformed Churches of Pennsylvania, the terms "Puritan" and "Puritanism" are usually distasteful terms, suggesting a stiffer and less pleasant form of religion than existed among the *gemütlich* Pennsylvanians. The term "Yankee" had an even more distasteful connotation, and such New England customs as Thanksgiving were long sneered at by Pennsylvania editors, and ridiculed, as Yankee importations which had no real reason for existing on Pennsylvania soil. For some of this feeling, see Don Yoder, "Harvest Home," *Pennsylvania Folklife*, Fall 1958.

24. "Second Christmas" is a Pennsylvania term which I find unrepresented in any of the dictionaries of American English. It was widely used not only in Pennsylvania, but also in the areas where migrating Pennsylvanians settled in the colonial period.

25. M. Diehl, *Biography of Rev. Ezra Keller, D.D.* (Springfield, Ohio, 1859), page 173.

26. William A. Helffrich, *Lebensbild aus dem Pennsylvanisch-Deutschen Predigerstand, Oder Wahrheit in Licht und Schatten* (Allentown, Pennsylvania, 1904), page 204. A similar item from an Allentown newspaper in 1859 describes the Fogelsville Sunday School Festival, to be held on Second Christmas, at 1 P.M.: "The Fogelsville Brass Band and Claussville String Band will be present, to entertain those present with good music. Sutlers are strictly forbidden to appear with their wares." (*Friedens-Bote*, Allentown, December 21, 1859)

27. *Kerwe* is the Palatine dialect form, from *Kirchweihe*. Grimm, *Deutsches Wörterbuch*, volume 5, part 1, page 822, under *Kirchmesse*, deals briefly with the history of the institution. Originally a church festival in German villages, dedicated to the saint of the village church, they early lost much of their religious character and became village fairs. The Northern English cognate is "kirkmass," the Holland Dutch *kermis*. Insight into the popular meaning of the holiday as a time devoted to pleasure is seen in the Dutch proverb *Het is neit alle dagen kermis*, "Christmas comes but once a year."

28. Roman Catholic clergy can also be somewhat Puritan in dealing with popular customs, dress, display, etc. There has been at times and in some areas a Roman Catholic equivalent of Puritanism. In fact, scholars like G. G. Coulton would go so far as to trace Protestant Puritanism from medieval Puritanism as seen especially in the clergy and monastic orders. See G. G. Coulton,

"The High Ancestry of Puritanism," in *Ten Medieval Studies* (Cambridge: Cambridge University Press, 1930), pages 58–71.

29. "The Heathenism of Christmas. A Protest Against Santa Claus," in the *Lutheran Observer*, Philadelphia, December 21, 1883. It was written for the *Lutheran Observer* by a correspondent calling himself "Germanicus."

30. M. Diehl, op. cit., pages 134–135.

31. Ibid., pages 173, 333.

32. The "donation" (donation visit, pound party, pounding, or surprise donation) was an American church social, involving a practical gift of food to the pastor and his family from his congregation. While usually connected with Christmas or New Year's, we sometimes find it in the fall, or at any time of year when a new pastor arrived in the parish. The *Reformed Church Messenger* mentions, for example, a "donation visit" to a new pastor, October 9, 1867; a "surprise" party for the pastor, December 16, 1868; a new set of teeth for the pastor as a New Year's present, February 3, 1869; a "donation visit" to the new pastor and family, January 20, 1869; and a "donation visit" on New Year's Eve, January 19, 1870. Even the Presbyterians honored their minister with gifts at Christmas: "The time has again arrived when Congregations, Bible Classes, and others, are in the habit of making presents of Books, &c. to their pastors and friends." (*Presbyterian*, Philadelphia and New York, December 15, 1838)

33. George B. Russell, *Creed and Customs* (Philadelphia, 1869), pages 400–401.

34. See the General Conference hymnal, *Gesangbuch mit Noten* (Berne, Indiana, 1890), which has a section of *Adventslieder* (hymns 40–47) and *Weihnachtslieder* (hymns 48–55), most of them by standard German writers, some of them to historic chorale tunes, others to "American" tunes by Lowell Mason, William B. Bradbury, and others.

35. C. M. Bomberger, "Almanacs and Herbs," *Pennsylvania Dutchman*, May 15, 1950.

36. Jehovah's Witnesses quote the same verses in their current opposition to Christmas. Mennonites seem today to be in a transition state between the old plain stable rural culture and "Third Force" revivalism and apocalypticism. See "The Third Force in Christendom," *Life Magazine*, June 9, 1958, which says of all the "Third Force" groups: "Their membership dismisses most present-day Christian customs and ritual as obstacles to the close relationship between man and God." It is also true that the apocalyptic Third-Forcers are interested not in growth and continuity in religion, based on past revelation, but rather on their own myth of the future, based on first-century apocalypticism. Hence such ideas as Christmas—which means for Christians a supreme example of the approach of God and man, in a specific moment of the past—mean nothing to them.

CHRISTMAS MUMMERS

1. Evelyn Schuler, who did a series of articles in the Philadelphia *Public Ledger* in 1930 on the history of the various units which participated in the New Year parade, wrote a revealing letter in the November 24 issue in reference to the terminology *mummers:* "From this they became known as 'shooters,' the only name the present-day mummers know and understand. 'Mummers' is a newspaper word, they explain, and to put it frankly, they will have none of it."

2. I fear that the connection with the Mysteries would be rather hard to trace, yet this horseplay was not likely of English origin, and flourished only while colonial manners retained distinctions of class. There is a dim likeness to the sports of holidays in England.

BARRING OUT THE SCHOOLMASTER

1. In the Lehigh Valley and sporadically elsewhere in eastern Pennsylvania, Shrove Tuesday was the traditional day for locking out the teacher. On Shrove Tuesday the last child out of bed in the Dutch Country is called the *fawsanacht* and is kidded all day long. Likewise, the last pupil to arrive at school that morning was similarly named and too came in for much teasing. To make sure one would not be the school *fawsanacht*, the children started for school very early on this morning, some even before daybreak. What did they do with all the free time before the first bell? They barricaded the inside of the schoolroom, locked out the teacher, and demanded the declaration of a holiday.

2. The term *barring-out* was also used as a noun. For example: "The one whose leg was caught under the window at the 'barring-out,'" from Abel C. Thomas's *Autobiography* (Boston, 1852), page 377.

3. Dr. Clifford J. Shipton, the librarian of the American Antiquarian Society and a leading authority on the history of education in New England, tells the author that he has never come upon the custom of barring out the schoolmaster anywhere in New England. There is early evidence for it in Virginia, however. Jane Carson, research associate at Colonial Williamsburg, informs that for a brief period, 1669–1702, the grammar students at William and Mary barred out the teacher before Christmas. The evidence for this practice is an affidavit of Commissary James Blair, President of the College, dated May 1, 1704; it was printed in a pamphlet, *Affidavit Made by His Reverence James Blair . . . against Francis Nicholson, Esq: Governour of the Said Province* (London, 1727), pages 1–6, and reprinted in William Stevens Perry, *Historical Collections Relating to the American Colonial Church* (Hartford, 1870), vol. 1, pages 131–138. The next and last reference to the custom in Virginia is for 1773. In the *Journal & Letters of Philip Vickers Fithian, 1773–1774: A Plantation Tutor of the Old Dominion* (Williamsburg, 1943), page 45, under entry of December 18, 1773, Fithian noted that a fellow tutor on a nearby plantation had been barred out of his school.

4. Phebe Earle Gibbons's article "Pennsylvania Dutch" in the *Atlantic Monthly* for October 1869, page 485: "We still hear of barring-out at Christmas. The pupils fasten themselves in the schoolhouse, and keep the teacher out to obtain presents from him."

METZEL SOUP AND CHRISTMAS MONEY

1. Sener's account of the metzel soup is copied almost verbatim from a description in the Harrisburg *Telegraph*, which was reprinted in the Lancaster *Daily Examiner* of December 29, 1880. For comparison's sake we here give part of the Harrisburg story:

There is an old story among Germans that on one occasion, near Strasburg, the King (father of Frederick the Great) was riding with the Prince, and passing a farmer's house where a metzel soup was being indulged in with all its disgusting revelries, the irate monarch, incensed at the exhibition, leaped from his horse, grasped a cudgel and began belaboring men and women indiscriminately, and breaking the arms of a number before the Prince could induce his royal father to desist.

MATZABAUM, MOSHEY, AND BELLYGUTS

1. Drepperd article in the February 1, 1956, issue of the Lancaster *New Era:*

"What is a Mojhy?" This question, we suspect, designed to "floor" us, came from a Berks Countian who we just know was grinning behind his genial exterior, grinning at what he thought would be our complete failure. He was right. We knew nothing about the thing called a mojhy. But we were in ignorance only a short second after our admission. "The mojhy is a Pennsylvania German candy that is like a hard patty for awhile, but then reduces to a chewy candy as you suck it," he explained. Having more than a teaspoonful of skepticism on tap at all times we determined to investigate the mojhy. When Barton Sharp asked us to go to the Reading Antiques show with him on the day we had planned to go to the Daniel Boone homestead, we agreed . . . and lo, there at the Reading Show we saw a jarful of mojhy's and bought some. They do not melt down into a chewy patty. They are essentially the same as the famed "cleartoy" which many of us remember as Christmas candy. They are made by boiling sugar in syrup and coloring. . . . Sometimes they are cast in very small pans of "bite size" and sometimes in big pans of maple sugar size. Every now and then apples on sticks are dipped in the mojhy sugar and become glaced . . . patty apples.

We looked in vain for the term mojhy in our German Dictionary. We did not look in vain for a similar term in our French Dictionary. This is what we found there—Moyeu (pronounced m'wahje), a sugar plum, or plum preserved by a glace process. Not the dragee. The French pronunciation, m'wahje is almost precisely that of mojhy. So, isn't it pertinent to wonder if the Huguenot settlers of Berks, in the Oley valley, did not introduce the moyeu and, after many years, it became more nearly the name its pronunciation suggests mojhy. Where, we asked, did this candy seem to have its roots? You guessed it. In the Oley Valley! Of course, our several informants may have been wrong in their facts. But there is no question that moyeu, pronounced m'wahje, means a preserved plum . . . a sugared or glaced plum. Now who in Lancaster County knows anything about this candy called the mojhy? We can tabulate the results under Domestic Economy; Candy, in our final files! There is no doubt about it, names of things, and of people, were strangely transformed in our colonial years.

2. Elizabeth Kieffer of Lancaster, Pennsylvania, informs the author that she remembers her grandmother, a native of Harrisburg, making a sweet she called moshey. Miss Kieffer says it was a cross between candy and cake—something vaguely like a praline.

3. The *Independent Balance* of April 8, 1818, has the following use of the word bellyguts: "There is an astonishing similarity between our esteemed friend and worthy agent Mordecai Bellyguts Noah and John Binn."

CHRISTMAS DEW

1. There is a similar description in the Irwin M. Hering manuscript "Boyhood Memories" (Muhlenberg College Library). Regarding Christmas in the period 1880–90 in Weisenberg Township, Lehigh County, Mr. Hering wrote:

Dew of Heaven. This was a practice never forgotten at our home and came into practice in our family directly from the generation before. On the evening before Christmas, father would place some grain, corn, hay, out in the open below the sky above where the morning's dew would fall upon it; hay for the cows, grain for the horses, corn for the swine and fowl. If he forgot to do this before dark or was not at home earlier in the evening, he would go out later on in the dark and take care of it. The first thing father did in the morning when he got up and out to the barn was to dole out to the animals, the feed that had the benefit of the dew of heaven.

In the house, mother would place some cakes, usually cookies, a piece of sausage perhaps in a basket and hang them on the clothes line where animals would not get at it during the night, and where the dew of the morning would fall upon them. The first thing we boys were supposed to do after we got up and downstairs was to partake of the cookies even if only to the smallest degree.

To do this faithfully was supposed to keep the animals, fowl, and other barn inhabitants from sickness during the following year; and the same of course applied to the folks in the house.

CHRIST-KINDEL TO KRISS KRINGLE

1. Before 1840 we located but three references to Santa Claus in our Pennsylvania Christmas literature. The earliest is from the Philadelphia *Saturday Evening Post* of January 7, 1826. The very next one is from the Lancaster *Union* of December 27, 1836: "and when the Christmas trees have all been wondered at . . . 'St. Claus' and his tiny chariot and horses will have ceased whirling through the brains of our little readers." The third is from the Philadelphia *Herald and Sentinel* of December 25, 1837: "where that old graybeard, 'Santa Clause,' or St. Nicholas, finds so many beautiful articles which he afterwards distributes in his rambles."

The definitive article on the origin of Santa Claus in America is Charles W. Jones's "Knickerbocker Santa Claus," in the *New York Historical Society Quarterly* for October 1954, pages 357–383. This article is the best piece of Christmas research in America to date.

2. Unlike Santa Claus, who came down the chimney, the Christ-kindel entered through the keyhole. We herewith reproduce two keyhole items: the Harrisburg *Democratic Union* of December 25, 1844: "Let juvenile innocence, when it rises from its pillow, discover its strained expectations satisfied by the nocturnal visit of St. Nicholas to the suspended stocking, or the mysterious entrance of *christkindle* through the key-hole"; the Carlisle *American Volunteer* of December 23, 1858: "the mysterious entrance of *christkinkle* thro' the key-hole."

THE CHRISTMAS TREE IN PENNSYLVANIA

1. The history of research into the beginnings of the Christmas tree in America follows: The first scholars who concerned themselves with the problem were Alfred F. Berlin and Henry Mercer. Berlin's two-page article "Introduction of the Christmas Tree in the United States" appeared in 1917 in the *Bucks County Historical Society Proceedings* (volume 4, pages 553–554); Mercer's followed on pages 555–557.

Since 1943 three scholars have devoted themselves to documenting the first Christmas tree in this country: Dr. William I. Schreiber of Wooster, Ohio; the late Rudolf Hommel; and Dr. Philip A. Shelley of The Pennsylvania State University. Dr. Schreiber's initial article, "The First American Christmas Tree," appeared in the December 1943 *American-German Review*. His most recent contribution, "Wie der Weihnachtsbaum nach Amerika kam," appeared in 1957 in *Christ Unterwegs* abroad. Rudolf Hommel's contributions are a pamphlet (privately printed in 1947), *On the Trail of the First Christmas Tree*, and an article in the December 1949 *Pennsylvania Dutchman*. Dr. Shelley's findings have appeared in his annual Christmas letter to his friends, as well as in *College Affairs* of December 1951.

The 1948 yearbook of the Department of Agriculture carried an article on the American Christmas tree tradition by Arthur M. Sowder, an extension forester in the Department of Agriculture. The Sowder article added no new information, but succeeded, unfortunately, in spreading anew all over the country the statement that trimmed Christmas trees were first used in the United States during the American Revolution by Hessian soldiers and later at Christmas festivities in 1804 at Fort Dearborn in Illinois. There is absolutely *no documentation* for the foregoing, neither in the diaries of the Hessian troops, nor elsewhere. And as to the

1804 tree, the author does not even bother to indicate his source. (It derives, incidentally, from the *Fort Dearborn Magazine* of 1920, which states that one Captain Whistler, a native of Ireland, ordered his soldiers to put up a Christmas tree. The suggestion is made that the Irish officer learned of Christmas trees from Hessian soldiers during the Revolutionary War!)

A roster of "first" Christmas trees outside of Pennsylvania, from documented sources, follows: 1832 in Massachusetts; 1834 in Illinois; 1835 in Ohio; 1840 in New York; and 1846 in Texas and Mexico.

For many years, at Christmas time, around the turn of the century, American newspapers all over the country were carrying articles stating that a German immigrant, August Imgard, of Wooster, Ohio, put up the first Christmas tree in this country in the year 1847. A commemorative plate gotten up by the ladies of the First Presbyterian Church of Wooster as recently as 1954 continues spreading this misinformation.

Pennsylvania newspapers and periodicals, through the years, advanced highly preposterous statements regarding the origin of the Christmas tree, among them the Lancaster *Semi-Weekly Intelligencer* of December 22, 1897: "The first Christmas tree in America was decorated and lighted up in New Amsterdam when Manhattan Island was a colony of the Dutch"; *Godey's Lady's Book* of December 1885: "The birthplace of the Christmas-Tree is Egypt, and its origin dates from the period long antecedent to the Christian era"; the *Saturday Evening Post* of December 30, 1882: "The Christmas-tree dates as far back as the seventh century." Legion are the references in the press that the Christmas tree is a practice deriving from the Druids.

2. *Lancaster County Historical Society Proceedings*, volume 47, page 64.

3. Evergreens—not Christmas trees—have been used to decorate Episcopalian and Catholic churches at Christmas time from their very first establishment in Pennsylvania. Peter Kalm described the decoration of the Catholic Church in Philadelphia on Christmas Day, 1749: "Pews and altar were decorated with branches of mountain laurel." The Pottsville *Miners' Journal* of December 24, 1859, alludes to this practice:

We will go out with the boys into the woods and get the "greens" for Christmas wreaths, and dig in the snow for the beautiful pine, and will ride to the church on top of the loads of pines, and hemlocks, and Kalmia, and will help the girls to weave them into festoons, and wind the pillars and hang the galleries, and make the star and work the green letters for "glory to God."

From the Easton *Express* of December 26, 1867, we learn that five hundred yards of evergreen were employed in the decoration of the Episcopal Church. As a final reference to the use of evergreens in Pennsylvania at Christmas time we shall quote the Philadelphia *North American* of December 23, 1867:

Now is the time that people decorate the churches, halls and saloons with spruce, holly and pine. The barrens of New Jersey now yield their only crop. Raids upon them are made at this season, and many an "honest penny" is turned from a soil whose only other productions are huckleberries and garter snakes. The ravages

upon these barrens for Christmas trees are by no means inconsiderable, and whole tracts are denuded every winter to supply the demand for Philadelphia customers. In their thrift and industry the farmers along these barrens engage in another enterprise that a few years ago was never thought of. They gather the fronds of the hemlock and the holly, and making them into continuous strands, sell them by the yard for wreaths and festoons, as if the material were ribbon or tape. A congregation therefore who wish to decorate a church can buy from these Jersey people ready prepared for hanging, all the material they require.

4. In the early years of the Christmas tree in this country, certain German-American institutions in Pennsylvania—Lutheran orphanages in Philadelphia and Pittsburgh—lit the tree and distributed gifts on Christmas Eve.

CHRISTMAS DAY

1. A second Dutch-English poem, "To My Sussy" (Reading *Chronicle of the Times*, January 10, 1826), has a stanza alluding to Christmas dinner:

My Sus Kan milch dhe Kows—unt pake—
  (Peshure she's not ashamt to do it)
Ahn ghrist-tag do, my Sus kan make
  Budding mit abbles, meal unt suit.

SECOND CHRISTMAS

1. The best volume to date on the history of gambling in America, Herbert Asbury's *Sucker's Progress* (New York, 1938), fails to mention either raffling or hustling.

OF PYRAMIDS AND PUTZES

1. The *Moravian* of April 30, 1863:

Moravian Sugar Cake. To gratify one of our lady subscribers, and in compliance with other repeated solicitations, we furnish herewith a recipe for making the genuine home-made sugar cake which we have taken down from the lips of several experienced housekeepers. Recipe: Of well-risen wheaten bread dough take about two pounds. Work into it a tea-cupful of brown sugar, quarter of a pound of butter and a beaten egg. Knead well and put into a square pan dredged with flour. Cover it and set it near the fire for half an hour to rise. When risen, wash with melted butter, makes holes in the dough to half its depth, two inches apart, fill them with sugar and a little butter. Then spread ground cinnamon and a thick layer of brown sugar over the whole surface. Sprinkle with a little essence of lemon. Put into the oven and bake in fifteen minutes.

FIRECRACKER CHRISTMASES

1. Around 1900 Helen Grimes, in an article in the Pittsburgh *Gazette Times* on the Pittsburgh of seventy years before—the 1830s, therefore—wrote:

The shouts of the children, the popping of firecrackers, the jingle of sleighbells, the laughter and chatter of gayly dressed people, exchanging pleasant greetings—for everyone knew everyone else—imparted a festive holiday air to the town, such as would be difficult to create today.

Further Reading

Aurich, Gustav. *Hagios Nikolaos: Der Heilige Nikolaus in der griechischen Kirche.* 2 vols. Leipzig: B. G. Teubner, 1913.

Barnett, James H. *The American Christmas: A Study in National Culture.* New York: Macmillan, 1954.

Bauman, Richard. "Belsnickling in a Nova Scotia Island Community." *Western Folklore* 31, no. 4 (1972): 229–243.

Baur, John E. *Christmas on the American Frontier, 1800–1900.* Caldwell, Idaho: Caxton Printers, 1961.

Belsnickle's Gift, Or a Visit from Saint Nicholas. A Holiday Present for the Young. Dedicated to the Girls and Boys Who Obey Their Parents. Lancaster, Pa.: James H. Bryson, 1843.

Benson, Evelyn A. "Pennsylvania's Own Christmas Differed from All the Rest." Lancaster (Pennsylvania) *Sunday News,* 21 December 1958.

Berky, Andrew S. "Christmas Customs of the Perkiomen Valley." *Pennsylvania Dutchman* 4, no. 8 (1952): 2–3, 7.

Bischoff, Oskar, ed. *Das Pfälzische Weihnachtsbuch.* Neustadt an der Weinstrasse: Pfälzische Verlagsanstalt, 1970.

Bogner, Gerhard. *Das Grosse Krippen-Lexikon: Geschichte, Symbolik, Glaube.* Munich: Süddeutscher Verlag, 1981.

Bokum, Hermann, ed. *The Stranger's Gift: A Christmas and New Year's Present.* Boston: Light and Horton, 1836.

Bradley, David. "Merry Kwanzaa." *Pennsylvania Gazette* 93, no. 3 (1994): 42–47.

Bringéus, Nils-Arvid. *Årets festseder.* Stockholm: Seelig, 1976.

Brody, Alan. *The English Mummers and Their Plays: Traces of Ancient Mystery.* Philadelphia: University of Pennsylvania Press, 1970.

Bronner, Simon J. "Shoemaker vs. Shoemaker: The Debate on Pennsylvania Germans in American Tradition." *Der Reggeboge/The Rainbow: Journal of the Pennsylvania German Society* 30, nos. 1–2 (1996): 3–30.

Brower, D. H. B. *Danville, Montour County, Pennsylvania: A Collection of Historical and Biographical Sketches.* Harrisburg, Pa.: Lane S. Hart, 1881.

Buck, William J. *History of Bucks County from its Earliest Settlement to the Close of the Eighteenth Century.* Doylestown, Pa.: John S. Brown, 1855.

———. "Manners and Customs." In: *History of Montgomery County, Pennsylvania,* edited by Theodore W. Bean, 335–338. Philadelphia: Everts & Peck, 1884.

Canter, Irving. "Uncle Sam, the Hanukkah Man: Assimilation or Contra-Culturation?" *Reconstructionist* 27, no. 9 (1961): 5–13.

Cassel, Paulus. *Weihnachten: Ursprung, Bräuche und Aberglauben.* Berlin: Ludwig Rank, 1861.

"Christmas . . . An Ethnic Experience." *Cultural Columns* 4, no. 1 (1984): 6–7. Harrisburg, Pa.: The Governor's Heritage Affairs Commission, 1984.

Clouse, Jerry A. "The German Element in Perry County." *Der Reggeboge/The Rainbow: Journal of the Pennsylvania German Society* 31, nos. 1–2 (1997): 3–26.

Coffin, Tristram Potter. *The Book of Christmas Folklore.* New York: Seabury Press, 1973.

Cox, Harvey. *The Feast of Fools: A Theological Essay on Festivity.* New York: Harper and Row, 1970.

Davis, Susan G. "'Making Night Hideous': Christmas Revelry and Public Order in Nineteenth Century Philadelphia." *American Quarterly* 34 (February 1982): 185–199.

DeGroot, Adriaan D. *Saint Nicholas: A Psychoanalytic Study of His History and Myth.* New York: Basic Books, 1965.

DeJonge, Eric. "The Origins of the Pennsylvania Belsnickel." *Pennsylvania Farmer* (Harrisburg, Pa.) 165, no. 12 (December 23, 1961); 4–5.

Diehl, M. *Biography of Rev. Ezra Keller, D.D., Founder and First President of Wittenberg College.* Springfield, Ohio: Ruralist Publishing Co., 1859.

Drinker, Elizabeth. *The Diary of Elizabeth Drinker.* Edited by Elaine Forman Crane, et al. 3 vols. Boston: Northwestern University Press, 1991.

Duane, William, Jr., ed. *Extracts from the Diary of Christopher Marshall.* Albany, N.Y.: Joel Munsell, 1877.

Egan, Maurice. "A Day in the Ma'sh." *Scribner's Monthly* (July 1881): 343–352.

Erich, Oswald A., and Richard Beitl. *Wörterbuch der deutschen Volkskunde.* 3d ed. Edited by Richard Beitl and Klaus Beitl. Stuttgart: Alfred Kröner Verlag, 1974.

Fisher, Henry L. *Olden Times; or, Pennsylvania Rural Life, Some Fifty Years Ago, And Other Poems.* York: Fisher Bros., 1888.

Fogel, Edwin M. "Of Months and Days." *Pennsylvania German Folklore Society* 5 (1940).

———. "Twelvetide." *Pennsylvania German Folklore Society* 6 (1941).

Gibbons, Phebe Earle. *Pennsylvania Dutch, And Other Essays.* Philadelphia: J. B. Lippincott, 1882.

Golby, J. M., and A. W. Purdue. *The Making of the Modern Christmas.* London: B. T. Batsford, 1986.

Gross, Leonard. "The Jew and Christmas." *Look* (28 December 1965): 22–24.

Halpert, Herbert, and G. M. Story, eds. *Christmas Mumming in Newfoundland: Essays in Anthropology, Folklore, and History.* Toronto: Toronto University Press, 1969.

Harbaugh, H[enry]. *The Star of Bethlehem! A Christmas Story, for Good Children.* Lancaster, Pa.: Pearsoll and Geist, 1862.

Harding, Annaliese. *John Lewis Krimmel: Genre Artist of the Early Republic.* Winterthur, Dela.: Henry Francis du Pont Winterthur Museum, 1994.

Helffrich, William A. *Lebensbild aus dem Pennsylvanisch-Deutschen Predigerstand, Oder Wahrheit in Licht und Schatten.* Edited by N. W. A. and W. N. Helffrich. Allentown, Pa.: privately printed, 1906.

Herberg, Will. *Protestant, Catholic, Jew.* New York: Doubleday Anchor Books, 1960.

Higgins, Emily Mayer. *Holidays at the Grange; or, A Week's Delight. Games and Stories for Parlor and Fireside.* Philadelphia: Porter & Coates, 1886.

Hofmann, Hans. *Die Heiligen Drei Könige: Zur Heiligenverehrung im kirchlichen, gesellschaftlichen und politischen Leben des Mittelalters.* Bonn: Röhrscheid, 1975.

Holliday, Albert E. "Mummers Strut Their Stuff on New Year's Day." *Pennsylvania Illustrated* 2, no. 2 (1977): 20–25.

Hoskins, Janina W. "Christmas in Europe: A Selective List of References in English." *Library of Congress Information Bulletin* 38, no. 49 (1979): 499–504.

Hostetler, Beulah S. "A Christmas in Germany." *Pennsylvania Farmer* (8 December 1956): 5, 23.

Jones, Charles W. "Knickerbocker Santa Claus." *New York Historical Society Quarterly* 38 (October 1954): 357–383.

———. *Saint Nicholas of Myra, Bari, and Manhattan: Biography of a Legend.* Chicago: University of Chicago Press, 1978.

Kane, Harnett F. *The Southern Christmas Book: The Full Story from Earliest Times to Present: People, Customs, Conviviality, Carols, Cooking.* New York: David McKay, 1958.

Kieffer, Elizabeth Clarke. "Christmas Customs in Lancaster County." *Papers Read Before the Lancaster County Historical Society* 43, no. 6 (1939): 175–182.

Klinefelter, Walter, ed. *A Bibliographical Check-list of Christmas Books.* Portland, Maine: Southworth-Anthoesen Press, 1937.

Kohler, Erika. *Martin Luther und der Festbrauch.* Köln-Graz: Böhlau Verlag, 1959.

Kretzenbacher, Leopold. *Santa Lucia und die Lutzelfrau: Volksglaube und Hochreligion im Spannungsfeld Mittel und Südosteuropas.* Munich: R. Oldenbourg, 1959.

Kriss Kringle's Book. Philadelphia: Thomas, Cowperthwait, & Co., 1842.

Kriss Kringle's Christmas Tree. A Holiday Present for Boys and Girls. Philadelphia: E. Ferrett & Co., 1845.

Kriss Kringle's Raree Show, for Good Boys and Girls. New York: William H. Murphy, etc., 1847.

Künzig, Johannes. *Die alemannisch-schwäbische FASNET.* Freiburg, West Germany: Institut für Ostdeutsche Volkskunde, 1950.

Lanz, Josef. *Krippenkunst in Schlesien.* Marburg: N. G. Elwert Verlag, 1981.

Lauffer, Otto. *Der Weihnachtsbaum in Glauben und Brauch.* Berlin: de Gruyter, 1934.

Levy, Paul. *The Feast of Christmas.* London: Kyle Cathie, 1992.

Mannhardt, Wilhelm. *Wald-und Feldkulte.* 2d ed. 2 vols. Berlin, 1905. Reprint, Darmstadt: Wissenschaftliche Buchgesellschaft, 1963.

Mantel, Kurt. *Geschichte des Weihnachtsbaumes und ähnlicher weihnachtlicher Formen: Eine kultur- und waldgeschichtliche Untersuchung.* Hannover: Verlag M.u.H. Schoper, 1975.

McNeill, John Thomas, and Helen M. Gamer. *Medieval Handbooks of Penance.* New York: Columbia University Press, 1948.

Méchin, Colette. *Saint Nicolas: Fêtes et traditions populaires d'hier et d'aujourd'hui.* Paris: Berger Levrault, 1978.

Meisen, Karl. *Nikolauskult und Nikolausbrauch im Abendlande: Eine kultgeographische- volkskundliche Untersuchung.* Düsseldorf: L. Schwann, 1931.

Miles, Clement A. *Christmas in Ritual and Tradition, Christian and Pagan.* 2d ed. London: T. Fisher Unwin, 1913.

Myers, Richmond E. "The Moravian Christmas Putz." *Pennsylvania German Folklore Society* 6 (1941).

Nitzsche, George E. "The Christmas Putz of the Pennsylvania Germans." *Pennsylvania German Folklore Society* 6 (1941).

Papa, Joan Springer. "When Santa Was the Terror of Christmas." *Today: Philadelphia Inquirer Magazine* (12 December 1971): 6–8, 10, 12, 14–15.

Perry County: A Pictorial History. Newport, Pa.: The Perry Historians, 1978.

Program 6th Annual Pennsylvania Dutch Folk Festival June 30 to July 4, 1955—Kutztown, Pa. Lancaster, Pa.: Pennsylvania Dutch Folklore Center, 1955. [Biographies of Alfred L. Shoemaker, Don Yoder, and J. William Frey, pages 28–31.]

Reichard, Harry Hess. "The Christmas Poetry of the 'Pennsylvania Dutch.'" *Pennsylvania German Folklore Society* 6 (1941).

Reid, Ira DeA. "The John Canoe Festival." *Phylon* 3 (1942): 349–370.

Restad, Penne L. *Christmas in America: A History.* New York: Oxford University Press, 1995.

Richards, Katharine Lambert. *How Christmas Came to the Sunday-Schools: The Observance of Christmas in the Protestant Church Schools of the United States.* New York: Dodd, Mead, 1934.

Robacker, Earl F. "Art in Christmas Cookies." *Dutchman* 6, no. 3 (winter 1954–1955): 2–7.

————. "Christmas Back Along." *Pennsylvania Folklife* 16, no. 2 (winter 1966–1967): 2–13.

Robbins, Walter L. "Notes & Queries: Christmas Shooting Rounds in America and Their Background." *Journal of American Folklore* 86, no. 339 (1973): 48–52.

Rominger, Charles H. "Early Christmases in Bethlehem, Pennsylvania (1742–1756)." *Pennsylvania German Folklore Society* 6 (1941).

Russell, George B. *Creed and Customs of the Reformed Church.* Philadelphia: Reformed Church Publication Board, 1869.

Samuelson, Sue. *Christmas: An Annotated Bibliography.* Garland Folklore Bibliographies, vol. 4. New York: Garland, 1982.

————. "Nativity Scenes: Description and Analysis." *Folklore and Mythology Studies* 3 (spring 1979): 5–16.

Sansom, William. *A Book of Christmas.* New York: McGraw-Hill, 1968.

Sauermann, Dietmar, ed. *Weihnachten in Westfalen um 1900.* Münster: F. Coppenrath Verlag, 1976.

Schreiber, William I. "First Christmas Trees in America." *Journal of German-American Studies* 15, no. 1 (1980): inside back cover.

Shaeler, A. D. *The Story of the Christmas Putz.* Herrnhut, Germany: Gustav Winter, 1927.

Shoemaker, Alfred L. *Christmas in Pennsylvania: A Folk-Cultural Study.* 1st ed. With an introduction by Don Yoder. Kutztown, Pa.: Pennsylvania Folklife Society, 1959.

————. "Fantasticals." *Pennsylvania Folklife* 9, no. 1 (winter 1957–1958): 28–31.

Snyder, Philip V. *The Christmas Tree Book.* New York: Viking, 1976.

Spamer, Adolf. *Weihnachten in Alter und Neuer Zeit.* Jena, Germany: Eugen Diederichs, 1937.

Spencer, Frances Kipps. *Chrismons: Christian Year Series.* Danville, Va.: Lutheran Church of the Ascension, 1965.

"Ueber die Christ- oder Weihnachts-bescherung." *Neu-Verbesserter Nord-Americanischer Calender 1785.* Lancaster, Pa.: Francis Bailey, 1785.

Usener, Hermann. *Religionsgeschichtliche Untersuchungen Erster Teil: Das Weihnachtsfest.* 3d ed. Bonn: H. Bouvier, 1969.

Van der Linden, R. *Ikonografie van Sint-Niklaas in Vlaanderen.* Lederberg: Drukkenrij Erasmus, 1972.

Van Gennep, Arnold. "Cycle des Douze Jours." *Manuel de Folklore Français Contemporain* 1, no. 7, 1958.

Waits, William B. *The Modern Christmas in America: A Cultural History of Gift-Giving.* New York: New York University Press, 1993.

Weaver, William Woys. *The Christmas Cook: Three Centuries of American Yuletide Sweets.* New York: Harper Perennial/Harper Collins Publishers, 1990.

————. *Pennsylvania Dutch Country Cooking.* New York: Abbeville Press, 1993.

Weber-Kellermann, Ingeborg. *Das Weihnachtsfest: Eine Kultur- und Sozialgeschichte der Weihnachtszeit.* Luzern: Verlag C. J. Bucher, 1978.

Weihnachten in Vergangenheit und Gegenwart: Ausstellung des Ludwig-Uhland Instituts für Volkskunde an der Universität Tübingen 1964–1965. Tübingen: Ludwig-Uhland Institut, 1964.

Weiser, Frederick S. "Pennsylvania's Folk Religion: The Raw Materials of Repentance." *Lutheran Forum* 1, no. 12 (1967): 4–6.

Weiser, Lily. *Weihnachtsgeschenke und Weihnachtsbaum: Eine volkskundliche Untersuchung ihrer Geschichte.* Stuttgart: F. A. Perthes, 1923.

Weiser-Aall, Lily. "Jul." *Kulturhistorisk Leksikon for nordisk Middelalder* 8 (1963): cols. 6–14.

Welch, Charles E., Jr. *"Oh, Dem Golden Slippers."* New York: Nelson, 1970.

————. "Some Early Phases of the Philadelphia Mummers' Parade." *Pennsylvania Folklife* 9, no. 1 (winter 1957–1958): 24–27.

Winey, Fay McAfee. "Belsnickling in Paxtonville." *Pennsylvania Folklife* 19, no. 2 (1969–1970): 10–13.

Wolf, Eric R. "Santa Claus: Notes on a Collective Representation." In: *Process and Pattern in Culture: Essays in Honor of Julian H. Steward,* edited by Robert A. Manners, 147–155. Chicago: Aldine, 1964.

Yoder, Don. "Christmas Customs: Folk-Cultural Questionnaire No. 10." *Pennsylvania Folklife* 18, no. 2 (spring 1967): 49.

————. "Christmas Fraktur, Christmas Broadsides." *Pennsylvania Folklife* 14, no. 2 (1964): 2–9.

————. *Discovering American Folklife: Studies in Ethnic, Religious, and Regional Culture.* Ann Arbor: UMI Research Press, 1990.

Zentz, Wendy. "Solstice: A Holiday for Atheists." *Philadelphia Inquirer* (16 December 1984).

Index

Page numbers in *italics* indicate illustrations.

Alderfer, E. Gordon, 42
Alexander, M. R., 13
Allison, Mrs. Robert, 53
"Among the Christmas Trees" articles, 67–74
"Amusements in Rural Homes around the Big and Little Mahoning Creeks" (Jack), 42
Annals of Philadelphia (Watson), 36
    excerpts from, 78, 102
anxieties, Christmas, 148
apees, 102–104
    recipe for, 104
Arthur, T. S., 105
Autobiography of Rev. Abel C. Thomas (Thomas), excerpt from, 8

Bache, Anne, 43
Bacon, Samuel, 23–24
Barba, Preston A., 103
Barr, George R., 12
barring out the schoolmaster, 7–14
Bassler, J. H., 13
Bauman, Richard, 139
Bausman, Benjamin, 10, 29, 38, 80
Baver, Russell and Florence, ix
Bayard, Samuel P., 129
Beam, C. Richard, ix
Beck, James N., 121
Behney, J. J., 19
bell-ringing, holiday, xiv
bellyguts, 21, 23–24
Belsnickels, 3, 76, 84
    Nova Scotian, 139–140
    research, 137–142
    today, 140–142
Belsnickling, 75–90
    in groups, *141*
"Belsnickling in a Nova Scotia Island Community" (Bauman), 139–140
Berky, Andrew S., 89
Berlin, Alfred F., 46
"Birth of Christ, The," broadside (Peters), *xv*
Bischoff, Oskar, 134

Blue Hills, The (Weygandt), excerpt from, 22
Bokum, Herman, 48
Book of Christmas Folklore, The (Coffin), 134
Book of Christmas, A (Sansom), 134
bookplates, 145, *145*
Brandt, Francis B., 3–4
Brendel, John B., 89
British Isles groups, xiii
broadsides, 144–145
Brophy, Bertha, 42
Brower, D. H. B., 11
Buck, William J., 85, 105
bushwhacker Christmas, 121–126

Carnival of Horns, 91–98
Center for Pennsylvania German Studies, Millersville University, ix
Century of Moravian Sisters, A (Myers), excerpt from, 126–127
Children's Friend, The, plate from, *129*
Chrismon trees, 148
Christ Child, 137–138
Christ-kindel, 33–36
    containers for, 38–44
Christmas
    activities, 107–114
    colonial, xiv–xvi
    controversy, xiv–xvi, xvi–xvii
    in multicultural America, 147–148
    Open-Hearth, 1–2
    Woodstove, 1, 29–31
    see also Second Christmas
Christmas addresses, 144–145
Christmas in America: A History (Restad), 134–135
Christmas cards, 44, 79, 147
    early, *xxviii*
Christmas Cook, The (Weaver), 144
"Christmas Customs of the Perkiomen Valley" (Berky), excerpt from, 89–90
Christmas Fairs, 110–114
    opposition to, 112–14
"Christmas at Home" (Bache), excerpt from, 43
Christmas money, 19–20

Christmas Mumming in Newfoundland (Halpert and Story, eds.), 140
"Christmas Presents" (Arthur), 105
Christmas stockings, 42–44
"Christmas Tree, The," 52
Christmas trees, 45–55
    on Christmas morning, 55
    corner, 68
    decorations, 57–65
    during 1830s, 46–47
    during 1840s, 47–49
    earliest documented reference to, 45
    earliest printed use of term, 46–47
    earliest use in Sunday schools, 49–52
    early, 48, *70, 71, 72*
    first community, 55
    humorous, 64–65
    Moravians, 53
    ornaments, 59–64
    post 1850 period, 52–55
    stereopticon card, *73*
    twentieth-century developments, 55
"Christmas When I Was a Boy" (Kremer), excerpt from, 12–13
Christmas: An Annotated Bibliography (Samuelson), 148
"Christmas-Eve Reverie" (N. A. M. E.), excerpt from, 100
Cochran, Thomas E., 8
Coffin, Tristram P., 134
Continental groups, xiii
cookie cutters, 99–106, *101, 102, 103, 105*
cookies, 99–106
    apees, 102–104
    leb-cakes, 100–102
    sand tarts, 104
    see also doughnuts; Dutch cake
Council of the Alleghenies, ix
Cuyler, Theodore, Ledyard, 48–49

Danville, Montour County, Pennsylvania (Brower), excerpt from, 11
Darley, F. O. C., print by, *116*
Das Pfälzische Weihnachstbuch (Bischoff), 134
Das Weihnachtsfest (Weber-Kellermann), 134

Davis, W. W., 17, 88
"Day in the Ma'sh, A" (Egan), excerpt
   from, 6
"Descriptive and Historical Memorials of
   Heilman Dale" (Heilman), 14, 100
Dictionary of Americanisms (Mathews), 22
*Dictionary of the Non-English Words of the
   Pennsylvania-German Dialect*, 22
Die alemannisch-schwäbische FASNET
   (Künzig), 139
"Die Metzel Soup" poem (Behney), 19
Dieffenbach, Victor C., 23, 110
Directions for Cookery (Leslie), apees
   recipe from, 104
divining rod, instructions for making, 26
"Don't forget the poor," 17–18
doughnuts, 104–105
Drepperd, Carl W., 22
Drinker, Elizabeth, xvi
Dunkelberger, Ralph D., drawings by, *xxx*,
   9, 28, 76
Dutch cake, 105–106
   recipe for, 106

Earle, Alice Morse, 16
Early, J. W., 14
Easter Rabbit, 75
Egan, Maurice F., 6
entertaining, Christmas, xviii–xix
Episcopalians, Christmas of, xxii–xxiii

Fackenthal, Mrs. R. W., 16
fantastical parades, 109–110
Fastnacht, 138–139
Fehr, Robert F., 89
firecrackers, 129
   advertisements for, *130*
   in Pittsburgh, 129–130
Fisher, Henry L., 12, 16, 18, 25
Fisher, John, 19
folk art, 144–147
folklife studies, viii
"Folk-Lore of Lebanon County"
   (Grumbine), excerpts from,
   13, 87, 100
foods and feasting, 107–108, 144
   cookies, 99–106
   doughnuts, 104–105
   Dutch cake, 105–106
fraktur
   sketches, *xx, 146*
   texts, 145–147
Friends, xvii–xxi

Gay Dutch, xxvii
   Christmas of, xxiii–xxiv
   church vs. Santa Claus, xxv–xxvi
   Reformed Church attitudes,
      xxviii–xxvix

Second Christmas of, xxiv–xxv
   see also Lutherans; Reformed Church
Gibbons, Phebe Earle, 11, 16, 21,
   79, 102
Gingrich, David H., 24
Godey's Lady's Book, engravings, *53, 54, 62*
Goshenhoppen Historians, ix
"Granny Forney's Cake and Beer Shop"
   (Stein), excerpt from, 23
greased pig catching contests, 108–109
Grischtkindel, 137–138
Grumbine, Ezra, 13, 23, 87, 100
Grumbine, Lee, 23

Haldeman, Samuel S., 16, 80, 117
Halpert, Herbert, 140
Hanukkah, 147
Harbaugh, Henry, xxviii, 1, 107
Hark, Ann, 42
hats, setting, 40–41
Heilman, U. Henry, 14, 100
Helffrich, William A., xxiv, 52
Henninger, L. B., 41
Herberg, Will, 147
Hering, Constantin, 47
Hex Marks the Spot (Hark), 42
Hill, Henry, fraktur by, *xx*
Hill Country Tunes (Bayard), 129
History of Bucks County (Buck), 105
"History of Ephrata" (Barr), excerpt
   from, 12
*History of the Moravian Church in Philadel-
   phia* (Ritter), excerpt from, 101
History of the Protestant Episcopal Church
   (Tiffany), 50
Hocker, Edward, 42
hog bristles, market for, 19–20
Hollenbach, Raymond E., 20
Homan, John George, 26
Home Life in Colonial Days (Earle),
   excerpt from, 16–17
Hommel, Rudolf, 45
How Christmas Came to Sunday-Schools
   (Richards), 49
"How Christmas Was Observed in Olden
   Times," excerpt from, 100
"How to make Molasses Candy, vulgarly
   called Paley Cutts" (poem), 24
Hoyt, Ivan, art by, *137*
hustling, 115–117
Hutchison, Ruth, 22

"Introduction of the Christmas Tree in
   the United States" (Berlin), 46
Irving, Washington, 33

Jack, Phil R., 42
Jeremiah 10:1–6, xxix
Jones, Charles W., 137

Kauffman, A. W., 33
Keller, Ezra, xxiv, xxviii
Kiebach, Raymond E., 103
Kimmel, John Lewis, watercolor
   by, *xxvii*
Kreider, Charles D., 128
Kremer, A. R., 12
Krippenkunst in Schlesien (Lanz), 142
Krisher, Dorothy, 42
Kriss Kringle, 33–36
   containers for, 38–44
   establishment of term, 36–38
"Kriss Kringle" musical composition
   (Oesten), 40
Kriss Kringle's Book, 36
   cover, *34*
   excerpt from, 37
*Kriss Kringle's Book for All Good Boys
   and Girls*, 43
   cover, *41*
Kriss Kringle's Christmas Tree, 33, 36,
   48, 49
   cover, *39*
   excerpt from, 37
   title page, *51*
"Krist Kindle" (Hermann), excerpt
   from, 82
Künzig, Johannes, 139
Kurtz, Benjamin, xxvii–xxviii

Lambert, Marcus Bachman, 22
Lancaster *Daily Evening Express*,
   "Among the Christmas Trees"
   articles, 67–74
Lancaster—Old and New (Law), poem
   from, 13
Lanz, Joseph, 142
Law, James D., 13
leb-cakes (lebkuchen), 100–102, *144*
lebkuchen. See leb-cakes
Leeds, C. H., 14, 23, 102
Leslie, Eliza, 104
"Little Folks' Christmas March" musical
   composition (O'Kane), 93
Long Lost Friend (Homan), excerpt
   from, 26
Loos, I. K., 85
"Loveliest Tree, The" (poem), 60
Lutherans
   Christmas of, xxiii–xxiv
   New, xxvii–xxviii
   see also Gay Dutch
Luther's Christmas Tree (Stork), 50
Lykens Twenty Years Ago (Miller), excerpt
   from, 11

McClure, David, xiv
McKnight, W. J., 13
McKnight, R. M., 112

McNeill, John Thomas, 138
"Manners and Customs" (Buck), excerpt from, 85
Marshall, Christopher, xiv
Mathews, Mitford M., 22
matzabaum, 21–22
"Matzabaum and Metzel Soup" (Sener), excerpt from, 15
Méchin, Colette, 136
Medieval Handbooks of Penance (McNeill), 138
Mengel, Matthias, 86
Mercer, Henry C., 41
"Merry Christmas, A" (poem), 106
metzel soup, 15–19
    feeding the poor, 17–18
Miller, Charles H., 11
Miller, Daniel, 87
Miller, Lewis, drawing by, *45*
Montgomery Country Store (Alderfer), 42
Moore, Clement Z., 33
Moravian Christmas Eve service bulletin, *xxiv*
Moravians, 119, *121*
    bushwhacker Christmas, 121–126
    Christmas of, xxiii–xxiv
    Christmas service, *123*
    Christmas trees and, 53
    putzes, 119, 126–128, 142–143
    pyramids, 119
More, Hannah, 17
Morris, James L., 78
moshey, 21, 22–23
Muhlenberg, William A., 49
Mumaw, John Rudy, 42
mumming, 3–6, 75, 140
Myers, Elizabeth, 126
"The Myerstown Academy" (Bassler), excerpt from, 13

"Nativity Scenes: Description and Analysis" (Samuelson), 143
Nead, Daniel Wunderlich, 40
Nelson, George, xvi
"New Christmas Hymn, A" (More), verse from, 17
New Lutherans, xxvii–xxviii
"New Year's Day" (Sedgwick), excerpt from, 47
New Year's Present, A, verses from, 42–43
Newell, William H., 15
Noell, D. K., 24
Nova Scotian Belsnickels, 139–140

"O Little Town of Bethlehem" (Hark), excerpt from, 42
"Old Fashioned Christmas, The," 38
Old Home Week Letters (Leeds), excerpts from, 14, 23, 102

"Old House of Bethlehem, The" (article), 119–121
"Old-Time Christmas in a Country Home, An" (Bausman), 29–31
    excerpt from, 80
Olden Times (Fisher)
    butchering scene from, *18*
    excerpts from, 12, 16, 18–19, 25
"On the Trail of the First Christmas Tree" (Hommel), excerpt from, 45–46
ornaments
    advertisements for, 59–64
    early, 59–64
"Our Schoolmasters" (Bausman), excerpt from, 10–11

"Palmyra, Its History and Its Surroundings" (Early), excerpt from, 14
parades. *See* fantastical parades
Pasavant, W. A., 49
"Pennsylvania Dutch" (Gibbons), 16, 102
Pennsylvania Dutch (Gibbons), 21
    excerpt from, 11
Pennsylvania Dutch (Haldeman), 16, 117
    excerpt from, 80
Pennsylvania Dutch Cook Book, Reading, 22
Pennsylvania Dutch Cook Book (Hutchison), 22
Pennsylvania Dutch Country Cooking (Weaver), 144
Pennsylvania Dutch Folk Culture Society, ix
Pennsylvania Dutch Folk Festival at Kutztown, viii, ix
Pennsylvania Dutch Madonna, *xviii*
Pennsylvania Dutchman, The, viii
Pennsylvania Folklife, viii
Pennsylvania Folklife Society, viii
Pennsylvania German Cultural Heritage Center, ix
"Pennsylvania Idioms," 24
"Pennsylvania Yuletide" (Krisher), 42
"Pennsylvania-German in the Settlement of Maryland, The" (Nead), 40
Peters, Gustav S.
    broadside by, *xv*
    engraving by, 145
Pictorial Scrap Book, The, engravings, *64*, *136*
Pioneer Outline History of Northwestern Pennsylvania, A (McKnight), 13
Plain Dutch, Christmas of, xxix
plates, setting, 41–42
ponhaws, 17–18
potato picking contests, 108
Presbyterians, Christmas of, xxi–xxii
Protestant, Catholic, Jew (Herberg), 147

Publications of the Pennsylvania German Folklore Society, 143
Puritans, xiii
    argument against holy days, xix
putzes, 119, *126*, 126–128, *143*
    origins of, 142–143
pyramids, 119

Quakers, xvii–xxii
    argument against holy days, xix

raffling, 115–117
Rakestraw, Joseph, 49
Rathvon, Simon Snyder, 21, 45, 84
recipes
    apees, 104
    Dutch cake, 106
Recollections of the Old Chambersburg of Sixty Years Ago (Henninger), 41–42
Recollections of Samuel Breck (Scudder, ed.), 4
    excerpt from, 5
Reformed Church
    attitudes, xxviii–xxvix
    Christmas of, xxiii–xxiv
    see also Gay Dutch
religious groups, xiii–xiv
Restad, Penne, L., 134
Richard, Kathryn, 42
Richards, Katharine Lambert, 49
Risk, Robert Blair, xxi–xxii, 44
Ritter, Abraham, 101
Russell, George, xxix

Saint Nicholas, *ii*, *135*, 135–137
Saint Nicholas of Myra, Bari, and Manhattan (Jones), 137
Saint Nicolas (Mechin), 136
Samuelson, Sue, 143, 148
sand tarts, 104
Sansom, William, 134
Santa Claus, xix–xxi, 135–137
Sauermann, Dietmar, 134
Schach, Paul, 103
Schaefferstown, historic, ix
"Schools of our Fathers, The" (Alexander), excerpt from, 13
Schwarze, William N., 119
Schwerdgeburth, Carl August, painting by, *58*
Scott, Anna B., 104
scrapple, 17–18
Scudder, H. E., 4
Second Christmas, xxiv–xxv
    activities, 115–118
Sener, Samuel M., 15, 21
Setley, Abram, 17
"Seventy Years Ago" (Noell), excerpt from, 24

Seventy-five receipts for pastry, cakes, and sweetmeats (Leslie), 104
Shelly, Colsin R., 14
Shoemaker, Alfred L., vii–ix
shooting matches, 115
Showalter, H. A., 118
Small, J. Edgar, 22
Snyder, Jaret L., 20
solstice movement, 147–148
"Spring Garden Watchman's Address, The," *113*, 145
Stauffer, G. W., 17
Steffy, J., 7
Stein, Thomas S., 23
stereopticon card, *73*
stockings. *See* Christmas stockings
Stork, T., 50
Story, G. M., 140
straw bread baskets, setting, 38–40

Templeton, Fay, 44
Thomas, Abel C., 8
Thompson, D. W., 23
Thomson, Charles, xiv
Thomson, Hannah, xiv
Thomson, W. W., 130
Tiffany, Edward, 50
trade cards, *136*
Trein, Jennie C., 142, *143*
Trilby socials, 110

University of Pennsylvania, Department of Folklore and Folklife, ix

Valuska, David, ix
"Verses on Vanity and Superstitious Manner" fraktur (Hill), *xx*
Vogelbach, Jacob T., 50

Voices in the Temple. . .The Christmas Tree, 49
Volkskunde der Schweiz (Weiss), viii

Watchman's Addresses, *111*, *113*, 114, 145
Watson, John F., 36, 78, 102
Weaver, William Woys, 144
Weber-Kellermann, Ingeborg, 134
Weihnachten in Westfalen um 1900, 134
Weiss, Richard, viii
Weygandt, Cornelius, 22
wheelbarrow matches, 117–118
White, Charles S. J., 143
Wieand, Paul R., 7
Christmas card by, *79*
Wright, Samuel, 19

Young, Henry, 22

Zahm, Matthew, 45